Man and Society
IN DISASTER

Man and Society
IN DISASTER

Edited by GEORGE W. BAKER
and DWIGHT W. CHAPMAN

Foreword by CARLYLE F. JACOBSEN

BASIC BOOKS, INC. *Publishers, New York*

LIBRARY OF CONGRESS CATALOG CARD NUMBER: 62-15100
MANUFACTURED IN THE UNITED STATES OF AMERICA
DESIGNED BY JOAN WALL

CONTENTS

FOREWORD

Carlyle F. Jacobsen

THE SOCIAL NEEDS that produced this volume as a scientific report on behavior of individuals and groups in response to stress can be traced back to one of our country's great disasters—the Civil War. It was at that time that the National Academy of Sciences was established to make available to officers of government the knowledge and judgment of scientists and scholars. In order that these officers might plan courses of action reflecting the most adequate technical information of their time, the National Academy of Sciences and its component member, the National Research Council, has from time to time assembled committees of scientists to advise government on urgent problems. The Committee on Disaster Studies, established in 1952, was one such committee.

The charge given this Committee had urgent and immediate purposes. Although much had been learned concerning the behavior of people under stress of bombing and other catastrophies during World War II, the creation of the atomic bomb, and later the hydrogen bomb, added new dimensions to the problems of coping with physical, personal, and social disaster in the event of all-out war.

The questions confronting the Armed Forces and the Federal Civil Defense Administration were many. At one period evacuation of people from densely populated areas seemed to be the most suitable means of protection, but evacuation is slow and its outcome uncertain. The prospect of the delivery of warheads by fast moving missiles so shortened the warning period that it was doubtful that evacuation could be accomplished in a meaningful way. The better understanding of the hazards of radioactive fallout required further changes in the plans of civil defense.

What might be expected in the behavior of people under stress? What could be anticipated about morale, emotional shock, and depression in the recovery period after bombing? Would advanced training make people more knowledgeable and presumably more rational under threat? These are but a few of the questions which were addressed to the Committee on Disaster Studies by officers of the Armed Forces and the staff of the Federal Civil Defense Administration.

It was the privilege and purpose of the Committee on Disaster Studies to review and evaluate current information in the literature and to conduct further studies on the behavior of people under the stress of natural disasters. The value of the Committee's reports and studies is best judged by the users of the information. One can devoutly hope that the ultimate test of this aspect of the Committee's work will never come.

As a field of scientific inquiry the study of behavior of people under stress, particularly in its psychological and social aspects, is very new. Indeed, its major development has taken place during the past fifteen or twenty years. Much new information has been assembled and, more importantly, theoretical and conceptual frameworks have been developed for bringing together some of the diverse and sometimes conflicting data. It has been the tradition of the National Academy of Sciences–National Research Council to encourage comprehensive, scholarly reviews of the current status of new fields of inquiry. *Man and Society in Disaster* is such a review.

Since 1957 the work of the Committee on Disaster Studies has been carried out by the Disaster Research Group. The present volume is a satisfying outcome of the earlier work of the Committee. Four of the authors of this volume were long associated with the work of the Committee on Disaster Studies. The growth of interest in the field is reflected in the contributions of the other social scientists who have prepared the remaining chapters.

PREFACE

WHILE THE CONDUCTING of periodic and systematic inventories has long been an established practice in business and industry, it has not become rationalized and routinized in science and technology. Given the degree of freedom which scientists require in their work and their varied organizational affiliations, it is unlikely and probably undesirable that the custom will ever become ritualized to the same degree that it has in business. True, the director of each new research project traditionally undertakes a search of the literature before proceeding very far with his own effort. However, for a variety of reasons, the total program area to which a project contributes is not so likely to be subjected periodically to assessment and the subsequent development of fresh approaches.

Since the Disaster Research Group has been familiar with much of the work that has been done in disaster research during the past decade, it is both convenient and fitting that the Group assume some responsibility for a fairly extensive review of the field. The present book was designed (1) to achieve, for selected aspects of disaster, the codification of the substantive and theoretical knowledge that has been accumulated, and (2) to suggest various strategies and tactics for further advances that will contribute to our ability to understand, predict, and control human behavior under disastrous or stressful circumstances. It is appropriate that the reader know the considerations that were adopted for the guidance of the contributors to this task.

Throughout the period when the Committee on Disaster Studies stimulated and directed work in the disaster area, 1952-1957, it was generally believed that the supporting federal agencies would be best served if the scope of the Committee's work reflected a relatively large multidisciplinary interest. (In addition to social scientists, the membership of the Committee on Disaster Studies included representatives of such other fields as law, engineering, and medicine.) Since the inception of the Disaster Research Group in 1957, however, human behavior in disaster has been the exclusive concern of the Group. As the professional identity of the contributors to *Man and Society in Disaster* would suggest, this volume is limited to substantive and methodological questions of prime interest to the behavioral sciences.

Within the framework of the behavioral sciences, we asked selected scholars to look intensively and critically at a number of the specific subjects (e.g., the family, the aged, the community, research methods) that have been and will be of continuing concern to both the scientific community and the administrators and planners who have disaster-related interests and responsibilities. The approach to the selection of topics was fairly programmatic. I do not presume that it is exhaustive.

The press of time often causes some field workers who are developing a new research interest to ignore the relationships between their immediate subject (e.g., human behavior in a Kansas tornado) and a general phenomenon (e.g., human behavior in modern American society under stressful or extreme circumstances). Being aware of this human tendency, we asked the contributors to *Man and Society in Disaster* to devote themselves to the further development of those existing sciences that are most appropriate for an understanding of human behavior in disaster. We have not encouraged any tendency to spawn a "disaster science."

While most of the completed disaster field studies have generally focused on disaster agents that damage property and kill people in sudden and dramatic fashion, we assumed that other classes of events, such as economic depressions, false alerts, and wars—as well as experimental studies of human stress—also provided appropriate data for the development of knowledge of human behavior under stress. This view has been adopted and made explicit by the present contributors whenever it was appropriate.

Since Pitirim Sorokin wrote *Man and Society in Calamity* (1942), orientations toward social theory have changed. Many of the reformulations were initiated by Robert Merton in his *Social Theory and Social Structure* (1948). No longer do our social theorists strive to explain all behavior by means of one grand theoretical system. During a period when man has achieved spectacular increases in the range and power of his mechanical and electronic systems, he has regrouped his intellectual forces and reoriented his expectations regarding the power and the range of his social theories. In codifying present knowledge about human behavior in disaster, our expectations are even more modest.

When the disaster program was initiated within the National Academy of Sciences-National Research Council, the first consideration was that federal administrators and planners need to understand and predict the kinds and ranges of human behavior that would be manifested in the event of a nation-wide atomic attack. Fortunately for humanity, none of the subsequent research opportunities have furnished data on this subject. Reports on the studies of natural disasters have not generally endeavored to extrapolate to thermonuclear disaster. While there still is much to learn about human behavior in natural and relatively small man-made disasters, there is no reason for further delaying a more concerted and systematic inquiry into behavior in a potential thermonuclear disaster. Therefore we asked the contributors of substantive chapters to try to extrapolate their findings from the completed disaster studies to a kind of disaster that is difficult to envisage. The lack of such information may be one of the most important gaps in our security system.

It is generally recognized that most publications reflect an indebtedness that is more widespread than the author or editor realizes; the present book is no exception. There are several sources of influence, guidance, and encouragement, however, which I do recognize and take special pleasure in acknowledging. In generally identifying a new area of research and stimulating participation in it, the members of the Committee on Disaster Studies, under the chairmanship of Carlyle Jacobsen, performed significant services for the scientific community and the agencies having operational disaster functions. The staff which served the Committee and was subsequently constituted as the Disaster Research Group, directed by Harry B. Williams from 1952 until late 1959, earned the gratitude of a wide number of people for their enthusiastic and wide-ranging staff and research work. The present book would have been neither necessary nor possible if they had not performed so well.

A number of behavioral scientists early responded to the stimulus created by the Committee on Disaster Studies. Some of these scientists have continued to devote a significant portion of their creative and productive efforts to the study of disaster. The consolidated bibliography reflects in some small measure our indebtedness to their contributions.

Association during the past few years with the men whose chapters comprise this book has been both pleasant and rewarding, and I want to express my enduring gratitude. Their selection as contributors was guided by a number of considerations. Quite naturally, I leaned in the direction of scholars who I believed generally shared the orientation toward research and theory building so ably expressed by Robert Merton. Since the most enduring middle-range propositions about human behavior in disaster must be tested in rigorous empirical work, I was equally interested in securing the cooperation of those who applied this conviction. In order to maximize opportunities for obtaining new suggestions for conceptualizing and conducting future behavioral studies of disasters, contributors were sought who had achieved distinction in their several specialties but who had not previously touched base with disaster research. More than half of the contributors are in this category. I am equally pleased to note that the remaining contributors bring to our task considerable experience both as accomplished scientists in other specialties and as seasoned contributors to disaster research. Three of these authors, Dwight Chapman, John Gillin, and Irving Janis, served on the original Committee on Disaster Studies.

Very special thanks are due my associate, Dwight Chapman. To our common project he has brought a most welcome mellowness, derived in part from his senior experiences in psychological research and editing. We have benefited greatly from wise suggestions provided by Leonard S. Cottrell, Jr., based on his reading of an early draft of the manuscript. During the early planning stages of this project, John H. Rohrer provided helpful guidance. From Martha Crossen we obtained both the rich benefits of her craft and a warm intuitive understanding of the editing process.

My own small secretarial staff has endured with good grace the burdens which have necessarily been imposed by the addition of this publication to our "normal" load. The work of two assistants is gratefully acknowledged. Mark J Nearman provided facile bibliographic guidance during early planning and drafting stages, and Mary Lou Bauer did much to ensure the completeness and accuracy of the published work. Finally, the general work environment of the Academy-Research Council's Division of Anthropology and Psychology, functioning under the direction of the Executive Secretary Glen Finch, has provided freedom to initiate and complete a major project.

The bulk of the financial support necessary for the creation and writing of *Man and Society in Disaster* came from a National Institute of Mental Health grant. Additional financial support was secured from a Ford Foundation grant and from contracts from the Office of Civil and Defense Mobilization and the Office of Emergency Planning.

G.W.B.

January 1962

List of Contributors

GEORGE W. BAKER, PH.D., Technical Director, Disaster Research Group, National Academy of Sciences-National Research Council.

ALLEN H. BARTON, PH.D., Director, Bureau of Applied Social Research, Columbia University.

DWIGHT W. CHAPMAN, PH.D., Professor of Psychology, Vassar College.

IRA H. CISIN, PH.D., Research Specialist, State of California Department of Public Health.

WALTER B. CLARK, M.A., Research Assistant, State of California Department of Public Health.

H. J. FRIEDSAM, PH.D., Professor and Director, Department of Economics and Sociology, North Texas State University.

JOHN P. GILLIN, PH.D., Professor of Anthropology and Dean, Division of Social Sciences, University of Pittsburgh.

HAROLD GUETZKOW, PH.D., Professor of Political Science, Psychology, and Sociology, Northwestern University.

DONALD A. HANSEN, PH.D., Lecturer, Educational Sociology, University of Otago, Dunedin, New Zealand.

ROBERT W. HAWKES, PH.D., Assistant Professor of Psychology and Sociology, and Senior Research Associate, Administrative Science Center, University of Pittsburgh.

REUBEN HILL, PH.D., Professor of Sociology and Child Development, and Director, Minnesota Family Study Center, University of Minnesota.

IRVING L. JANIS, PH.D., Professor of Psychology, Yale University.

CARLYLE F. JACOBSEN, PH.D., President, Upstate Medical Center, and Dean, College of Medicine, State University of New York.

GIDEON SJOBERG, PH.D., Associate Professor of Sociology, University of Texas.

JAMES D. THOMPSON, PH.D., Professor of Sociology, and Director, Administrative Science Center, University of Pittsburgh.

ROBERT N. WILSON, PH.D., Associate Professor of Sociology, Yale University.

STEPHEN B. WITHEY, PH.D., Professor of Psychology, and Research Program Director, Survey Research Center, Institute for Social Research, University of Michigan.

Part One

DEVELOPMENT OF A NEW RESEARCH AREA

▶ *one*

A BRIEF INTRODUCTION TO CONTEMPORARY DISASTER RESEARCH

Dwight W. Chapman

THE AWESOME FASCINATION intrinsic to disasters together with their social consequences has long insured the growth of a vast literature that describes, interprets, or seeks to reconstruct such events. Any great catastrophe—the destruction of Pompeii or of Hiroshima—leaves behind it some permanent residue of public record, however fragmentary or distorted. Depending on its place and its era, a disaster gives rise variously to accounts of eyewitnesses, letters and diaries, stories that circulate and are somewhere set down, details of the findings of official investigations, journalistic reconstructions pieced together from scattered information, or recordings on film and soundtrack. And when any disaster strikes with the sort of human impact that is long felt in its culture, this public record is further perpetuated by becoming woven into histories, novels, and plays that anchor it in a durable context of personal and social meaning.

There is, then, nothing novel nor even modern about men's concern to know what happens in disasters, and nothing new in the feeling that because disasters are often profoundly consequential for human beings and their society the facts about them should be preserved for study. The huge literature thus accumulated is something to which contemporary students of disaster have often turned for its wealth of suggestiveness.

Several features of the present-day study of disasters are so new, however, that they mark a distinguishable boundary between the past and the present. The first is that interest has turned from an idiographic, historical account of disasters as particular events to a nomothetic approach, in which any particular disaster is examined for what it may tell us about the nature of disaster generally and about the validity of tentative theories.

This change of interest arises from a second new development: the disaster student nowadays is typically a social scientist, and his general objective is to bring the human phenomena in disaster into the realm of systematic understanding—that is, to apply to them the ordering concepts of psychology, sociology, anthropology, and other human sciences, as well as to use them to amplify and criticize the existent working concepts in those disciplines.

Consonant with the systematic point of view is a third characteristic of contemporary disaster research—that its methods, too, have become much more systematized, and that the investigator now moves into the scene of a disaster not only with explicit plans for studying a manageable number of the manifold aspects of disaster but also armed with technical procedures for sampling, interviewing, and data-collecting that contrast sharply with the planlessness of most historically available information.

It was between World Wars I and II that sporadic pieces of disaster research were carried out which tested or applied some of the systematic concepts of the social and behavioral sciences. Prince's (1920) study of social phenomena following the explosion of a munitions vessel in Halifax harbor is the pioneering example, and Cantril's (1940) unique study of reactions to the widely credited radio broadcast "invasion from Mars" performed a significant psychological analysis of human behavior under the simulated threat of a terrifying disaster.

Only after World War II, however, did actual programs of disaster research begin to form. The impulse for a planful attack on the human problems of disaster came, of course, from the implications of atomic and thermonuclear weapons; government agencies responsible for planning for the hazards of a nuclear age began to organize and support research that would advance our understanding of human beings in situations of acute stress and wholesale destruction. Under federal auspices, the United States Strategic Bombing Survey (1947c, 1947d) studied restrospectively the human consequences of the massive bombing of cities in Germany and Japan. Janis' (1951) analysis of these data for the varieties of behavior produced by the emotional stress of bombing developed concepts and principles that have taken an important place in the theory of disaster. The British government sponsored research (Titmuss, 1950) on the problems encountered in evacuating a large population from London during the wartime blitz. In Canada, Tyhurst (1951) carried out a number of immediate post-disaster studies and was able to identify several recurrent phases of disaster behavior. Project East River (1952), set up in this country under federal auspices, was in part concerned with applying concepts of the human sciences to problems of training and preparation for civil defense. The National Opinion Research Center at the University of Chicago, the Operations Research Office of Johns Hopkins University, and the University of Oklahoma undertook for government agencies a program of research on disaster behavior through field interviews of survivors of natural disasters.

In 1952, at the request of the Army, Navy, and Air Force medical services, the National Academy of Sciences-National Research Council appointed a Committee on Disaster Studies (reorganized in 1957 as the Disaster Research Group). With resources from federal agencies and foundations, this committee undertook to encourage research on human problems in disaster, to advance communication and planning among students of disaster, and to provide consultative services to such agencies as the Federal Civil Defense Administration. Since the time of its establishment, this group has supported a wide-ranging program of studies. Most of these, using the frequent opportunities given by natural disasters of all sorts, have been field studies carried out in stricken communities as soon as possible after the impact of tornadoes, floods, explosions, and similar catastrophic events. They have used interviews with samples of survivors and with officials and rescue agencies to identify the basic phenomena that occur among people during the approach, the strike, and the aftermath of disastrous occurrences.

Including both research sponsored by the Disaster Research Group (listed by Nearman, 1959) and numerous independent studies (e.g., Bettelheim, 1943; Bucher, 1957; Diggory, 1956; Green and Logan, 1950; Iklé, 1951; Logan, Killian, and Marrs, 1952; Schneider, 1957; University of Oklahoma Research Institute, 1952), the scientific investigation of disaster behavior has reached large proportions. A recent inventory (Disaster Research Group, 1961) of field studies lists the following numbers of disasters thus treated: twenty tornadoes, thirteen fires and explosions, twelve floods, twelve hurricanes and typhoons, eight earthquakes, eight incidents involving poisonous or asphyxiating chemicals, six false alerts, five epidemics or threatened outbreaks, four airplane crashes, three blizzards, and two mine disasters, as well as six miscellaneous emergencies. Eleven civil defense exercises have also been studied. The total number of recorded interviews available from these studies is 14,461. In addition, research on World War II bombings involved 7,163 interviews.

Aside from the much-used field survey, research has profited from work in the laboratory and in artificial situations contrived to reproduce conditions similar to those that prevail around the time of actual catastrophes. Hudson's (1954a) study of the conditions governing anxiety in threatening situations was done in the interests of scientific understanding of disaster behavior. In the Army, research (Schwartz and Winograd, 1954) has tested the effects of indoctrination upon the morale of troops taking part in training maneuvers close to live atomic explosions. Recently there have been studies of groups of people occupying experimental shelters such as those called for as part of civil defense planning (Baker and Rohrer, 1960). In several test evacuations of American cities, problems of communication, organizational behavior, and the response of citizens have been studied by research teams present by pre-arrangement during these drills (e.g., Livingston, Klass, and Rohrer, 1954), and some major problems in obtaining efficient public cooperation have been thereby identified. There has been some research on the information-processing and decision-making of staff organizations manning civil defense control centers during practice alerts and exercises. Attitudes of national samples of the public toward matters bearing on civil defense preparedness have been surveyed at intervals by the National Opinion Research Center and by the University of Michigan's Survey Research Center. The most recent one was conducted by Michigan in the fall of 1961.

Publications on disaster, besides reporting research on particular disasters, have included papers analyzing the major phenomena and socio-psychological problems that recur in such situations, as well as papers presenting theoretical formulations and methodology relevant to disaster research and illuminated by it. Monographs such as those by Wallace (1956) and Killian (1956b) have contributed important conceptual schemes for ordering the facts and problems uncovered in a wide range of disaster studies.

As of 1959, the total number of unrestricted publications by, or under the sponsorship of, the Disaster Research Group alone was 99, in addition to a large number of unpublished working papers and research memoranda as well as papers published for the restricted use of government agencies.

It is evident, then, that the field of research on the human and social aspects of disaster has reached a state of considerable maturity of effort. The accumulation of data and knowledge is substantial. The identification of key problems, both of a practical sort and of the kind that challenge theory in the behavioral sciences, has steadily progressed. New concepts of considerable power in creating an orderly understanding of the effects of threat and impact of mass-destructive forces have been moving into wide use and agreement. And, in general, as a professional field of research this area of study has developed its own corpus of data and its own systematic directions.

Like any realm of investigation reaching self-sustaining maturity, however, it has reached the point at which it is both able and eager to take stock of itself, to mark out for attention the things about which it knows least, to evaluate competing formulations, to look for concepts in psychology and sociology that have been neglected as sources of further understanding, and to state unsolved problems for work to come.

The contributors to this volume have had those purposes in mind. The variety of aspects of disaster research which they treat is wide. Some of the authors are "old hands" at disaster research; others are, rather, social and behavioral scientists who have accepted the invitation to apply their special competencies to an examination of disaster research and to contribute what their fresh consideration of its literature leads them to discern or to hypothesize. Consequently, each author's point of departure is that state to which the past several years have brought disaster research. From that base he moves forward to contribute his synthesizing and exploratory ideas.

Since this book is not primarily a survey of past disaster studies as such, but is rather a pushing forward from what they offer, those readers unfamilar with the main trends of disaster research need and deserve some substantive background. That is the purpose of the rest of this chapter—to sketch the most prevalent human phenomena found by disaster studies and the most prominent research problems and concepts to which those findings have given rise among recent investigators.

Some Important Products of Disaster Research

The first systematic studies of human behavior in disasters had the task, as does all pioneering research in any field, of determining the major descriptive categories of events that take place. This phenomenology of disaster can be usefully systematized by reference to typical periods of time within the course of a disaster, since these periods are presumably related to types and problems of behavior. In an early paper, Powell and Rayner (1952) proposed the division of disaster time into seven phases:

1. Warning during which there arises, mistakenly or not, some apprehension based on conditions out of which danger may arise.

2. Threat during which people are exposed to communications from others, or to signs from the approaching disaster force itself, indicating specific, imminent danger.

3. Impact during which the disaster strikes, with concomitant death, injury, and destruction.

4. Inventory during which those exposed to the disaster begin to form a preliminary picture of what has happened and of their own condition.

5. Rescue in which activity turns to immediate help for survivors, first aid for the wounded, freeing trapped victims, fighting fires, etc.

6. Remedy during which more deliberate and formal activities are undertaken toward relieving the stricken and their community, both by survivors and by the outside relief agencies that have now moved into the scene.

7. *Recovery* during which, for an extended period, the community and the individuals in it either recover their former stability or achieve a stable adaptation to the changed conditions which the disaster has brought about.

These periods have indeed been found to evoke typical behaviors, and their usefulness as a basis for suggesting research problems has been great enough to have brought this time-schema (or minor variations thereof) into general acceptance. The reader will find such periods of disaster time mentioned frequently in the chapters of this book.

The division into time periods also serves well the present purpose of reviewing the main findings of disaster research. We now turn to what problems have been most studied and what has been found in each of these phases of a whole disaster sequence.

THE PERIOD OF WARNING

Precipitate disasters, like those involving sudden explosions, may not be preceded by any period in which the victims are aware of mounting danger. But in disasters whose slower approach gives cues and opportunity for public apprehension, as in the case of a mounting flood or a developing epidemic, the period of warning becomes an important part of the sequence of human experience.

The special significance that research has ascribed to this premonitory period is that human reactions to warning and threat involve both anxiety and ways of handling anxiety, and that the devices by which people deal with their feelings of apprehension are forms of early preparation for their more clear-cut responses to immediate danger and impact. Some of the conditions for effective or futile behavior at the time of the disaster, therefore, lie in what has gone on under the milder, vaguer stress of early warning, and it has been characteristic of research on pre-disaster periods to seek to connect these two variables.

Wolfenstein (1957), examining interview data obtained post-impact from many disaster survivors, found in these recollective accounts considerable evidence for a marked repression of anxiety on the part of some and a patent over-reactivity on the part of others. These two extremes of response to ambiguous signs of danger continue to operate when warnings become clearer and more urgent, and they thus bear on how quickly and how rationally people will finally act to protect themselves. However, it seems clear that these contrasting extremes of denial of threat on the one hand, and uncontrolled terror on the other, are deviations from the bulk of human reactions to warning, in which most people act with reasonable courage and prudence, carrying on with essential activities but keeping a wary eye to the weather and taking some precautions. As Wolfenstein has noted, the data suggest that the minority who are distinctly over- or under-reactive to the threat of disaster are often those whose general emotional situation is already precarious and for whom the handling of a neurotic reservoir of anxiety has chronically been an expensive preoccupation. For them, warnings of an approaching disaster have the effect of intensifying an already existent apprehensiveness or of arousing habitual defenses against it.

Less dependent on interviewees' recollections of pre-disaster feelings and behavior are studies in which reactions are investigated during or immediately after a real or simulated warning. Hudson (1954a) has used an experimental situation in which college students attending a lecture were distracted by recorded sounds of explosions, sirens, and shouting from without. His results show that there is a wide range of emotionality in responses to such ambiguous and potentially alarming stimuli; that people in this situation rapidly develop interpretive hypotheses and that where these hypotheses are confused and in conflict their anxiety grows; and that the more anxious subjects perceive others in the group around them as anxious, so that they develop a considerable cognitive support for their own apprehension.

Janis (1958b) has studied the attitudes of pre-surgical patients to the prospect of major surgery and has found the same range of reactions—from rigid denial of threat to exaggerated fear—that Wolfenstein drew from retrospective interviews following actual disasters. It appears from Janis' research that behavior during the period of threat has predictive value for the period of recovery after the fear-provoking event: patients who in the pre-operative period experience and work-through a realistic amount of anxiety withstand more serenely the discomforts of post-operative recovery than do patients who experience either no anxiety or more anxiety than they can handle. The hypothesis that in the periods of threat and warning an optimal amount of anxiety and a successful experience of handling it make for effective behavior in the later phases of disaster has thus been finding wise bases of support. A related idea, that there is some optimal degree of social stress which prepares communities, groups, and families to make good recovery from disaster, has also been emerging and will be found reflected in several chapters of this book.

Surveys of the attitudes of national samples of the public toward civil defense matters likewise confirm the existence of a wide variety of responses to the continuing uncertainties and threat imposed by the Cold War and the menace of atomic destruction should it grow hot. From these sources there is evidence that a good many people who are overtly most apathetic toward civil defense precautions nevertheless overestimate the destructiveness of atomic weapons, as if an exaggerated cognition of the danger and an outward denial of its threat went hand in hand.

It is evident from all such findings that the period of warning is one in which, because of the fragmentary and ambiguous signs of danger, minor changes in the stimulus situation are able to produce great differences of reaction; these reactions can in turn alter or reinforce interpretations of what little information is available. The shape of a cloud of smoke produced by a fireworks factory explosion in Houston (Killian, 1956a) led some residents of that city to suppose that it had undergone atomic attack. Cantril's (1940) study of reactions to the radio program simulating an "invasion from Mars" turned up respondents who, looking out to see what was going on in the streets, had in some cases interpreted the flow of traffic as normal and reassuring, in others as unusually heavy and as a sign that people were fleeing the city. It is clear as a practical matter that the prevailing situation in the period of warning is that of human search for certainty in the absence of reliable information. Whenever officials have failed to structure this period as soon as possible by explicit warnings and relevant information, the studies of disaster have found the consequences of public confusion and overanxious behavior. A related finding is that persons who have had previous experience with similar dangers or who have been trained in detecting and combating the danger are usually better able to resolve their doubts in favor of rational self-protection. The implications for the usefulness of indoctrination and training in preparation for possible disasters are obvious.

THE PERIOD OF THREAT

Since urgent warnings of immediate danger are the important conditions in this period, much of the research on this phase has looked for the psychological conditions under which warnings are well identified, accepted, and acted upon, as well as for the effects of the timing, source, and content of such messages. The public agencies responsible for issuing warnings have also been studied as problem-solving groups, liable to errors arising from defects in their internal communication, their hierarchical or competitive relationship to other agencies, the pressures of their public relations, their quality of leadership, and other sources of malfunction that are familiar to the student of organizations.

In this phase of approaching disaster, human beings face more urgently the same problems of resolving perceptual ambiguity that they did in the phase of warning. Signals that suggest a drill rather than a real emergency, official cautions that leave unspecified the nearness of danger or the protective steps to be taken, conflicting advice, or calls to action from prestigeless or resented authorities may easily support disbelief or inaction. Studies of false alarms suggest that a complicated set of factors bears on consequent public reactions. Sometimes alerts which do not eventuate in any great danger are nevertheless not depreciated, and they may even have the effect of improving the response to alerts on later occasions; sometimes they work in a "cry wolf" fashion to evoke only apathy or anger when the next alert comes along. The crucial conditions that decide these contrasting outcomes are not at all well understood. There is evidence (Killian, 1954a) that warnings of possible but unrealized disasters are well received if people are convinced that the disaster could indeed have occurred, as where a warned-of flood or wind strikes with less than disastrous force. On the other hand, there is also evidence of a considerable latent readiness to resent even well-intentioned warnings that turn out to be premature, overcautious, or stupid. Wolfenstein (1957) points out the analogy between this attitude and the drive of the child to assert his autonomy against parental control: he covertly hopes that parents' warnings will be proved false, and he defends himself against them by interpreting them as nagging and officious. For such reasons, agencies officially charged with alerting a community must sometimes walk a narrow plank between latent public resentment of excessive warnings and public condemnation if the warnings turn out to be too mild or too late.

With respect to the content of warning messages, there persists the problem of determining the limits of reassurance on the one hand and alarm on the other. Janis (1958b) has shown that warnings outside a middle ground of informative content may engender either more apathy or more terror than compliance. The most effective warnings appear to combine enough threatening information to arouse ego-involvement (but not so much as to arouse defensive repression) with assurance that specified preventive action will be effective.

Some theorizing (Nicholson and Blackwell, 1954; H. B. Williams,

1956), though not much empirical research, has approached the decision-making of individuals in the period of warning as a problem in game theory. It is plausible to think that personal decisions about what to do in the face of danger take place within a complex of implicit personal estimates: (1) how likely the threatening event is to occur, and how soon; (2) how great a loss the person will suffer if it does, and if no countermeasures occur; (3) what measures of protection are open to him; (4) how effective each measure will be; (5) the cost of such measures in money, time, effort, anxiety, and other deprivations. A change in any of these estimates should be reflected in what the individual will do in response to warning and in how quickly he will act. Although there is little opportunity to study these variables systematically in an actual disaster situation, interview data do provide casual illustrations of the influence of each of them on the behavior of people trying to decide what to do as disaster approaches.

Elaborate studies have examined the problems of protecting large populations, as by evacuating cities, in a period of clear warning and peril. British research (Titmuss, 1950) on their experience in removing London children and nonessential adults from that city for the duration of its bombing found some stubborn facts of psychology that would not yield to the sheer logic of protection-by-evacuation. Where families were split up by the departure, the adverse emotional effects upon children were often greater than the emotional hazards run by children who remained in an intact family in London under periodic bombardment (Bowlby, 1952; A. Freud, 1946; A. Freud and Burlingham, 1943). For both city children and adults, adjustment to their hosts and to the ways of life in the countryside was often difficult and sometimes impossible. Joyce Cary's novel *Charley Is My Darling* draws a touching individual portrait of what research has confirmed on a massive scale. The filtering back to London of a large proportion of evacuated residents, who finally preferred the rigors of buzz-bombing to those of a strange and remote rural culture, continued to frustrate the official protective measures.

Studies of rescue and billeting at the time of the great Holland floods (Instituut voor Sociaal Onderzoek, 1955) show, like the British research, that tensions between evacuees and their hosts are in part a function of the size of social-class differences between the two. But the Dutch studies make it seem likely that this may hold true only within a limited range of such differences: when the evacuated family and their hosts are extremely far apart in backgrounds the effect seems to be reversed, and this apparently for the reason that greatly disparate pairs of families have so little in common that they find no fundamental ground within which to develop mutual hostility. After all, Shaw's Pygmalion and his protegée got along reasonably well so long as they could regard themselves as in no wise sharing (and therefore not competing within) the same culture. But whether certain cultural differences are crucial for this phenomenon is not yet known.

The United States Strategic Bombing Survey (1947c) found that, under the particular circumstances in Nazi Germany, repeated bombings and threats of bombing had failed to produce any significant absenteeism in defense plants. Economic and political sanctions against absenteeism had been far more important influences on workers. In short, the body of research on protective measures contradicts the popular belief (e.g., Peterson, 1953) that human beings under threat of disaster are motivated sheerly by a simple drive for physical safety. The imminence of danger, it is evident, produces a complicated social situation capable of engaging a wide variety of motivations and attitudes.

THE PERIOD OF IMPACT

Research has furnished several important descriptive generalizations about the behavior of people at the moment of actual impact of disaster, and some of these generalizations differ sharply from the picture often given in fictional and journalistic accounts.

The folklore of cataclysm frequently asserts that panic—in the sense of wild, terror-stricken behavior—is natural and commonplace. Quite to the contrary, panic has seldom been found in the study of actual disaster. The accumulated mass of interview data from survivors concerning what they themselves did during acute danger and what they saw others doing shows that behavior under the impact of tornadoes, floods, wrecks, and other crises is surprisingly rational, courageous, and calm. Panic behavior has consequently come to be recognized by students of disaster as an exceptional phenomenon arising under exceptional conditions (Janis, Chapman, Gillin, and Spiegel, 1955). The few cases of mass panic that can be found have the following conditions in common: (1) people perceive an immediate, severe danger to themselves; (2) they believe that there exists only a limited route of escape and that this route is about to be blocked; and (3) they receive no contradicting information. Only a few disaster situations fulfill those conditions—for example, rapidly spreading fires within a confined space, as in the Coconut Grove fire in Boston.

We know also that in any disaster some few people may give way to extremely emotional behavior, screaming or running wildly, or "freezing up" in stunned immobility; but their personal panic usually remains a restricted occurrence without much group significance. Indeed one of the fascinating by-products of disaster research has been to raise the question: Why has this myth of inevitable mass panic enjoyed such durable popularity? That it adds to journalism and fiction an extra dash of drama is obvious; and this is probably one reason why it has been perpetuated. But the myth clearly invites some explanation on grounds of its more covert psychological utility. Wolfenstein (1957) has related it to the fears and fantasies of unbridled impulse seen in the neurotic struggling against the threat of his own tightly leashed impulsivity. More generally, an element of self-distrust in us all may make us overly hospitable to the belief that in danger most people will go to pieces. Then, too, when for such reasons the myth has been nourished in popular literature, panic in disaster inevitably takes on the character of an expected narrative or dramatic convention and acquires the rugged truth value of any easy consensus that few bother to question.

Where people are caught in groups during disaster, leadership has its influence upon group behavior. People first look to designated leaders for guidance; but since most groups overtaken by a catastrophe are without official leaders, the emergence of informal, undesignated leaders has claimed considerable research interest. The appearance of *ad hoc* leaders and the effectiveness of their behavior in guiding group activity are frequent in the findings of disaster studies. Examination of the recorded cases of successful emergent leaders shows that they arise in excellent confirmation of the principles of leadership that social psychology has developed; they are not persons somehow destined by an enviable cast of personality to take charge in all situations, but rather those in whom some skill, knowledge, insight, or other fortune of personal resource matches an urgent need in a group's situation. Thus, in the residential section of a city in which houses began to blow up as a result of a rush of illuminating gas released by a faulty main reducer-valve, delivery-truck drivers in the neighborhood—who happened to know how to use a wrench to shut off the house valves—took on highly effective rescue roles among a population of helpless housewives (Marks and Fritz, 1954). At an air show during which a falling plane killed and wounded many spectators, the announcer realized that his public-address equipment would enable him to control a crowd that was converging on the wounded and dying; and a priest who began to move among the injured in order to give extreme unction soon developed an accessory role as organizer of first aid (Marks and Fritz, 1954). Since training for specific roles furnishes these leader-making skills and knowledges, the utility of pre-disaster indoctrination for protective and rescue functions is clear. In the same air crash mentioned above, the local switchboard operator quickly began using the telephone system for organizing ambulance, medical, and police services—a role she had never previously played but which her training had provided in latent form, ready to be triggered by the demands of an emergency situation.

Corresponding to the importance of appropriate knowledge and skills in creating emergent leaders is the pervasive finding that officially designated leaders who are incompetent to meet the real needs of the disaster situation come to be ignored or deserted, or at best they retain a quasi-status only by abdicating actual decisions and leadership to more competent subordinates.

THE PERIOD OF INVENTORY

Stock-taking begins, after the strike of a disaster, with the efforts of the stunned individual survivors to come to an understanding of the catastrophe that has just taken place. The evidence shows that an immediate effect of the impact is to produce a momentary fragmentation of the social scene into isolated individuals, each overwhelmed by the event and each believing for the moment that only he and his immediate companions have been the victims. As the survivor struggles for a comprehension of his condition, he comes rapidly to some realization of the mass destruction that has taken place; the interviews taken in disaster studies speak eloquently of the shocking sense of catastrophic loss and abandonment that this realization can produce. As the survivor begins to find that there are others who also felt and survived the blow, these feelings give way to a powerful sense of gratitude at still being alive and of concern and warmth for other survivors.

Thus for most who are alive after the impact, emotional relations to others are very rapidly rebuilt. Those who are lightly injured or unhurt soon become active, rescuing victims who are trapped or badly hurt, and moving over the scene in an effort to find their loved ones and to comprehend the extent of the tragedy. The second of these actions is of course subject to the same difficulties as were the earlier efforts to appraise the threat of disaster. Rumors, vacuums of information, ambiguous sights and sounds, all become sources of shifting and anxious interpretation. Prominent in this search for comprehension is the powerful need to know the fate of one's family, and much of the roving, worried behavior of survivors is motivated thereby. It is typical, too, that this search may be interrupted from time to time for efforts to rescue strangers under the pressure of sudden appeals or demanding situations. It has been pointed out that the apparent confusion of activity that the unpracticed observer sees immediately after disasters is not, after all, aimless for most of the persons involved in it. Individually they are acting in highly purposeful directions. It is only because their activities are not socially coordinated at first that the appearance of random confusion arises. It follows that the first acts of rescue by survivors are often heroic, typically rational, and sometimes successful—but also relatively unorganized and inefficient.

This human fragmentation immediately following impact, together with the subsequent discovery that much of the hitherto orderly environment has been shattered, has at least two important consequences. First, it highlights the family as the still-functioning unit of social organization, because no social catastrophe can destroy kinship, and any adversity heightens the sense of family ties. The prominence of family-related roles in post-disaster behavior has been repeatedly shown. Survivors immediately turn their anxiety toward the possible fate of their families; even officials with well-defined community rescue roles find these in severe and occasionally hopeless conflict with their felt responsibilities as fathers and husbands. This dominance of concern for the family is strong in any case, but it appears to govern behavior even more powerfully in cultures in which the extended family is accorded an importance greater than in our own. A flood which threatened towns on both the Mexican and the United States sides of the Rio Grande (Clifford, 1956) permitted a comparison of behavior in a more family-oriented community with that in a less family-oriented one. In the Mexican community, evacuation took place generally within the organization of the extended family, within which most mutual aid, advice, and coordination occurred, as against the greater influence of neighborhood, community, and governmental organization in the stateside town.

The second effect of the social fragmentation caused by impact is that it makes possible the distinctly new social situation that the survivor enters from the moment of the actual disaster on. We have mentioned that most survivors experience keen emotions of gratefulness for survival and of warmth toward other survivors as they regain contact with the disaster-struck scene around them. Most studies, too, have found that survivors—in both this inventory period and the later period of rescue—are impressed by the sympathy, helpfulness, friendliness, and emotional accessibility of others. They recall that differences of status seemed to have been swept away, that you could share your concerns and emotions with almost everybody, that strangers acted like friends. The interviews gathered during later recuperation sometimes find an actual nostalgia for the emotional warmth of the post-impact period, saddened and anxious as it may have been. They also find a good many cherished memories of the help respondents were able to give to others—sometimes feelings of having felt important and useful for one of the few times in their lives. This indication of a latent Admirable Crichton lurking in many a man, ready to respond to the elementary democracy and the seriousness of social involvement that rise in the wake of disaster, provides the social scientist with material for a uniquely critical commentary on some aspects of everyday community life.

THE PERIOD OF RESCUE

The phase of rescue is divided from that of immediately-preceding impact by naturally indistinct boundaries. Most people in the impact area of a forceful disaster agent are momentarily stunned. But most of them soon recover mobility, and as they start to assess their situation and take steps to cope with it, the rescue phase may be said to begin.

Although rapid recovery from the immediate shock of impact is the rule, a number of survivors manifest what has come to be known as the "disaster syndrome" (Wallace, 1956). They do not quickly emerge from the stunned condition but continue to act dazed, withdrawn, and relatively immobile; or, if they move about, they do so in an aimless, abstracted way. They are suggestible and passive, and medical workers observe in their docility a striking contrast to the more common querulousness of people who have suffered an ordinary street accident. The syndrome may persist for many hours, not only among those who have been physically injured but also among those who are essentially unharmed. How prevalent this phenomenon is in any disaster remains debatable, since various studies have found it in anywhere from none to about one-third of survivors. Its cause has been thought to be the sudden, wholesale destruction of the physical and social environment—a conjecture based on the fact that the disaster syndrome has been identified only under conditions of mass disaster and not under conditions of more individualized stress. Whatever its specific causes and however variable its incidence from one disaster to another, the disaster syndrome is nevertheless a clinical concept with both a teasing theoretical interest and some obvious practical implications for managing the care of survivors.

We have noted the intensification of family roles induced by disaster and we have observed that family loyalty is potent in guiding a good deal of individual behavior as people move into post-impact activities. The influence of other roles and role conceptions has, of course, been clearly found, especially among professional rescue personnel—community officials, police, firemen, doctors, civil defense workers, and all others who have been trained and motivated to perform certain services if emergencies should occur. The roles that their indoctrination has prepared them to assume in an emergency usually sustain in them a channeling of effort and a continuous relation to coordinating plans and authority that are lacking in the casual rescuer.

However, some nondisaster roles and habits that could, with modifications, be applied effectively in disaster may be carried over into the emergency situation so rigidly that they fail to be useful in important respects. Thus, a study of the hospital management of the wounded following a tornado in a large city (Bakst, Berg, Foster, and Raker, 1955) showed that some procedures had been ill-adapted to the extraordinary demands imposed by the catastrophe, particularly to the handling of the large number of casualties arriving at hospitals in a short space of time and in the surgical procedures used on wounds contaminated by the debris hurled by a tornado at and into its victims. Measures for separating those wounded needing immediate surgery from those who could wait or for whom surgery was hopeless, as well as for transferring patients from overburdened hospitals to less crowded ones, were inadequate. Surgical teams in the most glutted hospital worked continuously and beyond the point of diminishing efficiency and adequacy of supplies, while a group of volunteer doctors from another city were thanked for their trouble in coming but were not in fact incorporated into the local effort. In short, much of the medical activity in this unusual situation followed roles and habits that are quite appropriate to the everyday practice of a hospital in handling its usual load of ordinary emergency cases, but which must give way, in the event of mass casualties, to practices more like those used on the battlefield. Consistently enough, the study found that doctors with front-line military experience had best adapted their procedures to the extraordinary demands of the disaster.

Within a short time after a disaster, many people from the surrounding communities begin to pour into the area. This "convergence behavior" (Fritz and Mathewson, 1957), brings not only official rescue agencies but also crowds of people who are anxious about friends and relatives, who are eager to volunteer their help, or who are simply curious. A few may also arrive who move in to exploit the situation; but the looting that appears so frequently in fictional and journalistic accounts is actually infrequent, even when guards have not been assigned to prevent it.

The convergence on the disaster scene generally creates a severe traffic problem. Roads are slowed or blocked to the passage of essential vehicles, crowds get in the way of rescue teams and apparatus, and telephone lines needed for coordination of relief are choked by anxious or inquisitive calls into the central area. Nor is the inpouring of people and communications the only convergence problem; supplies of all sorts begin arriving—extremely useful to a point, but beyond that, running over into a plethora that is hard to accommodate. A phrase familiar to disaster research is that in America, and pretty much throughout the Western world, disasters take place in a "cornucopia society." Let a disaster occur, and the horn of plenty floods the site with a surfeit of goods, services, and well-intentioned human beings—as can be expected in a culture with quick concern for the afflicted and with the affluence to relieve physical hardship. The cornucopia phenomenon makes treacherous the necessary attempts to project from ordinary disasters the state of affairs that would prevail under nation-wide nuclear attack, for in that awesome case the cornucopia would itself be severely damaged, if not destroyed outright.

What amount of serious mental illness results from the tension, crisis, and deprivation that a disaster entails? The general answer to this question now seems clear: Very little indeed, particularly if one defines mental illness as more profound than the transitory emotional disturbances that do occur over a period of weeks following disaster. The supposition that disaster might significantly increase the incidence of mental illness was certainly a plausible one. Leighton (1959) posits "a recent history of disaster" as one putative index of that social disintegration which should heighten the occurrence of neurosis or psychosis in a community. Nevertheless, our studies have not found disasters eventuating in any wave of psychological illness—possibly, of course, because we have investigated only relatively short periods following impact. British students of their wartime experience (Titmuss, 1950) found statistical grounds for concluding that mental illness actually declined in incidence during the protracted period of bombing and threat of destruction. In view of our knowledge and our ignorance, a cautious general statement would be that the short-term effects of disaster do not include significant amounts of serious mental illness, and that the emotional mobilization required of survivors may in fact counteract some existing cases and prevent some incipient cases from becoming florid. It must be added, however, that we know very little about whether disasters contribute to psychiatric disorders that may be long delayed in their appearance.

THE PERIOD OF REMEDY

The flowing in of relief to a disaster-crushed community is of course the beginning of that healing period in which the community moves to planful and longer-term measures of recuperation. In some cases such a process may presumably last for years, particularly if one includes in it such slow recovery as the rebuilding of obliterated areas or individual adjustment to the death of family members.

This is not to deny that symptoms of stress (of course including possible exacerbation of pre-existing symptoms) are observed during the days immediately following disaster. Such reactions—insomnia, digestive upsets, "nervousness," and other familiar products of emotional tension—may appear in a sizable proportion of survivors, but they tend to subside within a matter of days. For a time they create some practical problems: they put a considerable load on physicians and hospitals just when medical services are most needed for serious cases, and they can be easy to confuse with symptoms of real injury if the disaster involves toxic materials. Thus in one American city a considerable number of people became victims of poisonous whiskey that got into bootleg channels of distribution. Public warnings issued at the height of this episode brought to hospitals and clinics not only victims who were developing symptoms of poisoning but also many others worried about what might have been in last night's drink and showing stress symptoms not unlike those of actual poisoning. In atomic disaster, stress reactions such as vomiting or debility could be interpreted as early symptoms of severe radiation and could overload diagnostic centers.

Emotional effects of disaster upon children of school age were for the first time carefully studied following a tornado which struck a motion-picture theater during a matinee attended by many children (Perry, Silber, and Bloch, 1956). Most of the young survivors lost siblings or friends. They manifested various temporary disturbances, in some cases lasting several months: regression to more infantile behavior, sleeplessness, increased dependency on adults, fear of leaving the house, and withdrawn and autistic behavior. The quickest recovery from such disturbances was found among children in families that accepted their regressive behavior and encouraged them to talk out their tragic experiences, to accomplish the "work of grieving," and thereby to express and learn to accept their feelings of sorrow and horror. Other families showed a "dissociative-demanding" response to their emotion-laden situation; that is, they created a tense atmosphere in which the child had to repress his memories and hurts in deference to the parents' struggle to deny their own emotions, often revealed in stern or overly sensitive behavior. In effect, the usual roles of parents and children became reversed. Children in such families showed the slowest rate of emotional recovery.

The same study found evidence that family structure generally permits the grieving role to only a limited number of members at a time—frequently only to one. Other family members are thereby held within supportive and comforting roles during that period. As the grief-stricken member recovers, his role may shift to another person in the family, who then, for the first time after the tragedy, finds full expression for his sorrow as well as a pattern of surrounding roles directed to comforting his misery. For this reason, delayed emotional reactions to personal loss in disaster may appear in individuals after a considerable period during which their role has been mainly one of comforting, and at a time when the mourner's role finally opens up to them in the emotional economy of the family.

A subsequent study (Perry and Perry, 1959) of children surviving a schoolhouse disaster further confirmed these observations, although it did not find emotional disturbances to be so prevalent among the bereaved, evidently because this community was one in which extended families offered abundant emotional support. Both studies indicated that the emotional recovery of children who have lost members of their families through disaster will be helped if they can find somewhat new roles in the family and if they are encouraged to see and take pride in these as part of the family's explicit plan for rehabilitating itself. Thus a child who takes on some of the farm or household duties that a lost brother used to perform can find in these a valuable and heightened identification with the supportive family and with its movement toward recuperation; however, there are cases in which this creates role difficulties for siblings.

The period of remedy takes place, at least initially, in an atmosphere often notable for its robust morale. The recovering community is generally found to be drawn together by problems and activities which the majority of its members agree are important and which easily challenge their cooperative energies. Furthermore, the considerable softening of class barriers and the heightening of interaction among people who were formerly strangers contribute to solidarity. Shared sorrows, sympathy, and plans for the future keep visible the common, indispensable values of the community and bring to light a foundation of coherence that is harder to find underneath the pluralism of ordinary times. Rescue and rehabilitation agencies coming in from outside have sometimes ignored or underestimated the in-group tightness of disaster-hit communities. When they do so, their policies for the administration of relief can run into dismaying conflict with new and strongly held values in the community, or their initiative in making decisions can become disappointingly unwelcome to people intent on their own ideas for recovery.

Studies of the recuperation of communities show that the utopian human relations of the early recovery period tend gradually to disappear as the survivors return to their more usual ways of life. Social distinctions submerged by the common fate of disaster reappear as the community becomes again capable of supporting a complicated pattern of tasks and class stratification and as it re-engages with the intact social system.

We do not know much about the long-term changes that may be wrought by disaster, because almost no research has undertaken to follow a stricken community over any great number of years. In theory, it appears unlikely that a social system struck by a major disaster could return to a state precisely like that before the catastrophe; but whether the inevitable changes might in some cases be trivial is a matter of conjecture. Interview material suggests (but only suggests) that a recovered community may retain a heightened sensitivity to some of the life-and-death issues it confronted in the moment of disaster. A good many survivors are found to be strikingly articulate about philosophical and religious values that have become sharper for them. We should expect some consequent modification of relevant social institutions. Also we know that in disasters for which it is possible to assign some human responsibility, there may take place a prolonged informal working-out of allocation of blame and innocence; this is bound to have an effect on the subsequent status of some individuals and organizations. There are, too, ecological effects in the wake of destruction, some of which can be quite striking —as when Udall, Kansas, following a devastating tornado, grew in its recovery to a much larger population than it had had before, mainly because friendly banks offered builders in that area a lowered rate of mortgage interest as an aid to reconstruction and thereby also attracted potential home builders from nearby towns (Hamilton, Taylor, and Rice, 1955).

Such, then, are some of the principal features of what has been called the "natural history of a disaster," and some of the phenomena and problems examined in disaster research. So general and sketchy an account, of course, fits no single disaster with any precision; every mass catastrophe takes place in ways and under circumstances that make it unique. But this brief survey of the field may make evident in rough form the pattern of knowledge that has been emerging from careful empirical study—a pattern to which the following chapters add greater detail and greater range of theoretical interpretation.

▶ *two*

THE METHODOLOGICAL CHALLENGE OF DISASTER RESEARCH

Ira H. Cisin
with **Walter B. Clark**

THE PRINCIPAL PURPOSES of this chapter are to encourage discussion of methods used in research on human behavior in disaster situations and to invite attention to some important questions connected with the selection of methods in social research in general, and in disaster research in particular. Strictly, we cannot speak of the methods of disaster research; there are no special methods unique to this field. Its methods are the methods of social research, the available techniques are those of social research, the essential logic is that of social research. Why, then, does disaster research deserve special methodological consideration?

Part of the answer lies in the necessarily impromptu nature of many disaster studies, particularly those which attempt to study behavior on the site of a disaster immediately after (or, to magnify the difficulty, during) a disastrous event. Research planning takes time and, as Killian (1956b) points out, time is what the researcher has least of in many disaster studies. Difficulty piles upon difficulty at each step of the research, and the researcher often finds himself incapable of applying the rules that he knows so well. The carefully defined population that he would like to study is thoroughly disrupted; his sampling plan deteriorates into a nonrandom selection of the persons he can locate; his data-collection procedures suffer from transportation and communication troubles. He reaches the analysis-and-report-writing stage somewhat bewildered by the information he has collected, certain that there are important insights and vital conclusions hidden somewhere in the pile, but unable to find analytic techniques applicable to data which meet none of the assumptions and conform to none of the procedural rules available from his course work, his reference books, and his previous experience. In short, improvisation has replaced method, and the quality of the results seems to depend more on the researcher's ingenuity than upon his scientific skill. Of course, the temptation exists to "throw away the book" when the going gets tough. Perhaps the most important message of Killian's review of the difficulties lies in its emphasis on the need to hug the book even more tightly with one hand while frantically improvising with the other.

The need for improvisation to overcome administrative and technical difficulties is only part of the reason for concentration on the methods of disaster research; there are at least two other reasons. First, disaster research is of practical importance: it can contribute information and offer guidance to increase the efficiency of efforts to minimize destruction and to restore necessary facilities in disaster areas; in fact, it may be argued that disaster research represents the major contribution social science can make to national survival in the event of nuclear war. Second, disaster research is of great theoretical interest—it presents, at least as well as any other subject matter area, certain pre-methodological questions of the utmost importance in the planning of research efforts. The first reason requires no further explanation. The second is, perhaps, the most elementary point in any discussion of the methods of social research: the specification of the purpose of the research and the problem to be investigated. It is universally agreed that methods can be selected optimally only in the framework of the problem to be dealt with. But it is probably safe to say that, in spite of this lip service, there is confusion between operational problems and research problems, between basic and applied problems, between problems of prediction and problems of control.

We lack systematic procedures for decision on a purpose for research, and for definition of research problems in terms of that purpose. This lack has plagued much of the past disaster research. Is it possible, then, to formulate procedures for problem definition or problem selection? Is it possible that this important first step in research can be formalized like the procedure for selecting samples or computing chi-square? Perhaps, but it is not within the scope of our capabilities to do so. Rather what will be presented here is a discussion of the kinds of conceptualization available to the researcher, the kinds of considerations that influence his choice, and the methodological implications of the choice, both for the future of disaster research and for the studies done in the past.

Our plan is, thus, a simple one. In the first part the reader will find a brief summary of Killian's work on the special technical and methodological difficulties of field research on disaster—the difficulties one has in constructing and executing a plan in the light of a realistic evaluation of existing situations. Subsequent sections will be devoted to a discussion of pre-methodological considerations of a theoretical rather than a practical nature; here the reader is invited to face the variety of conceptual frames in which disaster research may be viewed. He is offered a challenge to reason deductively from these frames, to select methods which optimize the contribution of the research to the specified problem, and to select or improvise techniques which maximize the utility of the methods.

Method and Technique

Strictly speaking, a discussion of methodological and technical difficulties in disaster research presupposes that decisions have been made with regard to conceptualization, model selection, and problem definition—in short, that pre-methodological problems have been solved. The discussion might then be limited to problems in the execution of previously made research plans. The special situations in which disaster research occurs, however, make such rigorous, time-bound thinking unrealistic. The student of disaster research is well aware that the field situation will require a maximum of ingenuity and improvisation. He cannot plan his research for ideal situations; he cannot pretend that he will be able to exercise laboratory control or even the quasi-control frequently associated with the somewhat anomalous "field laboratory." We shall give first consideration, then, to the practical problems of carrying out systematic research in disaster situations, drawing heavily, for both content and organization, on Killian's work.

Killian has said, "There is no area of social research in which the scientist must operate with less freedom than in the field of disaster study. Controlled experiments, except with small-scale, simulated models, are forbidden him. Since disasters are highly unpredictable, he rarely has the opportunity to select the locus of his study before the disaster has occurred. . . . Insistence on the control of a large number of variables may lead to no research at all" (1956b, p. 4). Killian is not advocating less rigorous methods when disasters are the problem under consideration. He points out that the lack of knowledge as to the time, place, and nature of the disaster "means that a *specific* research design must be crystallized hastily, with a limited knowledge of the situation" (1956b, p. 5).

Perhaps the greatest problem in disaster research stems from the lack of time for careful investigation of the particular situation prior to data collection in the field. This leaves the investigator with no choice but to work out a basic design in advance, and then to fit the chosen design to the disaster. Killian examines this question of determining whether the "available" disaster will permit the application of the prepared design and recommends that the investigator keep not one but several suitable flexible designs in readiness. Then, "if he has a more general model and set of hypotheses about the effects of different kinds of warnings (for example), . . . he can go into a wide variety of disasters and test some of his hypotheses" (1956b, p. 13).

Similarly, the problem of adequate controls and measures is always with the investigator. As Killian points out, there can be no simple solution here, but adequate criteria are needed for comparisons of the variables deemed important for the particular problem under investigation. Killian points to the development of criteria for the rating and comparison of organizational performance in disasters (as suggested by Form, Nosow, Stone, and Westie, 1954) as a hopeful indication that even knotty problems of this kind are not insuperable.

Given a flexible research design, the social scientist is faced with the problem of selecting the subjects from whom the data can be gained. Here again, previously made decisions will provide a framework within which final decisions can be made. As Killian has put it, "Certain precautions must be observed to insure that the subjects selected are adequate for testing the hypotheses of the study. This requires attention to the physical and ecological situation in the disaster and foresight in sampling the sub-populations which logically can be expected to have been involved in the actions or to have been subject to the variables being studied. These logical expectations, to some extent, can be checked empirically by preliminary interviewing before the final sample is drawn" (1956b, p. 14).

Probability sampling has found little use in the study of disasters, because "the conditions . . . make it difficult to define, locate and reach the universe to be sampled" (Killian, 1956b, p. 15). Despite the apparent difficulties, however, rigorous sampling techniques have a great contribution to make in permitting statements about the frequency of behavior patterns found to be associated with disasters, even though physical destruction may make reconstruction of the pre-disaster situation and population difficult if not impossible. Killian mentions such useful existing aids as land-use maps for a description of the pre-disaster community.

Of course, the procedures in sampling—as in every other area of research—depend upon the problem at hand. Killian's example here is the special sample of those who were in the Impact Zone, or who participated in the rescue operations. Locating such respondents is a problem that often can be overcome by following leads given by already-located informants. This approach may also be useful in collecting data on group processes, particularly when the groups emerged spontaneously under the stimulus of the disaster itself.

Another interesting and important suggestion is found in Killian's discussion of sampling "points of observation." Here the researcher gains information by using a subject as both respondent and informant on the behavior of others. Using this procedure in the study of formally structured organizations, he recommends observations from "(1) persons at different levels in the hierarchy of the same organization, (2) persons at corresponding levels in different organizations, (3) persons in any organization which had higher or wider jurisdiction or coordinating functions, (4) persons not in an organization who were (a) in a position to observe its work, (b) recipients of its services" (Killian, 1956b, p. 18).

The securing of data relatively free from bias is important to all social research, but the great emotional impact of disaster may bring about greater distortions than are found in most situations. The problem of securing the cooperation of the subjects does not seem to present great difficulties. Killian points out that people are generally willing to speak of their disaster experiences *if* they feel that these experiences are not being exploited: "They want to be convinced that the research will do somebody some good" (1956b, p. 20). An occasional exception to this rule may be found among officials who either are sensitive to publicity about their own roles in the disaster or feel that it is unwise to "bother" the population at such a time.

Interviews have been the mainstay of data collection in the field of disaster research. Here there are no special problems that cannot be overcome with careful attention to the effectiveness of the schedule and the skill of the interviewer in obtaining and recording the data. Killian notes that the disaster victim may find it difficult to describe his experiences in orderly detail; frequently the account will be rambling and disorganized, if rich in content. But he notes, "if answers are permitted to flow in this unstructured fashion, frequent probing questions must be used to insure complete, systematic coverage of the questions in the schedule. . . . the interviewer must be prepared to listen to, and even to probe responses which are gruesome and tragic in spite of the effect which they arouse in him. . . . The greatest danger is not that the interviewer will appear unsympathetic to the respondent but that he will become so identified with him that he drops the role of the scientific observer" (1956b, pp. 23-24). The close supervision of interviewers is highly recommended to preserve interviewer detachment and to minimize interviewer bias. A further caution: People who have discussed their experiences with others in the community can rapidly assimilate inaccurate versions of the disaster. These "group versions" may quickly come to be accepted by a large segment of the population (Killian, 1956b, p. 30).

The questionnaire has not been widely used as an instrument of data collection in disaster research. Killian points out that the difficulties in approaching disaster victims may have discouraged such use. He feels that the questionnaire could be used, however, if the following conditions are observed: "(1) A clear convincing covering statement indicating the sponsorship, the purpose, and the possible significance of the research, accompanies the questionnaire; (2) The research objective is specific enough to permit the requisite data to be obtained with a brief instrument consisting of limited-choice questions; and (3) The sample, or the entire population, can be reached more easily, efficiently, and quickly through the distribution of questionnaires than through personal interviews" (1956b, p. 21).

The projective test is another instrument which has not found wide use in disaster research, possibly because such tests are time-consuming and difficult to administer. In addition, however, some theoretical considerations intrude, for no one knows "to what extent results of tests administered after a disaster reflect stable, pre-existing personality characteristics rather than reactions to the disaster experience itself" (Killian, 1956b, p. 27). Because of these difficulties, Killian would recommend the use of projective techniques only in combination with other techniques.

Sociometric techniques may also play a part in disaster investigation. If one can assume or demonstrate that social structures return to something approximating "normality" at some time after the event, then sociometric measures may permit investigation of the changes in social structure believed to accompany the impact of a disaster on a community. The ideal, but most frequently unobtainable, case would of course permit measures both before and after the event.

A final data-collection technique mentioned by Killian involves the use of documents. He inserts a word of caution since the most easily obtainable records—newspapers, for example—may not contain accurate relevant information. Although the requirements of journalism and those of science are infrequently coincident, information can be gleaned from newspaper and radio accounts, personal documents such as diaries and letters, and the reports of surveys and investigations made by police, insurance agents, relief agencies, etc.

In discussing the analysis of disaster research data, Killian remarks that the techniques are those common to all research. One must keep in mind only the new factors presented by the disaster itself. For example, the physical forces of a tornado or a flood certainly make some behavior difficult if not impossible. Such forces will affect all behaviors from communication through rescue operations but may not affect the several areas equally. Data collected in the field then must also contain pertinent information as to the physical characteristics of the particular area from which they came.

Killian mentions finally the problems of entree in field studies. The possibilities of pending lawsuits, fears of responsibility, etc., may lead to caution on the part of respondents. Killian feels that this can be at least partially overcome by selecting a suitable identity for the investigation. This problem of auspices, he feels, must be "played by ear." In some cases a university might be the best sponsor, in others some government agency. In any event, assured anonymity for the respondent, backed up by a trustworthy interviewer representing a trusted organization, is highly recommended.

The Many Faces of Disaster

The practical difficulties of conducting research in disaster situations may legitimately discourage the research worker. But social research has a history of difficult situations that have been met with imaginative improvisation and creative intuition. Characteristically, the social researcher does not flee the difficult situation; he attempts to buttress himself with a strong theoretical background, he concentrates on the development of flexibility in the planning process, and he strives to compensate, through more adequate conceptualization, for some of the imposed technical inadequacies. The remainder of this chapter is devoted to a discussion of the early planning of disaster research, the pre-methodological considerations that distinguish this fascinatingly difficult area of inquiry.

What is a disaster and what kind of theory is available to facilitate our thinking about disasters? Obviously the choice of theoretical models is important in the selection of optimum methods and techniques. If a single model can serve for all disasters, then planning must concentrate on the improvement of tools for execution of studies conforming to the unitary model. If, on the other hand, every disaster is in itself a theoretical entity, then sheer improvisation must be the specialty of the research worker. Certainly no unitary model will suffice for all research purposes in all disasters; it is equally certain that there is some identifiable communality among at least some disasters. Then what kinds of models are most appropriate for what kinds of disasters, and what implications can we draw from the selection of models for the decision on research problems and procedures?

First, however, what is a disaster? It is an event (or series of events) which seriously disrupts normal activities. Probably every individual has experienced, at some time in his life, some form of personal disaster: the death of a loved one, a serious accident, a sudden illness, a fire in the home, a flooded basement, loss of a job or some other financial crisis. Familiarity with these personal experiences makes it easy to project one's thinking to the community level and to visualize, in somewhat the same terms, the disruption of a larger group of persons in a community disaster.

Marks and Fritz (1954, *1*, p. 3) have defined a disastrous event in systematic terms:

1. The event affects a community of persons—i.e., a collection of people who occupy a common territory and are bound together in relatively permanent social relationships.

2. The event confronts a large segment of the community with actual danger or threats of danger and loss to cherished values and material objects.

3. The event results in deaths, injuries, the destruction of property, and other losses and deprivations to the population, e.g., the disruption of community utilities and other community services.

4. The direct or indirect consequences of the disaster affect a large proportion of the population in the community, i.e., the repercussions are diffused throughout the community rather than focused on a particular group or collection of individuals.

Powell, Rayner, and Finesinger (1953) have sought to establish a framework permitting comparison between disasters in terms of the stages through which they passed. The seven stages—warning, threat, impact, inventory, rescue, remedy, and recovery—are used to construct a profile of specific disasters, which can be related to individual and group responses to the disaster as mediated by such intervening variables as pre-disaster conditioning and the nature of the destructive agent involved.

A narrow reading of disaster definitions might lead the unwary to conclude that only *destructive* events can be considered disastrous. The requirement that a destructive event actually occur would be unnecessarily restrictive in disaster research. But a potential disaster may be just as disruptive of individual and community behavior as the actual event. The responses generated by hoaxes and false alarms clearly demonstrate that disaster behavior can and does occur in the absence of objective danger. It is the perception of threat and not its actual existence that is important.

The methodological implications of a broadening of disaster definitions to include potential as well as actual destruction may be of tremendous importance. If, on theoretical grounds, we concentrate our attention on the disruption of human activities and on human response to the disruption, then some of our practical difficulties may be at least mitigated. For example, the sampling of populations following an actually destructive disaster is extremely difficult; but such sampling may be quite easy in a situation where the population has perceived a threat although no crippling destruction has occurred. Thus, studies of false-alarm behavior and such studies as *The Invasion from Mars* (Cantril, 1940) can contribute immensely to the body of knowledge about disaster behavior under circumstances that are virtually ideal as compared to those surrounding the actually destructive disaster.

Perhaps the earliest disruption attributable to a disaster occurs when the possibility of disaster is entertained. This *early recognition of possibility* may not affect the behavior of the individuals involved, and the recognition of possibility may come too late for any effective action. But it may be argued that unless early recognition of possibility occurs, and unless the disruption which it causes is tolerated, the effect of disaster if it actually occurs will be magnified. Early recognition of the possibility of a school fire disrupts normal school behavior to the extent that fire drills are scheduled; early recognition of the possibility of flood disrupts normal behavior because dikes may have to be built; early recognition of the possibility of earthquake modifies building codes. Many examples can be cited, at the personal as well as the community level, from equipping a home with fire extinguishers to the scheduling of elaborate air raid drills. In each case, a modification of what previously was regarded as normal behavior occurs, and a new definition is substituted. When we speak of *unexpected* disasters, we are really referring to those whose possibility was not recognized—or, more precisely, those considered to have so little probability that the disruption necessary to prevent them or to prepare to cope with them was not considered worthwhile. An example is provided by the study of the tornado in White County, Arkansas (Marks and Fritz, 1954, *1*, pp. 77-80), where a portion of the population considered a tornado extremely unlikely because of the particular topography of the area in which they resided; this despite the frequency with which similar disasters had struck farther south in "tornado alley." Expectation, the first stage of preparation for disaster, thus involves early recognition of its possibility, an evaluation of the probability as sufficiently high to justify some disruption of normal behavior, and, of course, implementing action calculated to avert disaster or to minimize the severity of its effect. We are led then to consider as the cost of early recognition a certain tolerable disruption of normal living, as insurance against the major disruption the disaster would bring.

The second period of disruption occurs, in some disasters, in a *period of expectation.* The dam upriver has broken, the forest fire is raging out of control on the other side of the hill, enemy airplanes have been sighted crossing the channel. The probability that a disaster will occur in the not-too-distant future has increased enormously, and any plans for coping with the disaster are put into effect. The retreat to the storm cellar, community evacuation, the alerting of rescue agencies outside the community—these exemplify expectation behavior. We must note that this expectation is at least partly dependent upon the prior recognition of the possibility of disaster. If a possible source of danger has not been recognized as such, the cues of impending disaster may be ignored; some individuals in the path of the Arkansas tornado attributed the sounds to normal events such as the noise of a passing train. Similarly, the bell and siren system used in Holland to warn of flood danger was ignored or misunderstood by many, even though the system was well known and had been in existence since the Middle Ages (van Dijk and Pilger, 1955, pp. 84-86).

The third stage of disaster is the *period of impact.* In one sense, this stage represents the maximum disruption of normal modes of behavior. But in another very real sense this disruption is entirely different from the disruptions that have preceded it and those that will follow it. While the bombs are falling or the tornado is blowing, the individual and the community can do very little to affect the outcome. Certainly unintelligent behavior at this period can magnify the effect of the disaster; the person who refuses to stay in the shelter or who panics at the sight of the floodwaters carrying away his home and decides to swim after it, the person who refuses to leave his car because it is his most precious possession—these not only can intensify the effect of the disaster on themselves but also can injure the entire community because they disrupt discipline and demand special attention from authorities who have other things to do. But apart from these people, the behavior of individuals *during* the disaster would frequently seem to be less related to survival or to minimization of effect than the behavior that has occurred earlier and the behavior that will occur during the next period.

Immediately following the impact period, in the wake of disaster, comes a *period of reaction.* From the observer's point of view this is the period of maximum disruption—while the community counts its dead, surveys the destruction, cares for its wounded, and attempts to survive in the face of communication difficulties, transportation problems, water pollution, inadequacy of medical facilities, and the staggering problems of "convergence behavior" (Fritz and Mathewson, 1957). Here the curious, the vicious, the inept, and the competent from outside descend upon the community to gawk, to loot, to sympathize, to organize.

For many persons the period of reaction is one of high anxiety: dazed and confused, they may behave in ways no longer appropriate to the situation while they strive to locate loved ones and to realize the extent of damage to themselves and their community. Much evidence is accumulating to substantiate that, from the individual's viewpoint, the disorganization of this period is not real but apparent. Fritz and Marks (1954) interpret their data to indicate that "the immediate problem in a disaster situation is neither uncontrolled behavior nor intense emotional reaction, but deficiencies of coordination and organization, complicated by people acting upon individual definitions of the situation." This aspect of disaster is often erroneously identified as panic.

Having survived this period of maximum reaction, the community is now ready for a *period of reconstruction.* This is the beginning of a return to normality, in which disruption takes the form of unfamiliar work, planning for the future, rehabilitation of survivors, and, frequently, feverish activity to prevent the recurrence of a similar disaster. Thus the cycle is complete and the community returns to the period of recognition of possibility, where this recognition is encouraged by its recent experience.

Does a disaster-hit community ever return to "normal"? Probably not, if in "normal" we include every detail of the way of life prevailing before the disaster. Certainly the building codes of San Francisco and Tokyo still recognize the possibility of repetitions of earthquake disasters; communities that have suffered school fires tighten up their rules for drills and inspection; London has retained and improved its bomb shelters. When death occurs in a family, it is impossible for the family to reproduce its previous way of life. The gradual return to normality after a disaster can better be thought of as adaptation to modified behavior patterns than as a return to previous behavior patterns. The amount of modification and its permanence can probably be expressed as a function of the severity of the disaster and the manner in which the community is reminded of it during the years following. Some of these modifications are dictated by the disaster itself; thus, the occupational pattern of the affected area in the Holland floods was drastically changed when farm lands were inundated with salt water (Haveman, 1955, p. 8). In other cases the direction of modifications may be a function of the "costs" of the modifications. For example, Marks and Fritz (1954, *1*) have described the increase in fatalism and religiosity among survivors of the Arkansas tornado who could not afford to build storm shelters.

A "unitary theory" of disaster behavior, such as exemplified in the foregoing account of the cycle of disruption, argues, essentially, that all community disasters can be characterized by the following facts: they affect a relatively large number of persons; they are disruptive of normal behavior, requiring sacrifice in the pre-disaster stages and rapid change in behavior modes during and following the disaster itself; they frequently impose new norms and new ways of life as the price of survival; social structures and social controls are frequently destroyed and new structures and new means of control must be improvised; recuperation from disaster frequently involves a community in an unfamiliar dependency on other communities and on larger governmental structures.

Such a unitary theory appeals to the researcher who wants to study the effects of disruptive events on forms of behavior and organization in which he is particularly interested. Thus, for the student whose primary interest is in community organization and the functioning of formal groups such as the family, any disaster will serve equally well, in that it places a strain on the criterion variable he has chosen. This is analogous to the study of the effect of psychological stress on individual behavior. The researcher whose principal interest is automobile driving behavior can be satisfied with a unitary theory of stress, since he can observe disruption of normal driving behavior whenever any one of several kinds of stress occurs. He need not concern himself with the varieties of stress and their differential effects so long as they seem to affect equally the behavior he is studying.

For a student of personality, social systems, political systems, economic systems, or subcultural systems, a unitary theory of disaster is probably adequate. In many field studies of disaster it is clear that the dependent variable is the operation of one of these systems; the disaster itself represents a vehicle for study of the system—or, more usually, the disruption attributable to the disaster represents a variation in the value of one or more of the independent variables whose relation to the dependent variable system is to be studied. For example, when we ask: "What is the effect of disaster on community organization?" we really ask, "What is the effect of sudden destruction of life and property on community organization?" A study of the disruption of a social system is, effectively, a study of that system, and it is thus legitimate to deal with the disruptive phenomena interchangeably.

But what of the researcher whose interest is in the disruptors? Can he be satisfied with a unitary theory of disaster? In particular, what of the researcher who is interested in the process of disruption, the forces leading to disruption, the resistance to disruption? This researcher, for example, asks how a community or individuals behave when they first sense the possibility of a disaster, how decisions are made on the probability of a disaster, what disruption is tolerable in the pre-disaster period to minimize the disruption during and after disaster?

Our purpose here is not to draw a sharp distinction between the two kinds of research mentioned—that in which the disaster is a vehicle through which a social or other system can be studied in other than its normal state, and that in which the process of disruption and the potential control of behavior to minimize the disruption are the principal objectives. The point is that while a unitary theory of disaster behavior may well serve for studies of systems suffering disruption, it may be necessary to distinguish among kinds of disasters if the emphasis is to be on the disruptive process itself.

Some distinctions frequently made in classifying disasters are of little value for either kind of research. For example, disasters can logically be classified as man-made (bombings, dynamitings, and some fires) or natural (tornadoes, hurricanes, earthquakes). There is little evidence, however, that this classification makes much difference in the reactions to disaster. Perhaps it may be important, in pre-disaster stages, in determining the expectation probability values placed on disaster occurrence; perhaps it has something to do with the willingness to tolerate the disruption requisite for disaster preparation—but these effects are yet to be demonstrated. It would seem reasonable to expect many people to be more fatalistic about natural disasters than about man-made disasters; yet the Strategic Bombing Surveys (Janis, 1951; U.S. Strategic Bombing Survey, 1945, 1946) seemed to indicate that many persons in the affected populations regarded the bombings with an air of resignation to the inevitable. This suggests that fatalism may be more closely associated with the preventability of the disaster or with the mitigability of its effects than with its origin in nature or in man.

Another important distinction can be made, between expected and sudden disasters. This distinction has been subsumed in the disaster disruption cycle at the beginning of this section. An expected disaster is merely one on which a high probability value has been set by the community and, usually, one for which the pre-disaster disruption required for preparation has been deemed tolerable. A sudden disaster, on the other hand, is one on which, for one reason or another, a low probability value has been set or for which advance preparation has been deemed economically or socially too disruptive. It is this type of disaster that poses some of the most important problems in social control to be discussed next. In particular, it poses special problems for research in cases where a disaster must be prepared for even though it is not likely to occur.

In discussing the willingness of a community to tolerate some disruption in the form of preparation for disaster, it may be worthwhile to distinguish between those disasters whose primary threat is to property and those which represent a threat to human life.

Certainly no attempt has been made here to exhaust the possibilities for classification in distinguishing among types of disasters. Our purpose has been to suggest that for certain types of research problems it may be necessary to distinguish among disasters in terms of form, origin, or effects.

In summary, then, disaster is conceived for purposes of research as an event or set of events which may or may not actually occur, but which is perceived as sufficiently probable to justify the disruption of normal behavior that preparation for the event requires. Field studies of disaster-related behavior have, in the main, concerned themselves with disruption of social and other behavioral systems during and after disasters which have occurred, and have concentrated on the effect which the disaster had on these systems. An alternative conceptualization is one in which the disaster disruption appears as the dependent variable and the behavioral or adaptive systems appear as independent variables; the primary focus of these studies would be to increase understanding of tolerance for disruption in preparation for disasters which may never occur.

The importance placed on this latter point clearly reflects a bias of the author that should be made explicit before we discuss the kinds of research available to the disaster researcher. Given that some kinds of disasters can be foreseen, and that advance preparation may prevent disaster or mitigate its effects, then it behooves the researcher to devote a considerable portion of his energies to studies of social control—to research that will provide information of practical as well as theoretical importance. For example, it may be argued from one point of view that one of the most important contributions of disaster research can be to help the people of the United States prepare themselves for the possibility of a nuclear war; it may even be that the preparation itself will serve as a deterrent to the occurrence of the disaster—this alone would be sufficient justification. In addition it may be argued that the destructive power of a nuclear disaster is so great and the probability of national survival so low without preparation that every effort must be bent in the direction of modifying behavior *now* and increasing the tolerance for disruption *now* in order to reduce in some way the almost total disruption that would face an unprepared nation if the disaster were to occur.

This, then, is the course of disaster research: to describe disaster behavior so that it can be better understood; to analyze disaster behavior so that it can be better predicted; and, above all, to construct dynamic models of disaster behavior so that it can be better controlled. Because of the great importance of a kind of disaster that may never occur, emphasis should be put on the kinds of behavior involved in the preparation for disaster. The study of behavior during and after disasters is justified to the extent that it aids in the understanding, prediction, and control of future behavior aimed at the prevention of disaster and the mitigation of its effects.

The Kinds of Research

The principal thesis of this chapter is the rather obvious point that the method chosen for research derives from the formulation of the research problem and that research technique derives from method and from the state of the art. In the previous section, various orientations for formulation of research problems were examined. Now we must categorize the kinds of research appropriate to each. It is assumed that the research is ultimately geared to a practical problem, that the research is to be evaluated in terms of its contribution to prevention of disaster or mitigation of its effects—or, more specifically, that the research is to be judged in terms of its contribution to understanding and control of the motivation of populations, to prepare for defense against disaster. Because this is a discourse on method rather than on purpose, the specification of any particular purpose is somewhat arbitrary and is to be regarded as an example providing guidelines for the mode of classification adopted. Ideally the classification scheme should have generality extending beyond the limitations of one practical purpose; at the same time it is clear that, except for the most basic kinds of research, research problems must derive from practical problems, with the hope that the solution to any research problem may contribute to the solution of more than one practical problem.

This formulation is sometimes oversimplified into a dichotomy between basic research and applied research. Thus a basic research problem is conceived as one divorced from any practical problem existing or foreseen, one contributing new information or a new descriptive or classificatory model for the explanation of events or observations. At the other end of the continuum, applied research is conceived as providing the solution for some single, specific practical problem, with no reasonable expectation that the solution may have application to any other problem. Obviously, few studies in social research, and particularly in disaster research, can be placed at either extreme of this continuum. Even if we accept a rather limited practical purpose—for example, increasing our ability to prepare a population for some particular disaster—it is certainly feasible to cast research problems so that they will contribute to more than this limited purpose. The fact that we can entertain a unitary theory of disaster behavior at all testifies to this possibility.

Remembering, then, that the behavior under study occurs at several periods of time—before, during, and after a disaster, and assuming that the ultimate practical purpose is to achieve minimum disruption in the event of disaster, what kinds of research are available? How can disaster research problems be formulated, and what research methods derive from these formulations?

Clearly, the opening wedge in disaster research must be a set of *descriptive* studies, detailing the behavior with which disaster research is concerned. Descriptive studies tend to be informal observational studies that attempt to answer the question: "Just exactly what happened?" Since, in any disaster, a great many things happened, it is perhaps inevitable that descriptive studies characteristically reflect the selective perception of the observer. The newspaper reporter sees one thing, the psychologist another, the sociologist still another. The descriptive studies serve the principal scientific purpose of introducing the researcher into an unfamiliar area and of steeping him in the phenomena to be studied more formally in the future. The principal purpose of descriptive studies is the generation of hypotheses, the encouragement of insights, and the beginnings of explanation.

Those who have undertaken descriptive studies have generally concentrated their efforts on the details of the disaster itself and on behavior during and immediately after the disaster. The methods have ranged from the most informal observation to precise sample surveys.[1] Unless the observer has himself been involved in the disaster, descriptive studies have had to depend upon recollective interview techniques, either structured or unstructured. For describing the details of the disaster and its effect on the community, descriptive studies have tended to rely on interviews with knowledgeable informants selected for their

[1] There are many excellent bibliographies of disaster research studies, emphasizing descriptive studies. Perhaps the most readily available is *Field Studies of Disaster Behavior: An Inventory* (Disaster Research Group, 1961). See also bibliographies in *The Annals of the American Academy of Political and Social Science*, 1957, *309* (January), and the *Journal of Social Issues, 10* (3), 1954, and Rayner, 1957.

position in the community structure. For detail on the effect of the disaster on individuals and on small groups (families), descriptive studies have tended to rely on interviews with individuals selected as a sample of the pre-disaster population. The technical difficulties of these kinds of studies—the problems of recall and retroactive inhibition (or exhibition); the problem of rapport in interviews with people who are still dazed by their experience; the difficulties of classification and analysis in unstructured interviews—have been discussed earlier in the section summarizing Killian's (1956b) work.

Despite the obvious technical difficulties, the descriptive study has played a very important part in the development of disaster research. Researchers have been trained and hypotheses have been developed, so that the scientific study of disaster behavior might proceed to its next stage of development. Undoubtedly, important research opportunities have been missed.[2] For example, there is a remarkable paucity of descriptive studies on preparation for disaster. It is possible, of course, in a study conducted after a disaster has occurred, to estimate what preparations a community had made for the disaster. And yet how much more valuable these data might be had they been gathered before the disaster occurred. It would be possible, and perhaps not prohibitively expensive, to anticipate disasters in certain communities and to study community behavior at or before the period of recognition of the possibility.

A few studies have made this attempt in other areas of social research. In studies of ethnic relations, attempts have been made to gather "before" data in areas where tensions seemed to be rising; then, when an interracial incident occurs, "after" data can be secured in the knowledge that the "before" data are protected from contamination. Similarly, in studies of childhood injuries, data are being gathered on families in which accidents have not occurred. Then, if and when accidents do occur in these families, the pre-accident data will have been shielded from a retrospective bias. In disaster studies, description of the normal functioning of a community could be extremely valuable in evaluating disruptive effects revealed by descriptive studies after disasters have occurred. In particular, where preparation for disaster as a deterrent to its occurrence is a matter of public policy, it might be especially enlightening to find out what preparations people are making for their own protection.[3] A descriptive study of attitudes and behavior regard-

[2] Many writers have been concerned with missed opportunities for descriptive studies (see especially Killian, 1954b; J. W. Powell, 1954a).

[3] Studies of existing protective measures used in false alarms have revealed the inadequacy of preparation in terms of planning, organized action, and, per-

ing preparation for nuclear war could conceivably make an important contribution to an appreciation of the magnitude and the variety of social control problems.

Descriptive studies, particularly those employing formal survey methods and structured interview techniques, tend to develop into *analytic* studies, studies reporting relationships between disaster behavior as a dependent variable and other characteristics of the individual or family or community as independent variables. To accomplish the purpose of reporting correlation coefficients, differential probabilities, or distributions of proportions for people who behaved differently during a disaster, these analytic studies must forego the artistic insight-seeking of the descriptive studies and adopt more formal methods so as to insure, for example, that every respondent is asked for information on the characteristic to be reported in relation to the disaster behavior. Similarly for the dependent variable, the forms of disaster behavior must be standardized so that relationships may be shown unequivocally. In planning such studies employing sampling survey methods and structured interview techniques, the researcher is obligated to decide in advance what items he will put in his questionnaire, and is restricted to those items throughout his analysis. This restriction is the price he pays for taking the next step toward hypothesis-generation beyond what he was able to accomplish in descriptive studies. The results of analytic studies must perforce be regarded as hypotheses rather than as conclusions because analytic studies require no explanatory model; they are intended to round out descriptions of behavior by demonstrating that people with different characteristics have behaved differently. At best, an analytic study can be said to test hypotheses of relationship rather than hypotheses of explanation or causation. But without going through this step of observing relationships, it is extremely unlikely that an explanatory model can be constructed and explanatory hypotheses tested.

Disaster research today can perhaps be best described as in a late stage of analytic studies; a considerable body of agreement has developed on the variables which tend to be correlated with disaster behavior, and similar agreement is developing in the area of the dependent variable—the facets or dimensions of disaster behavior to be studied.[4] It should be noted, however, that this body of agreement relates to behavior during and after disasters. Very little is known about in-

---

haps most important, public attitudes—the assumption that "it can't happen here" (see particularly Mack and Baker, 1961; Scott, 1955).

[4] The development of usable measures, classification schemes, and analytic hypotheses, as well as the beginning of explanatory hypotheses, are well exemplified in Fritz and Marks, 1954.

dividual differences in disaster preparation behavior and about the correlates of such behavior.

As we indicated in the discussion of analytic studies, the next step in the progress of disaster research is in the direction of what might be called dynamic analytic, predictive, or *explanatory* studies. The shift from analytic to explanatory studies is a giant step, one that seems to require a large body of analytic data, possibly more than now exists. But it is a step that is vitally necessary if disaster research is to progress toward its goal of social control.

In general, explanatory studies try to make sense out of the relationships observed in analytic studies, and to gather those relationships into a motivational model which explains the behavior under study as the dependent variable. In a sense, the analytic study uses a form of regression analysis to "post-dict" behavior. The explanatory study attempts to select and interrelate post-dictive variables into a structure that will permit *pre*-diction of the dependent variable. The process by which this transition occurs is ordinarily a tedious one. As data from analytic studies are amassed, regularities are observed, consistencies are noted, hunches are generated, dynamic hypotheses emerge.[5] These dynamic hypotheses take various forms, of which the most primitive is: "Whenever X occurs to persons with characteristic Y, the probability of behavior Z is increased relative to behavior W." This form of statement translates itself readily into a predictive hypothesis which can then be checked back against the existing analytic studies. Having passed the checking-back test, the hypothesis may now be exposed to formal test in a new survey, in a quasi-experiment (an after-the-fact experiment built from materials available in a survey) or, if the situation is appropriate, in a controlled experiment.

Dynamic explanatory hypotheses are beginning to emerge in disaster research and this bodes well for the future. An example of such a hypothesis is this: "In disaster situations, if the lines of authority are maximally similar to the lines of authority in normal nondisaster situations, the effectiveness of social control is increased." This hypothesis is supported in a variety of ways in both disaster research and other fields. In military situations, for example, it is generally recognized that when faced with a crisis situation a unit will perform better under its familiar trusted leader than under a newly appointed leader. The success of evacuations in school fires lends support to this hypothesis.

[5] Excellent examples of the kind of thinking required for the move from analytic to explanatory dynamic hypotheses, from post-diction to pre-diction, and of the way in which social control hypotheses are generated, are to be found in Foreman, 1953; Fritz and Mathewson, 1957; Fritz and Williams, 1957; and Quarantelli, 1954.

And, on a quasi-experimental basis, the data from Operation Four-Thirty support it (Mack and Baker, 1961). A word of caution is appropriate, however. A well-supported dynamic hypothesis, even one that has been experimentally tested, is not necessarily an adequate guide for action. Even if the above hypothesis were to stand up against subsequent test, how safe would it be to arrange that the Civil Defense hierarchy be identical with the administrative hierarchy of normal operations? The danger of such a course is dramatized by the report of the school fire in which the children remained immobilized in their classroom because no teacher appeared to lead them to safety. In short, the step from explanatory theory to social controls is another giant step.

In the planning of explanatory studies, perhaps the most important research step is the selection of the level or form of explanation. In a way, the distinction between analytic studies and explanatory studies is not a useful one, because analytic studies are indeed explanatory at one level. At the very least, they put the dependent variable of interest in a constellation of variables related to it. In another way, an insufficient distinction has been made, and a special category of predictive studies should be set up. As an example of this last distinction, consider the well-recognized correlation between height and weight. In an analytic study with, say, height as the dependent variable, this correlation would emerge; it would then be obvious that we could, for the population studied under the conditions of the study, post-dict height from weight. Psychometric cross-validation would then support this relationship in a predictive study—but would the relationship stand up as an explanatory model? Certainly the ability to *predict* one phenomenon from another is not to be interpreted as enabling us to *control* the dependent variable by inducing modification of the independent variable.

The explanatory hypothesis, then, seems to call for a model in which predictive relationships can be interpreted as causal, or at least dynamic in the sense that induced change in one will tend to produce change in the other. Only such hypotheses can lead toward the shift from explanation to control. It would be foolhardy, of course, to expect that a simple explanatory model would work very well. Certainly the complex causation systems of disaster behavior will not lend themselves to simple explanation. What are sought are explanatory models that will make significant contributions toward increasing the probability of occurrence of desired patterns of behavior; that such increases are likely to be small should be regarded as a challenge rather than a source of discouragement to the social science theorist.

The fact that explanatory studies demand essentially causal hypotheses can lead to a futile search for first causes. If it is believed that cigarette smoking contributes to the probability of lung cancer, is this a sufficient explanatory hypothesis in itself; or must the model be expanded so that we account for the cigarette smoking in terms of orality in the personality structure; or are we then obligated to account for the development of orality in terms of early childhood sucking deprivation? When can we stop? There is no easy answer to this question of level of explanation, just as there was no easy answer to the question of what to look for in a descriptive study or in an analytic study. In general, planners of explanatory studies tend to avoid explanatory variables at the same level as the dependent variable—just as they would avoid explanation of height in terms of weight, or the explanation of one attitude in terms of another attitude. This cannot be adopted as a general rule, because it is sometimes possible to explain a demographic characteristic, such as income, in terms of another demographic characteristic, such as educational level, which has preceded the dependent variable in time. In the construction of explanatory models, the general procedure seems to be to seek explanatory variables which precede the dependent variable in time, or from which a causal arrow can reasonably be drawn to the dependent variable, or which seem to be at a "deeper" level than the dependent variable. Thus behavior is frequently explained in terms of attitudes, attitudes are explained in terms of personality structure, personality structure is explained in terms of early childhood treatment.

It should be re-emphasized that the choice of explanatory models is the option of the researcher. If the objective of explanation is control, however, he would do well to elaborate his explanatory model at least to the point where he specifies explanatory variables that satisfy these two conditions: (1) they are related to the dependent variable in a dynamic way—i.e., induced change in one will tend to produce change in the other; and (2) they can somehow be placed under control—i.e., change in them can be engineered. Unless these conditions are met, the explanatory model serves little function that cannot be fulfilled by analytic studies.

What, then, is the role of demographic characteristics in explanation? What shall we do with the frequent findings that sex, age, and economic status are correlated with the dependent variables in which we are interested? Since such variables can rarely be placed under control, are we to say that they are inadequate for explanatory models? The answer must be that they are inadequate as members of zero-order explanatory models for entire heterogeneous populations. They are certainly not inadequate for models built in some analogue of a partial-regression form. What is meant here is that the demographic variables function in explanatory models as control variables, defining subpopulations of specific interest, conceivably defining important subpopulations that require separate explanatory models—one for each subpopulation—or defining subpopulations for which the shift from explanation to control must be accomplished by different means. At the practical level, any advertising researcher knows that men and women have different motives for buying soap; in trying to exploit these motives, due account is taken of the difference in explanatory models and different appeals are used.

A final word of caution may be appropriate. It is very easy to paint oneself into a corner: Explanation of undesirable disaster behavior in terms of highly cherished social values promotes only conflict and futility in the researcher whose goal is social control. Sometimes the easily available explanation creates insoluble moral problems. It is as though the investigator of childhood injuries were to find that many such injuries were caused by a healthy and highly valued exploratory tendency among children. Shall he recommend that the exploratory tendency be curbed? It is unpleasantly frequent in research on health and welfare that one finds explanations of undesirable occurrences in terms of desirable behavior or attitudes. The researcher who advances such explanatory models must face the fact that the shift from explanation to control may simply not be worth the social cost. How unhappy the lot of the researcher who explains in terms of manipulable variables that no one wants to manipulate! How frustrating it must have been for Bernert and Iklé (1952) in their study of behavior during World War II bombing of London that "the principal enemy of evacuation was solidarity of family life among the mass of the people"!

Special Problems of Social Control

The sequence of descriptive, analytic, and explanatory studies does not, alas, necessarily solve the problem of social control. The kinds of studies described can, at best, answer questions about why people behave as they do. But even the most successful explanatory study can offer only hints about how the dependent variable might be modified through modification of the values of the independent variables. And explanatory studies stop far short of solving the problem of how the values of the independent variables can be modified. In short, a systematic sequence of descriptive, analytic, and explanatory studies of disasters can represent only a beginning toward solution of the problem of how to convince people that they ought to behave in some desired way.

Consider the problem of securing the cooperation of some defined population in a program of preparation for large-scale disaster. What special research problems does such a practical problem suggest? To what extent can the kinds of research we discussed contribute, and what additional kinds of research are required if a pre-disaster campaign calling for behavioral modification is to be successful? It is our purpose now to discuss the methodological implications—or rather the pre-methodological implications—of conceptualizing and formulating research programs to deal with problems of social control and the engineering of consent. Our orientation is essentially that of marketing research. The objective of the researcher is no longer the understanding or the explanation of human behavior. Clearly, his objective is control, and he has resolved for himself the difficult philosophic questions that have arisen in the course of his decision that the public needs to be aroused and that he and his colleagues are somehow wiser, better informed, and more far-sighted than the people themselves in deciding what the people should do.

The following discussion is built around the social control problem of civil defense preparation for nuclear attack, including the problems of deciding on the optimum course of action and engineering the consent of the public toward behavior consonant with the decision. Interest in this extreme form of disaster should not be permitted to obscure the fact that the decision and action steps discussed below are applicable to any organized community program of preparation for disaster.

The first requisite of a social control program is specification of objectives, in terms not only of goals but also of means for the achievement of the goals. At the level of goals, clearly the objective is survival of all or of a maximum proportion of the population. Are these goals realistic and acceptable to the public? As they are stated, these goals would undoubtedly rank, for the great majority of Americans, at the top of their hierarchy of values. Perhaps more important, what sacrifices are the people willing to make to obtain these goals? Would they be willing to evacuate their cities and subsist for a time on roots and berries in the woods? How much inconvenience will they tolerate? How far back are they willing to turn the clock of medical progress in order to survive? It is important that such questions be answered, because in deciding on the means to be proposed, it is necessary that the means as well as the goals not clash violently with the value system of the affected public. Previous field studies of disasters would indicate that the survival goal is of such over-riding value that almost any inconvenience is tolerable. Of course, in previous disasters the people may have been bolstered by confidence that help was on its way and reconstruction was possible in a reasonable period of time. Perhaps the question boils down to: For how long a period of time will people tolerate what kinds of inconvenience bolstered by what kind of expectation of return to "normalcy"? Systematic sociological and anthropological surveys of value systems and their elasticity are necessary as a precedent step before the planning of any program of social control.

Acquiescence of the public to the goals and even to some rather extreme means for the accomplishment of the goals does not provide planners with a workable program. Even if the public were willing to tolerate almost any means to maximize survival probability, what means shall be recommended? Shall the people be asked to dig their own shelters, as some have proposed? Shall they be assembled in central shelters in the pattern of World War II London? Shall they be ordered to evacuate cities? What tools and what supplies must everyone keep in his car at all times? Shall different communities be encouraged to follow different means, or is there one best solution for all situations?

Past field studies of disaster offer few answers to these and similar questions. We are not concerned here with what people would do in a disaster if no preparations had been made. We are concerned with the kinds of preparation that would best meet the emergency. By studies of values and by reference to disaster field studies, we may be able to make some guesses about the acceptability of various procedures; but the question here is essentially an engineering question: What are the best procedures? To say that this is a problem for operations research is to dodge the question with an obvious response. What kind of operations research is required and to what questions shall the operations analyst address himself? Probably the most practical use that can be made of operations research at this time would be a series of simulation studies, falling generally into two classes: those which assume that a given plan is put into effect in a given situation and report out the results of its implementation; and those which assume only that a given situation prevails and try to extract an optimum procedure from the conditions of the situation. In addition, the techniques of operations research must be applied to provide estimating parameters for the evaluation of new ideas. For example, how long would it take to evacuate a city of a given size at a given time of day utilizing the existing network of roads and taking into account deterioration of driving skill under stress and the probability of tie-ups? The sheer engineering practicality of any proposal must be subjected to test by operations research techniques before the proposal is seriously considered. To the extent that existing operations research techniques are inadequate to handle some of the problems of this step, then the development of new operations research techniques must be supported.

Even a solution to the problem of practical feasibility is by no means sufficient. Just as the goals of the survival program were checked against the value system of the public, so the means devised must also be acceptable to the people. This stage of development requires a rather delicate balance among three forces: optimum solutions arising from operations research; the initial willingness of the public to adopt the solutions, as revealed in sociological surveys; and the ability and willingness of the planners to modify public acceptance of proposals. If the public is unwilling to accept the plans as originally devised, then either the plans must be changed or the planners must make the judgment that the attitude of the public can and should be changed. The achievement of this balance at some point where a reasonably optimum plan can be judged practical may be a matter for expert judgment rather than for research; observation of past successes and failures and results from disaster field studies may be helpful.

If the public is to accept a plan and act upon it, three important communications steps must be performed. The public must (1) know of the plan; (2) accept the plan and believe in it; (3) learn to practice the plan and behave according to it. In speaking of the public at this point, one should not neglect the role of the emergency leader in the implementation of the plan. No matter how well versed the individuals are in the execution of an emergency plan, its success will undoubtedly depend on the information, conviction, and efficiency of a hierarchy of appointed leaders charged with the responsibility of directing the public in the execution of the plan.

Studies of false alarms (Mack and Baker, 1961) can be cited as examples of many of the problems just mentioned. In the case of at least one alarm, the general public did not know, for minutes or hours, that it was a false alarm. The sirens signaled an evacuation of the city. Many persons reported that they felt it must have been a false alarm, an unscheduled drill, or a scheduled drill of which they had not heard. In other words, for many persons the period of early recognition of the possibility that the disaster might occur simply had not been reached. Many persons did not correctly interpret the message of the sirens; many scoffed at the idea of evacuation; many sat by waiting for instructions.[6] The appointed leaders were no more convinced than their followers that the emergency was real and that the evacuation plan should be put into effect. Some local officials felt it was within their prerogative to decide that evacuation was not a good idea at all, and that the correct procedure was to direct their followers into sub-

[6] That these events are not unique is indicated in the following studies, among others: Instituut voor Sociaal Onderzoek, 1955; Katz, Kessin, McCoy, Pinto, and Strieby, 1960; and Scott, 1955.

terranean shelters. This behavior did not arise from ignorance; they did not misread the signal; they simply decided for themselves that their plan was superior to the official plan.

The purpose of this retelling of the false-alarm story is to direct attention to the critical communications needs of a successful survival program. The public and its leaders must know and accept the plan and must be practiced in its execution; otherwise the plan is likely to fail, no matter how good it is. Research needs in this area are critical, ranging from surveys on the acceptability of various plans to laboratory studies on the interpersonal communications process and the role of various sense modalities in the achievement of conviction.

Emphasis on the need for research should not be read as an evasion or a deferral of solution to the problem. An excellent argument might be made for the development of procedures "until the doctor comes."[7] If the problem is immediate and the research is likely to take a long time, must we wait? To what extent can expert judgment now assist us? Scientific conservatism might lead us to say that we cannot generalize from existing research to situations that have not yet been investigated, but this position would rank with that of the psychologist who maintained that his years of studying how rats learned could offer no guidance at all to those faced with the problem of improving classroom teaching. Since interim solutions are required, our choice is not between deciding and waiting; our choice is between deciding without using available information and deciding after an imaginative application of available information. All that is suggested here is an interim decision procedure *and* support of the necessary research on the communications process. Such an interim decision requires codification and application of relevant theory from studies of learning and from social-psychological studies of attitude change. This is the kind of synthetic research that is probably least gratifying to the researcher: the review of barely relevant material against the requirement of taking huge leaps of logic to tentative conclusions whose probability of verification is likely to be only slightly better than chance. Gratifying or not, this synthesis and application of available psychological and social-psychological theory is required if waiting for the results of new research is intolerable.

This review of the research requirements implicit in the development of a program of social control for disaster preparation makes it clear that the empirical studies carried out represent only one of several kinds of disaster research that must be incorporated into a rounded program. With the over-all problem formulated as one of social con-

[7] Important first steps toward this development have been taken (e.g., Fritz and Williams, 1957; Janis, 1951; Marks and Fritz, 1954, *3*).

trol, it becomes obvious that such a research program must include:

1. Operations research, employing existing techniques or developing new techniques, for the simulation of disaster situations, estimation of disaster parameters, and development of optimum plans for disaster preparation and disaster behavior. It is essential in carrying out a program of operations research in this area that the human parameters be estimated from research of the other types mentioned below, and that the interaction among these methods of research be maximized, so that the plan that emerges from the operations analysis be consistent with human capabilities and human acceptability.

2. Empirical sociological surveys of disaster behavior under a variety of conditions, with particular emphasis on studies of predisaster preparatory behavior in situations where no plan exists or where a variety of plans have been proposed, with variable community support.

3. Social-psychological surveys on the acceptability of various plans for disaster preparation, with special emphasis on the potential acceptability of optimum plans and the means and motivational devices that might be employed in order to maximize acceptability.

4. Sociological observational and interview studies on the organizational structure of communities, emphasizing the role of designated leaders in disaster preparation and disaster behavior, and recognizing the importance of the acceptability of plans to community leaders.

5. Psychological studies on communications, including both field studies and laboratory experiments on the transmission of information, the modification of attitudes, and the means to be employed to maximize the probability that learned behavior will persevere under conditions of stress.

6. Interim multidisciplinary synthetic study of existing findings, hypotheses, and theories geared to provide best-guess solutions as early approximations of what might emerge over time from the systematic research suggested above. In this exercise, maximum imaginative use would be made of a variety of materials ranging from journalistic reports of disaster behavior through empirical studies in related areas, such as the wartime stress of soldiers, to the most formal theoretical laboratory studies of the experimental psychologists. One of the most important contributions to be achieved from an effort of this kind is the identification of areas of particular weakness—those areas where the integrator finds himself at a virtual loss for information—as a means for generating research requirements in the other categories mentioned above.

Part Two

BEHAVIOR OF INDIVIDUALS IN DISASTER

THE SEQUENCE OF TIME phases that governed our exposition in Chapter One has proven useful for describing the events and facts that emerge as one follows a disaster through its course. But the most fruitful study of disaster behavior must follow systematic concepts which link phenomena in this area to the formal structure of the behavioral sciences.

One gross distinction helpful in relating disaster phenomena to the systematic concepts of relevant sciences is to distinguish research that seeks an understanding of the behavior of individual human beings from research concerned with the behavior of social units that comprise numbers of individuals. On the one hand, we may ask questions about the effects of threatening or actual disaster upon a particular man in the light of his personal predispositions to fear, anxiety, cognitive interpretations, repressions, etc., and with regard to his personal resources of information, skills, and ego strength. On the other hand, we may ask equally important questions about the activity of an official public agency, a chance group of survivors, a family, or a community as a collective entity. And in each case, the appropriate dimensions of behavior and the nature of the unit useful for analysis are quite different.

This distinction, which we follow in the next two sections, is of course the one that has permitted psychology and sociology to go their largely separate ways, developing their different and peculiarly useful sets of fundamental concepts. In disaster research, as elsewhere in the social and behavioral sciences, it is best that each discipline first work out the models and variables most immediately demanded by the human phenomena that it chooses for study. The work of developing the correspondences between the differing conceptual units and vocabularies of any two sciences becomes fruitful only when the two are advanced enough to offer a good deal of substance to each other.

The chapters of the following section are essentially psychological in their analysis of disaster behavior. They look to psychological principles to explain individual behavior under disaster conditions; at certain points, they utilize observed features of disaster behavior to throw critical light on psychological theory. Their deductions and generalizations bear also on highly practical problems of human fate in disaster. However large the social area that a catastrophe plunges into confusion, to some inevitable degree each individual must survive or succumb to disaster in ways that are privately his.

Chapter Three deals with human behavior during the period of approaching disaster, when the major question is what measures the individual will undertake as a result of signs and messages that warn him of impending danger. Chapter Four extends its examination somewhat further into a period when the individual must cope with increasing disruptions and threats, including the actual assault of the disaster itself. While these two chapters consider highly related and sometimes overlapping realms of behavior, they illustrate how rather different theoretical approaches to disaster behavior may be equally profitable. Thus Chapter Three uses as its main tools the concepts of anxiety and of reflective fear and the difference between these —a difference which it sharpens and clarifies. Chapter Four centers its analysis around the vast literature of stress (and "threat," the anticipation of stress), deducing a model for disaster behavior from the various reactions known to be consequences of psychological stress.

In Chapter Five we turn to problems of mental health. There is first of all the question of what effect disasters have on the psychological well-being of individuals. There is also the fact that what research finds to be true about the likelihood of personal breakdown or resilience under disaster conditions tells us a good deal about those conditions which, in a more normal community, might be expected to affect the level of mental health.

As we noted in the Introduction, we are fortunate to have some studies of children who have undergone disaster. Chapter Six chooses for examination another age group—the elderly—about whom we have no direct studies but concerning whose special strengths and vulnerabilities in times of catastrophe it is important to draw together all that may be gleaned from bits and pieces of relevant research.

▸ *three*

PSYCHOLOGICAL EFFECTS OF WARNINGS

Irving L. Janis

IN ANALYZING DISASTER behavior it is essential to determine the conditions under which warnings are taken seriously and whether they evoke adaptive or maladaptive responses. Earlier reports by the author and his collaborators have presented experimental evidence bearing on the effects of different dosages of fear-arousing material in warning communications (Hovland, Janis, and Kelley, 1953; Janis, 1958a; Janis and Feshbach, 1953) and have shown how personality predispositions are related to high and low responsiveness to mass media communications (Hovland and Janis, 1959; Janis and Feshbach, 1954). This chapter will analyze the pertinent evidence from field studies of large-scale disasters in order to obtain some new leads bearing on the psychology of warnings.

A set of hypotheses will be presented which provide some tentative answers to the following questions:

1. When signs of potential danger and informative communications about an impending disaster are presented, what factors determine whether they will instigate *effective preparatory behavior*, enhancing the recipients' ability to cope with subsequent adversity?

2. Under what conditions do warnings and informative communications about potential unfavorable events produce *emotional sensitization*, increasing the likelihood that maladaptive behavior will occur as a consequence of overwhelming anxiety, obsessional fear, or demoralization?

3. What are the main factors that promote *underreactions* to warnings—apathy, indifference, wishful thinking, and various forms of denial which interfere with successful preparation?

Despite obvious shortcomings of the available observations, numerous bits of available evidence can be pieced together to obtain clues concerning the key variables that are likely to influence the way people will respond to disaster warnings. The empirical generalizations in this chapter, together with the explanatory hypotheses derived from a theoretical analysis of "reflective fear," are presented as a summary of a more extensive monograph in which I have attempted to systematize what is now known about the conditions under which warnings and other preparatory communications are most effective in inducing adaptive behavior (Janis, in press).

Reactions to Warnings during a Poison Liquor Episode

To illustrate the various types of reactions to which the theoretical constructs and empirical generalizations are intended to apply, let us examine what happened when people were given warnings about the threat of being blinded or killed by poison liquor during a toxicological disaster in a large American city. J. W. Powell's observations on this crisis (1953, pp. 87-103) provide some statistical data on the incidence of extreme emotional disturbances evoked by warning communications and, at the same time, call attention to various types of inappropriate actions that created serious problems for the civil and medical authorities who were attempting to control the danger.

In October 1951 nearly 300 gallons of illegally distilled whiskey, containing lethal doses of methyl alcohol, were distributed in various sections of Atlanta, Georgia. Within one week, 39 people were killed, 9 were totally blinded, and over 100 others were suffering from one or more symptoms of methanol poisoning—stomach cramps, severe vomiting, impairment of vision, dizziness, breathing difficulties. A few victims were white, but the majority were colored. Shortly after the first victims arrived at the emergency ward of the local colored hospital, warnings were disseminated throughout the city, especially in those colored sections where the poisoned whiskey was known to have been distributed.

As more and more warning messages came to public attention, hundreds of apprehensive persons asked for medical attention because they thought they might have been poisoned. According to Powell, the symptoms of many people who asked to be examined were purely psychological. Records from the medical staff of Emory University's Grady Hospital indicated that 433 clinic interviews were conducted with persons who thought they had been poisoned. Altogether, 183 cases (42 per cent) were found to be negative on standard medical tests and completely asymptomatic. These persons were suffering from nothing more than extreme apprehensiveness in response to the alarming warnings and rumors that spread throughout the city. Of the remaining cases, 75 reported definite physical symptoms which were found to be negative on the medical tests. These people had apparently developed hysterical reactions which mimic the symptoms of methanol poisoning. Thus, it is estimated that only 40 per cent of those examined at the emergency clinic proved to be genuine casualties. As J. W. Powell puts it, "Of every ten people who took up the doctors' time during those five crucial days, four had had no poison or showed no symptoms; two more had had no poison and did report symptoms; and only four had actually had the poison and did require treatment" (1953, p. 91).[1]

Other types of psychological problems were also encountered in the Atlanta poisoning disaster. At the opposite extreme from the hypervigilant, apprehensive people who unnecessarily overloaded the emergency medical facilities were the disaster victims who, despite clear-cut physical symptoms, ignored the warnings concerning the need for prompt medical attention and did not come to the clinic. An illustrative example of a denial reaction in response to repeated warnings is to be found in one of J. W. Powell's (1951) intensive interviews. Mrs. F., a forty-year-old colored waitress, spent one evening sharing a bottle of bootleg whiskey with a woman friend, Louise, and her brother. Early the following morning, Louise awoke Mrs. F. with excited complaints of being unable to see anything and of feeling terribly sick. Within fifteen minutes, while Mrs. F. was phoning for a doctor, Louise died. Shortly thereafter, Louise's brother, who slept in the same house, developed the same symptoms of blindness and nausea. With Mrs. F.'s help, he was rushed to the hospital by ambulance. This was followed by a visit from a police detective who examined Mrs. F.'s liquor bottles, told her about the poison whiskey that had been sold in Atlanta, and informed her that her friends were victims of menthanol poisoning. Up to this time, Mrs. F. had assumed her woman friend died of a heart attack and had remained puzzled about the similar symptoms of her friend's brother. But now, despite the clear-

[1] The incidence of apprehensive and hysterical reactions found in this study may be extraordinarily high, but the lack of systematic data from other disasters precludes comparative assessment. In any case, one cannot rely upon the estimates obtained from this study for predicting the incidence of emotional overreactions in other disasters because there are two special features of the Atlanta poisoning episode that could augment the occurrence of such reactions: (1) The threat of poisoning seems to be especially potent in eliciting hysterical conversion symptoms; (2) Most of the people directly affected were southern Negroes of a low educational level—a subgroup that might be more predisposed than others to develop hysteria and somatic complaints.

cut warning information given by the detective, Mrs. F. did not think of herself as needing medical help. A few hours later, when she developed her first symptom of poisoning, she merely took a home remedy to alleviate gastric distress.

A short time later, Mrs. F. suddenly became "blind as a bat" and felt "scared to death." Only then did she begin to think of getting medical attention. In accounting for her failure to take adequate account of the series of warning events, Mrs. F. gave some indication of the latent fears that lay behind her maladaptive attempts to deny the danger.

> INTERVIEWER: "You said before that perhaps you were so busy worrying about the others rather than yourself."
>
> MRS. F.: "Yeah, I think if I would of ever thought that it could have happened to me, I would of had a heart attack or something would have happened to me."

Denial reactions in the Atlanta disaster resulted not only in delay of treatment, as in the case of Mrs. F., but also in failure to follow other urgent medical recommendations. Powell reports that a sizable number of clinic patients ignored the physician's instructions to carry out the prescribed self-treatment for preventing symptoms from growing worse, with the result that they were brought back to the hospital in critical condition. Another serious form of underreaction to the official warnings was noted in a few recorded cases treated for minor symptoms at the clinic, who, after returning home, evidently drank more of the poisoned whiskey. Some of these victims may have failed to comprehend the warnings or, later on, may have denied the danger as a result of the temporary psychotic state induced by methanol poisoning.

In contrast to the maladaptive behavior of those who overreacted or underreacted to the warnings, some of the potential victims reacted with discriminative vigilance, watching themselves carefully for possible symptoms, checking on the liquor they had recently drunk, and seeking further medical information about the danger. Adaptive reactions of this type may have occurred in some of the nonpoisoned cases who came to the clinic, especially in those who were uncertain as to whether minor symptoms of gastric upset might be the prelude to more serious symptoms of methanol poisoning. The mood of cautious watchfulness also led some of the high-status members of the Negro community to check on rumors that Negro victims were being sent to the morgue before they were dead and were being mistreated in the medical clinic. According to Powell, these rumors gained credence from local beliefs about the past history of police brutality and from earlier stories of drunken Negroes who had been beaten to death but were listed by the authorities as having died from poison whiskey. Vigilance reactions occurred in a number of well-educated Negroes affiliated with the local university. Some of them surreptitiously entered the morgue and the hospital wards to see for themselves whether the rumors were true. Their eyewitness testimony evidently helped to alleviate suspicion and to counteract the spread of disruptive rumors.

Studies of other community disasters, and of psychological stress engendered in individuals facing the threats of ill-health or surgery, call attention to essentially the same varieties of reactions to warning communications as were seen in the Atlanta toxicological disaster. On the one hand, there are many people who respond to an external threat by becoming vigilant in a highly discriminative way, watching for signs of oncoming danger, seeking for information about how to cope with the crisis, and getting set to carry out protective actions. On the other hand, there are people who behave in a maladaptive way. Some overreact to warnings by becoming excessively excited or by developing acute psychoneurotic symptoms; others underreact by denying the threat and by failing to take essential precautions (cf., Diggory, 1956; Janis, 1958b; Wolfenstein, 1957).

Functional Properties of Reflective Fear

Many psychologists have followed Freud in distinguishing between "normal fear" (or "objective anxiety") occurring when a person is aware of a known danger, and "neurotic anxiety" arising from inner dangers linked with the person's unconscious impulses. Freud recognized, however, that the question of whether or not the person is aware of an external danger is not an entirely dependable criterion, inasmuch as the same external conditions that elicit normal fear can also elicit neurotic anxiety (see Freud, 1936, p. 148). Detailed studies of people facing objective danger situations bear out Freud's observations that reality-oriented fears are sometimes heavily overlaid with neurotic anxiety or neurotic guilt, so that criteria other than the eliciting stimulus must be used to differentiate nonneurotic from neurotic reactions (see Janis, 1958b, pp. 107-125). In the following discussion, I shall attempt to describe the criteria that enable a consistent distinction to be made. In doing so, I shall attempt to make explicit a number of functional properties of reality-oriented fear that Freud alluded to implicitly but did not specify in his writings on anxiety. Since the construct will be somewhat redefined, I shall give it a distinctive label in order to avoid confusion: "reflective fear." (The adjective "reflective" is used both in the sense of deliberative or thoughtful and in the sense of reflecting the realities of the external danger situation.) Elsewhere

(Janis, in press) I have shown that this construct can be anchored to empirical observations by positing the following functional properties:

1. INFLUENCE OF ENVIRONMENTAL CUES

The arousal of reflective fear is assumed to depend upon perceptions of actual threat stimuli, warning communications, and other environmental cues that convey information about impending danger. Thus, for example, in a pre-disaster situation, a person's level of reflective fear will increase or decrease depending upon whether he receives new warnings about the imminence of catastrophe or new reassurances from the community authorities. This functional property is in direct contrast to the relatively unmodifiable character of neurotic fear or anxiety.

2. AROUSAL OF NEED FOR VIGILANCE

A major behavioral consequence of reflective fear is a strong need for vigilance. The manifestations of this need include a broad class of observable changes which can be generally described as increased attentiveness to environmental events and readiness to take protective action in response to any cue perceived as indicating the onset of danger. Adopting a vigilance set involves cognitive as well as action changes—scanning the environment for signs of danger, attending to information pertinent to the danger, planning alternative courses of action for dealing with emergency contingencies, and the like. On the action side, a vigilance set involves a lower threshold for executing plans involving precautionary measures, heightened muscular tension, and increased gross motor activity oriented toward avoiding the anticipated danger. In the Atlanta poison liquor episode, some of the dominant forms of vigilant activity consisted in paying close attention to feelings of physical discomfort and coming to a medical clinic to be checked by a physician.

3. AROUSAL OF NEED FOR REASSURANCE

Another consequence of reflective fear is a strong need for alleviating emotional tension by obtaining convincing reassurances. Like "vigilance," the "need for reassurance" is a dispositional construct; we assume it is positively correlated with the level of reflective fear and entails changes in both the cognitive and action aspects of behavior. For example, an increase in the need for reassurance is manifested by selective attention to and recall of communications that minimize the danger or play up the protective resources available for coping with it. Heightened need for reassurance is also manifested by changes in beliefs and attitudes—the adoption of a fatalistic outlook or a greater faith in divine protection, the use of magical or superstitious practices for warding off bad luck, and the acceptance of rationalizations for continuing on a business-as-usual basis (see Hovland *et al.*, 1953, pp. 60-89). Corresponding changes in action include overt efforts to avoid exposure to danger warnings and greater adherence to conventional morality in an effort to avoid offending the "powers that be."

The most extreme forms of reassurance are those involving anticipations of total invulnerability: the person feels convinced either that the danger will never materialize in his vicinity ("It can't happen here") or that, if it does, he will be completely protected from it ("Others may suffer, but we shall be safe"). Such extreme anticipations, referred to as "blanket reassurances," may dominate completely over vigilance tendencies, as was seen in those victims of the Atlanta toxicological disaster who ignored the warnings and failed to seek medical aid even though suffering from obvious symptoms of poisoning.

4. DEVELOPMENT OF COMPROMISE FORMATIONS INVOLVING DISCRIMINATIVE VIGILANCE AND REASSURANCE

On the one hand, vigilance and reassurance are potentially conflicting tendencies, in that they can impel a person toward incompatible cognitions or actions. ("I must watch out because something dangerous is likely to happen at any moment," *versus* "I can relax and forget about it because the danger will not affect me.") On the other hand, the two tendencies do not *necessarily* conflict every time both are aroused. It is possible to develop *compromise formations* which combine vigilance (anticipating danger, seeking information about it, remaining alert to signs of threat) and reassurance (expecting to be able to cope successfully with the danger or to be helped by others if the danger becomes extreme). In the Atlanta study, the examples given of well-educated members of the colored community becoming agitated by scare rumors about maltreatment of fellow Negroes and then checking the reliability of the rumors by visiting the local hospital wards and the morgue, clearly represent such compromise formations. Presumably these persons obtained emotional relief when their investigations failed to confirm the rumors.

A common type of compromise formation among men in hazardous occupations involves *danger-contingent* reassurances: The person acknowledges vulnerability to the potential disaster and makes plans for carrying out protective actions that can be relied upon to enable him to survive *if* one or another form of danger actually arises. Such an attitude, combining discriminative vigilance with discriminative reassurance, is likely to be much more adaptive than an attitude of either blanket reassurance or indiscriminate vigilance. Thus, the development of compromise formations is conceived as one of three alternative modes of responding to threat situations which arouse reflective fear.

The diagram in Figure 3-1 shows the three alternatives specified in the foregoing assumptions about the functional properties of reflective fear. The likelihood that a person will develop one or another of the three modes of defense is assumed to depend upon a large number of situational as well as predispositional variables, some of which will be described in later sections of this chapter.

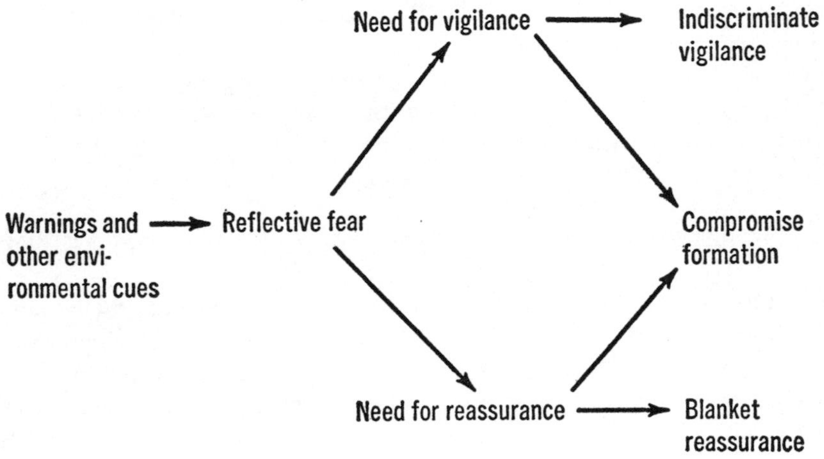

FIGURE 3-1.

The capacity for adopting a sustained vigilance set presupposes a relatively high level of development of the "ego" functions essential for testing reality, since it requires the person to forgo an immediate gratification—the warding off of dysphoric feelings—in exchange for an anticipated reward—greater safety in the future. Evidently children learn only gradually to bear the emotional tension that goes along with vigilance. Even many adults find it extremely difficult to adopt a set of watchfulness, alertness, and readiness to take protective action in the face of known danger. Whenever they are not exposed to constant reminders of the danger, they seem disposed to abandon this vigilance set in favor of a more comfortable attitude of blanket reassurance. But if danger signs are present, vigilance tends to be aroused. Later on we shall see that discriminative vigilant reactions will be fostered if fear does not mount to a high level. If it does mount, however, the person may make impulsive decisions and display "panic" reactions that objectively increase the danger.

Basic Reaction Patterns Evoked by Warnings

Figure 3-2 (see p. 64) indicates the main causal sequences implied by the foregoing discussion of reflective fear. Five main sequences are represented here, and these appear to be consistent with the available empirical findings concerning the varieties of pre-disaster reactions displayed by normal personalities (Janis, in press).

1. NORMAL REACTION TO LOW THREAT

The first normal sequence in Figure 3-2 (1→2→3→4) usually occurs in response to warnings about potential dangers or losses that the community generally regards as relatively unimportant or improbable. In response to such threats, clinically normal people tend to react with *mild* reflective fear, which is promptly reduced by means of blanket reassurance, with the consequence that behavior remains essentially unaffected by the warning. If the initial estimates prove to be correct (i.e., either the danger does not materialize at all or, if it does, it entails little suffering and only minor losses), such reactions can be said to have adaptive value in that the person avoids wasting time and energy on useless preparation and conserves his resources for more important tasks. Few people will suffer adverse consequences from ignoring low-threat warnings in a community where such warnings generally predict external events accurately. If serious dangers were to materialize, however, this sequence would prove to be just as maladaptive as Number 5 below.

2. HYPERVIGILANT REACTION TO LOW THREAT

Occasionally, signs of low threat are grossly misinterpreted by clinically normal persons, who consequently anticipate being victimized or possibly annihilated by the impending danger. This exaggerated fear reaction can give rise to either of the following subsequences: 1→6→7→8, or 1→6→9→10. Examples of the latter sequence, which can have markedly disruptive effects on the community, were observed in a few people who thought that the huge, mushroomlike cloud following an industrial explosion in South Amboy, N. J., had been caused by an atomic bomb (see Green and Logan, 1950).

3. NORMAL REACTIONS TO MODERATE OR HIGH THREAT

When warnings of moderate or high threats occur, the normal sequence of reaction is assumed to be 5→6→7→8. Thus, in clinically

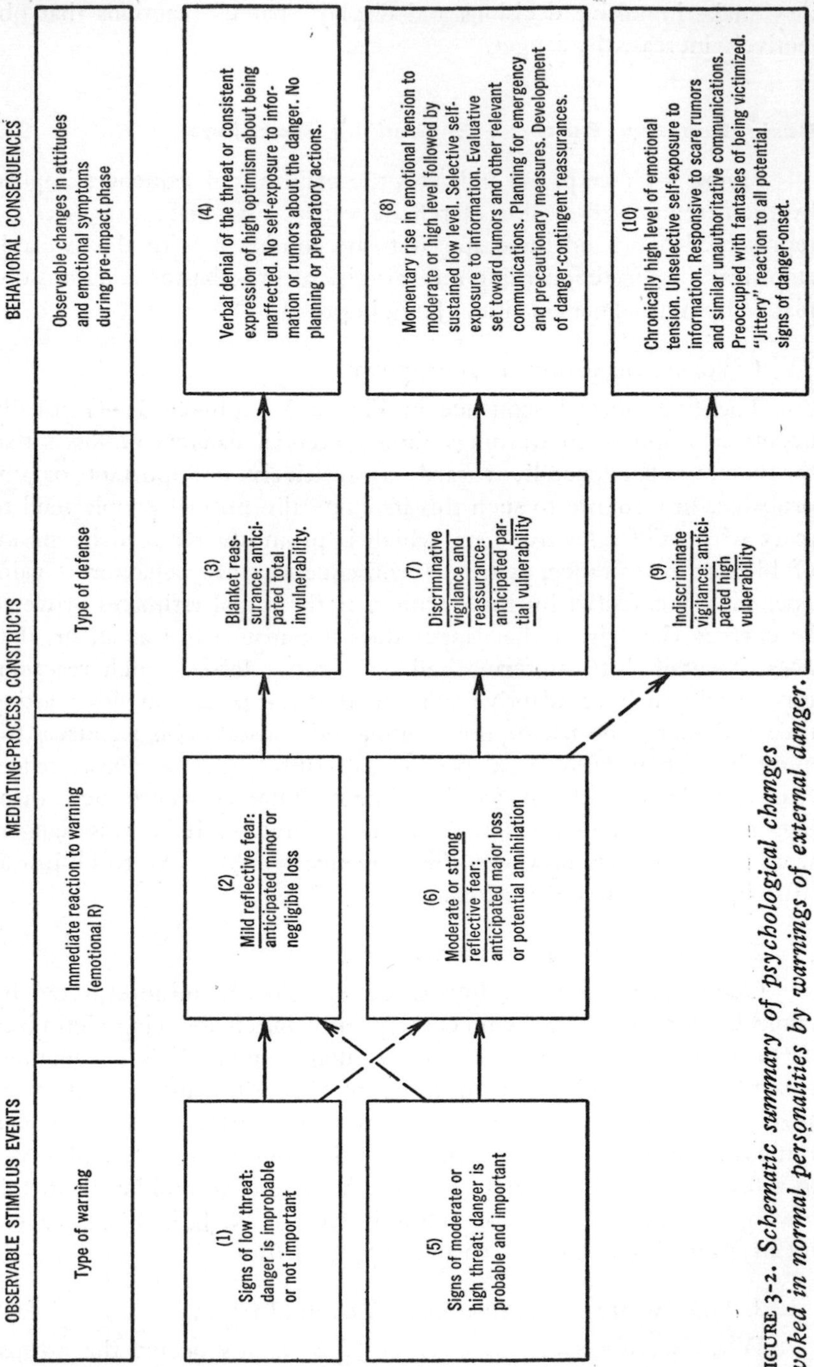

FIGURE 3-2. *Schematic summary of psychological changes evoked in normal personalities by warnings of external danger.*

normal persons the arousal of reflective fear is expected to lead to reality-oriented compromise formations which satisfy both vigilance and reassurance needs in a discriminative way, with corresponding changes in attitudes and behavior. This sequence generally is adaptive in that the person is better prepared to cope with the danger situation if it subsequently materializes.

4. HYPERVIGILANT REACTION TO MODERATE OR HIGH THREAT

When a warning of serious danger occurs, hypervigilance is assumed to be a maladaptive type of overreaction that does not necessarily imply neurotic anxiety, the sequence being 5→6→9→10. The crucial feature of this pattern is that reflective fear becomes so strong that it prevents compromise formation. Any normal person, whether or not he is hypersensitive to a given threat, is assumed to be capable of indiscriminate vigilance if he apperceives an impending danger as far greater than his limited resources for coping with it. Because this sequence is likely to result in impulsive or inefficient behavior if serious danger actually materializes, it is regarded as maladaptive.

5. HYPOVIGILANT REACTION TO MODERATE OR HIGH THREAT

A different type of maladaptive outcome results from extreme underreaction to a serious threat, as represented by the sequence 5→2→3→4. This reaction pattern, which resembles the denial symptoms encountered in some psychotics, does not necessarily imply preexisting emotional disorder, since it occurs in clinically normal persons under special environmental conditions. (The environmental conditions which promote this type of underreaction will be discussed in the next section.) If the danger does not materialize, hypovigilant reactions have no specially negative consequences; but if the danger does materialize, maladaptive behavior and sustained symptoms of psychological trauma are likely to occur. Studies of surgical patients and observations of soldiers' and civilians' reactions to wartime dangers indicate that when warnings arouse a moderate degree of reflective fear prior to the occurrence of a stressful life situation, they will function as a form of "emotional inoculation" (Janis, 1958b). For example, among people who are scheduled to undergo dangerous surgical operations:

> . . . the patients with low anticipatory fear tend to feel convinced that they will remain wholly unaffected by the surgical experience, and sometimes also expect to obtain unusual gratifications. They are apt to adopt a joking or facetious attitude and make use of simple slogans, such as "there's nothing to it," to bolster their belief that the stressful occurrences will prove to be of a very trivial nature. When actual suf-

fering occurs, it comes as a somewhat shocking surprise and is frequently interpreted as meaning that someone has failed to treat them properly. The usual pains, discomforts, and unpleasant postoperative treatments tend to be regarded as unnecessary accidents caused by the hospital staff. Thus, instead of regarding their suffering as an unavoidable consequence of surgery, they are inclined to place the blame upon danger-control personnel, who are now apperceived as being inept, unprotective, or malevolent. [In these patients, the] level of postoperative emotional disturbance . . . tends to be comparatively high, the symptoms of which include low frustration tolerance and externalized rage. . . .

The evidence bearing on the relationship between preoperative information and postoperative emotional reactions forms the basis for the following inferred generalizations concerning the probable effects of preparatory communications: If a person's anticipatory fear is stimulated to a moderate degree by impressive warnings or by other forms of information, the probability that he will subsequently overreact emotionally to actual stress stimuli and develop sustained attitudes of resentment toward danger-control authorities will be markedly lower than if his anticipatory fear is not at all stimulated during the pre-crisis period. . . .

Within the low anticipatory fear group there is probably . . . a sizeable subgroup of more or less normal personalities who will spontaneously develop and cling to pathogenic attitudes of denial unless their anticipatory fears are deliberately stimulated by impressive communications. For such persons, no special psychological devices may be necessary for successful emotional inoculation beyond conveying purely factual statements from a prestigeful source. In order to guide the work of worrying in such a way that the person will end up with an effective set of reality-oriented reassurances, it will probably prove to be advantageous to present well-balanced communications with respect to two general types of content: (a) fear-arousing statements which describe the impending dangers and deprivations in sufficient detail so as to evoke a vivid mental rehearsal of what the crisis situations will actually be like, thus reducing the chances that subsequent adverse events will be frighteningly ambiguous or surprising; and (b) fear-reducing statements which describe realistically the favorable or mitigating aspects of the threat situation, calling the person's attention to the ways the authority figures will help him and to the things he can do for himself (Janis, 1958b, pp. 399-402).

Conditions Fostering Vigilance versus Reassurance Tendencies

From the foregoing analysis, it is apparent that one central research problem is to determine the environmental conditions which foster high vigilance *versus* high reassurance needs when people are warned of impending dangers. During the pre-impact phase of a disaster, clinically normal personalities are capable of the extreme complacency accompanying an attitude of blanket reassurance or the extreme hypervigilance characterizing states of acute panic. What types of information about the danger foster vigilance and what types foster reassurance? When pertinent information about the danger is held constant, what additional factors need to be taken into account in order to predict overreactions and underreactions to warnings? What types of events and communications promote adaptive compromise formations?

The remainder of this chapter will present tentative hypotheses concerning situational factors which appear to affect significantly the probability that people will react one way or another when a warning is issued. Some of the hypotheses are based on assumptions about the origins of vigilance and reassurance tendencies, which are assumed to develop early in each person's life history, as a joint product of personal learning in fear-arousing situations, and social training in those norms of the community that prescribe where, when, and how one should take account of various types of anticipated dangers. Additional hypotheses are suggested by empirical findings from disaster studies which deal with reactions during the pre-impact phase. Each hypothesis will be discussed briefly without attempting to review all the pertinent findings, but references will be made to a few cogent disaster studies.

Effects of Different Types of Information

The level of reflective fear induced by a warning stimulus determines to a large extent whether the person will adopt a discriminate or indiscriminate reaction. One main assumption is that when a very low degree of reflective fear is aroused by unambiguous warnings dealing with remote, improbable, or relatively trivial dangers, the average person will tend to ignore the warnings ("Nothing will happen to me, I don't need to worry about it"). As fear mounts, however, blanket reassurances become less and less successful in suppressing awareness of danger; at the same time, previously acquired habits of vigilance become increasingly prepotent. The probability of developing discriminative compromise formations appears to be greatest when reflective fear is at a moderate level (see Hovland *et al.*, 1953, pp. 66-88). When reflective fear reaches a very high level, there is an increase in indiscriminate vigilance reactions, manifested by reduced mental efficiency and a predominance of regressive thought processes involving poor discrimination between safe and unsafe features of the environment (see Janis, 1958b).

Thus, we expect a curvilinear relationship between the level of reflective fear and the probability of discriminative reactions to warnings. At the low end of the fear continuum, reassurance tendencies are likely to predominate; in the middle range, both reassurance and vigilance tendencies will be aroused to a moderate degree; at the upper end, vigilance tendencies will tend to dominate the person's behavior. The information factors that determine the person's level of reflective fear are therefore assumed to have a marked influence on his mode of defense.

The arousal of reflective fear is assumed to depend upon two types of information. One type, which tends to increase reflective fear, consists of unambiguous information about the magnitude of oncoming danger. The second type, which tends to reduce reflective fear, consists of unambiguous information about the magnitude of personal and community resources for coping with the danger. The first type also includes information indicating that the danger has a high probability of occurrence. Similarly, the second type includes information indicating that a given resource for coping with the danger will be available and effective at the time it will be needed. The highest level of reflective fear, and hence the greatest likelihood of indiscriminate vigilance, will occur when there is a great deal of information of the first type and none of the second type.

Thus, for example, when an urban population has been alerted to signs of an impending flood or tornado, the average person tends to show an increase in reflective fear if subsequent warnings issued by a credible source assert any one of the following four themes: (1) the potential disaster, if it happens to hit here, can cause more destruction or more casualties than had previously been predicted; (2) the chances of being hit here are now substantially greater than had previously been predicted; (3) our rescue teams, fire fighters, first-aid units, or other disaster-control organizations do not have enough manpower or equipment to cope with the potential disaster as effectively as most people hope; or (4) our disaster-control personnel cannot be mobilized in an emergency as quickly as people expect, or cannot be of much help until after the initial destructive impact. Conversely, the level of reflective fear and the probability of vigilance reactions tend to be lowered if subsequent communications reverse the content in any of the four categories. (The term "reassurances" is used to refer to any assertion to the effect that the potential disaster will cause less destruction, or is less likely to materialize, or can be more effectively dealt with than had been expected; we shall continue to designate as "warnings" those communications and physical signs that convey any of the four types of themes that heighten awareness of vulnerability to danger.)

Only when unambiguous information about impending danger is available to the warned population can we apply the rather obvious propositions presented in the preceding paragraphs. But what happens if the information available during the pre-disaster period is so inadequate or confusing that people cannot obtain a clear-cut conception of what is in store for them? Especially when the threat is an unfamiliar one, involving a nonrecurrent type of personal or community disaster, people may be confronted with an abundance of vague folklore, uneducated guesses, and conflicting rumors (see Allport and Postman, 1947).

From a survey of existing studies of ambiguous threats, the following hypothesis is suggested: *Under conditions where a serious warning has aroused fear to a moderate or high level, the recipient's vigilance tendencies will tend to be increased by any subsequent communication or physical sign that he perceives as containing ambiguous information about his vulnerability.*

This "ambiguity" hypothesis is intended to apply whenever the significance of a verbal message or physical event is obscure or equivocal. In the case of verbal communications, ambiguity is usually due to imprecise wording. Ambiguity can also arise from the use of highly precise technical language with which members of the audience are partially or wholly unfamiliar, so that for them parts of the message become equivalent to double-talk. Similarly, when a person is unfamiliar with the nature of the danger or with the environmental setting in which the danger cues occur, he will often be puzzled and wonder what is happening. Thus, ignorance can endow purely neutral events with ambiguous status, whereupon they may be interpreted as mysterious or potentially ominous signs.

The "ambiguity" hypothesis, it will be noted, does not refer to instances of low-threat warnings. When the initial warning arouses only a slight degree of fear, we would expect subsequent items of ambiguous information either to be ignored or to be interpreted as confirming the recipient's low-threat expectations, thus reinforcing an attitude of blanket reassurance. There are numerous indications in the disaster literature that ambiguous signs and communications pertaining to oncoming danger do, in fact, foster complacency if the threat is initially regarded as unimportant (Fritz and Marks, 1954; Wolfenstein, 1957). Perhaps the most widely observed instances occur in flood disasters; examples will be cited in a later section on factors that give rise to hypovigilance (pp. 78-81).

It seems likely, therefore, that ambiguous signs and communications are capable of increasing or decreasing vigilance, depending on whether the level of fear aroused by antecedent warnings is high or low. Withey (this volume) has suggested that there is a general tendency to assimilate any new information as reinforcement for whatever psychological set is dominant at the time of the exposure. He points out that when a person is not expecting disaster, any threat cues will tend to be interpreted "as unthreatening until such interpretation can no longer be made" (p. 113). But when a person is set to expect disaster, he tends to become so oversensitive that even a minor suggestion of possible threat will be capable of stimulating emergency reactions.

Withey's assumptions are essentially the same as those presented here, except that we add a further assumption which makes explicit the importance of the ambiguity factor: unambiguous information about impending dangers will evoke marked changes in the level of fear and there will be little or no assimilation; but the more ambiguous the cues, the more likely that they will be assimilated into the pre-existing psychological set.

Illustrative Examples of Reactions to Ambiguous Threats

One implication of the foregoing assumptions is that a marked shift from extreme hypovigilance to extreme hypervigilance is to be expected whenever: (1) highly ambiguous threat signs appear at a time when people are not expecting any danger at all, and then (2) the signs persist or reappear after one or more additional warning signs have induced awareness that a serious, albeit unknown, threat is actually present. A shift of this kind is illustrated by the reactions of a group of factory workers who were exposed to the threat of carbon monoxide asphyxiation in Chicago on December 8, 1952. In contrast to most industrial disasters, this one involved an unknown and undetectable causal agent, the insidious presence of which could be inferred only from the ill effects it produced in the victims (Marks and Fritz, 1954, *3*, pp. 144-166). Early in the morning on an ordinary work day, a few employees in the plant developed characteristic asphyxiation symptoms—headache, nausea, dizziness, weakness. At first neither they nor their fellow workers thought of them as anything more than isolated cases or "flu" or "a hangover," but gradually their frequency mounted, and it became apparent that something was *generally* wrong. The employees then became extremely agitated and stopped their business-as-usual activities to devote all their energies to discovering the source of the unknown danger and trying to escape from it. One worker said, "I got almost hysterical because I couldn't put my finger on what it was."

Prolonged reactions of hypervigilance have been especially prominent when the residents of a disaster area were unfamiliar with the source of the disaster or its consequences and therefore did not feel sure that signs of apparent safety could be trusted. Outstanding examples of this type of ambiguity occurred following the series of gas explosions on September 21, 1951, at Brighton, New York (Marks and Fritz, 1954, *3*, pp. 21-28). The residents did not know just what had happened and why; as one of them said, "We didn't know if the ground right under us would blow up." In neighboring areas, scare rumors soon began to circulate, some of which greatly exaggerated the threat. One such rumor asserted that hundreds of houses had already exploded and another that a raging fire inside the gas mains would soon blow up the entire town. During the following week, many residents in and near the stricken neighborhood were jittery, unable to sleep, and constantly apprehensive about the possibility that the explosions might suddenly start again, despite repeated assurances by the authorities that the area was safe. The authoritative communications were probably no longer perceived as unquestionable signs of safety, as they would have been before the unanticipated explosions, because attitudes of resentment and distrust toward the authorities had developed as a result of their apparent failure to detect the hazard and to prevent the calamity. In general, whenever an unfamiliar and unexpected disaster occurs, many signs and communications that ordinarily would function as reassurances become ambiguous, not only because the authorities are perceived as untrustworthy, but also because of a change in attitude toward the entire environment. The world is no longer felt to be a safe place in which to live after a disaster has demonstrated that unknown dangers can be lurking anywhere at any time.

Ambiguities often arise even in those disasters involving familiar dangers whose origins and manifestations are well understood by the threatened population. Conflicting signs and messages concerning the imminence or actual onset of the danger are a common source of uncertainty and confusion. An example of hypervigilance arising from this type of confusion is provided by the unwarranted mass evacuation of Port Jervis, New York, in August, 1955 (Danzig, Thayer, and Galanter, 1958). After having been hit by heavy rainstorms from Hurricane Diane and then inundated by the Delaware River, the stricken populace of Port Jervis was kept in a constant state of alert uneasiness by rumors and unofficial reports concerning a possible recurrence of the flood. Over a period of three days, while pumping out cellars, cleaning up debris, and restoring the city to a normal condition, the flood victims became concerned that their town might be completely destroyed if the nearby dam were to burst. In an attempt to reassure them, the police chief issued a statement that the dam gates were going to be opened to relieve pressure. This ambiguous message was regarded by many residents as a confirmation of the threat and evidently contributed to the widespread speculation about the dam. Soon after the message was issued, numerous exaggerated rumors began to circulate, one of which asserted that the dam had actually broken. When a fire captain radioed this rumor to his headquarters, a number of firemen heard his message over their radios and, without bothering to check on it in any way, assumed that "this was it." They immediately turned on their sirens and drove firetrucks through the town, shouting that people should get out because the dam had burst. Within a few minutes the firemen were halted by their chief, but the receptive populace continued to spread the false alarm and within a half-hour hundreds of people were in the streets, rushing to get out of town.

The local officials, having ascertained that the dam was in excellent condition, promptly used radio stations, loud-speaker systems, and all other available media to tell the people that the evacuation was wholly unnecessary. But in their aroused state, the evacuees were relatively unresponsive to the official denial messages. Interviews of a random sample of 107 residents of Port Jervis indicated that "although most of the people who fled had left after hearing only one threat message, less than a quarter were content to return to Port Jervis after hearing one denial" (Danzig *et al.*, 1958, p. 50).

This episode of unwarranted evacuation illustrates the extreme readiness of a population to react uncritically to minimal threat cues after prolonged exposure to ambiguous signs concerning the possible recurrence of a familiar source of danger. A single ambiguous message by a local official appears to have been the precipitating event, giving rise to a chain reaction that culminated in an extraordinary mass outbreak of hypervigilant action.

A somewhat different type of ambiguous situation arises when a disaster-stricken population is unfamiliar with, or unsure of, the instrumental means available for escape. In the North Sea floods of 1952, for example, some of the people in the inundated areas of Holland refused to accept the repeated urgings of rescue personnel to come aboard helicopters in order to be evacuated to a safe area. For these Dutch farmers and villagers, the rescue operation meant entering an untrusted vehicle which would take them to a strange place, away from others in their family or neighborhood group (Balloch, Braswell, Rayner, and Killian, 1953). Thus, in contrast to the Port Jervis episode, hypervigilance among the Dutch flood victims took the form of unwarranted *resistance* to evacuation. Their refusal to be flown to a safe refuge calls to mind Shakespeare's characterization of the dread of death, which may apply equally to lesser threats: "[We] rather bear those ills we have than fly to others that we know not of."

In general, unfamiliarity with any important feature of the environment in which danger cues occur makes it difficult for the threatened person to interpret correctly any new event or communication, since he remains uncertain as to whether it is a sign that the danger is mounting or lessening. The greater the degree of unfamiliarity at a time when reflective fear is strongly aroused, the higher the probability that environmental signs will be ambiguous stimuli that touch off hypervigilant reactions. When sick people are brought to the hospital for the first time, they frequently become upset about the strange procedures and suspect that something has gone seriously wrong if a strange piece of apparatus is brought into the room or if they see some of the hospital staff dressed in green uniforms rather than the expected white ones (Janis, 1958b, pp. 360-370).

In addition to field studies of personal and community disasters, a few quasi-experimental investigations have been reported bearing on the effects of ambiguous threat stimuli. Hudson's (1954a) studies of threat stimuli indicate that an ambiguous warning signal is capable of inducing a vigilance set in the perceiver which sometimes disposes him to misinterpret subsequent communications from others. During regular college classroom meetings, the investigator introduced sounds resembling those that might occur in the event of a surprise A-bomb attack. The drone of distant planes, fire sirens, excited vocalizations, and the like were projected from loudspeakers placed outside the building, and these sounds were followed by additional extraordinary events. The classroom instructor was suddenly called to the phone or was handed a message by someone who burst into the room in a manner that conveyed the greatest urgency. Immediately thereafter, an air-raid alarm sounded, followed by a flash of bright light accompanied by the sound of distant explosions. The subjects were then told about the experiment and were asked to describe their reactions on a questionnaire.

Some subjects remained calm throughout the entire twenty-five minutes during which the ambiguous threat stimuli were presented. Others became manifestly upset and reported having thought that an all-out war was being started by the Soviet Union. A common tendency was to look to the instructor, as the group leader, or to fellow classmates for cues concerning the seriousness of the threat. Many subjects evidently found confirmation of their own fears in the gestures and verbalizations of the others around them. In support of this tendency, Hudson reports a fairly high positive correlation between the individual's self-rating of his own level of fear and his rating of fear in the group as a whole ($r = .63$, based on 61 cases). Other ambiguous stimuli were also interpreted as justifying strong feelings of fear.

"The hilarious amusement of a group of students who were aware that they were the objects of an experiment did not interfere with the developing anxiety of persons in other sections in the lecture room. Instead, their uproarious behavior was perceived as evidence of their anxiety" (Hudson, 1954a, p. 54).

These field observations and research findings indicate the plausibility of the assimilation tendency as a purely descriptive phenomenon, but there is little evidence bearing directly on alternative explanations. A number of complex psychological mechanisms undoubtedly enter into the assimilation tendency, and the specific processes underlying low-threat assimilation probably are quite different from those underlying high-threat assimilation. For example, the latter seems to involve not only selective attention and emotional interference with normal apperception but also a special form of projection whereby the person overestimates environmental dangers once he becomes acutely frightened. Kris (1941) pointed out that when the source of external danger is vague or unfamiliar, many people fill in the gaps with exaggerated fantasies, which they project onto the unstructured environment. Thereafter, they remain excessively preoccupied with the prospects of being victimized unless the fantastic elements are deflated by realistic information.

Situational Factors Influencing Actional Readiness

We shall now examine some implications of our earlier assumption that vigilance tendencies will be increased by any verbal or physical signs that lower the person's appraisal of his own or his community's resources for coping with an anticipated disaster, even though his appraisal of the magnitude of the external danger remains essentially unchanged. A series of four hypotheses will be presented which specify situational factors that change a person's self-appraisal and thereby influence his readiness to take action. Like the ones presented earlier, these hypotheses have not yet been adequately tested but appear to be plausible in the light of existing evidence from disaster research.

1. ANTICIPATED INACESSIBILITY OF EXISTING ESCAPE ROUTES

Under conditions where a personal or community disaster is anticipated, the strength of vigilance tendencies will be increased by any warning communication or physical sign interpreted by the perceiver as indicating that a currently available escape route will become inaccessible to him once the danger materializes.

The term *escape route* in this hypothesis refers, broadly speaking, to any behavioral sequence or course of action that will lead to avoidance or mitigation of the danger stimuli. Anticipated inaccessibility may involve expectations about deficiencies in the physical or social environment (e.g., "Roads will be so overcrowded that they will be useless to us") or in one's own skills (e.g., "I might become too excited to be able to drive my car"). Regardless of the perceived source of the deficiency, the net result is that the person anticipates a loss in his power to cope with mounting danger if the emergency situation should arise. In a summary statement on the problem of panic prepared for the National Research Council (Janis, Chapman, Gillin, and Spiegel, 1955), it was pointed out that the most extreme forms of indiscriminate vigilance occur at times when people expect great danger to be imminent and, at the same time, perceive the last remaining escape routes to be rapidly closing. Studies of the effects of pre-disaster warnings suggest that even when a threat is perceived as entailing a relatively low magnitude of danger, the strength of vigilance tendencies will increase if new information is received about the closing of escape routes (see Danzig, *et al.*, 1958). Hence the hypothesis has been formulated in such a way as to include low- as well as high-threat situations.

On the assumption that the relationship specified by the hypothesis is mediated by a change in the anticipated degree of victimization, we would expect the following complementary hypothesis to hold: Vigilance reactions will be diminished by any communication or physical sign interpreted by the perceivers as indicating that existing escape routes will become more accessible to them or that new ones will be opened up if an anticipated threat materializes. Some of the observed effects of reassuring communications appear to be consistent with this hypothesis (see Janis, 1958a; 1958b).

2. ANTICIPATED NEED FOR SELF-INITIATED ACTION

The strength of a person's vigilance tendencies will be high or low, depending on whether the available verbal information and physical signs lead him to expect that, if the anticipated danger materializes, his own actions will have high or low importance with respect to mitigating danger. Vigilance increases when the person is exposed to signs indicating that adequate protection for himself and his family will require self-initiated action; vigilance decreases when the person is exposed to signs indicating that he can rely on others to protect him and his family.

The individual's expectations concerning the importance of his own actions determine whether or not the anticipated danger is in the category of those events for which the person acknowledges a sense of responsibility. There are numerous indications in the disaster literature that a marked lowering of vigilance activity is produced among the residents of a potential disaster area by authoritative communications which convey that community leaders or specialists in disaster control can be expected to carry out whatever protective measures are required (Janis, in press). The reassuring effects produced by such communications may stem partly from a reactivation of childhood attitudes of trust in the protective powers of the parents. But we would expect that, as a result of social training and distressing life experiences, the individual learns to discriminate between danger situations in which other people can be relied upon to protect him and those in which his safety is partly or wholly his own responsibility.

3. ANTICIPATED RESTRICTION OF ACTIVITY

Under any conditions of threat, including those in which a person does not expect his own activity to play a significant role in reducing his chances of being victimized, the strength of his vigilance tendencies will be increased whenever he is exposed to communications or physical signs indicating that at the time of danger impact his own activity will be restricted.

This proposition applies to restrictions of perceptual as well as cognitive and motor activity. For example, during World War II both combat troops and civilians became more agitated when air-raid warnings came at night rather than during the day (Garner, 1945; Glover, 1942; Janis, 1951; U.S. Strategic Bombing Survey, 1947c and 1947d). Reflective fear may be more readily aroused at night partly because people expect that poor visibility will interfere with their ability to find and use escape routes. Many Japanese civilians reported that they were especially fearful of night raids because they knew it would be more difficult to escape from fires and collapsing buildings when they could not see clearly (U.S. Strategic Bombing Survey, 1947d). Such instances of anticipated restriction are equivalent to anticipated interference with escape opportunities and hence can be subsumed under the hypothesis concerning the effects of the anticipated closing of escape routes (pp. 74-75). But in many instances the heightening of vigilance seems to occur even when the person believes that the limitation will not alter his chances of survival. A surgical patient is likely to become extraordinarily jittery and hypervigilant when the cues he receives in the operating room make him realize that the physicians will impose severe restrictions upon his perceptual, cognitive, and motor activity, despite his conscious knowledge that such restrictions will reduce rather than augment the danger (Janis, 1958b). In such cases, expectations of enforced passivity may arouse reflective fear to a disproportionately high degree because of a reactivation of childhood situations of passive helplessness. Similar instances of irrational heightening of vigilance evidently occur during the pre-impact phase of large-scale disasters (Glover, 1942; Sullivan, 1941; Wolfenstein, 1957).

4. ANTICIPATED RESTRICTION OF SOCIAL CONTACTS

The strength of vigilance tendencies will be increased whenever a person is exposed to communications or physical signs indicating that during a period of oncoming danger he will be out of contact with authority figures, members of his primary group, or other significant persons upon whom he is emotionally dependent.

There is considerable evidence of a striking increase in affiliative needs under conditions of external threat (Glover, 1942; Janis, 1951; Schachter, 1959; Wolfenstein, 1957). Reliance on parent surrogates and primary groups evidently constitutes a major source of reassurance, alleviating fears of abandonment and annihilation, derived from childhood separation experiences, which are reactivated by threat situations in adult life.

When a person knows that authority figures, friends, or members of his family are nearby he feels reassured and his vigilance reactions tend to be lower than if he knows such persons are absent. But the net effect of the *actual* presence of a significant person depends partly on what that person says and how he says it. For example, if he makes dire predictions or displays acute emotional symptoms, a group leader will transmit fear, thus heightening vigilance rather than lowering it (Hudson, 1954a; Reusch and Prestwood, 1949).

The hypothesis under discussion, however, refers to *anticipated* rather than to actual separation from authority figures or other significant persons. Heightened vigilance has been observed among soldiers when they expect to be required to remain alone for a long period in foxholes, and among civilians when they perceive signs indicating the possibility of becoming socially isolated at a time of impending disaster. High vigilance is also to be expected when an individual is not physically isolated but separated by a great *social distance* from the people with whom he is in contact. Extreme instances of hypervigilant reactions have been noted, for example, when refugees were exposed to the threat of air raids in a foreign country or when wartime evacuees found themselves among people of a markedly different ethnic or social class background (Janis, 1951).

Cues evoking anticipated psychological separation are sometimes obtained from the *absence of communications* on the part of authority figures from whom information or reassurance is expected. When civic leaders and trusted news services fail to issue bulletins about what is going on during a large-scale community disaster, many people begin to lose confidence in them; they become increasingly preoccupied with signs of threat and display more and more hypervigilant reactions, such as accepting and spreading exaggerated rumors about the terrible things that are going to happen (see Glover, 1940).

There are, of course, many different signs that arouse vigilance by creating anticipations of psychological separation from significant persons. Such anticipations can readily be evoked by an impressive news story or exposé propaganda which describes the authorities in an unfavorable manner, making them appear to be untrustworthy, indifferent, or hostile toward the recipients. Similar effects are likely to be produced by authoritative communications containing weak or vague statements which generate doubts as to whether the authorities really intend to be helpful (see Janis, 1958b, pp. 134-138, 170-172, 302-325).

Adaptation and Sensitization Effects Produced by Antecedent Warnings

A major implication of the assumptions about reflective fear introduced at the beginning of this chapter is that the way a person reacts to any given warning will depend partly upon the type of information he has received from antecedent warnings. The available evidence, as we shall see shortly, indicates that in a pre-disaster situation a series of preliminary warnings can induce an "emotional adaptation" effect, decreasing the probability that any new emergency warning will evoke vigilance reactions. But other observations indicate that the opposite outcome can also occur: under certain conditions, a series of preliminary warnings can produce a "sensitizing" effect, with the result that the probability of vigilant reactions to a new emergency warning is increased rather than decreased. In the sections that follow, we shall attempt to differentiate between the conditions fostering adaptation and those fostering sensitization. First we shall examine some comparative findings bearing on the differences between "nonprecipitant" and "precipitant" disasters, which contain important leads concerning the conditions under which emotional adaptation is likely to occur. Then we shall scrutinize additional observations concerning the features of those pre-disaster situations in which preliminary warnings appear to have a sensitizing effect.

Nonprecipitant versus Precipitant Disasters

A report by a disaster research team at the University of Oklahoma Research Institute (1952) refers to disaster situations which build up slowly as "nonprecipitant" or "crescive." In this report, the characteristic reactions to warnings in nonprecipitant disasters are illustrated by a case study of the great Kansas City flood and fire of 1951, which damaged or destroyed the homes of nearly 20,000 residents. During the hour or so immediately before the city was inundated, the city's officials issued strong warnings of the imminent danger together with urgent orders to evacuate without delay. Despite these warnings, the majority of residents did not leave. The people who failed to respond remained skeptical that the flood waters would overcome the powerful systems of dikes. Most of them did not attempt to leave the stricken area until they actually saw the water coming into their homes, by which time the only way to escape was to climb to the roof and remain there until rescued by boat. From their interviews with flood victims and disaster control personnel, the authors conclude that a major factor contributing to the population's nonvigilant reaction to the final urgent warning was the series of preliminary communications, issued during the days preceding the actual crisis, warning the residents that the area might be endangered. "The very fact that it was possible to issue warnings long before the danger was immediate made possible a gradual, easy adaptation to the approaching danger, but, at the same time, rendered the warnings less effective" (University of Oklahoma Research Institute, 1952, p. 18).

Hudson (1954a, p. 57) reports similar observations in the town of Miami, Oklahoma, when the same flood waters reached there after having inundated Kansas City. Reports concerning reactions to many other floods in the United States and in other countries point to the tendency to ignore urgent last-minute warnings when they occur in a nonprecipitant type of disaster (Ballach *et al.*, 1953; Clifford, 1956; Spiegel, 1957).

Reactions to other kinds of nonprecipitant disasters are also characterized by indifference to last-minute emergency warnings. Logan and his collaborators have reported that in Pitcher, Oklahoma, a large number of residents refused to accept warnings by officials during 1950 that the long-standing threat of cave-ins from former mining operations had become so great as to endanger the life of everyone who did not immediately evacuate.

> It is evident that living on the dangerously unstable roof of a mine had become part of the normal existence of these people. Rumblings due to blasting in the mines almost every afternoon had become a familiar part of their lives, as had periodic warnings that they were living in an area which might suddenly sink. Hence, when the company issued a new warning, even one accompanied by an order to evacuate, they did not perceive this as a threat but as a normal, familiar event. They even made jokes about it. The day following the issuing of the evacua-

tion order, one man brought a parachute to a Lions Club meeting! (Logan, Killian, and Marrs, 1952, p. 94).

Similar reactions of indifference to serious dangers were observed toward the end of the air war in Britain among residents of London who had been extremely vigilant during the first air raids but then had gradually become more and more emotionally adapted to the recurrent threat (Janis, 1951, pp. 109-116).

In contrast, the reactions to emergency warnings issued in precipitant disasters differ markedly. Typical findings were reported in a study of the tornado at Leedy, Oklahoma, in 1958. During the half-hour before the tornado struck, official radio bulletins warned of the approaching storm and advised the residents to enter storm cellars. The warnings were heeded to such an extent that "almost the total population was in storm cellars when the tornado struck" (Tornado Warning, 1948).

In this case, the vigilant behavior evoked by the warning was of an adaptive character. But inappropriate vigilant activity sometimes results when an emergency warning is given without having been preceded by any preliminary warning. Fritz and Marks (1954) present some comparative data from an Arkansas tornado in 1951 which suggest that a last-minute warning in a precipitant disaster can evoke maladaptive behavior to such an extent that the population might be better off with no warning at all. Their evidence indicates that the incidence of casualties bears a curvilinear relationship to forewarning time (i.e., time interval between warning and disaster impact). Death loss and injury loss (to the respondent or his immediate family) were found to be higher for the group that received a warning less than one minute before impact than for either (1) the group with longer forewarning time or (2) the group with no forewarning at all. After calling attention to various uncontrolled factors that make it necessary to regard the apparent relationship with considerable skepticism, the authors present the following tentative conclusion: ". . . comparisons of actions taken with losses sustained would suggest that people who had only brief forewarning took action with a protective *intent*, but that the actions taken may have actually increased their danger or they may have been caught unprotected during the process of taking [inappropriate] protective action" (Fritz and Marks, 1954, p. 38). In other words, the people who received a forewarning of one minute or less may have become so excited that they exercised poor judgment or acted in an inefficient manner which increased their chances of becoming casualties.

The various studies mentioned above provide preliminary support for the generalization that *emergency warnings are less likely to induce vigilant reactions in nonprecipitant disasters than in precipitant disasters.* This proposition might be explained on the basis of a number of alternative hypotheses, all of which are compatible with the theoretical assumptions stated earlier concerning the nature of reflective fear:

1. Signs of urgency and imminence are more likely to be present in precipitant than in nonprecipitant disasters. The more imminent the disaster is perceived to be, the greater the likelihood that vigilance will be aroused.

2. Precipitant disasters may be regarded by most people as more dangerous and more difficult to escape than nonprecipitant disasters. If so, the propositions presented earlier concerning the anticipated magnitude of danger and the availability of escape routes could help to explain the higher incidence of vigilance behavior in precipitant disasters, since the warnings issued in such a disaster would tend to generate a higher level of reflective fear, which, in turn, would give rise to a higher degree of vigilance.

3. In nonprecipitant disasters numerous antecedent warnings are likely to be issued before the final emergency warning is given; whereas in precipitant disasters there is little or no opportunity to issue any warnings prior to the emergency warning. Any emergency warning will be less likely to evoke vigilant reactions if it comes relatively late in a sequence of warnings about familiar dangers insofar as people tend to become emotionally adapted to the threat.

Theoretical Implications Concerning Adaptation and Sensitization

The third hypothesis just presented has implications that go beyond the question of why nonprecipitant disasters evoke less vigilance than precipitant disasters. In its most general form, the "emotional adaptation" hypothesis asserts that *the vigilance tendencies aroused by any warning concerning a familiar source of danger will be dampened if the recipients have previously been exposed to one or more warnings pertaining to the same threat, provided that the warnings do not add any new information about increased vulnerability to the danger.* Little experimental evidence is available as yet, but field studies of disaster behavior provide some preliminary support for this hypothesis (see Janis, 1951; Janis, 1959, pp. 227-229; MacCurdy, 1943).

From our earlier theoretical assumptions, we would expect the level of reflective fear to decrease if preliminary warnings present new information about decreased vulnerability (e.g., convincing arguments to the effect that the danger is much less serious than had been thought). The adaptation hypothesis asserts that fear will also decrease if the antecedent warnings have conveyed no new information at all about vulnerability but merely have made the recipient realize that a known source of danger might materialize in the foreseeable future.

From what has just been said it is apparent that sensitization effects are likely only if antecedent warnings communicate that vulnerability is greater than had previously been anticipated. The following hypothesis seems to be consistent with the existing evidence from disaster studies: *when preliminary warnings provide information that heightens awareness of potential vulnerability to an impending disaster, the recipients will become more sensitized to new warnings, as manifested by a general increase in their fear reactions to all relevant threat cues and a corresponding increase in vigilance reactions to subsequent emergency warnings about the imminent onset of the danger.*

This "sensitization" hypothesis is intended to apply whether the source of danger is initially familiar or unfamiliar. It is also applicable to implicit or explicit warnings, no matter how slight the danger is perceived to be. But, of course, the over-all adaptive value of sensitization would be different for high- versus low-threat situations. If the final emergency warning refers to a *severe* threat, we would expect an antecedent sensitizing warning to increase *hypervigilant* behavior. But if the final emergency warning is perceived as referring to a very *mild* threat that can be safely ignored, the sensitization effect would promote *adaptive compromise formations*. When reflective fear has been heightened by a strong preliminary warning, a subsequent mild warning will be more likely to evoke discriminative vigilance reactions that lead the person to become alert to the danger and to seek for ways of mitigating it.

These generalizations concerning the conditions under which adaptation and sensitization will occur and the differential consequences that will ensue for high- versus low-threat warnings could be tested by carefully designed experiments or by systematic controlled comparisons. But, once again, when we look for pertinent evidence we must make use of studies that bear only indirectly on the hypotheses under discussion. We shall examine in detail a few studies that serve to indicate some of the subtle ways in which sensitization effects may be manifested and, at the same time, provide a few systematic comparisons that seem relevant for testing predictions from the sensitization hypothesis.

Illustrative Examples of Sensitization: Public Reactions to Warnings about Health Hazards

In 1948, the Survey Research Center at the University of Michigan studied public reactions to a publicity campaign conducted by the American Cancer Society. The two main slogans in the campaign consisted of warnings about the prevalence of the dread disease: "Every three minutes someone dies of cancer," and "One out of every eight people dies of cancer." The main purposes of the campaign were to solicit financial contributions and to encourage people with early symptoms to come to cancer-detection clinics. The campaign was carried out at a time when similar slogans were being circulated for other causes. Some people complained about being bombarded by dire warnings and a few made fun of them, sharing the attitude of the wit who suggested combining all the scare slogans into a single master slogan: "One out of every one person dies, period."

In order to determine the effects of the campaign the Survey Research Center interviewed a cross section of the U.S. population. As expected, they found a wide range of individual differences in responsiveness. Approximately 40 per cent of the sample knew that the campaign was going on and recalled or recognized one of the slogans; at the opposite extreme, 24 per cent knew nothing at all about it. The remaining 35 per cent showed partial awareness of the campaign (e.g., mentioned it spontaneously but did not recognize slogans).

Prior exposure to the threat of cancer was found to be related to awareness of the campaign. The group of respondents who had never known anyone with cancer showed significantly less awareness of the campaign that those who knew a relative or acquaintance with cancer. For the vast majority of the latter group, the prior experience with the threat consisted largely of observing and hearing about the unfortunate consequences of the disease (pain, poor prognosis, death). We would assume that exposure to negative information from contact with a cancer victim with whom one can readily identify would be equivalent to an antecedent warning, making the observer much more aware than he otherwise would be of the potential dangers of the disease. The findings from this study, therefore, are consistent with the expectation that prior exposure to adverse information about a threat will tend to build up an attitude of vigilance such that the person will pay more attention than others to any new communications that deal with the same threat.

Similar findings were reported by Leventhal and his co-workers (1960) from their survey of public reactions to the Asian influenza epidemic in the fall of 1957. The survey was conducted simultaneously in a northern and a southern U.S. city during a period when the number of Asian influenza cases had already reached epidemic proportions. Nearly 40 per cent of the families in each city had one or more persons ill. But partly because the cases accumulated slowly over a two-month period, with only a small percentage ill at any one time, the vast majority of people in the two cities did not acknowledge the existence of the epidemic and failed to protect themselves by being vaccinated. These hypovigilant reactions occurred despite the repeated publicity from public health authorities, local agencies, and large industrial organizations. One of the main findings of the survey was that respondents in families where respiratory illness had occurred during the weeks prior to the interview were more likely to believe that an epidemic was actually in progress than those in families in which there had not been any such illness. This and other supporting findings are interpreted by the authors as indicating that "contracting influenza or seeing it in one's immediate relatives increases sensitivity to similar illness in others and to news items and stories which stress the growing incidence of illness" (Leventhal *et al.*, 1960, p. 60).

Sensitizing Effects of False Alarms

A marked increase in vigilance would be expected to follow any false alarm which interferes with expectations of blanket immunity ("It *can* happen to me—and it almost did"). Unconfirmed warnings of dire disaster do not invariably produce the outcome described in the popular "wolf-wolf" story. This is indicated by Killian's study (1954a) of reactions to a series of hurricane warnings. In September 1953 the residents of Panama City, Florida, were informed by newspaper, radio, and other media that Hurricane Florence was approaching the Gulf coast and would probably hit them with the worst storm in Florida's history. The two local radio stations broadcasted hourly an official warning advising all people near the coast to move to inland shelters. An estimated 10,000 residents followed this advice. But the hurricane suddenly changed its course. Instead of hitting Panama City with its full force, the storm center crossed the coast about 100 miles away, so that Panama City experienced a relatively mild windstorm which produced only slight damage. It became apparent to everyone in the area that the people who had ignored the evacuation warnings lost nothing by doing so and were much less inconvenienced than those who had taken the trouble to go to shelters or to leave town.

In a series of intensive interviews, Killian investigated how people who had accepted the official evacuation advice felt about it afterward. He found that few of the evacuees complained about having been misled by the false alarm; the vast majority said they would evacuate again under the same circumstances. If their interview statements can be accepted as valid, these people remained as ready as ever to take emergency action in response to any new hurricane warnings.

Commitment to a decision concerning protective action is one of the factors that may foster the continuation of an attitude of vigilance. Having once decided to take the action recommended in the warning communications, those who did leave may have become motivated to reduce cognitive dissonance or to minimize postdecisional conflict by thinking up good reasons for what they did (see Festinger, 1957; Janis, 1959). Perhaps discussions of the potential disaster among fellow evacuees provided the opportunity to "pool" good arguments and rationalizations as well as to receive social support when it became apparent that the protective action had been unnecessary.

In the false alarm investigated by Killian, the commitment factor might have contributed to the outcome, but does not in itself provide an adequate explanation for all the pertinent findings. Killian noted that sensitivity to the hurricane threat was not restricted to those respondents who had decided to evacuate but also occurred in a sizable minority of those who had decided not to do so. Forty per cent of the latter stated unequivocally that they would evacuate in response to a new hurricane warning, even though they did not do so the first time. These people seemed to regret having rejected the evacuation warning despite the fact that it proved to be a false alarm. They made no attempt to bolster their decision even though it would have been quite easy for them to do so. Rather, they seem to have increased cognitive dissonance by adopting a new position which was not compatible with their recent decision. Evidently some additional information was obtained from the false alarm and its aftermath which induced them to regret their decision and to adopt a new attitude toward the threat.

It is important to take account of the fact that although the evacuation proved to be unnecessary, the alarm was only partially falsified. The residents' direct observations of the windstorm in their own area were reinforced by news reports which described the enormous damage wreaked by the 160-mile-an-hour hurricane in areas less than 100 miles away. Under such circumstances, many who remained in their homes may have been induced to think about what the full force of a hurricane would be like and to imagine what might have happened if they had not been lucky compared with others. Those near the waterfront, for example, could not help noticing the enormously high tide, which perhaps made some of them realize, for the first time, what a hurricane could do to a city like theirs, situated only fourteen feet above sea level. Had nothing at all happened, they might not have been stimulated to think about the potential dangers of being pounded by flood waters nor to notice the inadequate protection afforded by their homes in the event of a much stronger windstorm than the one they experienced.

Returning to the sensitization hypothesis, we must note that although the Panama City findings are consistent with it, alternative interpretations cannot be excluded. Perhaps it would be most accurate to say that the sensitization hypothesis offers a basis for understanding those instances where false alarms do not result in any lowering of vigilance. If a warning evokes vigilant reactions that subsequently prove to be unnecessary, as when the center of Hurricane Florence failed to hit Panama City, the net effect of the false alarm experience will depend upon the type of information conveyed about the threat. If no new information is obtained, or if the new information shows the threat to be less dangerous than had been supposed, a marked lowering of vigilance is to be expected, as occurred following the false alarms in British towns during the early days of the air blitz of 1941 (Glover, 1942; Janis, 1951; Vernon, 1941). But if new information is obtained which points up their personal vulnerability, people will react by becoming more vigilant than before the false alarm occurred. When such information has been conveyed, we can expect increased vigilance in those who had ignored the unnecessary warnings as well as in those who had become alarmed, although, as was suggested earlier, the effect might conceivably be more pronounced in those who had committed themselves to some form of protective action in response to the false alarm.

A Reinterpretation of "Near-Miss" Reactions

The sensitization outcome is much more likely to occur, of course, when a preliminary warning does *not* turn out to be a false alarm. As soon as it becomes apparent that an earlier warning should have been taken seriously, people are likely to regret their foolishness in having risked endangering themselves, and thereafter will become all the more responsive to future warnings (see Wolfenstein, 1957). Thus, whenever a warning is confirmed by subsequent disaster events, the intact survivors who ignored the warning would be expected to show a greater increase in vigilance than those who took it seriously (holding constant the degree of victimization entailed by the physical impact of the disaster).

A study of the Texas City disaster (Logan, Killian, and Marrs, 1952) provides examples of extreme sensitization to fire alarms after a series of devastating explosions demonstrated to the entire population that earlier warning signs should have been heeded. Similar changes in readiness to respond to warning signals have also been observed as a consequence of direct experience with other danger stimuli. Formerly unnoticed storm clouds and the sounds of rising wind come to evoke strong fear reactions in the survivors of tornado disasters, producing sleeplessness, obsessional watchfulness, and other post-traumatic reactions that can be properly described as hypervigilant in character (Fritz and Marks, 1954; National Opinion Research Center, 1953). Such traumatizing events have been described as "near-miss" experiences, in contrast to "remote-miss" experiences in which warning signs occur without being accompanied by any distressing danger impact (MacCurdy, 1943). Studies of wartime and peacetime disasters indicate that acute emotional shock, traumatic neurosis, and various transient forms of emotional disturbance are most likely to occur among those persons who undergo narrow escapes or who are actually victimized by the disaster (Fraser, Leslie, and Phelps, 1943; Glover, 1942; Janis, 1951; MacCurdy, 1943; Moore, 1958b; Wolfenstein, 1957). But these studies also indicate that remote-miss experiences sometimes induce sustained apprehensiveness accompanied by extreme vigilance reactions of the type ordinarily associated with near-miss experiences. Under what conditions does this exceptional type of remote-miss reaction occur? Are there also some exceptional near-miss experiences that have benign rather than traumatic effects, and, if so, under what conditions do they occur?

In a number of instances already cited, direct personal involvement in a disaster gave rise to discriminative vigilant reactions which had adaptive value. Many people who had been victimized by tornadoes, for example, developed apprehensive alertness to signs of a possible recurrence of the disaster, listening regularly to weather forecasts on the radio, watching carefully any unusual cloud formations, and preparing storm shelters. Moore (1958b) reports that after the 1953 tornado in San Angelo, Texas, which destroyed or damaged practically every home in the entire town, over one third of the surviving families built storm cellars, which were put to good use when another severe storm hit the town a year later. In many such instances the near-miss episode can be characterized as having a benign effect, inducing awareness of *partial* vulnerability and leading to adaptive compromise formations.

Thus, the distinction between remote-miss and near-miss experiences cannot be regarded as a basic one for explaining adaptive as against maladaptive reactions, even though there is some evidence indicating that the use of these concepts enables us to make better-than-chance predictions (see Janis, 1951). Accordingly, we shall reexamine the concepts briefly in the light of our theoretical analysis of reflective fear, focusing on the conditions under which danger episodes give rise to indiscriminate vigilance as against compromise formations.

In line with earlier discussions of the dynamics of near-miss reactions, our initial assumption is that attitudes of hypervigilance are produced by danger episodes in which anticipations of personal invulnerability are so completely shattered that the person is no longer able to ward off strong reflective fear when he encounters new danger cues. In contrast, the more benign type of near-miss experiences can be regarded as mildly admonitory in character, merely breaking down blanket-immunity reassurances, inducing the person to become aware of his potential vulnerability but without rendering him incapable of evolving new danger-contingent reassurances. Some of the people at San Angelo seemed to be referring to this type of change in self-concept when they described themselves as having "learned a lesson from the tornado," and when they spoke about their newly acquired desire to have storm shelters ready before there were any more tornado warnings (Moore, 1958b).

Martha Wolfenstein cites numerous examples of disaster victims who express a need to avoid repeating their mistaken disregard of warnings and to protect themselves from again being taken by surprise (e.g., "I'm not going to let them [storm clouds] slip up on me like that"). She points out that an attitude of alert watchfulness can satisfy the need for reassurance, by counteracting feelings of passivity and helplessness.

> One pictures oneself in action rather than overwhelmed by distress. The image of oneself as a rescuer pushes aside that of one's being a victim. . . . Confidence in know-how, with the image of oneself as doing skillful and useful things, strengthens the feeling one can remain in control in a danger situation (Wolfenstein, 1957, pp. 42-43).

At first, the vigilant reactions following a disaster are likely to accompany a moderate or high state of fear. But, later on, we would expect emotional adaptation gradually to set in, as the person builds up confidence in new precautionary measures and acquires various other new compromise formations that function as effective sources of reassurance. After the San Angelo tornado, for example, one woman stated that "a cellar helps your nerves a lot in any storm. . . . I just couldn't stay by myself at nighttime until the cellar was finished, if [there] was a cloud." Another spoke about the calming effect of being in contact with friends and neighbors in their big storm cellar: ". . . We have had as many as twenty-seven in there at one time. . . . When we're down there we just talk and laugh. We have a club meeting down there. . . . Kiddoes named it our 'Tornado Club'" (Moore, 1958b, pp. 271-272).

A similar development of new fear-reducing habits has been noted after many other disasters. In the final stage the person is ordinarily free from fear in his everyday life but is, nevertheless, in a habitual state of readiness to become vigilant if clear-cut warning signals occur. Taking account of the concepts introduced earlier in the discussion of "reflective fear" (pp. 59-63), we can view the learning effects of a near-miss experience as resulting in a set of discriminatory habits such that (1) in the normal course of events, when no warning signal is present, the person's level of fear remains very low, with blanket reassurance as the dominant reaction; and (2) when clear-cut warnings are perceived, the person's fear mounts to a moderate level that falls well above the threshold for discriminatory vigilance but below the threshold for hypervigilance. In contrast, when a person has been emotionally shocked by a near-miss experience, his level of fear will fall above the latter threshold and he will display hypervigilant reactions. If such reactions occur only at times when a person perceives clear-cut warning signals, his life adjustment may not be seriously impaired; but if they are also evoked at times when only very mild threat cues are present, the hypervigilance is much more disruptive and may be classified as a severe traumatic neurosis.

Using "near-miss" and "remote-miss" as purely descriptive terms to designate, respectively, a high *versus* low degree of victimization sustained in a disaster, we can say that the former is more likely to produce hypervigilance, whereas the latter is more likely to produce an attitude of blanket reassurance. Despite these differential tendencies, however, the effects of near-miss and remote-miss experiences can overlap to a considerable degree, and both types are capable of giving rise to adaptive compromise formations. In short, the sustained effects of any given disaster episode, whether near-miss or remote-miss in character, can range over the entire continuum, motivating the development of blanket reassurances or compromise formations or hypervigilance. The question of which type of outcome will ensue depends upon the two main factors discussed earlier in this chapter: (1) the type of information conveyed by the disaster experience, and (2) the person's level of fear in response to the threat stimuli (prior to the occurrence of the disaster episode). When the information conveyed by the episode is of the type specified by the sensitization hypothesis (p. 82), the predicted postdisaster reaction to any recurrence of the threat will be: (1) maladaptive hypervigilance if the person's fear level initially was moderate or high, and (2) adaptive compromise formations if the person's fear level initially was low. On the other hand, if the information conveyed by the episode is of the type specified by the adaptation hypothesis (p. 81), the predicted postdisaster outcome will be: (1) blanket reassurance if the person's fear level initially was low, and (2) compromise formation if the person's fear level initially was moderate or high.

These propositions serve to link the psychological impact of direct disaster experiences with the impact of purely verbal warnings. We assume continuity between the two types of situations in that the same type of emotional learning occurs in both and is influenced by the same basic factors. Direct disaster experiences, of course, are generally much more impressive than verbal messages, since one cannot easily ignore the relevant danger cues. In addition, direct exposure to danger stimuli entails more powerful rewards and punishments. Consequently, we would expect that more drastic changes in habitual reactions to threat stimuli will be produced by near-miss or remote-miss disaster experiences than by verbal descriptions or predictions about oncoming dangers. It is only in this respect that near-miss and remote-miss experiences take on special psychological significance, particularly when we are attempting to explain extreme changes such as those observed in cases of severe traumatic neurosis.

The assumption that the same principles of perception and learning operate whether people are exposed to actual danger events or to purely verbal messages about them, leads us to expect that when the appropriate conditions are present the latter can produce the same dramatic changes in emotionality as the former. That a purely verbal warning occasionally does so is a well-known fact to physicians who have the responsibility of communicating positive findings obtained from X-rays and medical tests to patients diagnosed as suffering from cancer or some other serious disease. When patients are told the truth by their physician, or learn it inadvertently from members of the family, they sometimes become as chronically hypervigilant as people who have been traumatized in a physical disaster or as depressed as those who have actually been bereaved (Bernstein and Small, 1951; Janis, 1958b; Lindemann, 1941; Wittkower, 1949 and 1952). In such instances, since the person is initially familiar with the nature of the threat, a terse authoritative communication is sufficient to make him perceive himself as seriously endangered. But when the source of danger is relatively unfamiliar, sustained emotional changes are not likely to occur unless vivid communications are presented which familiarize the person with the magnitude of the danger and stimulate him to imagine himself as being threatened by it.

In certain types of disasters, such as virus epidemics and mass poisoning episodes, where the source of the danger is known only to experts, the psychological effect on large numbers of potential victims is determined almost entirely by verbal communications. For example, when an explosion of radioactive thorium unexpectedly occurred at the Sylvania Laboratories in Queens, New York, the official messages communicated to the firemen, newspaper reporters, and others who came to the site of the disaster resulted in a drastic change in their anticipations of vulnerability to danger, transforming their perceptions of themselves as unaffected bystanders into potential victims of radiation disease (National Analysts, Inc., 1956). Similarly, the sporadic outbreaks of illness and blindness in the colored sections of Atlanta during the poison liquor episode were not recognized by the residents as signs of threat until verbal communications were issued explaining that poison liquor was causing the casualties (J. W. Powell, 1953, pp. 87-103). In both disasters the information conveyed by warning communications was sufficient to induce a marked increase in vigilance, leading to cautious, protective behavior of an adaptive character in some people and excited, inefficient overreactions of a maladaptive character in others. Although sensitization-inducing information is especially likely to occur during a near-miss disaster episode, such information can also occur and have the same effect during a pre-disaster warning period, during a remote-miss experience, or during a false alarm episode.

Additional Determinants

The factors singled out for discussion in this chapter are those that appear to be most plausible as determinants of alternative modes of response to warning stimuli. Among the numerous other factors mentioned in disaster studies are a few which at first seemed to be promising candidates but which, on further scrutiny, were excluded because of contradictory observations, indicating the need for further investigation in order to specify limiting conditions. One such equivocal candidate, of sufficient potential importance to warrant brief discussion here, is the factor of *role assignment*. Some investigators claim that this factor operates in the direction of preventing disorganized hypervigilant behavior. In a study of the excellent performance of firemen on a variety of disaster-control tasks carried out under the extraordinarily hazardous conditions of the Kansas City flood and fire of 1951, a major conclusion is that ". . . established role-conceptions, sustained and enforced by reference-group norms, enabled the firemen to keep going in the face of threat and danger" (University of Oklahoma Research Institute, 1952, p. 34). Other writers on disaster behavior also assert that emotional control is facilitated by assignment to a social role entailing some degree of responsibility for the welfare of others (Form and Nosow, 1958; Logan *et al.*, 1952).

One can readily surmise how a role assignment might counteract some of the negative effects of several hypervigilance-producing factors discussed earlier—e.g., by reducing ambiguity about what should be done in a confused disaster situation, by fostering group identification with others in the same role, by providing a form of anticipated (symbolic) contact, or actual telephone communication, with the authority figures who issue orders. But despite these and other possible advantages, the responsibilities attached to a role assignment sometimes interfere with emotional equanimity in an emergency by giving rise to intense role conflicts and new sources of anxiety (Glover, 1942; Janis, 1951; Killian, 1952; Schmideberg, 1942; Spiegel, 1953). Commenting on British reactions to the great North Sea flood, Spiegel (1953) points out that some men placed in a position to make decisions about what should be done to protect the community became obsessionally concerned about their responsibilities, devoted themselves to examining reconnaissance information, repeatedly checked on what was happening, and thereby deferred action. As a result, many lives were lost that could otherwise have been saved. Obviously, much more needs to be known about the conditions under which the advantages outweigh the disadvantages before we shall be able to state exactly which types of role assignment, if any, should be included among the vigilance-reducing or vigilance-enhancing factors.

Role assignment is but one example of the numerous additional factors that await systematic investigation. The various informational, situational, and sequential factors discussed in this chapter should not be regarded as an exhaustive list of all the pertinent variables mentioned in the extensive social psychological literature bearing on reactions to warnings. Nor are any of the hypotheses concerning the effects of the various factors firmly established as yet by systematic research data. Rather, they should be regarded as a highly selected set of descriptive and explanatory hypotheses which, in the light of the existing evidence, offer promising leads concerning the environmental conditions under which warnings will foster indiscriminate vigilance, compromise formation, or blanket reassurance.

► *four*

REACTION TO UNCERTAIN THREAT

Stephen B. Withey

THREAT IS A PERVASIVE PHENOMENON in human experience. As a concept it is fantastically inclusive—so much so that one finds oneself applying, with advantage, research findings from studies done with no particular notion of threat as a variable. An examination of the literature directly bearing on threat readily leads one into the vast and detailed research on stress, the whole topic of defense mechanisms, a large amount of the material on perception and thinking, the work on conflict and tension, a considerable portion of learning theory, and various new areas such as the growing literature on decision making, subjective probability, and systems theory. There is a sizable literature reporting field data gathered by people from various disciplines on reactions to impending disasters, increasing deprivations, aggression against minority groups, etc., and also the vast clinical material on reactions to individual situations of interpersonal and intrapersonal threat.

As a result of a sampling of this literature, the author developed a simple framework for predicting several psychological behaviors and explaining much of the available research on people in situations of threatening disaster. There should be no pretense that this is a theoretical formulation that integrates all the interdisciplinary material on threat. The rough schema is neither detailed nor precise at present.

The notion of threat is very akin to stress with the additional characteristic of degree of likelihood. Stress is, of course, an appropriate and important concept in the total study of biological and psychological phenomena. Moreover, the essential definition of stress remains the same regardless of the level of functioning to which it refers. Stress is the threat to the fulfillment of basic needs, to the maintenance of regulated (homeostatic) functioning, and to growth and development. The responses differ, depending on level, and range from cellular changes to individual and social phenomena such as panic and *anomie*.

The notion of threat specifically implies that the noxious stimuli are not actually present. Only the cues heralding their coming are involved. In some cases these cues themselves may have physiologically stressful characteristics, but we are not interested here in purely physiological adaptation to an extreme stressful condition but rather in reactions mediated by psychological processes such as conditioning, perception, thinking, defense mechanisms, and so forth that are triggered off by various available cues signifying impending stress. Apprehension is not the same as reaction to present stimuli of stress proportions though the difference may, to a large extent, be purely quantitative.

A search of the *Psychological Abstracts* or the *Annual Review of Psychology* reveals almost nothing under the heading, *threat*. The bulk of the material on this topic distributes itself through learning, motivation, emotion, abnormal perception, etc., under such items as: stress, anxiety, avoidance, fear, tension, panic, frustration, etc.

This dispersion is not sloppy indexing. These are all terms in good standing in various traditional organizations of research and theory. It just happens that the concept of threat falls athwart a great number of these classical divisions. In personality theory the notion of defense mechanisms was developed to categorize the various ways and means for handling threat to the personality. In physiology the notion of homeostasis gave rise to the notion of stress as those noxious conditions approximating critical limits for the organ or organism which result in various adaptive processes that restore a level of balance. In the large area of motivation the concepts of needs, frustration, punishment, fear, and tension were required. In learning theory the law of effect, avoidance learning, two-factor learning theory, and many other notions have dealt with aspects of the problem of adaptation to threatening or stressful stimuli.

It is impossible to encompass all of these topics in a single schema; this paper will present only a very general schema. Some of the disaster research bearing on the major items in this schema will then be summarily presented.

The presence of threat will be regarded as a form of stress in which the severity of the possible or impending event, its probability of occurrence, and the ability of the person to cope with the eventuality and the present tension result in various degrees of apprehension, worry, fear, or anxiety. Adaptive or maladaptive efforts usually follow.

We are dealing exclusively with a certain type or class of expectations in which the severity of the calamity is by no means the only measure of the degree of threat. To say that the threat of atomic bombing is a threat of complete annihilation is not to say very much about it, since most people adapt to living with such a threat by adding characteristics to it—its improbability of occurrence, or the improbability of its striking "here," or its possibility only in the distant future, or the ultimate possibility of defense. In a psychological sense these are elements of the threat as well as elements in the response through a feedback process.

To elaborate, it would seem that threat has at least five primitive characteristics. Other characteristics that come to mind, such as source of threat, individual versus group threat, the quantity of information about the threat, ability to handle or tolerate a certain level of tension, etc., can sometimes be subcategorized under the following primitive characteristics or, at other times, considered as determinants of various aspects of one or more of them.

1. Probability of occurrence of the threatened event.
2. Qualitative nature of the threat—physical pain, loss of loved one, etc.
3. Estimated magnitude of deprivation in the mode(s) of threat.
4. Timing—imminence and duration.
5. Possibility of escape or adaptation.

There is some research evidence on the role of each of these characteristics in threat and stress; for example, there is evidence that, given the same type and degree of objective stress, it is much more tolerable if its duration is known, and that subjects who rapidly eliminate uncertainty tend to decide at lower levels of uncertainty. There is also evidence with human and with animal subjects that stress over which one has some influence can be borne with much less evidence of stress reaction on the part of the organism whether it is measured by behavioral, physiological, or (with humans) subjective means.

It would seem that any threat can be defined by definition of these characteristics. The permutations possible under various combinations of them permit a description of a large number of threats.

Before we go on, it is pertinent to examine more thoroughly just what is meant by *threat*. We are dealing here with the second primitive characteristic. Regardless of timing, probability, etc., what makes an event calamitous?

A variety of suggestions are available from different areas of inquiry. They all involve some problems. The simplest approach is to say that any nonsatisfaction of a need is stress and its warning a threat. This can be adequate but there are some problems in listing needs and even more problems in determining their existence or their tolerance limits. In physiology the needs for healthy and efficient functioning may be defined. In psychology this precision has not yet been reached.

Some of the workers in the areas of stress and anxiety have recognized this problem quite clearly. In general, the conclusion has been that there is no escape and that only improved conceptualizing and continued research will enable us to specify more precisely the nature of psychological stress.

Lazarus, Deese, and Osler (1952) point out that there is no adequate definition in stimulus-response terms for the concept of psychological stress. The psychologist has no adequate way of defining the psychological condition that corresponds to the homeostatic steady state. Thus the term *stress* is of necessity a little looser than we would like it to be. The solution of most experimenters has been to produce situations which are *thought* to thwart the motives of most people. This is more or less adequate as long as one is not attempting to account for the reactions of any particular individual. This is analogous to the problem in studies of frustration in which a subject cannot be defined as frustrated unless he evidences some reaction, such as aggression, which is seen as a result of frustration. Thus stress stimuli are defined in terms of response or—less defensibly except at the extremes of stress—in terms of some arbitrary statement of the existence of stress stimuli. The only alternative to these two approaches has been to deal with situations or subjects in which subjective admissions of stress are reported or checked.

It is certain that motivation or drive or need must be involved, since it is clear from the research data that if a person is placed "unmotivated" in a situation which is frustrating to a "motivated" person, the results are vastly and qualitatively different. The whole notion of failure-stress, for instance, makes no sense with a person unmotivated to succeed in the experimental task.

It is on this sort of a base, however, that the homeostatic model, used in physiology, is based when it is used in the psychological realm. An elaboration of some concepts in this area, however, enables us to think about homeostasis in the psychological area a little more clearly.

Initially there are some simple notions about stress and behavior. Periods of stress may differ quite markedly from periods of relative ease. Still, the conditions of these two states should be analyzed together for two reasons: (1) stress and ease are relative concepts, since change, adaptation, and adjustment are continous functions, and (2) any formula that states the conditions for stress implies the limits for ease, and the conditions for the latter can be analyzed only against a background of "potential" stress.

Ashby (1952) provides some help here. He argues that one can record behavior as a line showing its quantitative changes against an ordinate of some measure of behavior and an abscissa showing the passage of time. This he calls the "line of behavior." It might be distance walked, amount of sugar used, oxygen absorption, or what you will.

On the plane through which this line of behavior moves one can imagine critical zones (critical variables); it would be threatening to the survival of the organism, organ, cell, etc. if the line of behavior entered these regions. One can walk only so far, then one drops from exhaustion; an insufficent amount of oxygen becomes stressful, and so forth.

Ashby then introduces the notion of step-functions to explain what happens when the line of behavior approaches these critical regions. The behavior of the organism changes suddenly. The reason is that some parameter in the situation, heretofore a steady variable, has suddenly changed. An endocrine is suddenly active. A warning reaches the threshold level. A nerve assembly is activated. This sudden change, whatever it is, radically alters the system, since a new variable (heretofore a constant, even if inactive) is now functioning. If the line of behavior does not veer away from the danger zone, then another step-function is likely to operate in another parameter until security or balance is restored.

It is clear what these step-functions are in much of physiology. They are by no means clear in psychology but it is interesting to speculate what they might be. They could be cognitions, associations, or the products of learning. The notion of step-functions is central to the choice of behaviors in stressful and threatening situations.

There is a wide range of adaptive behavior in many subsystems of the human organism before acute critical states are reached. Freeman and Fenn (1953) point out that, considering the body as a whole, oxygen consumption can range from 250 cc. per minute during the resting state to about 30 liters per minute during a 100-yard dash. Excessive demand results in Overutilization Anoxia, with the body making a sequence of sacrifices that are increasingly expensive to the total machinery of the body if the demand (or deficiency) continues.

Another example is offered by Selye (1956) in his General Adaptation Syndrome, involving as a first stage the "alarm reaction" with shock and countershock phases. If the noxious stimulus continues, a stage of resistance follows, ending in the stage of exhaustion. Each state results in processes expressed biologically in *different* ways but intimately connected with disturbances recognized chemically as disease states.

Basowitz et al. (1955) point out their ability to distinguish a hierarchy of stress sensitivity among biochemical variables. "With the least intense stress eosinophils disappear; as stress becomes more intense, glutathione falls; and lastly, hippuric acid rises." They simply raise questions about the relationship of this hierarchy to the psychological continuum of anxiety.

These illustrations from physiological fields bring us no closer to defining psychological stress or the critical variables and step-functions in psychological behavior. However, the evidence is strong that parallels will be discovered, and the model is helpful in directing the nature of our inquiry.

Another model that has striking similarities, though its origins and purpose are very different, is offered by Lewin (1947), in his notion of quasi-stationary equilibrium. Here again the states or behavior of a variable (or a system) is represented by means of a curve (line of behavior) in a graph where the ordinate represents the quantitative measure of the behavior and the abscissa represents time. The changes and consistencies in this line of behavior are the results of a process in which, figuratively, some forces are pushing the line down and other forces up. When the line is a more or less constant state (horizontal) these forces are in perfect balance.

Peaks or valleys in this line of behavior indicate points at which balance was restored with perhaps a resultant oscillation back toward a more normal level of behavior. The forces acting to maintain one or another state may not, of course, be simple opposition of two forces but the complex resultant of complicated fields of forces.

Excessive deviation from some normative level or pattern may, however, lead to a new pattern of behavior. If such a deviation occurs in everyday life, we would say that some one of the background variables had changed and the system was altered by the change in this parameter. This is what Ashby would suggest. These regions of the field define the critical states of the organism involving adaptation, though Lewin does not introduce the notion of critical states but rather fields of force which radically alter the line of behavior.

Realizing the value of these notions for a conceptualization of threat, one is still pressed to try to determine further the nature of these critical zones. It is difficult to improve on the lists of human needs offered by Murray (1938) and easy to assume that their frustration constitutes threat. However, when one lists the variety of things and situations that are, by common acceptance, seen as threatening, and if one then tries to carry out a content analysis or précis of such a list, an interesting development occurs. One comes up with such threats as:

Restriction Restriction or constriction of the area of free movement in one's life space.

Impotency Loss of potency in coping with the various situations with which one is confronted.

Isolation Isolation from all stimuli, social isolation, and so forth.

Irrationality Lack of understanding about what is going on, such as occurs in ambiguous situations, uncertainties, ignorance about cause and effect when such information seems necessary for behavior.

Conflict Conflict in demands, needs, or authority.

Nonacceptance Loss in acceptability of oneself by oneself or others.

Discomfort Physical discomforts of minor or extreme nature, physiologically determined.

A further précis of these threats at a high level of abstraction reduces to two: *conflict,* in terms of reality demands and one's idealized image, or conflicting authoritative demands, or conflicting motivational patterns that are incompatible, etc., and *deprivation* or severe restriction of activity, or stimuli, of contact with social groups, or of the physical factors required for survival, and so forth.

Each of these immediately suggests a mode of behavioral adaptation which is strikingly similar to the various adaptive and defense mechanisms in personality which, moreover, if taken in reverse, is strikingly similar to some definition of a threatening situation.

Anna Freud (1946), in her essay on the mechanisms of defense, comments on a kind of parallelism between the ego's defensive measures against external and against internal danger. As an example, she comments that repression gets rid of instinctual derivatives just as denial abolishes external stimuli. She suggests that the form of the defense mechanisms is derived as a consequence of particular juxtapositions of id, superego, and the events of the outside world.

Rationalization is a common defense mechanism needed to settle conflict, to restore self-acceptability, or to fill in information where irrationality or ambiguity (or nonacceptability of initial information) would constitute a threat. Withdrawal is a defense mechanism and isolation a threat. Apathy, too, is a defense that can be translated into the above list as a threat in terms of the resultant impotence and isolation.

It may be possible that all the defense mechanisms may define threat (and vice versa). Their use suggests some sacrifice by the organism in order to maintain the total integrity of the living unit. But sacrifice can be stressful, and is acceptable only when survival or prevention of some greater sacrifice is the alternative.

Systems theory (e.g., Bertalanffy, 1950; Miller, 1955; and others) provides another method for the categorization of threat or stress. In an open system there is an input of both energy and information, there are regulatory functions within the system, and an output of both information and energy resulting in feedback into the system again.

A deficiency in energy input results in stress. Similarly, demand for information that is not available results in stress and threat. Inadequate output of energy and of information similarly defines a stressful situation. Also the irreconcilability or inadequate regulation of the input-output or output-input picture is stressful, involving strains on "management."

Some further notions regarding the nature of threat are obtainable from the discussions by Hebb (1949) on central action. After developing his theory of phase sequences and assemblies on the neurological level, he offers possible explanations of various phenomena of behavior. Expectancy, attention, consciousness, voluntary behavior, set, attitude, and similar terms are explained by sensory-central interaction involving a *pattern* of neural activity. He does consider the "nature of pleasure," which becomes not the activity of particular structures in the nervous system, nor a particular kind of pattern of cerebral organization, but fundamentally a directed *growth or development in cerebral organization.* It is thus a transient state of affairs in which "conflict" is being reduced, an incipient disorganization being dissipated, or a new synthesis in assembly action being achieved. Those sensory conditions are called pleasant which contribute to the current *development* in the cerebrum, or which consist in the decline of a sensory process that interferes with development. However, sensory events should not support the phase sequence so strongly (short circuiting on motivation) that it runs its course immediately and cannot continue to dominate association-area activity. The well-developed phase sequence depends, for a continued existence, on repeated checks from the environment. Hence we see the preoccupation with what is new but not too new, with the mildly frustrating or the mildly fear-provoking. Many adult sports depend for their pleasure on the presence of some danger, and children frequently seek out the frightening situation in which the degree of emotional stimulation remains under control and can be terminated at will.

Unpleasantness then becomes a disruption of cortical organization, which can occur in several ways: the occurrence of incompatible phase sequences; the absence of a sensory facilitation that had always contributed to the phase sequence; "pain" stimulation that can be presumed to be innately disruptive of cortical activity; and chemical change of the blood content, altering the rate of firing of individual neurons and thereby disrupting a cortical organization that is fundamentally a matter of timing.

In cases of distinct disruption of phase sequences there can be a complete breakdown of adaptation because there may be no mechanism for adaptation. However, adaptation does frequently occur, in the form of rage, flight, attack, etc. The stimuli may themselves initiate other *established* phase sequences.

In addition, Hebb assumes that a disruption of timing tends to prevent the recurrence of the phase sequence which led up to that disruption, because of the cyclical (anticipatory and recurrent) organization of the phase sequence. The coordinated part of behavior, with unpleasant emotions, then has this constant function. It breaks the phase sequence leading up to the emotional situation, and, if other learned phase sequences are available (otherwise undifferentiated excitation), it substitutes behavior that puts an end to the original stimulation.

> *Aggression,* in rage, tends to change the irritating behavior of another animal, by cowing, driving off, or killing the annoyer. *Flight,* in fear, tends to prevent or terminate noxious stimulation. *Avoidance*—turning the head away from an unpleasant sight, covering the ears, holding the nose, or withdrawing the hand, as well as actually running away—tends to stop the stimulation that arouses either an irrational fear of some inert object or the practically equivalent disgust. *Fawning* may be a manifestation of fear as much as flight, and so may the desperate attack of a cornered animal; and each is a possible way of putting an end to the emotion-arousing behavior of another organism.
>
> *Failure to respond,* in shame, is a special case in which one's own behavior is the emotion-provoking stimulus; the effect of the emotional disturbance is negative, preventing the recurrence of that behavior, but this is also in line with the present thesis: All these effects may be achieved because *strong emotional disturbance tends to prevent the repetition of any line of thought that leads up to it,* and to eliminate the corresponding behavior (Hebb, 1949).

Similar notions about reinforcement of process, though worded in the language of social psychology, have occurred in studies of morale. Early investigations on morale inquired about dissatisfactions, the notion being that removal of these barriers would re-establish good morale in the studied groups. Later, the bulk of studies seemed to move to the notion of needs rather than barriers, with the action idea of gratifying needs (not just removing barriers); "satiation" almost became the paradigm for good morale. Recently, both of these ideas have given way to a third, which is that human activity and motivation is a process extending over time and acquiring a certain momentum (force, speed, pace, timing, etc.) toward rather complex goals. (The goals do not need to be very clear but they do need to exist.) Pleasure, interest, and activity then arise out of the progressive development of this ongoing process. If this be true, then some blocks to development are enjoyable, adding zest and meaning, and satiation would do nothing more than terminate the development; thus even deprivation—in limited amounts—becomes desirable.

Besides postulating the pleasure in some deprivation, some novelty, and some barriers, these notions, in reverse, imply that destruction of progress, momentum, etc., causes low morale—which is possibly a corollary of psychological stress and threat.

Two basic ideas appear in these concepts of threat and stress. One is a model typified by limitations of states, which describe critical zones. Approximation or invasion of these zones constitutes stress or threat for the organism. The other idea is that process is central and that stress occurs when adequate adjustive feedback breaks down. The two ideas do not seem to conflict, but they are not identical.

As a simple illustration, the driver of a car does not keep moving very long if the temperature of his motor invades certain critical ranges; nor does he continue if the environmental stimuli no longer support his notions of where he is going. If he gets lost, he gets anxious and stops. If his motor gets overheated, he also stops. Both require adjustment procedures. It would seem that both aspects must be included in any thoroughgoing examination of stress and threat.

It has already been stated that before psychological stress can occur, some motivation is required. Frustration or difficulty of accomplishment presuppose a motivation to succeed. Another way of saying this, since stimuli can be "demanding," is that the situation must involve some requiredness of behavior before stress can occur. If a half-million Chinese peasants are threatened with starvation, this may hold no threat for the average American observer. There is no requiredness for thought or behavior. However, if one identifies with human beings in suffering, if one sees the situation as requiring our assistance for political reasons, or if one suffers a loss of self-esteem in not fulfilling a moral obligation to alleviate suffering, then this situation could require some action. *It should be noted, however, that in each case the nature of the situation and even the principal actors are changed as the situation is defined by the hypothetical observers.*

The determinants of requiredness seem to arise from the ways the individual defines the event-gestalt to himself. Does he see himself or his identifications as one of the actors in the event? If he does, what values are engaged by the process and end product of the event sequence as forecast or imagined?

The notion of requiredness also suggests that certain behaviors are required rather than others; sometimes conflicting threats call for conflicting behaviors. Basowitz *et al.* (1955), in their work with paratroopers, found two types of threat operating in the situation—threat of harm and threat of shame. In objectively identical situations, these threats led to two very different behaviors. The threat of harm suggests avoidance of the task of jumping. The threat of shame suggests completing the task of jumping at almost any cost. The authors summarize:

> Shame- and harm-anxiety may differ in their effects on the adequacy of functioning at all biological levels. Although the evidence is still insufficient we believe that harm-anxiety may be more generally disruptive than shame-anxiety. For example, it has been shown that those individuals who fail in training are more clearly distinguished from their more successful comrades in their ratings of harm rather than of failure. Examination of individual case histories lends further support to this view. Moreover, it seems likely that at lower levels of intensity, shame-anxiety may more frequently lead to facilitation of performance while harm-anxiety has more disruptive consequences.

Experimental work on psychological stress has involved various procedures requiring different reactions. The presence of noxious stimuli requires alertness and speed in avoidance; stress in terms of difficult differentiation of competing stimuli requires delay and deliberation. The attention function in either case becomes so involving that other perceptual and intellectual functions are impaired, but the performance required in each circumstance is very different.

Stress imposed by failure in a motivated task requires a change of approach, which in turn requires fluidity in one's method; but persistent failure can only lead to rigidity of response (if the stress situation cannot be left) or to escape (if means can be contrived).

In Ashby's model (1952) the requiredness is in the approach to critical zones, and the step-functions operate randomly until stability is restored. In the physiological models for handling stress the structure and organization of the organism determine the "selection" and sequence of adaptive or defense processes. In psychological stress it seems necessary to include the higher mental processes, learned behaviors, intelligence level, and other complicating factors.

Various aspects of behavior in response to threat (or stress) have already been mentioned. Only general notions about the nature and sequence of behavioral reactions will be considered here.

J. G. Miller (1955), discussing various propositions in systems theory, says:

> *Living systems respond to continuously increasing stress first by a lag in response, then by an overcompensatory response, and finally by catastrophic collapse of the system.* Selye (1950) investigated the effects of varying degrees of many physiological stresses on the organism. He has employed such stresses as extreme variation in temperature and intravenous injections of glucose and typhoid toxoid into animals. The charts of his data show for each stress, an initial dip in the curve in the direction of the final collapse, which is the alarm reaction. It is followed by a rise of the curve above the level normally maintained by the organism, which constitutes a sort of overcompensation or overdefensiveness. As the stress is increased, more and more defenses are called into play until finally no additional ones are available and the system collapses suddenly into death.
>
> We have collected data which suggest that coded or symbolic stresses like those in battle may well elicit response curves similar to those of Selye. While extreme stress always worsens performance, moderate stress can improve it above ordinary levels.

In their account of psychiatric casualties in battle, Grinker and Spiegel (1945) state that the symptoms are regressive in a psychological sense—infantile reactions or "lower-level" visceral techniques causing new conflicts, anxieties, or crippling physical symptoms. For discussion, they group the casualties by symptoms: passive dependency, psychosomatic states, guilt and depression, aggressive and hostile reactions, and psychotic-like states.

In a theory of threat and defense in terms of "the self," Hogan (1952) emphasizes the cognitive determinants of behavior. Threat to him is, in the last analysis, a threat to the individual's perception of his ability to adequately reformulate his tension system. In response to such a situation he claims that only two reactions are possible: (1) to revise the structure of the self to be more consistent with continuing experience, or (2) distort, deny, or change inconsistent experience for self-defense. The first accepts the situation and alters the self, the second maintains the self and alters the phenomenology.

In a very thorough treatise on psychological aspects of the organism under stress, K. A. Menninger (1954b) takes the point of view that:

> All clinical phenomena may be advantageously viewed as belonging within a continuum between the state of adjustment which we call

health and an ultimate state of disintegration or extreme illness. Such a conception would render useless our designations such as nervousness, neurosthenia, neurosis, psychosis, etc., and would bring defense mechanisms into a dynamic organization.

In such a system the functions of the ego would be those of a homeostatic regulator. The purpose of the ego would be to maintain a level of tension which is tolerable, productive, and satisfying as well as consistent with growth. Since events persistently occur which tend to disturb the adjustment that the ego makes, these stresses require the ego to take steps to maintain the integrity of the organism. Minor stresses are usually handled by relatively normal or healthy devices. Greater stresses or prolonged stress excite the ego to increasingly energetic and expensive activity to maintain balance.

One of the first evidences of failure of the normal devices of the ego is the development or persistence of *stress awareness.* The subject is conscious of discomfort in connection with efforts at concentration or self control. Aware of this, he consciously exerts an extra measure of "will power" in the mastery or concealment of these phenomena. Perhaps *hypersuppression* is the most nearly normal of any of the secondary defenses. A less uncomfortable, because unconscious, method is the use and increased use of repression.

In outline form, the stages and symptoms of reaction to stress schematized by Menninger are the following:

1. The ego maintains psychosomatic homeostasis upon becoming aware of increased tension (a kind of pre-anxiety discomfort) and reacts by putting into effect one or some of the regulatory devices to relieve immediate distress. With increased stress, regulatory functions of the ego are taxed and result in: (a) exaggeration of "normal" processes; (b) manifestation described as illness (see following).

2. First-order regulatory devices are used when normal devices are overtaxed. Devices are usually exaggerations of normal functions but appear uncomfortably and unpleasantly. They are often described as "nervousness." First-order devices are transient, tending toward subsidence.

3. When first-order defenses fail (from inadequacy or exhaustion), second-order devices appear to relieve stress. Second-order devices are characterized by partial detachment from world of reality (impaired reality testing). They are "emergency" devices often incorporated into the psychological system.

4. Third-order devices (transitory ego rupture).

5. Fourth-order regulatory devices (psychosis, can be reversible).

6. Fifth-order devices (irreversible).

At this point it seems advantageous to think of the following steps or stages in reaction to threat. They may telescope so that they are virtually simultaneous; nevertheless, it is productive to keep them separate for conceptual purposes. These stages seem to be:

1. The presence of information about the threat (internal or external cues).
2. The perception or awareness of such information.
3. An estimate of the probability of the impending event occurring.
4. An estimate of the nature of such an event—sequence, gestalt, and consequences.
5. An estimate of the severity, to the individual, of such a development.
6. An estimate of means for coping with the threat.
7. An estimate of the probability of the success of these means.
8. An estimate of the cost to the individual of such means.
9. A resolution and decision about behavior.
10. A testing of behavior with success or return to a previous stage.
11. A selection of subsequent behaviors that are adaptive to the situation, in principle eliminating threat, but at increasing expense to the organism.
12. A selection of subsequent behaviors that are adaptive to the situation but protective to the organism, in principle "pulling through."
13. A selection of behaviors that are overly adaptive, excessively effortful, and seemingly overzestful and overcompensatory.
14. A selection of behaviors that are nonadaptive to aspects of the organism but preservative and defensive for part of the organism's integrity.
15. Breakdown.

The sequence can be terminated at almost any point.

The topic of uncertainty and psychological probability cuts across several areas, many of which are too tangential to warrant review here. These matters are not irrelevant to our topic but can, to a large extent, be assumed as general background knowledge, so that this development can restrict itself to those studies that particularly apply to the sort of schema we have been developing.

A great amount of work in perception has provided us with insights about the patterning and organization of presented stimuli, mutually dependent on the exterior organization and the internal patterning, habits, etc., of the observer. Some, but considerably less, work has been done in the particular area of perception of events or sequences of events as opposed to isolated stimuli. If experienced patterns are important in the learning of simple stimulus-response sequences, they are all the more important in the learning of perceptual meanings. It seems clear that in assessing the probability factors in the causal texture of the environment, the apprehensions of some people prevent their making simple or valid *actuarial* computations.

The whole notion of apprehensions, expectations, and "hypotheses" has been quite systematized by the work of Bruner and others. Problems have arisen involving subception, perceptual defense, reticence to report, etc., but these are too detailed for present consideration.

In this approach, perceiving involves three steps, starting with an expectancy or hypothesis, followed by the input of information and, finally, checking or confirmation procedures. The apparent smoothness with which this process goes on is no contradiction to this notion. The notion of "hypothesis" is by no means limited to specific, isolated expectancies; on the contrary, it is more related to integrated systems of belief or expectancy about environmental events in general.

Bruner (1951) states various properties of hypotheses that are relevant to present considerations:

> 1. The stronger a hypothesis, the greater its likelihood of arousal in a given situation.
> 2. The greater the strength of a hypothesis, the less the amount of appropriate information necessary to confirm it.
> 3. The greater the strength of a hypothesis, the more the amount of inappropriate or contradictory information necessary to infirm it.
> 4. The more frequently a hypothesis or expectancy has been confirmed in the past, the greater will be its strength.
> 5. The smaller the number of alternative hypotheses held at a given moment, the greater their strength will be.
> 6. The closer to monopoly a hypothesis is, the less information will be required to confirm it and the more tenaciously will it be retained in the face of stimulus contradiction.
> 7. The larger the number of supporting hypotheses or the more integrated the supporting system of hypotheses, the stronger the hypothesis.
> 8. The more basic the confirmation of a hypothesis is to the carrying out of goal-striving activity, the greater will be its strength.
> 9. Where stimulus conditions are such that information for either confirming or infirming a hypothesis is minimal, the hypothesis is minimal; the hypothesis may be strengthened by virtue of its agreement with the hypotheses of other observers to whom the perceiver may turn.
> 10. Variations in the attributes of the perceived self provide the most highly relevant stimulus information for confirming adjustmentally relevant hypotheses, i.e., hypotheses the confirmation of which are

crucial to adjustment. [In this connection, Bruner suggests *self-saliance* and *self-potency* as the two attributes of self which provide crucial information for guiding us in our adjustment.]

These notions are not all equally confirmed by experimental findings but they all fall well into the sort of schema we are developing here. It is noteworthy that many of these ideas are quite congruent with the ideas, on this level, that one might generate out of the work of Hebb.

McGregor (1938), examining the major determinants of the prediction of social events, says that as the structure of a situation becomes more fluid, through reduction of information, a subject's autism—emphasis on cognitive processes that are in the direction of need satisfaction—becomes more marked.

The work of the psychoanalysts, the users and theorists of projective techniques, the experiments of Brozek (1951) and many others, confirm the fact that under strong motivation and the absence of stimulus confirmation of satisfaction, ideation occurs, the content of which is, at least symbolically if not actually, related and identified with the desired or "confirming" end-goal. There is no reason to think that notions of likelihood are not similarly influenced by motivational directives.

Hudson (1954a) finds anxiety occurring in response to the unfamiliar, where lack of structure *and* threat exist as conditions. Threat seems to occur only as individual interpretation in such an ambiguous setting. Any stability in the present environment aids in reducing this anxiety, and the availability of some behavior pattern reduces anxiety. Anna Freud and Burlingham (1943) report that the children of London, during the war, increased their cues for the familiar by sticking close to their dolls and other possessions.

In an interesting experiment by Marks (1951) with children, it was found that expectancies were greatly affected by the condition of desirability of the occurrence. It was found, also, that the strength of effects on stated expectations were equal for the probability of the desirable and the improbability of the undesirable, but were not influenced by socio-economic status, grade, sex, or I. Q.

Although the test has not been made, one would predict the same sort of result from the work of N. E. Miller (1951) on avoidance, conflict, etc. Growing out of work on avoidance and approach gradients from maze-running experiments, the theory has been formalized so that one can generalize to a variety of conditions. The question is whether the gradients of generalization, time, or spatial distance can be used to include gradients of probability of occurrence.

Certainly a strong approach, *distant* from the goal, exercises more "pull" than similar avoidance at the same spatial distance. Perhaps subjective estimates of probability would work the same way, for the same reason.

Some interesting ideas in the area of uncertainty and probability are being developed by Thrall, Coombs, and Davis (1954). Their model uses the utility notions of economics. However, it has to be adapted somewhat to serve as a paradigm for a threatening or stressful situation.

An interesting development from their model is that a person faced with nearly certain threat should pay no attention to the cost of defense, the only additional factor being that he exhibits strong preference to win as high a prize as possible. This would account for the dreams of Utopia that often accompany tremendous defensive efforts on a social scale. At the other end of the scale, if the probability of an event is low, the severity of the threat (or the size of the prize) makes virtually no difference; all the individual wants to do is keep his effort, cost, and defense to a minimum.

This sampling of various research perspectives shows considerable coherence. The following schema of stages presents the sequences that these various researchers seem to have noted with differential emphasis. Initial stages may well continue on through later steps in the process and the separate elements can be telescoped until they may seem almost simultaneous. At other times, certain stages may cover a considerable length of time, as, for instance, a continued state of alert maintained after hearing a strange noise at night. This may last for minutes or hours filled with only scanning or other exploratory activities. The definition-of-the-situation stage might, in some cases, occupy months, as in the case of an international threat requiring the gathering of intelligence reports.

The cues for threat are assumed to be either continuous (or standing) or to follow some expected developmental sequence in accordance with the estimation and definition of the situation. Any change in this projected development would possibly lead to a new state of alert, the sequence then following a similar pattern of scanning for meaning and implications.

Stages

1. *Recognition* in which the threat is perceived by some cue or message.
2. *Validation* in which the input is checked for validity.

3. *Definition of the situation* in which the available information is organized so as to know the nature, timing, probability, etc., of the danger.

4. *Evaluation* in which defenses are initiated (or planned) so that the manageability of the situation and one's security become the prime matters of attention.

5. *Commitment* in which defenses are carried out (or thought about) with success or failure, the latter leading to a reevaluation and new commitment.

6. *Reassessment and overcommitment* in which failure begins to raise the level of fear and anxiety and the degree of effort devoted to defense, i.e., danger is greater than predicted.

7. *Progressive uses of a lattice of defense* in which the failure of one defense leads to another more expensive defense; but commitment to initial defenses may preclude the choice of certain defenses, so that not all defenses are available on a single continuum of increasing cost to the organism.

In this framework all activities are regarded as defensive, so that initial sensitivities and narrowing of attention, modes of organization of stimuli, and haste or reservation in speed of commitment are themselves aspects of defense tactics and strategy.

As speculative or actual reactions lead to failure, new tactics need to be devised. Initially, if the threat is not too severe, this can be challenging and pleasurable, as in a game. However, if the stakes are high, failure arouses rather intense anxiety which has to be handled along with the failure-provoking situation that persists.

It may be that a simple ratio of *threat* to the *means for meeting the threat* defines the situation. If so, as successive failures are encountered the threat becomes more severe as this ratio grows larger. Thus the recipient of the threat is faced with an increasingly difficult situation. The threat is becoming greater. The means for meeting it are disappearing. The conflict among notions of effective means becomes a frustrating affair, and the anxiety aroused by failure has to be handled at the ego level.

This notion suggests that a variety of means for meeting a threat are more effective in reducing anxiety and strain than is one defense that is ascribed a high probability of success. A Maginot-line defense may be very effective at the initial stages of threat, but once it is breached, even speculatively, the result is confusion and withdrawal.

It has been suggested by K. A. Menninger (1954b) that the choice of succeeding defense mechanisms can be expressed as various stages on a continuum involving increasing primitivization and disintegration. It would seem to the author that a better model might be a lattice, a mathematical device that would allow more than one mechanism to follow a given previous one and would also suggest that, once one device had been tried, the subsequent choices were somewhat restricted. In a continuum, either the sequence has to follow the order of the continuum, or one has to develop a rationale for "skipping" or "jumping." A lattice model, if it can be determined to be applicable, would permit a variety of paths.

It has already been noted that reactions to stress can be plotted as falling below "normal activity" during an initial alarm stage. Following this there is a stage of hyperactivity, involving excessive use of adaptive or retaliatory mechanisms. If the stress is continued, the activity sinks to the level of the catastrophic state. From a purely psychological point of view, the initial drop can be accounted for by the early scanning and defining processes and by the defense mechanisms that reduce the likelihood and expectation of threat, if they occur. As defensive tactics are initiated, their failure leads to heightened effort; the increasing severity of the threat (defined by its continuity and its nonsusceptibility to mastery) leads to even higher effort. As failure and stress continue, the organism becomes more involved in internal defense and survival and the hyperactivity abates to a level of complete quiescence.

The step-functions that lead to sudden reorientations in adaptation may be due partly to anxiety- or fear-provoked chemical changes, but they could also be due to new bits of information, the perceived behavior of other people, the chance occurrence of something in the environment, the reorganization of a perceptual gestalt, an acsociation, the revival of an old habit pattern, an unexpected success, the restructuring offered by an emergent leader, and so forth.

Implicit during the various ongoing central processes is the persistent effort to maintain a stable self-structure. This self-structure involves super-ego factors but also includes the various ego, reality-oriented, factors of one's habitual setting, role, and environment. This has been noticed by researchers in their mention of a threatened person's efforts to maintain contact with the familiar. Thus a person with deep roots in his local setting is more likely to "stick with the ship" than is someone with weaker roots.

Also, an individual whose familiar role is a suitable role for a disaster situation will be under less strain and will behave more adaptably than the others, because his reaction patterns are well entrenched, his role (and self-picture) is familiar, and the situation-reaction process actually requires less decision and adjustment. The effectiveness of the required role is also well proved by its past success. This aspect of disaster or threat reaction is applicable to doctors, nurses, firemen, policemen, etc., *when the situation requires the behavior for which they are trained.*

Within our schema, the phenomenon of a "near miss" operates in three ways: it substantially raises the probability of occurrence of extreme stress; it substantially reduces the effectiveness of such defenses as "I'm lucky"; and it raises new problems involving the handling of personal anxiety and guilt if the situation has involved loss of a close friend, associate, etc.

The schema that has been developed implies a number of hypotheses about reactions to uncertain threat that are linked together in sequential stages. This lattice assumes continued and sustained threat through various phases. If, for any single individual, one stage serves as an efficient defense, then the sequence is terminated. For another, the sequence may be continued until some other point of defense is obtained. At the later stages, the reaction is identical with reaction to actual stress; uncertainty is no longer a factor.

It would be valuable if a number of hypotheses could be checked against field or laboratory observations at a time of threat involving imminent stress. Since this particular grouping of hypotheses has not been formulated and ordered in this way before, no such comprehensive verification exists. However, if the schema is a valid one, the field data collected on disasters should substantiate bits and pieces of the schema. This scanning of field material is interesting, since most of the material out of which the schema was developed is laboratory work rather than field material.

Such an application of bits and shreds of evidence here and there cannot validate the schema, but it can add to its credibility and suggest its worth for thinking and research. Also, the exercise may clarify the hypotheses suggested in the schema and, perhaps, amplify them in terms suitable to a more valid generalization.

Most of the work on disasters has dealt with reactions to actual impact and the problems of rescue and recovery. A few catastrophies have been studied that included a warning time of sufficient duration that the validity of the threat and the decision regarding a course of action could be recalled and studied. In most cases warning time was a matter of seconds. In some cases the threat was so certain that uncertainty was eliminated and only the question of human reaction to present stress remained. In these latter cases the schema is applicable only as one looks at the individual desperately searching for a way of escape that is effective and less hazardous than sustaining the stress itself. In all, no contrary evidence has been found, but the pertinent information is scant.

In assaying a test of validity six points seem most promising:

1. The effect of previous experience and familiarity on threat reaction.

2. The tendency toward optimism and an estimate of low probability for the threatening and stressful.

3. The influence of set, apprehension, and anxiety on threat reaction.

4. The influence of feelings of effectiveness on sensitivity to information.

5. The effect of estimates of "cost" and worth of defense on threat reaction.

6. The influence of continued threat on threat reaction and defense.

These six points are crucial to the schema that has been developed. The only major omission seems to be the ordering of defenses in the later stages of threat reaction. The particular ordering of more expensive types of defense is not suggested, nor is there any evidence in existing disaster studies that would suggest possible conclusions.

Before attempting to find evidence for or against these six points, it may be worthwhile to review the notions developed about them so far.

1. There is a tendency for new stimuli to be interpreted within a framework of the known and familiar. This can work three ways:

  a. Under conditions devoid of threat and stress, if threat cues are introduced, the tendency will be to interpret them as unthreatening until such interpretation can no longer be made.
  b. Under conditions of recent but not repeated threat an apparent oversensitivity to stress cues will be developed.
  c. Under conditions of repeated exposure to threat (seasoned combat veteran) there will be a selective sensitivity not shown in a or b.

2. There is a tendency to estimate the probability of good events somewhat higher than the "objective" probabilities, and the probabilities of stressful events somewhat lower. Since "real" or even "subjective" probabilities are usually not measured, the prediction would be that even if cues are interpreted as indicating possible threat, rather than assimilated into a familiar, unthreatening setting, the likelihood of their leading to danger is underestimated. People will feel that the disaster to which they are alerted will not really happen or will not be as bad as predicted.

3. This tendency is parallel to those already covered, but restates in a somewhat altered frame of reference that the expectancies of an individual will influence his receptivity to warning and his choice and

mode of reaction. If a person is "set" to expect a disaster, a minor suggestion will raise the probabilities of occurrence in his mind considerably so that reaction to the disaster, whether it is imminent or not, is precipitated.

4. The degree of effectiveness in securing an escape or adaptation to the threatened disaster (or experienced disaster) will influence a person's sensitivity to information and his mode of response. People feeling more ineffective should be less sensitive to incoming information. People feeling overconfident should be equally indifferent, but not as a defense—just because they feel they do not need the information.

5. The higher the cost of a defense, the less likely is that defense to be adopted until less expensive forms of defense have failed.

6. Continued threat and a failure of adaptation or defense should lead to greater constriction of cognition, rigidity of response, and diffuse and primitive forms of reaction.

These points are not heavily emphasized in the field research data, but they are the points at which congruity of data and schema will be sought in an examination of the available material.

Almost all human experience involves the interpretation of stimuli within some familiar setting. Aspects of novelty are exhilarating, but anything that is genuinely strange seems to be somewhat traumatic and stressful. The experience of disaster can create a familiarity with such experiences, but since disaster is almost by definition an infrequent experience, the tendency is to interpret stimuli in terms of most probable occurrences, which implies interpreting them in nonstressful terms. In other words, what is most likely to happen is what has happened. Superimposed upon this tendency seems to be an "optimistic" set. People hope. They wish.

Nevertheless, when a set for the "worst" exists, this tendency may be reversed. A rumored catastrophe may create tensions and anxieties that need only a cry in the street to trigger them off. The rumors generate an atmosphere of "it could happen" and any suggestion throws the probability that much higher. Normally the set is against such expectancies. If it were not so, we would be in a continuing state of worry and apprehension.

Our control over tension requires that we expect to be able to cope with circumstances through effective accommodations and adjustments. When we drive our cars in traffic, we are not overly worried over the chances of a failure in the steering mechanism that would send us veering off into the other lane of traffic. Though such an event is possible, and might be fatal, past probabilities discount the need for concern. However, if someone competent to suggest such things put the idea into our heads that such a mechanical failure was imminent, a spot of oil on the road that momentarily affected our control of the car could create enough additional suggestion to send us into a garage. This is what is referred to as a state of alert or vigilance. Though our equanimity may be better maintained if our behavior takes such possibilities into account, it is, however, best maintained if we are not *overconcerned* with our welfare but save our energies for those events that do in fact require defensive or avoidance behaviors.

Effective warning becomes, thus, a function of the amount of information to be contradicted. Once a pattern of development has started, the amount of information needed to enforce the pattern's continuance is much less than would be needed to change one's expectancies. Put another way, one can think of information given by a warning as opposing the information receivable by the threatened person from other sources outside and inside the individual. The notion of information implies confirmation of one alternative among several possible ones. Thus a certain amount of redundancy is required in a warning, since these hypothesized or rationalized alternatives need to be contradicted.

To the extent that alternatives have a different subjective probability in a person's mind, more information may be required to effect a contradiction of the more probable event.

Since the frame of reference of one receiver will differ from that of another, and since the warning is likely to be other than definitive, people will be likely to report different meanings of any warning given the same objective words or signals of warning. In other words, they will think up various "alternatives" that are not contradicted effectively by the offered warning. Examples of this are offered in the following excerpts from disaster reports:

> *Conflicting warnings* (*Point 2*)
> In the Kansas City fire and flood the endangered population was faced with a rather ambiguous situation: the Army Engineers were maintaining that the dikes along the river would not hold, while the city engineers were maintaining that they would. Many people resolved this conflict by going to the water's edge to see for themselves. Since the dikes seemed to be holding, they resisted further attempts to be evacuated—with disastrous results (Balloch, 1953).
>
> *An air-raid alert* (*Points 1 and 2*)
> In the study of a false civil defense alert in Oakland, California, the great majority correctly interpreted the siren as an air-raid warning but the great majority also discounted its validity on the basis of war

not being likely and the apparent calmness of other people. The actual auditory cues were interpreted as caused by a short circuit, a practice or some other suitable rationalization (Scott, 1955b).

A hurricane (*Point* 2)
An element which seems to influence people's behavior during threat of crisis is the commonly found myth or legend that "it can't happen to me." This legend often seems to serve the function of minimizing the feeling of danger. More than half of the respondents claimed that Ocean City would never have a tidal wave or be washed away because "the sand bar was building up all the time." The fact that a portion of Ocean City had been washed away in a 1933 hurricane was used to rationalize and emphasize the "no danger" theme. Because "the 1933 hurricane tides had widened the inlet to the bay, there was even less danger from high tides" (Rayner, 1953).

A tornado (*Point 1*)
Even the roaring, the only cue of all those noticed in the immediate pre-impact period that respondents in impact areas reported they perceived more often than persons in non-impact areas, sometimes got assimilated to a normal definition. This was particularly true of those people who lived near the railroad tracks. They mistook the roaring for a train. One respondent reported her experience in this connection as follows: "I heard an awful roaring. Sounded like a train and I kept listening for a train to whistle and finally I heard a whistle and I was relieved you know" (Marks and Fritz, 1954, *1*).

A severe flood (*Point* 2)
An amazing number of people refused to believe that the flood could hit them, that it could come anywhere near to the previous severe flood of 1903. The result was that they would not move themselves or their belongings out of their houses. Many others piled furniture up in the center of the room, even though the warning had been issued that the flood water would destroy their possessions if left at that level. The result was that many had to be rescued out of the second stories of their homes. Of 10,000 homeless people, nearly 3,000 had to be rescued by boat (W. C. Menninger, 1952).

J. W. Powell writes, in *An Introduction to the Natural History of Disaster* (1954b):

> . . . *the predominant response to warning is the hope that nothing bad will happen.* In both Topeka (reported by William Menninger) and the Ohio Valley (verbal report by Col. Milani, who held command of the Army Engineers assigned there), thousands of people even after direct orders to evacuate, had to be taken by boat from their upstairs windows or roofs. The same was reported from Canvey Island in the English Channel, in the hurricane floods of February, 1953.

However, Powell continues:

> A small element goes to the other extreme, seeing an active threat in conditions which at the time only constitute warning. Thus some people in Arkansas were said to "go into a storm cellar every time a thunder storm comes up—even prior to the actual tornadoes." For these people warning is equivalent to threat. This is, in fact, true of general populations which have suffered a recent impact out of conditions that would ordinarily constitute only warning: e.g., the residents of Elizabeth, N. J., after the first two crashes, felt the continued presence of heavy planes low overhead not as a warning ("conditions from which danger might arise") but as threat ("actual presence of conditions promising local and personal peril"). In short, the appraisal at the stage of warning is either under- or, *in special cases,* over-cautious.
>
> It would seem that two processes are present:
>
> 1. An attempt to fit the "threat cues" into the familiar. The familiar is more probable than the unfamiliar thus having greater arousal strength from a learning theory point of view. Initially this leads to discounting the threat.
>
> 2. A formulation of expectancy as a continuation of present patterns of expectancy—in other words, in accordance with one's set. The tendency under "normal" or average conditions is to "predict" favorable events with a somewhat higher probability than one "predicts" unfavorable ones. Personality factors may identify exceptions in this tendency.

If one accepts a threat cue as validly indicative of danger, because of a built-up set, incontrovertible evidence, or a threat too serious and too imminent to be ignored even if improbable, the same processes operate. The danger is seen as "like some known danger" and the expectancy of avoidance (optimism?) leads to escape or protective behavior.

Actual impact is likely to be acutely disruptive to both of these processes. Shock and bewilderment may result in not only disruption but a blocking of the development of new "purposive" processes.

The definition of the situation is not purely a cognitive recognition of the occurrence of something called a tornado, flood, or fire. The severity of the situation includes a definition of the situation in personal terms of adaptation or defense potential along with the emotional impact accompanying these conclusions.

The acceptance of a threat implies the acceptance of an unstable cognitive structure. *Any disaster involves an increase in entropy,* and the organizing aspects of cortical functions seem to mirror this increase; such is the raw material of anxiety.

Hudson (1954a, 1954b) reports that some individuals under uncertainty say: "The worst would be better than this." The instability he refers to may be due to vagueness in the identification of an object or event, the meaning or cause of an event, the projected outcome, the projected action to be taken, etc. (Point 4).

There is much suggestive material implying that a generalized level of anxiety, feelings of ineffectiveness and impotency in one's personal life, and a set toward fatalism create a narrowing of the perceptual field and a limitation of the information that can or will be received. This narrowing occurs most conspicuously in the latter stages of threat and stress reaction. However, even during the less severe and earlier stages there is evidence for it.

Tyhurst (1951) writes that:

> It is quite clear with respect to behavior under situations of difficulty that helplessness is one of the most serious predisposing factors towards unfortunate behavior, and it is possible that problems of initiative are being largely neglected. I don't know what initiative is, actually, but it seems to me that it is the ability to make some sort of evaluation of a situation and develop self-initiating behavior of an appropriate kind.

A study by Douvan and Withey (1953) showed that those individuals who felt unable to manage and control their own personal affairs were unable to think of several ways of meeting emergencies; they had little confidence in the likelihood of others controlling larger affairs, they had less information about national events and showed less concern over such affairs because, they said, there was nothing they could so about such matters. These individuals paid little attention to what was available in the news about threats to the society at large. One might assume that the same picture would be true for the smaller society of which they were a part.

The converse—that effective people are more receptive to available information—might be restated as: where effective ways for insuring safety are available, information is more likely to be received without blocking or distortion. However, it seems that it is not the "objective" character of the information but the "subjective" evaluation of the situation by the individual that is important. Thus an individual's reaction to threat can easily vary from one circumstance to another. In the Vassar symposium ("Conference . . . ," 1955), comment was made that in Kline's work those that were rated highly by the assessment staff (successful) had a perceptual threshold that made them sensitive to cues of threat in the environment after they had been threatened, whereas those rated less successful were less able to perceive threat in the environment.

David Rioch, also speaking in conference at the Vassar symposium, remarked: ". . . and you have, quite routinely, men who go into the alerting action who fight efficiently and effectively but you find there is a *marked constriction* of the horizon" (Point 6).

He further emphasized that notions of effectiveness in sudden danger were speedily set:

> . . . when the first shell landed, I went two feet up in the air. By the time I landed on the ground, I knew I wasn't going to run away. . . . [A man] reacts to his own reaction and, in reacting to his own reaction, he discovers his own reaction is not going to take charge. He's going to take charge of his reaction (Point 4).

These factors also are shown to influence public reaction to the uncertain threat of atomic war. A study done in England by Fothergill and Lamberth (1950) showed that those who joined civil defense as a step toward "handling" this threat regarded the threat as more serious than others, but at the same time they felt less impotent—then perceived some tactic for reducing the threat—and felt and evidenced effectiveness in their personal lives (Point 4).

Another analysis of civil defense volunteering in the U.S., done by the University of Michigan Survey Research Center in 1952, showed that mild concern over the threat was more effective than extreme concern in eliciting participation. Also, knowledge of some tactics for coping with the threat and a positive evaluation of the worth of these tactics also gave weight to the forces toward participation. Regardless of information about the threat or about civil defense, or both, participation required a moderate evaluation, at least, of the effectiveness of civil defense programs.

Another part of the schema (Point 2) is supported by data obtained in a 1956 study on civil defense. Cognitively the great majority of the U.S. public think that the U.S. would be attacked heavily in the event of another war. But half of the adult population report that they do not need to pay attention to civil defense because they can discount any danger to themselves. With some it is a feeling of being in a safe area; with others it is a feeling that defenses will be adequate to fend off an attacker; with others the probability of an attack ever being initiated is seen as so low as not to deserve serious attention (Withey, 1956).

Apart from receptivity to information and consideration of tactics in terms of confidence-sets, the choice of behavior and the type of information scanned is heavily influenced by the guessed cost of defense (Point 5). S. A. Prins (1955) accounts for his own escape from the Nazis in Holland and the non-escape of virtually all of his associates as directly caused by the cheapness of escape to him. Others had a heavy investment in homes, families, friends, businesses, etc. He felt the same roots and attachments, and as long as he did so he postponed escape and rationalized the threat to one of minimal severity. His first rationalization for flight is a love for adventure and a willingness to revolt, to do wrong, to be an outlaw. But in his account he is forced to push further and admit that he had got to the point where he wanted to leave and never intended to return—there was no cost in leaving. He accounts for this partly in terms of early anti-Semitic experiences; his escape was finally precipitated by a break-up of his marriage.

The fact of cost appears again and again in reports of reaction to threat and disaster. Only a few examples need be mentioned:

> *In a flood*
> It would appear that past experience was a criterion for action in the case of many who refused initially to respond to warnings, but also for some to give up all hope; leaving a familiar environment and abandoning possessions to the elements were, undoubtedly, decisions that could not be made (Hudson, *Observations in a Community During a Flood*).
>
> The general provincialism of the Dutch farmers who were involved in the disaster greatly influenced their willingness to be evacuated from their villages. Many of them had never been off their island during their whole lifetime. Evacuation to the mainland seemed a much more terrifying experience to them than it might to victims in more mobile cultures.
>
> In the Netherlands, the evacuees were occasionally reluctant to enter the unfamiliar vehicles. This was most true of the smaller H-13 helicopter, but the seaworthiness of the unfamiliar DUKW was also occasionally questioned. The H-13 had the additional disadvantage of not being large enough to evacuate families as a unit. Because the victims felt some measure of security in just being together as a family group, they were reluctant to accept rescue if it meant temporary separation. Secondly, evacuees were reluctant to leave their homes and property for several reasons: fear of looting, fear that their farmlands would be taken over by others who remained behind, the knowledge that their farm animals would die without care, and finally just unwillingness to leave behind all the things that were familiar for strange new surroundings (Balloch, 1953).
>
> *In a tornado*
> "We couldn't decide where to go or what to do. So we grabbed our children and stuff and were starting to move outside. Where if it had been just ourselves, we might have taken out. But we didn't want to risk it with the children. The stuff was beginning to fly through the air by that time" (Hamilton, Taylor, and Rice, 1955).
>
> *In a hurricane*
> For [them] economic factors such as need to remain with property or fear of a subsequent financial loss if evacuation occurred, seemed to

> exert considerable force in the decision against evacuation. . . . Another . . . individual who had previous experience with hurricanes and had suffered no loss, rejected the appraisal of the authorities. However, this man, who is a hotel manager, did evacuate his guests. The feeling of responsibility for his guests overcame any reluctance to leave because of possible economic loss (Rayner, 1953).
>
> *In an air-raid alert*
> "I thought of going to the regular shelter in case it was perhaps a real alert or something but I figured others would think that was silly, since none of them went, so I stayed where I was" (Scott, 1955).

A study which tends to substantiate many of the notions already developed was offered by Diggory (1956). He showed that as threat was higher (due to proximity), there was more scanning behavior and a larger number of sources of information were used, that the incidence of word-of-mouth communication was raised, and there was a tendency of the estimates to be lower than the estimates made at a greater distance.

With the increasing magnitude of danger there is less opportunity for suitable action. Inability to formulate a defense reduces the probability that warning will lead to suitable effective action, and thus is likely to lead to the arousal of intolerable fear, acute disruption, and psychological disorganization. Continued anxiety and apprehension produce new stimuli which are productive of further anxiety in their own right.

But the threat need not grow in magnitude. Its mere continuance is sufficient to create the successive stages of threat reaction suggested in the schema. In a nonhuman condition this was shown in remarks by Rioch ("Conference . . . ," 1955):

> If you take cats and pinch their tails, the friendly cat will take a look and it's okay. We had one cat who patted me on the foot while I was pinching its tail. If you go on, here is very beautiful anticipatory behavior. Now, all of a sudden, there is a change, a rapid shift, and the cat takes one swipe. The swipe is at the hand with the forceps, then on the forceps, then where the forceps touch the tail. Then, if you don't stop, now the cat is making nice accurate movements with one part of its body. Now it goes into total action, screaming, biting, etc. This is very effective (for the cat), unless you have gloves and forceps. This goes on for a time, then you get a further change. The cat stops attacking and tries to pull away with all its earlier responses. Actually, I have never taken a normal cat across this total reaction. This goes on, then it changes, the cat falling flat in panic. As far as cats go, there is a series of steps which can be definitely separated. For the time relationship, there is a very sharp curve, and one can get this with no change in the input. This change is a function of the time of the ac-

> tivity and not of the input itself, so, I think, there is probably another thing that plays a part—just the continuation of the impact is going to make a difference in the capacity of the people to withstand it.

Further evidence on this is available from remarks by Glass (1955):

> Psychological breakdown occurs in these individuals subjected to severe traumatic conditions who are unable to utilize appropriate evasive or aggressive action and in addition cannot tolerate the consequent intense fear reaction. Relief is imperative for these terrorized persons. Individuals so affected *do not suffer a literal breakdown of psychic functions but exhibit a more primitive behavioral pattern that permits a decrease of personal involvement with intolerable reality.* [Italics added.] Emotional disorders of this type can be interpreted as meaningful behavior which has for its purpose the maintenance of the organism in situations of extreme personal discomfort even though such an adaptation may be deleterious insofar as survival is concerned. Support for this hypothesis has been furnished by Rioch, who states that neuropsychological mechanisms do not permit random or unorganized activity except possibly for a few seconds during transition from one organized functional pattern to another system of a higher or lower level of integration. The mute, stunned reaction commonly observed under disaster conditions illustrates the purposeful nature of these stress-induced psychological abnormalities. *Here the involved person appears isolated from the chaotic situation by apparently blocking the perception of external stimuli.* [Italics added.] Even more primitive is the uncontrolled, frantic behavior noted under circumstances of presumed imminent catastrophe, where the affected person seemingly responds to stimuli without discrimination or evaluation as if cortical control were lost and function was integrated at a brain-stem level. Less severe forms of emotional disorder due to stress exhibit a childish type of dependent adaptation that may be variously manifested by helplessness, trembling, hysterical paralysis, or marked suggestibility and docility.

One must keep in mind, however, that many threats can be tolerated when they are short of being actual stress. One can live under a Damoclean sword. In those cases of uncertain threat that is not precipitated, people manage to acclimate themselves to tense conditions such as those offered by the threat of inflation, the Cold War, and the continued, lurking threat of hot war. Much of this continued tolerance is a result, it seems, of an inability to detect any effective way to substantially reduce or eliminate the threat.

It would seem that the findings on reaction to physiological stress could be translated into terms that would also provide a model for psychological and behavioral reaction to threat. Such a translation and such a model have here been attempted. It is apparent, however, that the dynamics of progression through the phases suggested by the model are not yet clear. Intra-individual factors may well account for "choices" among defensive tactics, but environmental or event characteristics should also predict some of the patterning of attempts to cope with threat. Future research will probably make its major contribution in those investigations which closely link these two aspects into an information-processing model that includes new concepts not exclusively within or outside of the individual but interactional in character.

► *five*

DISASTER AND MENTAL HEALTH

Robert N. Wilson

Introduction

Extreme situations often teach us more about the behavior of individuals and groups than do normal or routine occurrences. This is not because something grossly different in the functioning of personalities or societies takes place in extremity, but because the dramatic intensity of unusual events serves to magnify significant features of the systems involved in them. The most important characteristics are more clearly seen because crisis has dramatically focused the observer's attention on essentials. Thus the traditional absorption of history in great happenings and great men is not so mistaken as was at first believed in the reaction against the grand manner of nineteenth-century historians. And thus, too, the contemporary social scientist and physician have often learned much, and learned it faster, as a result of observations provoked by crisis, or at any rate the unusual in human affairs. One need cite only the contributions of psychopathology to our understanding of personality, of war and economic depression to our understanding of social organization, of battle and disaster trauma to our understanding of surgery and medicine.

Disaster research during the past two decades has clearly contributed heavily to our knowledge of behavior in general, as well as of behavior in extreme situations. Perhaps the most distinctive trend in this knowledge has been the growing conviction that disaster is not a unique concatenation of phenomena, comprehensible only in and of themselves. Rather, disaster behavior is amazingly congruent with what we think we know about human intercourse in the large. Thus it is probably inappropriate to speak of a sociology of disaster or a psychology of disaster; rather, disaster research is guided by, and in turn stimulates, the basic threads of investigatory interest prominent in its parental substantive disciplines of social and medical science. To speak of disaster research and mental health, therefore, is not to carve out an esoteric slice of the human condition but to attack instead a set of fundamental, continuing problems in the analysis of behavior whereever it occurs.

Two emphases seem to emerge when one looks at disaster research from the point of view of general intellectual strategy and general propositions about social action. The first, intrinsic to behavior itself, is the overwhelming propensity of men as individuals and men as group participants to act in disaster in a purposive and competent way. If one were to ask in what way research has taken us beyond folk conviction, beyond the common-sense things that "everyone" knows about extreme situations, the first answer would inevitably be that disaster is not equivalent to total disorganization or panic.

The second dominant theme would seem to be the discovery that even these most confused and intractable sets of events—disasters—lend themselves to research activity. From the blooming and the buzzing, researchers have been shrewd enough and energetic enough to sort out categories of analysis, to gather data in a more than random manner, to construct a coherent representation of what seems at first glance to be rampant incoherence.

Disaster research and mental health research are two major fields of inquiry. Because they clearly share so many of the same concerns—both in questions of substantive interest and in problems of investigation—it would seem that some articulation of them is a matter of necessity as well as of convenience. Such a putting-together is rather hazardous, not to say audacious, because of the wealth of scattered findings and the anarchy of conceptual accommodations. It would probably be of slight profit to try to subsume either area of interest under the other, or to see both as part of some overarching scheme of analysis. One might argue that mental illness is a special case of inner, as opposed to outer, disaster, or that disaster is merely one of the kinds of stress to which men are exposed in the course of their ill and healthy lives. One might contend, perhaps with more justification, that both disaster and psychiatric disorder represent grave disturbances of social and psychological normalcy or equilibrium—and, further, that systems of interpersonal relationships ("society") try to right themselves by restoring some kind of balance within individuals and throughout their interactive networks.

A more modest effort is here proposed: to sift the relationships of the two broad areas of interest with a number of shockingly obvious questions in mind. These questions will center on two kinds of mutual implication, which might be somewhat inaccurately designated as "content" and "form." In the area of "content," we shall be interested in such questions as: What is the effect of disaster experience on the mental health of the exposed population? What does the prior health of the population enable us to predict about their response to disaster? What are the salient parallels between the occurrence of disaster and the occurrence of psychiatric disorder? Are there significant common elements in the recovery of a community from disaster and the recovery of an individual from illness? What individual strengths and what community strengths tend to minimize the impact of stress? What do these two types of event, both as separate happenings and as concurrent happenings, tell us about human behavior more generally construed? In the area of "form," our attention will shift to common elements in disaster research and mental health research, and hopefully to suggestions for common analytical orderings of the discoveries from the two fields. Questions of first import will be: What are the base lines of "normalcy" to which research is ordered? What are the proper units of analysis for these events? What are the equivalents of the laboratory which may be available to scientists interested in events largely sealed by morality from experimental procedures? How are these disruptive events, and research into them, related to the values of the societies in which they take place?

Effect of Disaster on Mental Health and Illness

There is no clear-cut generalization that will neatly cover the plethora of temporal, quantitative, and qualitative differences in the objective and felt severity of disaster. In at least five ways disaster, any disaster, may be confidently presumed to enhance the risk of illness:

1. In the short run, an individual exposed to the extreme shock of an explosion, fire, landslide, bombing, or whatever, will show some symptoms of disorientation and lessened ability to function with competence. The classic description is probably that of Tyhurst (1950-1951).
2. Physical trauma directly attendant on disaster may fix disorder or the propensity to it. The most obvious examples are brain damage due to a severe blow and toxic conditions due to some kind of poisoning. The sheer physical effects of disaster are not limited to somatic damage as such, but the damage may also promote drastic behavior changes. These effects are most often neglected by social scientists in their zest for interpersonal etiology.
3. A variety of psychosomatic and other symptomatology has

been observed in the victims of disaster during a period of one day to three weeks after impact. These symptoms, including vomiting, diarrhea, insomnia, and threatening dreams, usually are seen by those affected as a relatively "normal" and explicable consequence of strain. Little is known about the possible durability of the symptoms or their conceivable importance in engendering mental illness. At the present stage of knowledge most psychiatrists would probably deem these minor and transitory phenomena, although there is no evidence of a comprehensive check on any disaster population after a time sufficient for accurate judgment has elapsed.

4. Loss of a beloved object through disaster implies illness rather than health. This is the more true in our society, where the cards are stacked against facile or quick adjustment to interpersonal loss. The bereavement situation is the type illustration (Lindemann, 1944; Volkart, 1957).

There are many strong arguments for the belief that bereavement is an especially trying situation in modern Western culture. Lindemann's convincing clinical findings are supplemented by assumptions about certain distinctive patterns of social life which would tend to aggravate the loss. One of these patterns is that of the isolated nuclear family, whose members are so strongly dependent upon one another and so intensely involved in a tight emotional network. The intimacy of this small group implies that loss of a single member is almost automatically a catastrophic event; the rest of the family find readjustment exceedingly difficult, and there are few provisions for discovering replacements for the dead person or spreading the grief among collateral relatives. Further, our secular society is largely without ritual formulae for coping with the grief-work; the duration and quality of grieving are matters for individual choice, only minimally and informally governed by group prescription. There is also the value placed on unconditional romantic love, which means that the bereaved is supposed to be desolate and is almost certain to have great difficulty with feelings of ambivalence toward the lost person.

It should perhaps be noted, however, that clinical studies of bereavement have been largely confined to interpersonal loss in a stable society. We do not know how the bereavement patterns might be altered in situations of widespread loss. Conceivably, shared bereavement could have fewer pathological implications because of the very fact of sharing.

Separation, which might be said to recapitulate bereavement in miniature, is in some instances an important feature of disaster. Its effects on children are known to be particularly marked. Long periods of hospitalization and/or geographical isolation of children from one or both parents may be presumed to have resoundingly negative consequences for the mental health of children (Bowlby, 1952).

5. In overwhelming disaster, the impoverishment of the interpersonal and physical environment will lead in the long run to perceptual and cognitive difficulties classifiable as mental illness. Fortunately we do not (yet) have any instances of disaster on such a massive scale. Presumably the warfare of the future could recapitulate, for its survivors, the situation of isolation so graphically described in the experiments on sensory deprivation (Solomon, *et al.*, 1959).

It is reasonable to believe that the mentally unhealthy states attendant on shock and bereavement are of relatively short duration compared to the three other instances. Yet even though shock be an affair of a few hours or, at most, days, no one is certain that the remission of symptoms indicates entire recovery. We have enough experience of war neuroses to indicate the possibility of later arousal of buried trauma (Grinker and Spiegel, 1945). Bereavement, if best handled, implies a grief period with uncertain temporal limits; if worst handled, it portends depression or psychosomatic involvement or other consequences of possibly great duration.

It is probably fair to say that we know comparatively little about the long-run mental health consequences of disaster experiences. At least one observer (Leighton, 1959) has identified disaster as a background factor in community disintegration, with the implication that the mental health level of a given community is likely to be adversely affected by disaster. We need to know much more about the characteristics of community "recovery" if negative effects on the general level of mental health are to be forestalled. From the individual, clinical standpoint, treatment of long-run mental illnesses stemming from disaster is apt not to be appreciably different from conventional psychiatric therapy. It may be that the most important exception to this statement is the special desirability, in some cases, of recovering the traumatic experience through techniques of stimulating recollection and rehearsal of the original threatening situation. Hypnotic and narcotic devices may be prominently employed.

Kardiner (1959) emphasizes that war neuroses often arise in situations of great danger, when the ego feels itself to be overwhelmed by its environment. The ego, no longer capable of mastery, dedicates itself to defense rather than to enterprise. The result is a loss of confidence, a shrinkage and contraction of the ego, and a weak attempt to maintain contact with the world through "truncated resources." It is relatively easy to imagine similar syndromes based on disaster rather than on wars and to assume that their treatment will be typically prolonged and their outcome uncertain.

Some have argued that in a well-prepared population the usual mental health consequences are short-term jitters and that pathological anxiety states are not likely to occur. This stricture perhaps applies more forcefully to war than to peacetime disaster, since so few populations are in any degree well prepared for natural catastrophe. "Panic," or what is better termed "shock," may be treated, in Meerloo's (1958) view, with understanding, provision for oral satisfactions, and no recourse to narcotics. Meerloo notes that "first-aid hypnosis and first-aid catharsis can be easily planned for eventual mass treatment in times of catastrophe."

Galdston, in a summary comment on the topic of "morale," focuses on the importance of open communications networks in the period immediately following massive stress. This consideration seems to be extremely relevant to disaster situations. The maintenance of communication may be a means of "humanizing" disaster, making the experience more meaningful to the individual and thus serving as a measure of mental hygiene prophylaxis: ". . . Anything which operates to restrict the 'spectrum of feedback communication,' anything in other words that censors, limits, and otherwise reduces the spectrum, the breadth, depth, and scope of communication, impedes morale" (Galdston, 1958). It should be noted, however, that disaster researchers may occasionally embrace the "communications fallacy" of treating the free flow of information as a panacea. There may indeed be situations, especially in the immediate confusion of disaster, in which an overload of contradictory messages has negative implications for the perceivers.

It is probable that special attention should be given to the family group in disaster-related mental health and illness. All accounts (e.g., Fritz and Williams, 1957) stress the significance of family ties, the vigorous searching behavior of separated family members, the heightened interaction and solidarity within the family. Just as deprivation (e.g., bereavement) in the family system is seen as a pathogenic implication of disaster, so the strengthening of family bonds may be one of the chief counteracting forces to disaster-induced illness. Wallace (1956) very interestingly notes the importance of the "extended family" in mutual help in the Worcester tornado. Although this help usually involved material aid, such as shelter and food, it may be suggested that both immediate and extended families could form the first line of defense against mental illness following catastrophe.

The felt severity of stress is known to vary by individual physiological base, individual psychological base, and cultural norms (Funkenstein, King, and Drolette, 1957; Zborowski, 1952). The most general statement about the reaction base line with respect to mental health is that the healthier the individual is under normal conditions, the healthier he is likely to be under disaster conditions. This is true despite the occasional striking contradictions in which psychopaths and ne'er-do-wells perform heroically while apparently solid citizens funk. A record of competent behavior (disregarding for the moment how nearly "competence" may be equated with "mental health") is the best predictor of competent behavior in the future (Beach and Lucas, 1960). The generalization that competence begets competence appears to hold true at both individual and community levels. It is so important that it may deserve emphasis in a series of related propositions:

1. "While it is just as difficult to define 'mental health' as it is to define health in general, it is helpful to state some of the aims of mental health services and activities which are believed to promote and protect 'mental health.' Some of these aims, at least, involve the enhancement of people's capacity to cope with life crises, both endogenous and exogenous (Caplan, Working definition . . . , 1959), or the preparation of people to handle predictable or unpredictable stress" (Lemkau, Working definition . . . , 1959). If mental health is defined as the ability to cope with crisis and handle unpredictable stress, then mental health is either a requisite for (or the equivalent of?) effective behavior in disaster.
2. Behavior tends toward consistency, both in the maintenance of a secure self-image (Lecky, 1951) and in that past performance best predicts future performance. Thus the individual is likely to behave in disaster in a way consonant with his normal patterns of behavior. If a person has demonstrated health (ability to cope), he is likely to perform well in disaster (Perry, Silber, and Bloch, 1956).
3. Experience of disaster, and planning for future disaster, both equip populations to better handle extreme situations. Thus in Springhill, Nova Scotia, a community which had experienced mine disasters in the past performed highly effectively (knowing cues, waiting patiently, etc.) when a fresh disaster erupted (Beach and Lucas, 1960; see also Janis, 1951).

These propositions seem to imply that disaster behaviors at the level of community organization and at the level of individual functioning may both be in some degree predictable if we have some prior knowledge. They further indicate that just as civilian populations and military units may be prepared for disaster situations by training and education, so individuals may be prepared to maintain their mental health during extreme situations if they can be taught to cope with varieties of normal stress.

Unfortunately, all efforts to better fit people for crisis, whether it be "normal" life crisis or the more florid disjunctions of disaster, run into the paradox that training tends to groom for routines while what is required is some sort of training for flexibility. There are, however, new and imaginative types of education, such as that practiced by OSS during World War II or the psychodramatic role-playing sometimes used in psychotherapy, which promise much in the way of preparation for adaptability.

Perhaps the greatest ally in the attempt to promote effective handling of crisis is the general human propensity to strive for environmental mastery. This striving, recently elaborated for psychological theory by R. W. White (1959), appears to operate from earliest infancy through maturity. If the "concept of competence" (White) is critical to the understanding of normal behavior, it is even more important to the understanding of behavior in disaster. The intense desire to perform capably, in the deepest sense to *know* one's environment, offers substantial theoretical help in assessing the reasons for good disaster performance.

The concept of competence further suggests why research has demonstrated repeatedly that disaster is not necessarily and in all ways damaging to either individual health or social organization, and why it may indeed have curiously beneficial implications for mental health. There is a good bit of evidence that disaster experience may constitute for many people an "optimal stress," which promotes active mental harmony rather than psychiatric disorder. It is probably an open question whether the challenge of extreme situations really enhances health or whether it serves instead to replace a chronic and somewhat muffled inner threat (e.g., certain neuroses) with an immediate and drastic outer threat. Both phenomena may be occurring simultaneously in individuals whose pre-disaster mental health was not of the best. At any rate, concentration camp analyses indicate remission of symptoms during acute stress of imprisonment (Caudill, 1958), followed by symptomatic recurrence upon the return to normal life. On a less dramatic scale similar happenings are reported from natural disasters. Thus the victims of the Holland floods of 1953 are described as enjoying some alleviation of minor psychosomatic ailments during the most threatening phase of the disaster, with recurrence as communities returned to a more routine existence (Instituut voor Sociaal Onderzoek, 1955; Spiegel, 1957). Again, the trapped miners at Springhill in 1958 exhibited at least one instance in which an individual who had been previously hospitalized for psychosis performed quite well under the immediate stress of entombment (Beach and Lucas, 1960).

At the community level, one of the more astonishing research findings is surely that which has been described as "disaster utopia," "communism," or "euphoria" (Fritz, 1961). Social organization reduced to a relatively primitive level, in combination with severe outer threat demanding cooperative action, appears to enhance morale. The challenge is clear, the justification for the work one does is far more perceptible and reasonable than is the case with most occupations in a complex urban society. The payoff for effective behavior comes quickly and the imperatives of interdependence are obvious to all. There are very apparent positive implications in such a situation for the mental health of the community. These are bolstered considerably by the evidence from wartime morale studies which show morale at high levels during crises which were outwardly very threatening (Janis, 1951). Civilian populations in general did better under bombing and other massive threats than any planners had anticipated.

All these threads may be woven into a picture which makes disaster look like a desirable climate for mental health, at least in the short run. One could half-seriously suggest that we require a "moral equivalent of disaster" which, like William James's moral equivalent of war, would provide a stimulating and unifying outer challenge without unfortunate side-effects such as the destruction of life and property. Certainly disaster encourages Freud's dual prescription for the healthy mental life: love and work.

It should perhaps be remarked that the proponents of an extreme view of "disaster-as-a-good" generally confine their analyses to instances of clearly temporary, short-run disruption. Repeated and prolonged disaster would presumably have quite different and less positive implications, possibly in the vein of apathetic and asocial (if not anti-social) behavior such as that sometimes observed in the long-deprived or long-incarcerated.

Disaster, then, does not have any simple, unitary effect on mental health. Its deleterious consequences are most obvious and call for intensive research and therapeutic strategies. Its conceivably benevolent consequences are less obvious and more intriguing as a theoretical problem in human behavior. It has been proposed that the seemingly positive implications for mental health may be better understood through the notion of "optimal stress," or necessary and sufficient stimulation to effective behavior. Little is known, however, about the appropriate range of the optimal. It has been suggested that the concept of "competence" as an individual propensity for manipulating and mastering the environment offers clues as to why optimal stress should be welcomed and dealt with fairly successfully. Finally, the therapeutic or health-inspiring characteristics of extreme situations have led to speculation concerning some less drastic means of recapitulating their effect. It might be noted that some parts of the process of the "therapeutic community" in mental hospitals appear to lend credence to the notion that a severe threat cooperatively encountered may inspire healthy behavior. See, for instance, the apparently beneficial effects of realistic work schedules and the necessity for varieties of group coping behavior on seriously disorganized personalities at Belmont Hospital (Jones, 1953).

Parallels between Disaster and Mental Illness

> Perhaps society's interest in disaster at present is much the same as its interest in the mental patient. In other words, within our time, we have become less isolated from the affairs of other people, whether they be mental patients or people in disaster. Our interest in the emergence of schizophrenic-like patterns of life, whether man-induced or phenomena of nature, is an attempt to prepare for the possibility of such an eventuality erupting in our own lives. We need, ourselves, to have certain formulae for dealing with such disaster: A relative might become mentally disordered; or a relative might be hit by a tornado. By such devices we admit, however covertly, the possibility that it might happen to us.
>
> The very nature of the phenomenon of disaster is then reminiscent of one's worst fear—the nightmare that turns into reality. It is the uncanny, the schizophrenic-like, come to life. The first and most poignant necessity is to find some formulae for putting the disaster into some frame of reference. We cannot stay long sane and view disaster of catastrophic proportions without trying to fit it into some explainable framework furnished by society generally, by its institutions, such as the church, or if one is a child, furnished by significant adults (Perry and Perry, 1959).

The immense interest in research into, and hoped-for eventual control over, both disaster and mental illness, reflects significant facets of contemporary social organization and values of our own and all time. In part the interest hinges on perhaps the dominant social fact of modern life: man's fantastically heightened interdependence. We are involved in one another in a way never earlier foreseen; directly, in a fine-grained division of labor, and less obviously in the economic and spiritual web spun by technology, transportation, and mass communication. This pattern of tightly-woven interdependence is both extremely effective in the carrying out of many desirable activities and extremely vulnerable to the disruptive forces of illness and natural catastrophe. Society is thus driven to safeguard the balance of its several intertwined systems by anticipating and preventing interference, when possible, and by pulling the network quickly together again if upset has occurred. The attempt to control deviant persons and events and to maintain some variety of equilibrium is apparent in realms as diverse as international affairs and child care. In a real sense, modern societies cannot afford to let deficient links in their exchange and communications systems go unrepaired, whether these be the result of disaster with its gross disruption or of mental illness with its more subtle erosion of individual motivations and capacities.

From the point of view of the individual, these considerations are equally binding; our self-conscious and minutely coordinated lives do not inspire the kind of sufficiency that might ride out illness or disaster in isolation. As individuals we cannot afford the multiple costs of illness or disaster, we cannot get so far out of phase with the concert scored for the lives we all lead together. Because we lean so heavily on one another, whether we deliberately choose to or not, we lust after an answer to the accidents of life. And if this insurance is not forthcoming, we insist at the least that our fellows rally and be concerned if catastrophe occurs. It is almost certainly not fortuitous that John Donne should have provided a title for one of the most popular twentieth-century novels (*For Whom the Bell Tolls*), or that a statement from the same Devotion—"any man's death diminishes me, because I am involved in mankind . . ."—could now be paraphrased to substitute "illness" or "misfortune" for "death."

Wedded to our knowledge that drastic imbalance reverberates throughout the endless chain of interpersonal relationships is the belief that prevention and control are indeed possible. As Americans we are accustomed to finding answers, and to feeling angry or baffled if solutions are not fairly readily available upon the investment of time, energy, and money. The experiences of the last few decades, especially in technology and medicine, have inured us to miracles and made us impatient with problems to which no answer seems quickly possible. It is in a way outrageous that we should be so clever and resourceful and yet have to submit to capricious nature (in the case of disaster) and still more capricious human nature (in the case of mental illness). Our pragmatic tradition, our unexampled mastery of agricultural and industrial production, and our belief in activity as an intrinsic good all conspire to foster what an essayist in the (London) *Times Literary Supplement* (1959) identifies as "the universal error of believing that all good things can be deliberately procured." As researchers we would not, and probably should not, adopt an easy fatalism. It might, however, be salutary to consider how far specific, deliberate measures can alleviate the strains of disaster and illness, and how far those strains wait for resolution on more fundamental changes in the tenor of our national life.

A third common root of our similar interests in disaster and mental illness is the ancient question of Job. Natural disaster is more clearly an accident than is mental disorder, but the cry of "Why me?" remains. In both of these ruptures of the social tissue the lay mind requires some set of propositions to answer satisfactorily the query of why "it" happens here and now and to these people. Research into the framework of belief and the ways in which it is affected by varying types of disaster and illness might afford important knowledge of the basic tenets to which Americans order their behavior.

The parallels between disaster and mental illness are obviously not confined to the ways in which they fasten our attention on them. They are distinctly similar as phenomena. In both fields the amount of preparation for the critical event is severely limited, more by the patterns of human behavior than by the scarcity of preventive knowledge. If one has never confronted either disaster or mental disorder at close quarters, he is unlikely to devote much energy to learning to cope with them. Quite the reverse: most persons stave off the threat by not even attending to its possibility. Mental health education and civil defense education are both notoriously difficult because we do not like to think ahead to the time when they might be of real use, and we find it hard to apply known principles of behavior to the seemingly less drastic situations of everyday life. Disasters and illnesses are somehow "unreal" until encountered. Because they are critical disturbances in the perceptual world which we so carefully build for ourselves, the world where we feel in control or at least comfortable, they often continue to be unreal even when they are upon us. Thus persons in disaster tend to order the signals from their environment to a familiar, explicable happening; in a tornado the sounds may at first be perceived as the rumble of a passing train (Fritz and Williams, 1957). It is noteworthy, however, that a disaster-schooled community does not make such mistakes. Apparently no one in Springhill, Nova Scotia, took the "bump" of October 1958 as anything but a disaster signal. In mental disorder there is a similar tendency to cling for as long as possible to a definition of the situation as "normal." The wives of hospitalized patients are reported as having lived with bizarre symptomatology for several months or years before being driven to recognize their husbands as ill (Clausen and Yarrow, 1955). One of the hardest tasks we face in action programs in both fields, then, is that of convincing people that disaster and illness are real things, that they can be mitigated through preparation, and that they lie on a continuum of phenomena such that knowledge about them is relevant to apparently routine or normal situations.

Although many natural catastrophes are unpredictable and sudden, few mental illnesses are truly so. Yet they are both seen as sudden and dramatic events which fall outside mundane experience and require special reorganization of behavior. Perhaps the most important educational effort is to insist that although the special qualities of disaster and illness are fully recognized they may be assimilated to more usual experience and dealt with by the ordinary resources of competent people.

The concept of "linked open systems" (e.g., Caudill, 1958) points up still another common element. Both disaster and illness represent stresses that cannot be confined to a single behavioral context. Focal occurrences spread their effects to neighboring intrapsychic and interpersonal systems. We must therefore be prepared to see a translation of any given disturbance into other terms which seem to mask the direct consequences of the event. One of the most clear-cut examples is the expression of psychological upset in somatic terms, an expression that typifies reactions to illness and disaster. Another is the ramification of individual crisis throughout family networks and community life. It is obvious that we must, as we are indeed now beginning to do, consider the family of the mental patient, his effect in his occupational setting and in his informal community ties. In disaster, too, the most profound implications for mental health may not be limited to the individuals directly struck. In the Springhill mine disaster it was not the miners who had been trapped who sought emergency psychiatric aid; rather, the immediate psychological casualties were found among relatives and friends and persons not in any way close to the victims (Beach and Lucas, 1960). There is no way to calculate the hidden and long-range costs of these gross disturbances of interpersonal relations; we must be aware that they are probably considerable and alert our research to displaced manifestations of stress.

In common-sense terms the parallelism between disaster and illness breaks down in two significant ways. The unit of disaster is normally taken to be the community; the unit of illness is ordinarily conceived to be the individual. Strictly speaking, the occurrence of mental disorder might be seen as the equivalent of an accident rather than a disaster, except in those relatively rare instances of mass mental illness such as the medieval dancing manias. On the other hand, although the locale of illness is the individual, recent trends in social psychiatry have led us to think of the total social environment as the true point of application and etiological interest. It is perhaps unnecessary to label disaster as a group phenomenon and mental illness as an individual phenomenon. Both events involve both levels of analysis, and we can shuttle between them as long as we are clear about what we are doing. It is important that social organization, which has always been the province of disaster studies, is coming more and more often to be seen as a correct (if not *the* correct) province of mental health studies.

A hardier distinction than that between analytical levels is found in the natures of the presumed causal chains in the two events. Disaster comes from "outside" and is an act of fate; mental illness comes from "inside" and the agent is unidentified. In disaster there is with few exceptions no one to blame; despite the occasional scapegoating of someone for not foreseeing the crisis or not handling it better when it occurred, energy can on the whole be turned outward to deal with an immediate and concrete threat. Action of some kind can usually be taken and the satisfactions of environmental mastery enjoyed. Mental illness presents no such patent and readily understandable challenge. The locus of disorder is difficult for the psychiatrist to elucidate and often appears as entirely mysterious to those most closely related to the ill person. Guilt, appropriate or not, resounds in the people with whom the mental patient has been involved. Action other than sympathetic behavior and the seeking of professional help seems unavailable. Above all, mental illness lacks the causal intelligibility and the mandate to action which characterize disaster.

There are, nevertheless, certain striking consistencies in the "treatment of choice" for the victims of disaster and mental illness. Ordinarily in both instances an outside helping agency is required, and this agency tends to inspire ambivalent feelings in those to whom it ministers. Again, a chief aim in both disaster relief and psychiatric therapy is to help without promoting too grave a habit of dependency and to encourage the use of resources indigenous to the community or person affected. Support and permissiveness are freely granted, but leverage is exerted to foster independence and stimulate the desire to regain full functioning. Some immediate post-disaster behaviors may be likeened to the "therapeutic community" of psychiatric treatment (Jones, 1953). One remarkable similarity in this area may be found by comparing the activities of leaders in disaster with the activities of mental hospital personnel. In several instances, notably the Springhill mine disaster in which groups of men were trapped underground for long periods of time, leaders have been characterized as initiators and maintainers of interactive patterns. They kept things in motion, shoring up the less effective members of the group by suggesting activity and sustaining vigorous interpersonal relationships. All this is instructively reminiscent of programs of total-push therapy, habit training, and other techniques of coping with mental illness. It would appear that one of the preferred responses to a disturbance in the social system is to neither expel nor seclude the affected members, but to keep them functioning as far as possible as integral parts of the system. The maintenance of interpersonal ties and of communications of all kinds seems imperative to this effort at reconstituting a viable network.

Research in Disaster and Mental Health

Because these events are menacing and dramatic, they call forth an urgency of response which both aids and hinders research. The intense desire for actions and solutions implies high levels of financial support; it also usually helps the researcher gain access to situations in which disruption makes for a frankness and indeed a nakedness of behavior. Against these stimuli to creative investigation must be set the demand for results of immediate utility. We want firm answers in realms that are in their infancy as targets of full-scale scientific work. The desolation of a tornado-struck community and the desolation of a back ward in a state mental hospital are alike in their implicit injunction to roll bandages and boil water rather than to fuss over research designs.

There is little point in rehearsing the major problems of disaster research in the light of Killian's (1956a) excellent introduction to the methodology of this field. There is no comparably brief and lucid summary available in mental health research, although several substantial treatments of sections of the field do exist (e.g., Group for the Advancement of Psychiatry, 1959; Leighton, Clausen, and Wilson, 1959; Rohrer, 1956). We shall try to suggest parallels in research strategy and especially to identify areas in which research may meet common concerns of disaster study and social psychiatry.

In neither field do we have anything like the requisite base line knowledge of the phenomena concerned. We do not know the characteristics of a normal community or of a normally healthy individual. Both disaster and mental illness are types of significant change in preexisting states, but we are seldom sure how much or what kinds of change have occurred. The obvious reason why all studies face the problems of retrospective analysis is that we can predict neither disaster nor illness with much accuracy. It would be of immense value to have longitudinal research designs so that we might follow these events as processes, but the scope necessary to insure that any instances of the phenomena will occur in the followed population is clearly prohibitive. There are occasional "lucky breaks," as when an already-studied community suffers a disaster or a person who has been the subject of psychological analysis becomes mentally ill, but it is difficult to plan research to take advantage of happenstance.

There would seem to be some possibility of learning more about process in disaster and mental health by seizing on some more routine happenings as minimally satisfactory analogues to the events in question. Among these analogues might be death and separation, normal life crises, disaster drills, and inconvenient occurrences (such as storms or power failures) which are less than disastrous. A notable instance of such use of "available" data is the exhaustive study of emotional patterns in severely burned patients (Hamburg, Hamburg, and de Goza, 1953). Thus studies of the bereavement situation can be carried out at any time and have contributed a great deal to our understanding of one of the consequences of natural disaster for mental health. Similarly, research is now going forward on the mental health implications of normal but stressful events such as pregnancy and birth.

Comparative studies of disaster and illness in various cultures promise knowledge about community and individual coping abilities. Broad-scale cross-cultural research is leading us to believe that exceedingly stressful events are framed by the way of life of the people involved. This seems to be true of both different nations and different subcultures within American society. Examples of the latter might be the differential response by social class to tornadoes in Arkansas (Schatzman and Strauss, 1955) and to mental illness in New Haven (Hollingshead and Redlich, 1958). Lower-class groups seem at once more vulnerable to the effects of disaster and illness (they begin from a less adequate base of material, physical, and emotional well-being) and less able to deal with the crisis after it has occurred (impoverished perceptual frameworks, ignorance of the proper approaches to helping agencies, etc.).

The attempt to compare "true prevalence" and "true incidence" rates of amount and type of mental illness between differing communities, especially when those communities are sharply contrasting in cultural patterns, offers hope that socioenvironmental factors in the etiology of psychiatric disorder may be identified (Eaton and Weil, 1955; Leighton, 1959). There seems reason to believe that relevant dimensions of community response to disaster might be similarly uncovered. It is of course difficult to find comparable disaster events, although one notable research had the great advantage of treating two communities struck by the same flood (Clifford, 1956). One important thread in social psychiatric investigation is the study of the effects of rapid acculturation on the mental health of a society, a study increasingly relevant to the speedy Westernization of underdeveloped parts of the world. The hypothesis that rapid social change induces increased illness, if supported by solid findings, would appear important to questions of mental health in disaster. This would be particularly the case if the disaster were far-reaching and—as all disasters are to some extent—irreversible. It is not inconceivable that rapid acculturation might be viewed as sharing certain qualities with disaster, perhaps the most salient being a sharp restructuring of the perceptual field. Thus cross-cultural research on mental health and on disaster might in some instances make common cause and in many instances contribute one to another.

A major difficulty in investigating phenomena as complex as disaster and mental illness lies in the proper choice of units for analysis, the differentiation of global experience, and the implications of both of these for comparability and replicability of studies. This set of problems is obviously compounded when one tries to question the relationship of disaster to illness. Is one to discuss individuals, families, neighborhoods, or whole communities? In many disaster studies, for instance, relatively slight attention is given to just those facets that most interest the mental health researcher; we may have detailed descriptions of community organization and the operation of relief agencies, but little analysis of the *meaning* of disaster in the psychological life-space of the persons involved. Similarly, much psychiatric research presents the individual as an isolated entity, an intrapsychic world in himself, without telling us anything of his behavior as a family member or as the incumbent of an occupational role. In psychiatric research we seldom know enough about the world in which the ill or well person lives; in disaster research we seldom know enough about the inner worlds, the subjective manifolds, of those affected. Thus one must reiterate that reliable information about mental health in disaster requires both a plumbing of the depths of individual experience and a variety of interpersonal analyses, embracing the range from familial interaction to the relationships among official organizations.

As dramatic events bearing dramatic impact, both disaster and mental disorder tend to present themselves as global experiences; the overwhelming fact of *its happening* blurs distinctions of just when, where, of what kind, and to whom. The attempt to order these phenomena is still hazardous because we know so little and constantly mistake superficial differences in degree or color for basic differences in quality. But it is becoming increasingly clear that cumulative research is in great part a problem of the categories, that at least some settled categories are crucial to the affirmation and sharpening of extant findings. A bold start in this direction is exemplified in the "time-space model" of disaster elaborated by Wallace (1956) and others. The kinds of discrimination which characterize this model have clear relevance to studies of the effects of disaster on mental health. We cannot seriously ask, "What does disaster mean to the health of the population?"; we must instead strive for a much more precise phrasing, asking about health at various time periods from impact through the stages of rescue and rehabilitation and in locations from impact and fringe areas out through entire communities and regions.

Let us assume for the moment that the "time-space model" has become stabilized and is deemed applicable to most disasters we encounter. Now if we forget the differences among types of disaster (whether flood, hurricane, explosion, or whatever), what can be brought to bear from the mental health side to promote genuine comparability of effects? Unfortunately there is no consensual framework in studies in social psychiatry. It might be proposed that a combination of the following measures, linked to the time-space model, would afford us more refined data on disaster and mental disorder: age, sex, social class, ethnicity; the diagnostic categories outlined in the American Psychiatric Association *Manual;* a scale of impairment such as that employed by Leighton in Stirling County and Midtown. What is suggested is obviously something like a "true incidence" study of mental illness in disaster, a type of research notoriously difficult in nondisaster situations. Yet, despite the many provocative insights we have gained into the relationship of this sort of massive stress to mental health, it is hard to see how we can advance far in the long run without this suggested epidemiological strategy—a strategy that would require a vast investment of research talent. At least one attempt, although it is to be sure a less than comprehensive assault, is already on record in the case of the Springhill mine disaster (Beach and Lucas, 1960).

It has been cogently argued that disaster affords not only an opportunity to investigate the mental health implications of the experience itself but also a chance to pursue basic studies of the public mental health as such:

> It is our impression that one implication of the emotional reaction to disaster is that the common sense of human solidarity which follows a disaster experience can operate to further research in the intimate psychological bases of behavior. This leads us to suggest that disaster research per se can provide, under proper conditions, an entry to the study of psychological subjects not immediately related to disaster behavior. For example, one of the most difficult problems which confronts the public health study of mental illness and health is the assessment of some sort of baseline of mental health within a community or society. We feel that it would be easier to obtain the sort of cross-section of population necessary for answering research questions about such a baseline if a public mental health study were coupled with a study of a community disaster. That is, respondents in a disaster-struck

community will tend to be more amenable to research interests in the intimate matters of emotional well-being and emotional difficulties that are a part of their total life situation, and the opportunity provided by this post-disaster accessibility should be utilized for public health studies (Perry, Silber, and Bloch, 1956).

Toward a Frame of Reference

We have suggested several ways in which disaster research and social psychiatric research are related, ranging from the psychiatric consequences of disaster, to therapeutic parallels, to the possible use of disaster for general psychiatric investigation. At many junctures it has seemed that conceptual linkages of these two vast fields of study are not only feasible but mandatory. It is probably not enough merely to note striking convergences of interest or to employ the findings of one area for illuminating the other. We should, rather, aspire to a common universe of discourse which will clarify the relation of social disruption to individual disorder and generate research directed toward answering salient questions concurrently. It may be that a tentative frame of reference, however sketchy and unresolved, will lend itself to such goals.

The problems of relating disaster to illness do not appear to differ conceptually from what is the root dilemma of social psychiatry: the articulation of environmental patterning and the psychodynamics of the individual. Although there is a strong conviction among workers in the field that some of the most important clues to mental health and illness lie in the lifelong matrix of interpersonal stimuli to which the individual is exposed, most simple correlations between particular interpersonal exposures and illness have been inconclusive. Categories which will uncover clear relationships have yet to be devised. It has proved hazardous to try to join traditional psychiatric diagnoses to traditional sociological variables. What is required is some means of holding intrapsychic and interpersonal events in combined focus over fairly long periods of time, so that interpenetrations of process may be untangled.

Let us pose our basic query as follows: *What do we need to understand in order to mitigate the deleterious consequences of disaster for mental health?* There are at least three major sectors of information to be explored.

1. The pre-disaster state of personality functioning and of community organization. Most critically, we would need to assess the strengths and weaknesses of the individual and his social setting so that we could predict reactions to stressful experience and deliberately foster a learned competence in the face of unusual environmental pressures. How has the individual coped with stress in the past? How has the community coped with stress in the past?

2. *The immediate effect of the disaster experience as such on community mental health.* Here we are interested in psychiatric casualties from brain damage, shock, toxicity, and other readily identifiable trauma. Next, we would need to assess the magnitude of bereavement, separation, and social isolation. As to isolation in particular, we must consider the degree of dislocation in normal community services and organizational patterns, and the speed, quality, and quantity of outside help (the capacity of the helping "cornucopia" described by Wallace, 1956). The emphasis here is on emotional and sociological first aid, rather than on the indirect services of preparation and prediction alluded to above.

3. *The enduring consequences of disaster for the interpersonal environment and the individual's perception of his social world.* If disaster is irreversible, in what does its irreversibility consist? What changes in social organization accrue as a long-term effect of disaster, and how do these promote or retard the individual's health? We should investigate in what ways disaster experience may strengthen the social fabric, thereby bolstering individual rewards; if family bonds are tightened, friendships tempered in the fire of extremity, officialdom clothed in a mantle of grace and benevolence, do these things promote the health of the community's constituent personalities? Does the individual in post-disaster years perceive his world as a more threatening place, a system which has once disintegrated before his eyes and may do so again? Is he gnawed by the fear of an inadequacy proved or warmed by an old soldier's glow of obstacles successfully overcome? Above all we need to measure the disaster's meaning in terms of the over-all patterns of the individual life history, seeing his disaster experience not as an isolated occurrence but as a new thread to be woven into life's fabric or a rent to be well- or ill-repaired.

These sorts of questions are not different in kind from the ones that any sophisticated social psychiatry asks. Psychiatry always wants to know the effect of various kinds of stress on individuals who exhibit different degrees of immunity and vulnerability to those stresses. It has been proposed that one way of tackling social psychiatric problems is to look for "portals of entry" into the phenomena involved, rather than attempting a frontal assault on the entire field (Leighton, Clausen, and Wilson, 1959). Disaster may well be such a portal, and an especially suitable one.

Three primary requirements for a framework which will encompass disaster and mental health are that it exemplify chronology, process, and interactive forces. When these are combined with the central consideration of joining environmental patterns to individual character, the following scheme may recommend itself. This sketch owes much to many authors, but most to Alexander H. Leighton, whose frame of reference as fully elaborated in *My Name Is Legion* (1959) is unquestionably the most comprehensive social psychiatric model extant.

PERSONALITY

An holistic conception of personality is clearly essential to research, treatment, and prevention of psychiatric disorder. It is equally critical to a view of the individual in disaster, since extreme situations involve the whole man, all he has done and aspires to do, all that has happened to him in the course of life. A biosocial ordering of constitutional base, intrapsychic events, and a variety of interpersonal relations is seen as the favored mold for thinking about the person.

It is not enough to posit a stimulus-response model of behavior, in which individuals react to the stimulus of disaster. Rather, personal needs and the effort to fulfill them through striving and environmental mastery must form the starting point for analyzing how people behave in extremity. Man is purposive and goal-directed, in disaster and out. If personality is seen as a complex of needs and the struggle to realize them, then special attention must be paid to the ways in which the social environment shapes the expression of needs. Even in disaster, man is a resolutely social animal, satisfying himself much more in a learned than in an instinctual fashion.

The idea of the ego or self is a vital constituent of this conception of the individual. It may well be that one's identity, his notion of his essential self, is at the heart of health or illness in disaster; disaster may enhance or vitiate one's picture of himself as he is or as he would like to be.

Individual motivation affords us a guide to behavior and alerts us to what are likely to be the most important gains and losses from disaster in the personal experiences of those struck or closely affected. In addition to the more conventional arrays of need and paths to fulfillment, we might emphasize the concept of competence as developed by White (1959). The desire to behave competently, regardless of the substance of the situation and the more familiar propensities to be served, is a strong lead for understanding disaster behavior.

Two other aspects of personality are of special note here. The first is the need for social intercourse, the dependence of the individual on others for a definition of himself and the world he inhabits. Intense needs to communicate and to share experience in disaster have been often remarked. Linked to this facet is the whole realm of perception, which shapes the individual's security base and is most often disturbed by disaster. The perceptual implications of disaster are perhaps first in salience to immediate mental health levels.

ROLE

Although this is perhaps the most often discussed concept in the social sciences, it is important to emphasize several features of social role in relation to health and disaster. The growing individual may be seen as in one sense a bundle of roles, some already mastered at any point in time, some in the process of being learned, some only now envisioned as potentialities for the future self. In assessing health we need to know what the competence is for performing crucial roles. In particular, we ask what roles have proved especially difficult to assume and what ones are cherished as realms of proficiency. Further, which of the roles currently demanded of an individual seem to confront him with unresolved conflicts? Are these conflicts realistic clashes of incompatible pressure, or are they largely molded to irreconcilable shapes by the peculiar definitions given them by the individual or the people with whom he interacts? The analysis of roles in the life pattern is extraordinarily helpful in keeping before us the fact of interpersonal relatedness. Since roles depend for their structure on the mutual expectations of two or more persons, an inventory of individual roles always implies the existence of an interactive network. This network—past, present, and future—is the locus of mundane and disaster experience. As a guide to how he may relate to others in emergency, we thus ask how an individual has been related to those around him in everyday life.

There are at least three ways in which the study of social role may enable a researcher to ask provocative questions about mental health in disaster. First, how wide a repertory of viable roles is available to a given individual? If a person is limited to a few manageable roles, and these rigidly held, he is unlikely to respond well to the novel behaviors required by disaster situations. Second, since no person is infinitely flexible or talented, which are his areas of highest performance? In this vein, we want to know not only his capacity for any emergency roles in which he has been trained but also his strengths and weaknesses which may be transferred from normal roles to transitory roles. It has been found, for example, that the person who is most effective as a leader during the period of impact and immediately thereafter is not necessarily the person who can contribute most at a later time in the disaster. Finally, the talent for learning new roles is central to any consideration of a person's long-run adjustment to disaster. This is most strikingly seen in instances of separation and bereavement, when old role relationships must be dissolved and new ones instituted, but it is also important to changes of residence, occupation, and community structure which may be attendant on disaster. Familial roles may be the most critical of all in determining what mental health consequences may ensue; these are at once the relationships to which an individual in disaster looks first for solace and which will demand most from him in terms of effective behavior. Disturbances in the fulfillment of familial roles might be among the most telling pathological indicators to the researcher gauging disaster's long-range implications for mental health.

LIFE-ARC

As developed by Leighton and others, the idea of an individual's curvilinear motion through life to the pace of chronology is a useful frame for discussion. The life-arc, represented as stages of infancy, adolescence, maturity, and senescence intersected by critical conditioning events in the life history, is an elementary concept; its very simplicity and obviousness, however, may account for its neglect in research. The total life history is also often discounted just because longitudinal research is difficult and analyses confined to static cross-sections seem tidier.

Disaster seems a perfect situation for cross-sectional study, for it has a dramatic beginning and often represents a kind of community life history in miniature. Yet neither cities nor individuals are born in disaster, although some may die in it. It is likely that some mental illnesses can be dated from particular disaster experiences; even these, however, are almost certain to depend for their full comprehension and treatment on a knowledge of the individual's pre-disaster life. Much more often, surely, the mental health consequences of disaster are in reality the consequences of disaster *plus*—and the *plus* is exactly that portion of the individual's life-arc which occurred before the disaster. That is, we must search for the meaning of the disaster experience as part of a larger pattern of meanings characterizing this person in his course through life.

It is clearly important to know where the disaster caught the person in terms of age and development. The treatment of choice for a child in disaster is probably not the same as for an adult. Of equal importance to the question "Where has he been?" in assessing the individual's health at a given point in time, is the question "Where is he going?" Hazardous as it may seem to extrapolate, to project the life-arc into the unknown, it is only then that one can begin to think of mental health and illness as possible long-range precipitates of disaster.

As with the individual, so with the community, reaction to disaster will depend partly on where the community has been, partly on where it is moving. And the point at which disaster catches a community, in terms of cultural values, economic base, and many other forces, may have implications for the mental health of its inhabitants under disaster. One might conjecture, for instance, that the level of mental health in Worcester, Massachusetts, after the 1953 tornado (Wallace, 1956) would be superior to the mental health of Springhill, Nova Scotia, after the 1958 mine "bump" (Beach and Lucas, 1960). One disaster struck a thriving city, and had few implications for long-run occupational life; the other struck a dying town, part of a culture which feels itself to some extent bypassed and outmoded, and hit at the very core of the subsistence base of the majority of the townspeople. Most of the research on the vicissitudes of the life-arc in relation to health and illness has been able to hold only a few items "constant" (Hinkle and Wolff, 1957). In the case of disaster one finds a "uniform" stress whose effect might be gauged if one knew enough about the antecedents and consequents among a sample of individuals. Such research, taking advantage of disaster as a "natural experiment," would promise much information about both disaster and stress in the context of the total life history.

STRESS

We may, then, begin to view the individual in the frame of a developing personality, enmeshed in role relationships, moving through a life-arc. One of the inevitable accompaniments of his movement is recurrent stress. This stress is presumably of many varieties and has many differing effects on the individual; its effect will vary with the type of stress, the state of the personality at a given moment, the history of stress in this person and how it has previously been met. Although there are a host of discussions of stress (Selye, 1950; *Symposium on Stress . . .*, 1953) involving attempts to define it rigorously and especially to discriminate between the external agent —sometimes termed the stressor—and the effects of the agent on personality, social, and cultural systems, it seems most useful for our purposes to adopt Caudill's (1958) treatment: ". . . the words *stress* and *disease* are used to designate processes. In such processes there is an ongoing interplay between various stimuli and the defenses erected against them."

If stress is construed as an interplay of individual and total environment, we should then see disaster itself as such an interplay.

There are several aspects of the stress concept which merit special attention in the effort to assess mental health and illness in the context of disaster:

Stress as process The individual has a history of stress, and the massive intrusion of disaster cannot be seen except as part of a pattern. One would like to know how the person has reacted in the past, what situations of stress he has mastered, and what kinds of stress have found him unusually vulnerable. Has the cumulative stress of life been such that he is now tempered and strong, or battered and weak?

Stress as natural, optimal stress Stress may be seen as a condition of life and growth. Perhaps it is as dangerous for ultimate mental health to be exposed to too little as to be exposed to too much. What have been described as the benevolent effects of disaster on mental health may stem from the individual's being challenged sufficiently but not overwhelmingly. Research might well be directed to specifying the kinds of stress situations engendered by disaster; of these, it may be that the overt, unmistakable threats of impact are less critical to health than are certain more subtle effects which have not yet been fully elucidated.

Tyhurst's (1958) comment is relevant in reminding us that stress is ubiquitous and intrinsic to life: "We live . . . a life of conflict . . . in most cases in our daily living, stresses are good things."

Stress as differentiated To assess the meaning of disaster, it is of course not enough to think in terms of global stress. Rather, one must question the time-and-space coordinates of stress, asking what particular events occurred where. Differentiation of disaster events, in turn, demands differentiation of the target population by area, time, age and sex, ethnicity, and as many elements as possible of the total life history. Connections between stress and illness can probably never be established "in general."

Stress as enduring It should be reiterated that we know very little about long-run effects of disaster on mental health. There is no reason to think that stress promotes only dramatic change, instantly perceptible to the observer—or indeed to the subject. The enduring quality of stress seems to direct us toward extensive follow-up studies of health, toward an infinitely careful tracing of covert consequences.

COMMUNITY ORGANIZATION

It may be proper to fix community organization as an "intervening variable" between the raw disruption of disaster and the potential mental health consequences for the individual. The desirability of breaking down a rather amorphous concept like community organization into finer categories should be considered, but at least the following (presumably pathogenic) features are relevant to a community's ability to withstand disaster:

1. High frequency of broken homes
2. Few and weak associations
3. Few and weak leaders
4. Few patterns of recreation
5. High frequency of hostility
6. High frequency of crime and delinquency
7. Weak and fragmented network of communication (Leighton, 1959)

Some estimate of integration-disintegration of community patterns might help to provide the essential base line of pre-disaster functioning. At present this would tell us a good deal about the community; at a later stage of refinement it would hopefully also offer clues to the base line of the public mental health in the pre-disaster era.

Community organization is central to any frame of reference for two reasons: it may afford an estimate of the vulnerability of the population to psychiatric disorder under disaster; it may enable us to make judgments about the probable effectiveness of official and unofficial networks of relationship in coping with the post-disaster era—and hence in aggravating or mitigating individual illness. It should be taken for granted that in each of the concepts outlined above, and especially in community organization, the climate of cultural values is a salient element. How important these general life-ways can be is well illustrated by Clifford's (1956) comparison of Mexican and Texan cities during the Rio Grande flood.

THERAPY AND REHABILITATION

Certain gains may accrue from an attempt to see the therapeutic process in individual psychiatric illness and the process of community recovery from disaster in a common referential frame. Are there marked similarities which make these processes mutually reinforcing? Are there marked differences which sometimes set them at odds? If the period of post-disaster euphoria or "communism" serves some of the same functions as the "therapeutic community" of the small mental hospital, how may these functions be consolidated and prolonged in the interest of mental health? *Should* they in fact be prolonged, or would this foster an abnormal dependency which might make the individual unfit for nondisaster reality? If some variety of emergency counseling or brief psychotherapy is indicated for a given fraction of the population following disaster, how can this be articulated with what is happening in the community at large?

Perhaps the focal questions of the post-disaster period concern the amount and kinds of help that are desirable and attainable. Help in the form of physical necessities seems to be extremely plentiful in peacetime disasters in the United States. Is this the most important type of aid, once facilities have been minimally reconstituted? Are there less tangible types of assistance that might be important? One may question whether any sort of massive psychiatric effort is either required or feasible, whether the "cornucopia" should saturate a community with mental health aid as it does with food and clothing. Above all, it seems important to gauge the extent to which the disaster-struck should be regarded as genuine psychiatric casualties and given special treatment. Might we not discover that they are best handled in the fashion devised for certain mentally disturbed soldiers during World War II and the Korean War, i.e., reliance on "light duty," identification with the group, and *vis medicatrix naturae?*

Clifford's (1956) conclusion in his Rio Grande flood research provides a fitting last word for this report:

> The experiences of the research team in this study have convinced them of the extraordinary opportunities for research on general problems during a disaster situation. In the present case data were gathered on fundamental problems of inter-community relations that could hardly have been amassed under any other conditions. The disaster acted as a catalyst, in a sense, which suddenly brought many areas of relationships into sharp focus.

► *six*

OLDER PERSONS IN DISASTER

H. J. Friedsam

Introduction

There are two justifications for directing special attention to older persons in disaster. One is immediate and practical; the other is theoretical. On the practical level many older persons present problems which, at least in magnitude, are not to be found in other age groups. A simple example is the relatively high incidence of mobility-limiting chronic disease among the aged. This creates almost as much of a special consideration in planning for evacuation as does the need for continued schooling among children and adolescents. Again, there is some evidence that, compared with younger groups, older persons are less likely to receive warning and are more reluctant to evacuate. If this is correct, it is of obvious importance to disaster planning.

On the theoretical level the justification for investigation specifically directed towards the aged in disaster is to be found in the analysis of age statuses and age-related roles as a general theoretical problem. Although interest in this area is of long standing in anthropology, psychology, and sociology, well-known papers by Linton and Parsons can be used as convenient references to the general theoretical position of age-status analysis (Linton, 1942; Parsons, 1942). In the context of disaster research the case for the analytic importance of age roles has probably been stated most explicitly by Form and Nosow (1958).

Nevertheless it must be noted that age-status analysis, particularly where chronological age is used to designate age groups, often implies a higher degree of age-grading of role behavior than probably exists in most societies and particularly in the United States. This is of special importance where "the aged" are concerned, since such a term is usually categorical rather than behavioral in its reference. Thus, there is a tendency to use sixty-five as the chronological gateway to "old age" regardless of its relationship to roles. At the same time certain roles are often imputed to "the aged" which are not congruent with a chronological definition of the status or with each other. For example, there is a strong tendency to think of "grandparent" as a family role of the aged and of "retirement" as an economic role. Quite apart from the fact that some older people never become grandparents and that some of these in turn—and others—never retire, it is obvious that movement into these two roles occurs in quite different institutional and temporal dimensions and that they are completely independent of one another.

In addition to the lack of role congruence there is also the simple but important fact of great heterogeneity among "the aged," however designated. Thus, many are "married, living with spouse," and many are in various other family and household arrangements. Many of the latter are living alone; others are living with their children in a dependent relationship; still others are active heads of households including adult "children" and often grandchildren. Many are employed at jobs they have held for all or most of a working lifetime; many are retired; some have entered new employments after their initial retirement.

There are also wide variations in health (both physical and mental), income level, educational achievement, etc. To be sure, the range of variation may be no greater than it is in any other age group, but "the aged" differ in the percentage who are to be found at one or both extremes. In other words, some persons of all ages are ill, but the percentage is much higher among the aged; some families in younger age groups have low incomes, but the percentage is much higher in families with an older person as head, etc. Unfortunately, the data available for the present study allow only very limited attention to be paid to such variables.

"The Aged" in Disaster Research

Several implications for disaster research can be drawn from what has thus far been said. First, it should be obvious that any categorical designation of the aged, particularly in chronological terms, can yield only the crudest kind of generalizations; but it is also possible that generalizations on this level may be useful, and perhaps even necessary, preludes to a more sophisticated analysis in terms of roles. Second, sociological research on the aged in disaster should be framed, wherever possible, in terms of role models, or in terms of structural models which implicitly or explicitly embody role concepts. Third, the comprehensive study of older persons in disaster should be seen as having two fundamental dimensions: differences among older persons, and differences between older persons and younger persons. Fourth, the role concepts used may be either extrinsic or intrinsic to the disaster situation. Most of the references to roles of the aged mentioned thus far, e.g., "married, living with spouse," "retired," etc., are extrinsic. That is, they are the roles characteristic of older persons in what Anthony Wallace has called the "steady state," the "normal" state of affairs before disaster strikes, and they are standard variables in many areas of research. On the other hand, it may be equally important to develop victim models which derive from the disaster situation itself. For example, one could investigate differences in reaction to disaster between those who had lost a spouse or other close family member, those who were injured themselves, and those who suffered varying degrees of property loss (Fritz and Marks, 1954; Crawford, 1957). Either approach could be taken with reference to different types of disaster on the assumption that different disaster agents may be defined quite differently and have quite different consequences.

The present study makes little attempt to differentiate behavior by type of disaster. It is based almost exclusively on published and unpublished materials, including interviews with victims, relating to natural disasters. At some points, however, particularly with respect to problems of evacuation and casualties, the natural disaster materials are supplemented by data drawn from studies of World War II bombing. With its emphasis on natural disaster, the study has been organized largely in terms of the time-phase model introduced into disaster research by Powell, Rayner, and Finesinger (1953). It should be noted at once, however, that the available materials give unequal emphasis to certain stages in the time sequence at the expense of others. For example, data on several aspects of impact and evacuation are relatively plentiful, if unsystematic, but there is little on warning and not much more on rehabilitation. For this reason there is no attempt to adhere rigidly to the time-phase model.

Comparatively few studies of natural disaster have made the aged a prime focus of attention. A notable exception is the work of Moore and Crawford (1955) in their studies of the Waco and San Angelo tornadoes. Using a typology designed to take account of the varied patterns of family relationships which may exist for older persons, they investigated, for each type, the frequency of occurrence of a number of variables, ranging from injuries sustained to attitudes toward the future.

Although no other study has made the aged such a central focus of attention, some do offer more or less systematic data relating to this group. Lammers' (1955) research on the Holland flood, for example, utilizes age as an analytical category in the study of evacuation, most particularly in the study of tensions between evacuees and hosts. Although comparatively few of the data are quantitative, Titmuss (1950) has made invaluable contributions to the understanding of some of the direct and indirect social costs of the bombing of England in World War II borne by older persons. The United States Strategic Bombing Survey (1947) contains similar material, particularly in the report on *The Effect of Bombing on Health and Medical Care in Germany*. The National Opinion Research Center study (Marks and Fritz, 1954) of the Judsonia tornado includes some data utilizing age categories, but unfortunately much of it is presented only in categories of persons under forty-five and forty-five and over. A similar weakness characterizes the limited use of age categories in Form and Nosow's (1958) study of the Flint-Beecher tornado. A few other reports contain occasional references to older persons, either directly or by implication. What is most surprising is that studies which have made distinct contributions to the understanding of family relationships in disaster, e.g., Young (1954) on the role of the extended family, should have paid so little specific attention to the roles of aged persons.

The interview files of the Disaster Research Group were the richest single source of data for this study.[1] It should be said at once that the available interview materials could be treated only impressionistically. Although in many, perhaps most, of them the age of the respondent is given, in a surprising number it is not. In the latter it became necessary to look for cues to the respondent's age. Generally speaking, when a respondent referred to himself as old or when he identified himself as a grandparent, retired (or spouse retired), or in some similar role usually associated with older persons, the interview was accepted as being with an older person. Where ages were given, persons sixty and over were regarded as "older persons." The interviews will not bear the weight of the most rudimentary statistical

[1] The most useful interviews from the Disaster Research Group files were those with victims of the tornadoes in Worcester, Massachusetts, Waco, Texas, and Judsonia, Arkansas, and the hurricane ("Audrey") in Cameron Parish, Louisiana. The writer has also had at his disposal a number of interviews from the Waco-San Angelo study (Moore and Crawford, 1955), the Flint-Beecher study (Form and Nosow, 1958), the Dallas tornado study (Moore and Friedsam, 1959), and his own files on Hurricane Audrey. Unless otherwise noted, all quotations from and references to interview data are based on these files.

analysis, but it is useful and suggestive to examine them for possible hypotheses and for illustrative material.

This study, then, must be regarded as a beginning. It does not "prove" anything. Its aim is the almost infinitely more modest one of suggesting some hypotheses on older persons in disaster and supporting these suggestions with whatever materials and theory are currently available. In the end they remain hypotheses, but, it is hoped, hypotheses worthy of attention in future field studies of disaster.

Warning

Although studies or parts of studies which relate to the warning phase of the disaster sequence make up a considerable proportion of disaster literature, their total effect is weakened by lack of comparability.[2] Their range extends from the description of formal air-raid warning systems as found, for example, throughout the United States Strategic Bombing Survey to rather complete surveys of public response to natural disaster warnings such as that of Blum and Klass (1956). None of them has given special attention to the aged.

The fragmentary evidence which is available suggests the hypothesis that on the whole older persons are less likely to receive warning than are younger persons. On a most elementary level one would expect this to follow from the isolated living arrangements of many older individuals and couples and from the relatively high proportion who suffer from some sort of physical or mental disability that could interfere with reception of warning. The study of the flood at Zierikzee (van Doorn-Janssen, 1955, p. 180), for example, refers to twenty-one deaths, "mainly old and deaf people who had not heard the warning." The Kortgene study (Nauta and van Strien, 1955, p. 30) does not refer to the aged as such but does mention "gaps" in the warning net, persons who "were not called at all."

Unpublished data from the Dallas tornado study by Moore and Friedsam lend some support to the general hypothesis under discussion and to the implication that the Kortgene "gaps" may have been, in many instances, older people. Although large majorities of those respondents under sixty and those sixty and over reported that they had had no advance warning, the percentage of the latter, 86.3,

[2] It should be obvious that the warning phase itself is quite different, and perhaps not comparable, from one disaster to another. Thus, the period is usually well-defined and may cover days in a flood, whereas in a tornado it may be a matter of minutes, and for many victims, who have not been able to interpret the weather cues, virtually nonexistent.

was considerably higher than the percentage of the former, 73.4. Even more significant is the fact that over three-fourths of the difference is due to the percentage (18.3) of those under sixty who said that they received warning by word-of-mouth as compared to the percentage (10.4) of those over sixty. The implication of these data and the quotation from the Kortgene flood study is clear; they suggest the possibility that the aged are, for whatever specific reasons, more often outside informal warning nets than are younger adults.

Although it does not refer to warning in the usual sense of the term, Withey's study (1954) of public knowledge and attitudes on civil defense and atomic bombing is of interest here since it casts some light on the orientation of age groups to the mass media, particularly radio, as a source of information. He found not only that older persons rather consistently exhibited a lower level of knowledge of such matters than did younger persons, but a high percentage, 24, replied "Don't know" to a question as to how they would seek further information in case of warning that an A-bomb attack had started. This was twice or more the percentage giving the same response in any other adult group except those from fifty to sixty-four, for whom the percentage was 14. Furthermore, only 23 per cent of those sixty-five and over said that they would "tune in radio," whereas the lowest percentage for any other age group, again those fifty to sixty-four, was 32.

An aspect of warning for which no information seems to be available is that of possible differential age-group responses in interpretation of visual cues, particularly in tornadoes and hurricanes. Interviews with victims of tornadoes, for example, are replete with references to whether or not the person concerned correctly interpreted heavy black clouds, torrential rainfall, large hailstones, etc., as a warning of an impending tornado.[3] One can find instances of older persons saying that they made correct interpretations of such phenomena, but one can also find numerous instances of those who say they did not, and it is impossible to say whether either type of response occurs with greater or lesser frequency among older persons than among younger adults. There is of course one reason for suggesting that older persons may make a correct interpretation of visual cues somewhat more often than others: as would be expected, they more often report previous disaster experience. For example, Marks and Fritz report "some relationship between age and previous experience"

[3] The available evidence suggests that most persons fail to interpret such cues correctly. Wallace (1956) points out that, quite apart from hailstones, rain, etc., only fourteen of twenty-two persons interviewed who saw the funnel in Worcester recognized it as a tornado.

for the Judsonia tornado, and in their Dallas sample Moore and Friedsam found that the proportion of persons over sixty reporting previous disaster experience was twice that of respondents under sixty.

Pre-Impact Evacuation

Even when warning is received, there is no certainty that it always can or will be acted upon. Some individuals and families may be unable or unwilling to take protective action, particularly if, as in the case of pre-impact evacuation, it involves abandonment of home and familiar surroundings; but several studies suggest that a higher degree of both incapacity for and resistance to evacuation is encountered among the aged than in other groups. On incapacity, for example, Ellemers and in't Veld-Langeveld (1955) in their study of the flood at Kruiningen make reference to the inability of "old or sick people to leave their homes in response to warning."

The Strategic Bombing Survey report on evacuation from Japanese cities states explicitly that "old people were not evacuated; evacuees were younger than those who stayed in the cities" (1947d, p. 75). It attributes this to older people being less mobile and "less willing to pull up roots and move." Bernert and Iklé (1952, p. 138) have made a similar observation with reference to "elderly people in economically poorer districts" in European cities, who were "often unwilling to be evacuated" from their neighborhoods even when their homes had been destroyed. Titmuss (1950, p. 451) mentions the desire not to be separated from normal surroundings, of married couples to remain together, and "in some instances, the fear of being treated as a pauper" as factors in the resistance of older persons to evacuation.

In both England and Germany the aged population, or at least some segments of it, was regarded as a special group for evacuation planning purposes, and it is obvious that it turned out to be both more and less of a problem than the planning envisaged. German planning placed the "old and feeble" under "precautionary evacuation to safe areas of special groups whose presence in vulnerable areas was not necessary" (Strategic Bombing Survey, 1947a, p. 175). Unfortunately the Strategic Bombing Survey offers no concrete estimate of the number or percentage of aged persons involved, no indication of whether there was a greater or lesser reluctance to be evacuated on the part of the aged, nor any specific material on problems in reception areas. It does mention that precautionary evacuation of ". . . large numbers of women and children and of the aged and infirm . . . placed a severe strain on the medical organization in the areas to which they moved" (1947b, p. 225), hints that resistance to the break-up of families was a major factor in the development of a "later policy, which kept evacuees in the same district as the city from which they came" (1947a, p. 188), and indicates that late in the war refusal to issue food cards to persons over sixty-five was invoked as a means of forcing compliance with the evacuation programs (1947a, p. 185).

Titmuss' survey of the British experience of World War II is concerned for the most part with the evacuation of mothers and children, but some attention is given to the aged beyond that cited above. In addition to the reluctance of this group to evacuate, which was not a major focus of research attention, two points stand out in the discussion. First, the number of the aged evacuated was never very great. To a considerable degree this may have been due to reluctance on the part of the aged themselves, but apparently it was also due in part to a governmental decision not to try to billet aged persons compulsorily on householders (Titmuss, 1950, p. 359). What is significant in this is the rather explicit assumption that it would have been extremely difficult to establish satisfactory evacuee-host relationships on any other than a voluntary basis. As a result, official efforts to evacuate older persons were limited in scope and largely took the form of "assisted private evacuation" (pp. 359-360).

Second, the "aged sick" constituted a special case, not so much because of their own needs, which were great, but because of the low priority of their claims on hospital services. At various times during the war several thousand aged and chronically sick persons were evacuated from London hospitals to make beds available for anticipated air-raid and armed forces casualties, and some were shifted several times "until they ended up in institutions of the workhouse type." In extreme cases some old persons "were mentally or physically unable to notify relatives or friends," records were not kept or were lost, and the patients could not be located for weeks or months (Titmuss, 1950, pp. 500-501).

Impact and Rescue

Many field studies of natural disaster have concentrated on behavior at the time of impact and immediately thereafter to the neglect of warning and rehabilitation, particularly long-run rehabilitation. Despite this, the published reports and studies seem to offer less substantial material on the aged in impact and rescue than on most other phases of the disaster sequence. The Marks and Fritz (1954) study of the Judsonia tornado offers limited systematic data, but in general one must depend largely on the interview materials for suggestions.

Possibly the strongest impression received from the interviews is that whereas younger males tend to move from a family orientation during and immediately after impact to a more general community orientation, older persons (along with younger females) have a strong tendency to remain family-oriented throughout these phases. This family orientation may take a number of forms. During impact, for example, there is reason to believe that many older persons, even those who have adult children with them, assume leadership or quasi-leadership roles with reference to protective measures. For example, a sixty-nine-year-old woman in Worcester, whose daughter and grandson were with her when the tornado struck, describes what she did:

> "I was getting my supper ready and my grandson and my daughter was home . . . [when] the storm started. I could see the tree outside the kitchen window just twirlin' around so I said to my daughter, 'We'd better get out of there before the storm comes in' . . . an' I said to them, 'Hurry up and go in the back hall' because I thought we'd be more protected in the back hall and so we closed the . . . doors and was in the back hall and we threw ourselves on the floor. . . ."

Many of the interviews describe search activities by family members directed toward older persons, particularly, as Powell (1954b) has suggested, the search of daughters for their mothers. An excerpt from a summary of an interview with a nurse in Judsonia will serve as an example and also will suggest the intense emotional stress of a mature, married woman in her search for her mother:

> Mrs. R. . . . had not been hurt at all, but she fell upon Mrs. B. . . . when she saw her in the hospital saying, "I can't find mother anywhere. I've been looking in morgues and all over the place—looking at everybody and can't find my mother." The woman was quite upset—almost hysterical apparently, and just ran from place to place trying to find her mother.

As one might expect, there is evidence that the search is often reciprocal. In a Waco interview for example, a young woman, who lived with her mother—aged sixty-five—but who worked in the impact area, described at length her search for her mother, who had gone to a hospital during the afternoon to visit a relative. She was unable to find her, because the mother on learning of the tornado had hurried to the impact area to search for her daughter. They were reunited when both gave up searching and returned home.

Where an older couple maintain a household, it is to be expected that search and rescue activity will first be directed toward the spouse. In the following quotation a sixty-five-year-old woman in Worcester, who had been severely injured, describes her attempt to help her seventy-seven-year-old blind husband.

> ". . . I finally got on my knees and I heard my husband yelling and I didn't know . . . where I was. Finally I heard him yellin' and . . . I turned around on my knees and elbows . . . I went, I saw him, I saw that he had been thrown 50 feet in the front yard—I crawled on my hands and knees . . . but I finally, I don't know what I stood up against, but I picked myself up and I walked to him through all the plaster and everything, 'til I got to him and found him laying there . . . I knew he had been hurt—he was hollerin' so much, so finally I said to him, 'I'll take care of you.' He kept sayin' to me, 'Are you hurt, Louise, are you hurt?' I said, 'My arms are hurt'—wondering if they were broken."

Despite these examples one would expect that aged persons would not be as active in search and rescue as younger persons, since this is an area of behavior which is most likely to be affected by the strength, health, and mobility of the people concerned. Marks and Fritz (1954) found that "there was a substantially higher proportion of males and younger persons . . . among those who searched than among those who did not search" (p. 40). They also conclude that "the age-differential . . . may *partly* account for differences in the extent of rescue activity" (p. 408).

Marks and Fritz also offer some data which at least indirectly support the hypothesis that the older male is more likely than the younger to confine his post-disaster activities to the family. In their analysis of the "orientation of action to midnight, by household role," they found "male heads with dependents" were slightly more likely to orient action to the "general community" than were "male heads without dependents." Their analysis also shows that the latter group contained a higher proportion of older males. Furthermore, the percentage showing an orientation to the "general community" in their category of "non-responsibles," 50 per cent of whom were sixty-five and over, was not quite half that of "male heads with dependents," and was only a little higher than "females with dependents," a category made up for the most part of young mothers (p. 404).

If the assumption that older males are less oriented to activity outside the family is correct, it can be suggested that this may not be entirely due to their physical condition vis-à-vis younger males, but that there may also be sociopsychological factors which are important. Although it involves a quite different problem, Withey's study (1954) of attitudes toward civil defense, referred to above, is of interest in this connection. He found that 52 per cent, the highest in any age group, of his respondents sixty-five and over said that they were unwilling to participate in civil defense. More important, although 18 per cent gave health or physical handicap as their reason, 37 per cent simply gave age (pp. 103-104). Possibly this is indicative of the difficulty an older person has in defining his relationship to nonfamily groups and is a product of what E. W. Burgess has called the "roleless role" of the aged in American society.

The Extended Family as Refuge

It is a common finding of natural disaster studies that the extended family "comes into its own" in time of disaster.[4] For example, many field studies have noted that mass care facilities were little used because the victims moved immediately into the homes of relatives. Although sibling and other relationships are important to a full description and understanding of how the extended family functions in disaster, only aged parent-child or grandchild relationships will be considered in this section, and the evidence will again be drawn almost exclusively from the interviews.

A classic example of the role of an extended, almost patriarchal, family as a pre-impact refuge is reported in the Hurricane Audrey interviews. The ages of the grandfather and grandmother concerned were eighty-three and seventy-eight respectively. They had refused to be evacuated, as they had on previous occasions, and it is obvious from the following quotation that at least some members of the family who could have left the threatened area simply moved to another part of it to be with this patriarch and his wife.

> ". . . Somebody went to answer the phone, and they said that it would be the grandchildren from Creole—from Cameron that were coming over to stay in Grandpa . . . 's home here. They felt safe here . . . they're close families . . . they're always—if anything happens they're altogether. I mean they're the kind of people that would get together in anything like this. They wouldn't say, 'You go fight for yourself.' And that's why they were all tryin' to get to Grandpa . . . 's. He is more or less . . . a Southern aristocrat or something or other, but everybody goes to him in trouble or in time of stress. And that's what they were trying to do. They were all trying to get to Grandpa . . . 's house, 'cause they thought, well, they were safe if they were at Grandpa's."

Despite this case the interview materials relating to aged persons strongly suggest that it is mothers and daughters rather than fathers

[4] Fritz and Mathewson (1957), Klausner and Kincaid (1956), Wallace (1956), and Young (1954) in particular have emphasized the importance of the extended family in the early post-impact period and provide a broader view of its functioning than does the present study. Fritz and Mathewson also suggest that disaster "functions" for the extended family "in re-establishing and strengthening social solidarity among persons whose normal social relationships are tenuous or minimal" (p. 40).

and sons around whom extended family patterns tend to coalesce in time of disaster.[5] For example, a woman in San Angelo describes her experience in the immediate pre-impact period:

> "Well now, I wasn't here [in her own home] . . . I mean I was over at my mother's, see they live right here behind me, and I had just carried my husband to work . . . and I stopped by my aunt's sister's. And I stayed there about 10 or 15 minutes and the cloud kept looking bad . . . So I said 'Well, I'm going to get home.' So I called my mother and I said, 'What's happening out there,' and she said, 'Oh nothing, looks like the wind's gonna blow.' So I got in the car and here I come. And they had the street tore up out here and I couldn't get the car in the garage. So I went around the block and came back over at her house . . . She said, 'Well get out and come in, it's already here.' So I got in, went back and got as far as the kitchen when it hit."

Another woman in San Angelo describes the convergence of several adult children at their mother's home in the immediate post-impact period:

> "Well, I went down to my mother's . . . my brother come by and he got us and he took us down to our mother's . . . my sister come, she lives out on the San Antonio highway. And my other brother come over . . . We didn't think about my husband, how he was hearing about it. I mean, you know, we didn't think about him not knowing about it."

The foregoing quotations are excellent illustrations of the role of the older woman, the mother, as symbol of refuge and security in time of crisis. Other interviews suggest the importance of the daughter's role with reference to her parents. In several the daughter is reported as providing housing for a parent whose home has been damaged or destroyed; in others she is the nurse for a parent who has been injured or his spokesman to the outside world. In some cases she performs one or more of these services for her father, but it is the mother-daughter relationship which is ubiquitous. One is reminded of Peter Townsend's (1957) emphasis on mother-daughter relationships in his study of old people in a lower class section of London. His contention that there is a "special unity between grandmother, daughter, and daughter's child," that "the family system of care is largely built around these three," and

[5] This follows Powell's hypothesis (1954b) that the interview materials suggest that in time of disaster "men go for, or call, their wives; women, their children and then their mothers." The Hurricane Audrey interviews, the largest group available to the writer which post-date the formulation of Powell's hypothesis, appear to offer considerable support for it.

his illustrations of how the system functions, particularly in "many of the emergencies of life," are reflected over and over in the disaster protocols.

Despite the willing acceptance by one generation of its "crisis role obligations" to the other (Fritz and Mathewson, 1957), there is little doubt that in some cases a considerable amount of tension is produced, particularly where two previously independent households are forced to function as one beyond the immediate post-impact emergency phase. The following quotation from an interview with a woman in Judsonia provides an excellent example:

> "I feel if I ever got my mother's house rebuilt . . . we have it pretty well underway now and she thinks she'll be in it maybe next week . . . so I feel like once she gets settled . . . I can get settled again. I mean, after all, it's been four months . . . when you live by yourself, I guess, as long as my husband and I, you sorta get set in your ways and things like that get you upset after a period of time. Well, I feel like when I can get my house back in order then we'll live a normal life again . . ."

Age as a factor in host-evacuee tensions was investigated by Lammers (1955). He found a significant difference (at the 0.02 level) between evacuees aged fifteen to forty-four and those sixty-five and older, with the latter reporting less tension. However, when employment status and presence of children, the critical factors, were controlled, the relationship between age and reports of tension was no longer significant. Lammers therefore suggests that the initial correlation was probably spurious. Ellemers and in't Veld-Langeveld (1955) investigated interfamily adjustment of refugees from Kruiningen, and although their material appears to be more impressionistic than that of Lammers, they conclude that "age was a factor whenever old people were received by noisy young families, or vice-versa" (p. 120). In their study of the Farmington-Unionville, Connecticut, flood evacuees, Klausner and Kincaid (1956) mention that ". . . in some instances, it was the relation between the children and the 'old-folks' that was described as strained" (p. 61).

Lammers also investigated the integration of the refugees into the reception community. He defined integration operationally as "reported at-homeness" on the part of evacuee respondents. He found that "there is a worthwhile suggestion . . . that age might be connected with the evacuee's adjustment to the reception community," with persons sixty-five and older showing the lowest average integration score. As would be expected, he also found on studying the relation of "at-homeness" to employment status of head of evacuee family that the "retired, other" group had the lowest average integration scores (1955, p. 140).

The natural disaster materials presently available do not permit an assessment of long-run changes in intergenerational relationships which may result from the functioning of the extended family in time of crisis. It is possible that in most cases there are no significant changes; the younger—or older—generation may provide temporary refuge for the other, may help the other to re-establish itself, and then interaction is resumed on a *status quo ante* basis. However, the possibility of altered patterns of interaction should not be overlooked. During Hurricane Audrey, for example, an older woman who had been in a psychotic depression prior to the hurricane had responsibility for her grandchildren for a period of time and discharged it efficiently. Her doctor was convinced that this had altered her daughter's view of the mother's illness and that the daughter was taking a more active role in the mother's rehabilitation.

Older Persons as Casualties

Although most studies of disaster have been concerned in one way or another with victims, surprisingly little systematic attention has been given to that most striking of victims, the casualty. So far as the writer is aware, no one has undertaken to do even a thorough demographic analysis of the dead and injured of any major disaster. The nearest approach is his own analysis (1957a) of the data on dead and missing persons in Hurricane Audrey, which classified them in terms of place of residence, race, sex, and age. Wallace (1956) has also classified the casualties of the Worcester tornado by age and sex, and limited data on the direct and indirect casualty effects of World War II bombings are given by Titmuss (1950) and The United States Strategic Bombing Survey (1947a,b,c). Apart from these, most references to casualties are either gross summations of the total number of dead and injured or else are merely incidental or passing comments. Nevertheless, in the limited data available there is a very clear indication that casualties do not occur at random in age terms but that the young and the old, particularly the latter, become casualties with far greater frequency than their numbers in the impact populations would lead one to expect.

The data on casualties in Cameron Parish which resulted from Hurricane Audrey offer a good, although admittedly crude, basis for analysis in age-sex terms. Table 6-1 gives the percentage distribution by broad age groups of known-age deaths and known-age missing white persons and the age distribution for Cameron Parish in 1950.[6] A quick inspection of this table will show that for the white population the percentage of children (under ten) who died or were reported missing was slightly greater than the percentage of children in the Parish in 1950; the percentage of casualties between the ages of ten and fifty-nine was less than the percentage in these ages reported in the census, and the percentage of casualties sixty and over was considerably greater.

TABLE 6-1 *Age-Sex Distribution of Known-age Dead and Missing White Persons, Hurricane Audrey, June 1957, and of Cameron Parish, 1950*

	Known-age identified dead (per cent)		Known-age persons missing (per cent)		Age distribution Cameron Parish 1950 (per cent)	
Age group	Male	Female	Male	Female	Male	Female
Under 10	27.8	27.9	36.6	28.1	23.8	22.5
10 to 59	43.1	44.2	39.0	49.0	68.2	69.1
60 and over	29.3	27.9	24.4	22.8	7.9	8.2

SOURCES: Casualty data collected by author, 1957; Population data from *1950 Census of Population.*

TABLE 6-2 *Age-Sex Indexes of White Persons Dead and Missing, Hurricane Audrey, Cameron Parish, June 1957*

	Dead		Missing	
Age group	Male	Female	Male	Female
Under 10	117	124	153	125
10 to 59	63	64	57	71
60 and over	371	340	309	278

Table 6-2 converts the relationship of population and casualty data into an index for each of the white age-sex groups.[7] Presented in

[6] All references to Cameron Parish casualties are based on data collected by the author in July and August 1957. Nonwhite casualties are not included because of the high proportion of unidentified dead of unknown age in this group.

[7] The indexes were derived by dividing the casualty percentage for each age group by its population percentage and multiplying by 100. Any number of criticisms might be directed against this procedure. Among others, there was a seven-year time lapse between the census and the hurricane; the census data were for the entire Parish whereas the major impact area of the hurricane was essentially the lower half of the Parish. The answer to the first objection is that it is ex-

this fashion, the "relative vulnerability" of each of the groups is easily seen. There can be no doubt of the impact of the hurricane on the older population, but what is perhaps most striking is the consistency of the indexes for each age group.

Percentages of all known-age deaths attributed to persons sixty and over in Worcester, derived from data presented by Wallace (1956), are surprisingly close to those for older white persons in Cameron Parish. In Worcester, deaths to males sixty and over accounted for 26.7 per cent of all known-age male deaths; for females the percentage was 21.7. The comparable percentages in Cameron Parish were 29.8 and 27.9, respectively. However, if one combines the data for the dead and the missing in Cameron Parish—and it is fair to do so—the difference is even less. When the two groups of data are combined, males sixty and over account for 27.3 per cent of the known-age dead and missing males, and the percentage for females is 25.0.

Some additional evidence on the direct vulnerability of the aged to a disaster agent can be found in Moore and Crawford and in Titmuss. The former (1955, p. 21) found that the highest percentage of injuries occurred in families made up of aged couples. Furthermore, the percentage of families "with some member injured" was higher in three of the four family types having aged members than it was in their "conjugal type," which included no older person. The percentage of families reporting injuries in the fourth family type with aged members was equal to that in the conjugal type. Moore and Crawford also calculated the "average number of persons injured per total members for each type" and found that the averages for each of the four types with aged members were higher than that for the conjugal type. The two family types having only aged members showed the highest averages of all.

Titmuss (1950, p. 560) has indicated that older persons were admitted to hospitals for treatment of injuries due to enemy bombing of England in World War II in considerably higher ratios than were other age groups in the population. He attributes this to the fact that few were evacuated, the difficulty in taking shelter during raids, and a greater need for hospitalization when slightly injured.

Thus far, consideration has been limited to primary casualty ef-

---

ceedingly doubtful that the age structure of the Parish had changed much in seven years, and it is at least reasonably certain that it had not changed enough to alter the significance of the indexes. The writer, who spent a month doing field work on Hurricane Audrey, knows of no reason to assume that the age structure differed significantly in one part of the Parish from that in another. Even if some differences did exist, it is extremely doubtful that they would have been great enough to modify the indexes in any important respect.

fects, the deaths and injuries resulting immediately from the action of the disaster agent. But there are also what Titmuss has referred to as "secondary effects"—casualties resulting not directly from the action of the disaster agent but from intervening conditions produced by that agent. These indirect effects are much more difficult to measure than the direct effects, but the literature on World War II bombings indicates that they are very real and must be taken into account if one is to assess the total impact of a disaster. One of the most successful efforts to do so is found in Titmuss' estimate of the "excess mortality" from accidents to children and old people in the early years of the war. He calculates that in England the number of "excess deaths during 1939-1941 among men and women aged over 65 from accidents of all kinds" was 4,471. He also estimates that the number of excess deaths to children aged 0 to 15 in the years 1940-1942 was 2,026. To give significance to the total of 6,497 excess deaths due to accidents, he points out that it amounted to "just over ten per cent of the number of civilians directly killed by the enemy" and that it measured "only a part of the total mortality from accidental deaths attributable to the war" (1950, pp. 334-335).

Titmuss also draws attention to a quite different kind of indirect effect in his discussion of the utilization of hospital facilities during the war. He points out that "somebody had to pay the price of war by going without, waiting longer, getting less or being pushed about to make room for others." Apparently the greatest impact fell upon the aged (pp. 499-500).

It should not be concluded, however, that the medical picture for the aged was wholly bleak. Despite the "excess mortality" and despite the limitations on hospital services for the aged, death rates for all causes except operations of war for persons aged sixty-five to seventy-five fell during the course of the war. Actually there was a sharp increase for both males and females in this age group between 1938 and 1940, but from 1940 to 1945, death rates for both fell steadily except for a slight increase in 1943. In this decline, older persons were sharing in the general improvement of civilian mortality conditions that characterized wartime England (Titmuss, 1950, pp. 524, 529-538).

The most systematic attempt to assess the secondary effects of disaster is to be found in the Strategic Bombing Survey report on *The Effect of Bombing on Health and Medical Care in Germany* (1947b). Although calculations of age-specific death rates for various diseases could not be made, the report does set forth conclusions on the relationship of a number of causes of death which have a relatively high incidence among older persons and periods of or following heavy air attacks; deaths due to diabetes and cerebral hemorrhage declined; those attributed to "heart disease" increased as did deaths "registered as due to old age" and deaths from pneumonia and influenza; there was no clear-cut evidence that suicides increased (p. 158).

The report indicates that deaths of older persons due to coronary thrombosis during periods of bombing, which along with those of "old age" it attributes to stress, occurred so frequently that they were referred to as "the shelter death of the aged" (p. 100). In this connection it may be noted that in England between 1939 and 1946, according to Titmuss, the increase in "the recorded death rate from coronary disease and angina pectoris among men and women aged 45-55, 55-65, 65-75, and over 75 . . . ranged between thirty-three and forty-six per cent" (1950, p. 335).

The discussion of the impact of strategic bombing on hospital care suggests that in Germany, as in England, children and old people often suffered more than did others. The report mentions specifically crowded conditions, the necessity to evacuate wards and transport patients to air-raid shelters, and the worsening food situation which developed. With respect to each of these a greater impact on children and old people is noted (pp. 175, 223).

Little attention appears to have been given to secondary casualty effects in natural disaster. The study by Moore and Crawford (1955) shows that the percentage of respondents who reported post-disaster illness in their families was slightly higher than the percentage reporting pre-disaster illness in the two types having aged members only. However, in the other two types with aged members a decrease in adult illness was reported. Since the latter were multigenerational families, it is not possible to determine from the findings given what percentage, if any, of the decrease could be attributed to the older generation. In an unpublished report Albert S. Foley (1957) has indicated that two doctors whom he interviewed in Cameron Parish approximately a year after Hurricane Audrey apparently were convinced that the experience had "hastened" the death of "some people." Both doctors referred specifically to older persons in this context. In neither of these reports is there more than the barest impression that there may be significant secondary effects on older persons from natural disasters, but taken together they point towards the desirability of a future test of such a hypothesis.

Emotional and Psychiatric Casualties

Despite the acute emotional stress so characteristic of victim populations in all disaster situations, there is widespread agreement that the experience does not produce any significant increase in chronic mental disorders (Janis, 1951; Drayer, 1957). Fragmentary evidence indicates that this is as true for the aged as for younger persons. The Strategic Bombing Survey reports that "The increase in depressive states, especially in the involutional period of life, was negligible"; however, various neurotic symptoms, "especially in children and in older people," are attributed to bombing (1947b, p. 104). Vernon (1941, pp. 464-465) refers to a report by Kirman which indicates that many aged persons were "plunged into a state of agitated confusion" by destruction of their homes but added that most recovered in a day or two. Vernon (pp. 463-464) also notes that the impact of bombings on established patterns of family care of certain groups, including the senile aged, may have given rise to the appearance of an increase in psychotics, a position that is supported, at least by implication, by Titmuss (1950, pp. 447-448).

The acute emotional stress characteristic of the immediate post-impact situation, although widely described, has seldom been systematically discussed. Exceptions are found in Wallace's formulation of the "disaster syndrome" (1956, pp. 109-141) and the analysis by Marks and Fritz of affective and cognitive reactions and disturbances by "household role" (1954, pp. 413-415). The latter have noted that "male heads without dependents" and "non-responsibles" were slightly less likely than "male heads with dependents" and "females with dependents" to have shown "any strong affect" in the aftermath of the Arkansas tornado. At the same time, they were slightly more likely to have been "calm, unexcited." It is significant that persons in the first two roles were on the average older than those in the latter two. No implications can be drawn from these findings for the problems relating to long-run stress.

Among students of disaster, Moore (1958a, 1958b) appears to have the strongest reservations toward the idea that disaster experiences do not result in long-run emotional disturbances. However, a question of comparability of findings is raised by the fact that his approach to the question differs so much from that of others. Rather than depending on clinical symptoms of stress, he asked victims whether they had "noticed any emotional stress among family members as a result of the disaster." He has also used intensive interviews to gain supporting evidence. Furthermore, his research was conducted several months after the disaster. In this sense it focuses on "long-run" stress and differs fundamentally from the descriptions of immediate post-impact stress.

The victim responses secured by this method can be categorized as "reported emotional stress" (Moore and Friedsam, 1959). At the least they indicate to what extent victims have defined the emotional situation in their families as disturbed following the disaster. Whether they are indicative of mental illness is, as Moore has pointed out (1958b, p. 112), "a problem for expert opinion."

This approach has been used specifically in the study of aged persons (Moore and Crawford, 1955; Moore, 1958b). The percentages of families in each of the five family types used in the study reporting emotional stress were as follows: Type I—45; Type II—52; Type III—24; Type IV—54; Type V—35.[8] Since Types II and III are multigenerational families, one cannot be certain to what extent the reported stress is that of older persons. However, even if these two types are eliminated, a problem remains, since the percentage for Type I families (those without older members) falls between those for Types IV and V, which had only aged members. Two possible explanations for these findings are offered (Moore, 1958b). With reference to the Type V families (old persons living alone), it is pointed out that these respondents were necessarily reporting their own emotional states, and it is suggested that the respondents may "have rationalized to some extent any emotional stress they may have felt and, hence, would tend to report the absence of such feelings" (p. 143). The second suggestion is that families characterized by deep mutual understanding and constant communication "offer the greatest possibility for the expression of emotional stress" (p. 143). This presumably would account for the high percentage of Type IV families (aged-couple) reporting stress.

It is possible to rework the data presented by Moore and Crawford to produce a different explanation of their percentages for Type IV and Type V families. The 35 per cent of Type V "families" reporting stress is by definition 35 per cent of the individuals concerned. However, this is not the case for the 54 per cent of Type IV families in which stress was reported. For this group there are twice as many individuals as families, since each family is an aged couple, but a Type IV family was counted as reporting stress even though the report ap-

[8] Moore and Crawford describe the basis of the family typology used in their study as follows:

"1. The basic American family composition is of an unextended, conjugal type, containing only parents and children. . . .

"3. The most obvious criterion of differences in the family cycle will be the presence or absence of 'aged' members; 'aged' being arbitrarily defined as those individuals 65 years of age or older.

"4. Families containing aged members will vary in composition according to four patterns: (A) a complete extended family including three or more generations; (B) a broken extended family, usually with the parent generation broken, leaving the grandparent-grandchild relation or some other combination; (C) the aged-parent couple . . . ; and (D) one single aged person who represented a 'residual' family" (pp. 6-7).

The unextended, conjugal family was designated as Type I, and Patterns A, B, C, and D were designated as Types II, III, IV, and V, respectively.

plied to only one member. When the data are reworked to show the number of individuals rather than the number of families for whom stress was reported, the percentage is approximately 40 instead of 54, a figure which is quite comparable to the 35 per cent of individuals in Type V families reporting stress. Unfortunately it is not possible to determine whether these percentages are above or below the percentage of individuals in Type I families for whom stress was reported.

Despite this interpretation, the Moore and Crawford hypothesis that there is long-run post-disaster stress which varies with the structure of family relationships deserves further investigation, particularly for the aged who are involved in a wide variety of such relationships to a greater extent than are other age groups. Studies utilizing a similar hypothesis for nondisaster crisis situations might offer valuable comparative data for isolating what, if anything, is peculiar to the disaster situation.

Reactions to Loss: A Hypothesis of Relative Deprivation

The problem of stress is only one aspect of the more general problem of the reactions of victims to their experiences, and among these experiences few, if any, are so pervasive as that of deprivation. From one point of view a natural disaster is a situation characterized by sudden, mass deprivation to which victims and community must adapt. Despite this, few studies have undertaken a systematic, explicit investigation of this dimension of disaster. Among the exceptions one may note Marks and Fritz (1954), Moore and Crawford (1955), and Wolfenstein (1957). These studies have indicated strong tendencies for victims to understate their deprivations, to view the future optimistically in spite of deprivation, to define deprivation as supernatural punishment, and to accept the punishment as a lesson. Marks and Fritz go a step further in their analysis of "loss involvement" in the Judsonia tornado, but it is fair to say that the area of differential feelings of deprivation—relative deprivation—remains almost unexplored.[9]

On the whole surprisingly little use has been made of deprivation models in the study of disaster, particularly by sociologists. It may be suggested that this "scotoma" derives from their preoccupation with disorganization-reorganization models (e.g., Ellemers and in't Veld-Langeveld, 1955; Form and Nosow, 1958; Moore, 1958b; Nauta and van Strien, 1955; van Doorn-Janssen, 1955; Wallace, 1956). One well-

[9] Although a few studies of natural disaster have dealt with feelings about deprivation, so far as the writer is aware only Lammers (1955) has made explicit use of the concept of relative deprivation. His context is an attempt to account for some aspects of host-evacuee tensions in terms of social class factors.

known study (Form and Nosow, 1958) even seems to deny the relevance of deprivation: "In the every-day, common-sense definition, disaster is thought of as mass destruction of property and extensive injury and death to persons. Yet massive damage to property and persons on the battlefield is not considered a disaster. . . . the difference between disaster and nondisaster is that under disaster conditions social organization in some ways becomes disrupted" (p. 11).

However this may be for sociologists, it should be obvious that victims, convergers, and others apply "the every-day, common-sense definition" to their situations, and from this point of view a disaster is defined in terms of individual and mass deprivation, both absolute and relative. Actually, a disorganization-reorganization model implies a deprivation dimension, as such concepts as "convergence" (Fritz and Mathewson, 1957) and the "cornucopia theory" (Wallace, 1956) demonstrate.

There is no intention of suggesting here that a deprivation model is better than a disorganization-reorganization model in the study of disaster. Both are useful and necessary and direct attention to different aspects of the total situation.

In reading interviews with older disaster victims one gets the impression of what Marks and Fritz call a "high sense of deprivation" in many cases. As an example they quote the following from a Judsonia interview:

> " 'Ma, don't worry about it,' he says, 'you can live with us out at the house.' And I said, 'Yes, but I'd never be satisfied without a home, I've always had a home . . . as welcome as I could be . . . I feel like the young—I don't think it's right for two families in one house, that's the way I feel about it' " (1954, p. 340).

It is easy to find close parallels to this quotation, as the following excerpt from an interview with a Worcester victim illustrates:

> "That's another reason makes me feel so bad about the whole thing, you know. I did sacrifice, I admit that, like every other fella like me that tries to do these things, you know—buy a home. . . . Sacrificing —only to see it all wiped out . . ."

There are two instances of statistical data which support this impression. The Marks and Fritz analysis of loss involvement found that "the impact cases with high property loss only have a higher proportion of older people than any of the other loss categories" (1954, p. 456). Specifically they found that 77 per cent of the persons reporting high property loss only were forty-five years of age and over, although only half of the sample fell into this age group. In their study of the

Dallas tornado, Moore and Friedsam (1959) found that although most respondents of all ages reported that their loss was about the same or less than their neighbors and that they received about the same amount of help in evacuation and in restoring their homes, respondents sixty years of age and over were considerably more likely than those under sixty to give a "high deprivation" response. The older respondents reported their losses as greater and their help in evacuation as less with approximately twice the frequency of younger respondents, and they reported less help in restoring their homes with half again the frequency of younger respondents.[10]

The materials cited above offer no more than a hint, but a hypothesis involving the concept of relative deprivation seems to offer the best way to conceptualize the problem of differential reactions of younger and older persons to disaster-caused losses. One would expect to find that following a disaster, with the level of "absolute deprivation" controlled, the proportion of older persons indicating a sense of high deprivation will exceed the proportion of younger persons making similar responses. Since this position seems tenable, at least as a hypothesis, the discussion which follows will concern itself with the possible dynamics of a high sense of deprivation in the aged.

In common with many other victims, older persons stress the loss of symbolic assets, particularly their homes.[11] Excerpts from an interview with an elderly woman which Moore reports (1958b) are typical:

> "The other place was the first place we ever owned."
>
> ". . . we were very attached to it. Something dear to us . . . we both started and built it with our own hands, saved for it."
>
> ". . . I'll get out there and get to looking at the houses and I'll

[10] One criticism that may be raised is to what degree the evaluations of respondents are based on realistic appraisals of their condition and the help they received. It may be, for example, that the difference between older and younger persons in response to the question of help in restoring the home is less than the difference in responses to the question on help in evacuation because relatives who could not get to the scene in time to be of assistance in evacuation could be there to help in restoration. In some measure all evaluations may be reality based, but this begs the question. The crucial issue is who chooses whom and why when he is asked to compare his misfortunes with the intentionally vague "neighbors." As Merton and Kitt (1950, p. 52) point out, ". . . 'deprivation' is the incidental and particularized component of the concept of relative deprivation, whereas the more significant nucleus of the concept is its stress upon social and psychological experience as 'relative.' "

[11] Moore (1958b) has placed considerable emphasis on victim expressions concerning the home as a symbol: "When the home was intact, the family was intact; when the home was destroyed, the family was in peril. Further, . . . new houses did not mean new homes" (p. 252).

> think, 'Well, we've got a much prettier place than we did have to live, but it just ain't home.' "

Often the object of sentiment is nothing so dramatic or expensive as the home. An older woman in San Angelo and another in Judsonia refer to the losses of the trees around their homes. A sixty-one-year-old woman in Worcester says that she had "got a new pocketbook an' a new wallet an' that's what I kept asking for. Of all the things in the house, that's what I wanted."

Another older woman in Worcester states that case as well as it can be put when she describes her son's search through their ruined home:

> "I told him 'Go and get my diamond ring,' a few little things that I had and I said, 'Go and get those.' And every place that I sent him, it seemed as though everything was broken open but the things were there and he took them.
>
> "He found my diamond ring; he found his own ring and a few little things that you know, that I wanted to save—never could *replace*, memories that I cherish."

What appears to be most unique about the older person's view of his losses is his preoccupation with time. Many of the interviews include explicit references of this nature: "We worked 28 years"; "after working all those years"; "lived there twenty-seven years and lived there before for a long time"; "There's Mr. . . . , been there for thirty-five years, I guess"; "We've been married 52 years, happily married 52 years, and look what happened to her"; " . . . my career in there had been for 39 years . . ."; "losing your home and everything after twenty years of having—collecting things, you know, and losing them in a matter of minutes." These excerpts suggest that for many older persons what has been destroyed is not only an object but time itself.

In an attempt to explain the tendency of (American) disaster victims to understate their losses, Wolfenstein (1957, pp. 178-179) has emphasized "a very general American feeling that belongings are replaceable." Her emphasis on "this sense of easy replaceability" must be inverted to make it applicable to an interpretation of feelings of deprivation in the aged, but her discussion of the dynamics of that belief indicates how this may be done. She mentions "the prevailing feeling that one will find just as good or better as one moves along" and says: "Since the sense of one's own adequacy depends on the activity of getting, starting over again is less distressful than where self-esteem depends more on the static condition of having" (p. 179). Later, she adds: "The more belongings are included in the definition of the self the more vulnerable one is to losing parts of oneself" (p. 179).

If Wolfenstein is correct, it would appear to follow that if older persons are less able to see themselves in "the activity of getting," if they see themselves as unable to start over again, then belongings would be more important to the definition of self; "the static condition of having" (or "losing" in disaster situations) would be more important to them than to younger persons. Proof of these suppositions cannot be offered, but recent studies of the aging process (Henry, 1956; Henry and Cumming, 1959; Rosen and Neugarten, 1960) seem to support them. Rosen and Neugarten, for example, comment that the findings of their study "lend support to the hypothesis that with increased age there is less energy available to the ego for responding to, or maintaining former levels of involvement in the outside world. The implication is that the older person tends . . . to give up self-assertiveness, and to avoid rather than to embrace challenge" (pp. 65-66).

It is in this general context that the significance of quotations used to illustrate the preoccupation of older disaster victims with time becomes apparent. Although they are couched in terms which seem to make them measures of the past, they may be equally, if not more, evaluations of the future, for time—as the future—may be "seen" differently from different points on the life cycle.[12]

The interviews can be used once more for illustration. A sixty-nine-year-old woman in Worcester expresses her difficulty in defining the future by saying: "I'm beginnin', I'm beginnin' to wonder if . . . it's worthwhile thinkin' anymore." An older farmer who lived near Judsonia and whose economic status was high enough that he was denied Red Cross assistance in rebuilding his home says: ". . . they said we had a reputation that we could borrow any kind of money we wanted. I told him yes, that was all right, we could do that all right . . . I could get that money, but I said who's going to pay it back."

Not surprisingly, relatives and friends take a similar view of the aged and the future. A woman in Arkansas, herself an aged semi-invalid, speaks of friends and acquaintances: "Well, they're just like I am. They're old and about lived their life and they don't want to have to look at the wreck nor ruins of it and think it over." Another woman with an elderly mother and several other elderly relatives echoes:

[12] Kuhlen (1956, p. 25) has suggested that "the total psychological impact of serious losses" in health, economic status, and social relations may be less significant in early adulthood or middle age than in old age "simply because of the greater opportunity for repair offered by time yet ahead."

"I mean, uh, you find several people; not an awful lot, but older people, a lot of 'em feel that way . . . they think, they just don't have what it takes to come back. And something like this it is a big challenge for a young person that's lost everything."

An excerpt from an interview with a woman in Worcester includes virtually all of the elements under discussion:

"Well, we're lucky to be alive . . . I loved my little home . . . We had a nice little yard for the children an' everything. But we're young. We can rebuild . . . We can work and build *another* home because we're young and we have the rest of our lives ahead of us. The older ones are the ones I feel badly for. They've worked all their life and are probably all worked out now and haven't the will to go on like young people do."

Probably the one characteristic common to virtually all of the older people who have been quoted or discussed above is that they had something to lose. Several were obviously home owners, most were heads of households, several were still employed at the time that disaster struck, etc. In these respects they are "typical" of the aged, at least of the "younger aged," a majority of whom do own their own homes, are heads of households, and many of whom are still employed. But these cases are not typical of the many aged persons who are living on minimal retirement incomes, who live alone or with relatives in a dependent relationship or who are in institutional situations, and who in many cases are extremely isolated within their communities. These are the aged for whom a high degree of "absolute" deprivation exists before disaster strikes. With so little to lose, there is likely to be no difference between their pre- and post-disaster status. The interviews suggest that older persons so situated will be characterized not by feelings of deprivation, but by feelings of resignation, by the feeling that nothing has really been changed—neither self nor situation.

An excerpt from an interview with a very elderly, almost blind, woman who had been virtually at the center of the impact area in Waco illustrates this attitude:

"Well, when I have troubles, I just pray to the Lord to help me and to relieve me of certain things if it is His will and I think that maybe we might want things that if it would happen some other way, it would be better. He knows better than we do and that is the way I look at it. . . . You just have to learn to take it, that's all."

An elderly isolated male victim in Judsonia says:

"I'm getting pretty aged and I just couldn't hold out to work none by the day so I just plan on stayin' there and doin' what I possibly can do.

I guess I'll get me a house there sometime, or other, I don't know how soon. But I'll be thankful whenever they do fix it for me."

Very few interviews were located with aged victims who had suffered bereavement. Thus there is no basis for comparing the management of grief and feelings of desolation in older and younger persons. However, studies of bereavement by Lindemann (1944) and by Stern and his associates (1951) do offer a point of departure. The former has directed attention to the symptoms of acute grief in cases of disaster-caused bereavement (not necessarily of the aged), while the latter examined grief reactions in older persons (but not disaster-caused bereavement). Stern's findings indicate differences in grief in the older persons he studied as compared with Lindemann's subjects, particularly in the area of guilt feelings, which he notes as low among older persons. He also notes tendencies toward somatic illness and toward self-isolation among the bereaved aged.

Rehabilitation

Most studies of natural disaster have been done within a short period of time during or immediately following the post-impact emergency period and are of little use to a consideration of the problems of the rehabilitation phase. The notable exception is the study by Moore and Crawford (1955) which was undertaken several months after the tornadoes in Waco and San Angelo. Its data on rehabilitation are unparalleled elsewhere in the literature. Their findings suggest at several points that there are significant differences in rehabilitation processes between families with older members and those without.

Possibly their most important findings relate to the financing of home reconstruction. Their data indicate clearly that the percentages of families receiving aid in rebuilding their homes were considerably higher in each of the four family types made up of or including aged persons than in the non-aged or conjugal type. Furthermore, the average amount of aid received was greater in each of the four "aged family" types than in the latter. An investigation of the sources of funds used in reconstruction showed that the percentages of "aged families" using relief agency funds only were also considerably higher than that for the conjugal type. When it is recalled that relief agency funds are granted on the basis of "need," this finding takes an added significance. Curiously enough, they also found that the percentages of families using personal resources only in reconstruction were very slightly higher for the "aged families" than for the conjugal type. Whether this was due to lesser damage or greater resources on the part of a number of families is not known. As might have been expected, smaller percentages of three of the four "aged family" types incurred debt. The one exception was found in the intact three-generational family, which like the conjugal family usually has a younger person as primary wage-earner.

The two family types made up of aged persons only reported with considerably less frequency than those with younger members that only family members repaired or rebuilt the home, and conversely they reported with greater frequency the use of a contractor. A comparison of the average number of rooms in pre- and post-disaster housing showed no change for conjugal families but a decrease for three of the four "aged family" types, with the greatest decrease occurring in the one-person, residual families. The easily understandable exception was the intact, three-generational family which, like the conjugal family, had experienced no change. As the authors point out, these changes may be related to the "need" criterion of relief agencies.

The evidence described above leaves little doubt that families with aged members are likely to require more than their proportionate "share" of the activities of relief agencies following a disaster and points to the desirability of further study of the contact between older persons and relief organizations, particularly Red Cross. It is possible, for example, that the Red Cross use of the "need" criterion in making awards for disaster relief may have in many cases a considerably greater impact on the status of older persons than it does on younger persons. This seems to be the implication of the finding concerning the decrease in average number of rooms per house. In this connection it is worth noting that although he does not mention Red Cross in this context, Fogleman (1958, p. 303) reports that change in the size of houses was mentioned frequently in Cameron Parish during the rehabilitation phase. As one of his respondents put it, "Old people that had bigger houses has got smaller houses, and younger people who had smaller houses has got bigger ones."

The possible impact of the "need" criterion on older persons is also suggested by a case growing out of Hurricane Audrey in which a recommendation was made not to re-establish an elderly woman in a small business that she had operated because of her age. On the other hand Moore and Crawford (1955, p. 25) suggest the possibility that at least some of the aged families in their sample were probably better housed after the tornado than they were before. Presumably these were aged individuals and couples whose pre-disaster housing was substandard.

There is also an implication in the interviews that communicating relief agency policy to many older persons is difficult. For example, a

Red Cross official in Judsonia refers to the difficulty of explaining to an eighty-two-year-old woman "in her terms, on her level" why her house cannot be rebuilt immediately. That he was justified in his concern is evidenced in another Judsonia interview with a woman aged sixty-five who insisted that she had been denied Red Cross aid because of her age. A similar story of denial of aid to an aged couple resulted in the beginning of an independent relief campaign in a community near Cameron Parish. Upon investigation the difficulty proved to stem from the inability of the couple, whose English was poor, to communicate with the Red Cross worker.

Although Moore and Crawford imply that their four "aged family" types expressed negative attitudes towards Red Cross somewhat less frequently than did the conjugal family type, the extent to which older persons contribute to the criticism of Red Cross which is so often characteristic of the aftermath of disaster is not known. Several interviews contain intense criticisms, and although these criticisms are much the same as those made by younger persons, there are comments which suggest that older persons who do not receive awards are inclined to believe that their age was a factor. One might also speculate that those aged persons who do receive awards but who perceive their status as having been lowered would also be highly critical.

Summary and Prospect

At the outset of this chapter it was observed that the available studies and data on the aged in disaster were such as to make its conclusions tentative and to be regarded as hypotheses for future research rather than as firm findings. Among these hypotheses have been the following:

1. That older persons are less likely than younger to receive warning, and that this relationship will hold whether the source of warning is informal (from relatives, friends, neighbors) or from the more formal mass media.
2. That obstacles to pre-impact evacuation, including reluctance to evacuate, will be greater among older than among younger persons.
3. That older persons are less likely than younger persons to engage in behavior oriented toward individuals and groups beyond self and family in the rescue and immediate post-impact phase.
4. That where it is intact, the mother-daughter relationship will tend more than any other family relationship to structure intergenerational contacts in pre- and post-impact evacuation and in search activities.

5. That where older evacuees are sheltered by younger persons, particularly when children are present, significant tensions may develop.

6. That older persons are relatively more likely than younger persons to become physical casualties, both directly and indirectly.

7. That although some older persons may become temporarily disturbed by the destruction of their accustomed pattern of life, older persons are no more likely than younger persons to become psychiatric casualties.

8. That the sense of deprivation resulting from disaster-caused losses will be greater in older persons.

9. That extremely low-status older persons will experience strong feelings of resignation rather than deprivation.

10. That the relative needs of older persons in rehabilitation will be greater than those of younger persons, and that as a consequence they will make relatively greater "demands" on the services of disaster relief agencies.

11. That a "need" criterion, used by disaster relief agencies, may have differential effects on the status of older and younger persons.

Although the materials which have been reviewed lend varying degrees of support to these hypotheses, it is reasonably clear that older persons do constitute a special risk group in time of disaster. The data on their "relative vulnerability" to death and injury and on their need for aid in rehabilitation are among the best avilable. If they are not completely convincing, this is an area in which it should be possible to do further research, even on past disasters, without running too many of the usual risks of *ex post facto* design or of retrospective distortion. It should be possible to secure reasonably good data on deaths by age from one or more of several sources: state vital statistics offices, Red Cross, or local newspapers. Data on major injuries might also be available from the latter two or from hospitals. One could not expect any of these sources to yield data on secondary or psychiatric casualties.

Assuming that they could be opened to qualified research personnel, the Red Cross files and possibly those of the Small Business Administration could enrich understanding of the rehabilitation needs of many older persons. However, these sources could contribute only to studies of the immediate post-disaster needs of limited groups of aged victims. The broader approach to rehabilitation used by Moore and Crawford (1955) in Waco and San Angelo should be refined and replicated with reference to other disasters. Furthermore, a truly long-run study of rehabilitation, including all age groups, in which a community might be revisited at various intervals of time up to two or more years after a disaster, would yield data not now available in any form to students of disaster.

The hypothesis that the aged present special problems in warning and evacuation appears to be warranted, but the evidence, particularly concerning warning, is less convincing than that concerning casualties and rehabilitation. The several sources which touch on evacuation of the aged are in general agreement on the reluctance of older persons to evacuate, but there is little beyond speculation on why this is so or what its consequences may be. The materials on warning do little more than suggest hypotheses for future investigation. As pointed out above, research into the warning phase is often complicated by the very short period of time which it encompasses in some types of disaster and by the fact that in some disasters virtually no one, aged or young, receives warning; but it is also true that warnings without disaster, false alerts, etc., occur frequently enough to offer many research possibilities for this phase which cannot be paralleled for other phases of the disaster sequence.

Consideration of evacuation brings the role of the extended family into the foreground. There can no longer be any doubt of its importance in disaster situations, and as Wallace (1956, p. 95) has observed in his study of Worcester this "is particularly interesting in view of the commonly stated sociological assumption that extended family ties are relatively unimportant in urban life in America." But granting the significance of the extended family in disaster only raises further questions. Can Powell's hypothesis on the importance of the mother-daughter relationship, which receives strong impressionistic support from the interviews, be validated? If so, does it require an essentially psychiatric explanation in such terms as infantile regression, or can it be explained in terms of residential propinquity? To what extent does the latter reduce to the former? What happens when an extended family offers "alternatives," e.g., a sibling's home and the parental home as a refuge? How long do the "crisis role obligations" last and what areas of behavior do they entail? When and under what conditions does their fulfillment produce stress? In answering such questions, disaster research could make substantial contributions to the body of general sociological theory.

The conclusions relating to stress and to feelings of deprivation in the aged are the most impressionistic of all. In large part this is simply a reflection of the status of these problems in the study of disaster, and this status in turn largely reflects the difficulties of research into these areas. Problems of definition and comparability beset the presently available materials on stress, while the interviews used on deprivation were collected for other purposes and apparently on no other sampling basis than the availability of a victim and/or one or more of his relatives. But if a disaster has long-run consequences for its victims, they are most likely to be found in emotional disturbances and in changed definitions of one's life-space (and time). For this reason continued research on these topics is vital.

The hypotheses developed in this report have concentrated on the differential impact of disaster on older and younger persons. What is needed to test them is not so much research *on* as research which will *include* the aged. Each could be tested almost as a by-product of any well-designed project directed toward one or more phases of the disaster sequence, which utilized age categories. This is a way of saying again that they rest on an admittedly crude, categorical definition of "the aged," but to the extent that they can be verified, they will point to a need for the more sophisticated analysis which will rest on models that take into account the variety of roles that older persons play in today's society.

Part Three

BEHAVIOR OF SOCIAL UNITS IN DISASTER

IN THIS SECTION we approach the study of disaster behavior from a sociological point of view. Groups and institutions, social structures and functions—as they are affected by disaster—become the foci of research.

This approach permits, of course, the examination of a wide array of social units: families, agencies of government, formal organizations that operate in relief and rescue, units of social stratification, chance groups of survivors brought together by a common fate, and many others. The units taken up in the three chapters of this section are, then, merely representative and not exhaustive of the variety to which research is or can be directed.

Chapter Seven considers the small unit of the family. As the most intimate and enduring of primary groups, it can be expected to be peculiarly influential in mediating between individual human beings and the pattern of social disruption around them. To a considerable extent, the individual suffers disaster on a stage set by the family through its demands upon him, its support of him, and its unique identity with his personal vicissitudes. But also, as an entity in itself, the family as a feature of social structure will exhibit its own sources of resistance or vulnerability to acute crisis, and may either rebound or disintegrate in the wake of disaster—just as do individuals. How it will react must depend upon features of its internal structure in relation to the social system around it. The varieties of family structure and their implications for survival of disaster provide the focus of this chapter.

Choosing for attention a larger unit than the family, Chapter Eight looks at the various groups of people that perform important roles in rescue during disaster and its aftermath—groups that run from highly organized, formal agencies to relatively unorganized masses of people who must cope with danger and destruction as best they can. For each kind of group, the evidence shows that certain types of tasks are especially appropriate, and that certain crucial conditions govern whether or not these tasks will be effectively carried out. The discussion emphasizes particularly the demonstrable effects of differing patterns of communication within and among such working groups.

In Chapter Nine, the disaster-struck community is also approached from a broad point of view. However, it is treated as a total social system, and the examination of research findings is directed toward testing suppositions about the course of events in disaster that appear to be suggested by general social-systems theory.

▶ *seven*

FAMILIES IN DISASTER

Reuben Hill and Donald A. Hansen

WHEN DISASTERS STRIKE, families suffer. Members are killed or hurt, possessions are lost, homes are damaged. This we know. But what are the more specific effects of disaster on the family? Why do some families fall apart in the wake of disaster while others emerge almost unscathed, perhaps even strengthened by the stress? Are there general patterns of family activity in the course of the disaster? Conversely, what are the effects of family behavior on the response of a community to disaster? We do not know the answers to all these questions.

Wild guesses are not necessary, however, for if we play several streams of related findings over these questions, insights flow. These insights help us specify hypotheses and thus begin the steps toward useful theory.

In this chapter we draw together two sets of research findings: those about individuals and organizations in disaster and those about families under other stresses such as bereavement, war separation, and loss of job. Separately, each set of findings reveals little about families in disaster, for one ignores families and the other ignores disasters. Combined, however, they generate many promising hypotheses, which can be tested using the concepts and methods of family sociology.

We ask two basic questions in this chapter: How do families behave in disaster and how do disasters affect families? The first three sections deal with these questions, and emphasize the importance of community contexts for families in disaster. Then, with an eye on research, we suggest a number of theoretical frameworks that might be used in testing the hypotheses that emerge from our discussion. In the final section we attempt to move from present, sketchy knowledge, to implications for the family in thermonuclear attack.

Much in this chapter is speculative, and we urge the reader to question every statement. If our work does no more than arouse argument, it will prove valuable, for argument in turn may generate research. And research is needed.

Family Behavior in Disaster

THE EFFECT OF LOVE AND LOCATION IN DISASTER BEHAVIOR

When sirens scream of approaching disaster, minds turn to loved ones. If they are near enough, mothers run to protect their children, and men seek their families. They huddle together and support one another through the stress, and when it has passed, they rescue and nurse those they love.

Not until all intimates (primary-group members) within reach are safe, will an individual willingly lend his support and aid to other persons. Only then will an individual help less intimate friends and organizations (secondary groups) with whom he identifies. Strangers may be aided, and then possessions and property are looked after—first one's own, then those of close friends and relatives, and finally those of others less intimate.

In short, love dictates to the mind of the man in disaster. But the body cannot always follow the mind; if loved ones are beyond reach, the man may act toward those he loves less, or loves not at all.

Just before disaster strikes, an individual behaves according to the length of time he thinks remains before impact. When warning time allows, the individual who is separated from his family will leave friends to fend for themselves and rush home. When time does not allow, however, we suspect he will seek self-protection and may even seek to protect others near him.

What of the family grouped together before the impact? Will challenges be met quickly and members protected? It is hard to say. On the one hand we would expect the family to respond quickly and sensibly to danger warnings. The established authority and communication patterns, and the presence of loved and valued persons should increase sensitivity to threat and the readiness to act to meet that threat. On the other hand, the family is poorly organized to meet threats and hardships, for its very young and very old members are often ill-equipped to meet sudden challenges. Answers await research.

As the disaster hits, the individual continues to act toward those persons or objects available to him; if his loved ones are not near, he can be alert and even protective to others through the impact. But after impact, only the rare person can do anything but search until the fate of his loved ones is known. Usually he must actually see his loved ones face to face. Not until then can he be depended upon to enter into general rescue work, though he may make hit-or-miss attempts to help persons he chances upon. Once he is clear about his family, however, even if he finds them dead, the individual is often able to enter into community work, to all appearances calm and controlled.

After the family has been united, forced separation may cause renewed anxiety, and individuals may again be partially incapacitated. Just being together is deeply important following impact, even in loosely-knit families.

War research in both England (Titmuss, 1950) and Germany (U.S. Strategic Bombing Survey, 1947c) points up the importance of the family to persons under stress. In both countries, evacuation programs were seriously threatened because parents, having experienced the danger, preferred to keep their families together than to leave their children alone in relative safety. At times, there were more children returning to the city than leaving it. In Germany, official efforts to stem the flow of returning evacuees brought trouble:

> The morale of remaining members of evacuees' families was a particularly serious problem for the party, and there is evidence that both mood and behavior were adversely affected in this way. Desire of family members to be reunited was a major factor in the unauthorized return of evacuees. . . . Workers claimed that their willingness to work would be impaired unless members of the families were permitted to return . . . the counter-measures against returnees . . . provoked a storm of resistance, the effects of which were spread right to the front lines. The problems of family separation thus created a serious dilemma in the evacuation program (U.S. Strategic Bombing Survey, 1947c, p. 71).

The importance of the family to morale and to the success of any disaster program is further confirmed by the flood research in England and Holland. We see no serious reason to doubt that the same would hold for the United States.

THE EFFECT OF FAMILY ROLES ON DISASTER BEHAVIOR

Love and location may dictate whom or what the individual acts toward in disaster, but what he does is determined greatly by the roles he accepts.

Few if any roles hold more powerful command over an individual than his roles in the family. A parent alone with children, for example, may react far more quickly and effectively to danger than if he were alone. Sometimes his family roles may even lead him to act in ways an observer might think "crazy" or "panicky." The behavior of one father illustrates the effect of family responsibility: Sensing the approach of a tornado, he ran to the theater where his children were, and stood outside, holding the doors shut. It was not the tornado he had to hold back, but the people inside, who were shoving to get out. They didn't realize that if the doors were opened, the building would collapse. The father knew, however, and knew that those doors protected his children (Logan, Killian, and Marrs, 1952, p. 88). Again the effect of roles is seen in the preacher who, after the explosion of the "Grandcamp" started to flee town; then, to the surprise of his companion, he remembered his family and went back—in spite of, or perhaps because of, the fact that he thought the situation very dangerous (p. 88).

From his summary of studies of panic behavior, Quarantelli (in a personal communication) writes that having responsibility for someone else is an almost sure preventive of panic flight. "While I have almost never found any instances of a family group breaking in panic, I have found instances where the actions of family members to protect one another were interpreted by others as panic behavior." At times they may appear to be thoughtless individuals in flight, when really they flee as a group, their idea essentially being, "Let's get out of here before other people panic." As a general rule, though, intact families rarely panic.

In some situations, however, roles can hinder a family from meeting the threat of disaster. If the family is rigidly organized, "low status" dependent members may wait too long for the decision of the family head. When the high-status family member refuses to heed the warnings, or makes a poor estimation of the situation, the entire family may suffer. A similar status influence may have appeared in the schoolhouse disasters studied by Perry and Perry (1959). A white school inspector, present in the small Negro schoolhouse, purportedly failed to take charge until it was too late; the teacher and students, meanwhile, would not, or could not, act so long as the "high-status" white man was there. They were waiting for his cue and the delay set the scene for disaster.

Most often, however, the more clear-cut the responsibilities, the more effectively a person meets a disaster. Marks and Fritz (1954, pp. 426-428) have shown that, compared to persons without dependents, men with homes and dependents both prepared better and acted more rationally in all stages of disaster.

Why does responsibility make such a difference? The crucial element seems to be the way the person thinks of himself. "Others need me," he seems to think. "What I do may save or cost their lives." This thought helps him to stay in "emotional check" during the first moments of stress, and then quickly to rise to active aid. This thesis is supported by the observation that a woman will depend on her husband to protect the family, but when he is absent, she will quickly step into the protective, leadership role.

The thesis is also supported by the repeated findings that in stress situations small children take their cues for behavior from adults, and that the adults sooner or later notice the cue-taking, and from then on try to set better examples. In a concentration camp run by the Japanese in the Philippines, Vaughan reported that parents soon became aware that "what children believed about conditions under which they lived was more important than the actual conditions. Realizing this, value attitudes were deliberately patterned for children by their parents" (Vaughan, 1949, p. 136). The same strategy, though certainly more spontaneous and less well developed, is illustrated time after time in interviews with parents after disasters.

If everyone with dependents is caring for his family, is all the community rescue work done by those without families? Immediately after impact this may be the case, for even when he also feels loyal to other groups, the individual will almost always choose to stay with his family. Killian, surveying disaster studies a decade ago, decided:

> The choice required of the greatest number of individuals was the one between the family and other groups, principally the employment group or the community. . . . The great majority of persons interviewed who were involved in such dilemmas resolved them in favor of the loyalty to the family or, in some cases, to friendship groups (Killian, 1952, p. 311).

There are important exceptions, especially among those trained in roles that might be important in disaster. Refinery workers in Texas City stayed on the job until their units were safely shut down. Ministers, doctors, firemen, officials, executives, and others are expected to turn from their families, who are physically safe but perhaps emotionally upset, to perform their community roles.

As the hours pass, more and more men leave their families to help in the rescue. Who are these men? What kinds of families do they have? There is little evidence, though Friedsam (Chapter Six, this volume) observes that older men are most often family-oriented in disaster; younger men, after caring for their families, tend to enter into community work. Is this difference in the age groups due only to energy and enthusiasm, or might it be that the older men are either more dependent on their families, or less concerned with their communities? Westie (1954) has observed that juveniles—especially those labeled "irresponsible"—can be avid, if not effective, community workers. Their efforts, of course, might be explained by natural teen-age exuberance or the desire of adolesence to assert itself. We suspect, however, that comparison of irresponsible adolescents with those who are more family-oriented would show the irresponsible youth more active in community rescue and the others more engrossed with family efforts. And we suspect the same relationship between degree of autonomy and disaster behavior will be found in adults, with the exception of some who hold important disaster roles.

The importance of family roles affects the community in disaster, particularly in cases where the individual's role is crucial to the community. But more interesting to family research, and ultimately of great import to the community, is this observation: An individual who meets community needs may neglect the needs of his family and set off an array of disrupting reactions, decreasing family empathy and communication—in short, endangering his family's ability to adjust. Studies have not yet focused on this possibility, but it leads us to our next question: What are the effects of disaster on the family?

The Impact of Disaster on the Family

Disaster studies have noted differences in types of disaster agents (e.g., floods, explosions, hurricanes) and in characteristics of disasters (e.g., predictability, inevitability, controllability, origin, and intent). But within each of these categories there is also variation: though each family is victim of the same disaster agent, there is great difference in the intensity and duration of impact on the various victims, the breadth of destruction in the area surrounding each victim, and the types of destruction (death, injury, property damage).

To focus on the differences of impact, we must find a way to translate these variations in strain into researchable terms; this is done through use of the concept "family hardships." Hardships are those complications in a stress situation which demand family competencies that the event itself may have temporarily paralyzed or destroyed. Not all hardships brought on by the disaster agent are immediately felt. A shattered house is at once seen as shattered; a broken arm cannot be ignored for long. But a neurosis triggered by the shock of impact may be a long time in developing, and the family may not feel it until months later.

Though an impact may last only minutes, it can harshly test a family. Morale, solidarity, organization, and competencies may be strengthened or completely disrupted as family members give subtle cues about their feelings toward one another; the cues, often unintentional, may be forced from family members by the strangeness and intensity of the impact. We suggest that family recovery and development will be affected by the subtle communication of love and hate, trust and fear, respect and disgust.

More obviously, recovery is affected by the way members perform their roles. Family leaders, for example, are expected to direct others and, if necessary, to expose themselves to danger in order to protect and lead. If they fail, other members may take over the leadership roles, forcing a change in the entire organization of the family. Perhaps the shift is accepted at the time, but it may lead to tensions that erupt a year later in divorce, delinquency, suicide, or some lesser symptoms.

Postponed hardships can be as dangerous to the health and productivity of the community and nation as are the hardships brought immediately by the impact. Disaster research has not studied postponed hardships, but the studies of bereavement and of the depression of the 1930's have dealt with both immediate and long-term family stresses. From these we can get some insight into family reactions which might parallel the postponed effects of disaster stress. The insight is incomplete, however, for even in the immediate adjustment to hardships of disaster and other stress, research has discovered very little.[1]

Fogleman and Parenton (1959) noted that six months after impact family roles still are being readjusted to compensate for loss of family members and to rebuild damaged properties. Crawford, following Moore and others (Moore, 1958a; Moore and Friedsam, 1959), noted the "high resiliency" of tornado-stricken families: "In most cases the disruptions were severe, and although in most instances rehabilitations had not been achieved months after the disasters, the families were still functioning as families" (Crawford, 1957, p. 285).

Helmut Schelsky (1954), studying post-World War II German families who had lived through severe bombings and the postwar deprivations of denazification and underemployment, found families in general more solid as a consequence. He explains this as a reaction to the unstable larger society in which home and family are made into a haven from the uncertainty and insecurity of the postwar world.

At this point a few generalizations emerge from the studies of nondisaster stresses. Kent Geiger (1955), studying Russian refugee families in Europe and the United States, found that political persecu-

[1] Especially for immediate hardships, there is appreciable difference between studies of disaster and of other types of stress. Primarily, the distinction lies in the fact that the misfortunes experienced by families in disaster are shared. In disaster we do not expect to find the feelings of deviance and shame or of self-blame and blame of others often noted in other stress studies. In nondisaster situations we cannot hope for a "therapeutic community" to help the family find glory in its hardships. Nonetheless, stress findings do offer useful sensitizing theory for disaster study.

tion more often solidified than disorganized families. Economic deprivation, however, was detrimental to interpersonal solidarity in the family. Though the social structures differed in the two stresses, it appears that the crucial element was the family's definition of the hardship.

Cavan (1959) found that if families were well organized before the crisis of impoverishment, they tended to remain well organized; moreover, families that had had previous successful experience with crisis tended more often to recover in a new crisis. Angell (1936), too, found well-integrated and adaptable families invulnerable to crisis; that is, they took it in stride without marked changes in organization or role structure.

Koos (1946) focused on the troubles of low-income families in New York City over a two-year period and found, among those initially disorganized by crisis, evidence of permanent demoralization, a blunting of the family's sensitivity, and a tendency to be more vulnerable in future exposures.

FAMILY RESOURCES

If a desired end of community planning against disasters is continued family functioning, we must ask: How does a community disaster become a family crisis? We have noted the difference in the "hardships" families may experience in a disaster, yet there does not seem to be any direct relationship between severity of hardships and proneness to crisis. Why? The key seems to lie in the *meaning* attached to the hardships by the family members. These definitions are constantly changing and are closely connected to the resources a family can bring into play against the hardships it meets.

Family sociology, especially in studies of depression and employment, offers the most systematic investigation of family resources. But even here research is only beginning and many questions are yet unanswered.

Robert C. Angell (1936) was the first among sociologists to explore family resources intensively. He focused on the strengths of family organization and found some families to be "crisis proof" and others "crisis prone." He employed two concepts—family integration and family adaptability. By integration he meant the "bonds of coherence and unity running through family life, of which common interests, affection, and a sense of economic interdependence are perhaps the most prominent." Adaptability referred to the family's capacity to meet obstacles and to shift courses. With these twin factors, Angell was able to explain the different reactions to sharp decreases in income during the depression. A restudy of the cases suggested the greater importance of family adaptability.

Cavan and Ranck (1938) and Koos (1946) essentially agreed that a crisis-proof family must have an agreement on role structure, subordination of personal ambitions to family goals, family satisfactions which successfully meet the physical and emotional needs of its members, and goals toward which the family is moving collectively. Having all of these, the family is adequately organized; lacking any, the family is inadequately organized and may prove vulnerable to crisis-precipitating events.

The concept of family resources allows us to translate community structures and processes into more family-focused and researchable terms. Vulnerability to disaster stress, for example, is clearly related to the family's class status. The lower-class family is restricted not only in income but also in health, energy, space, and ideas for coping with crisis; because of its hand-to-mouth existence it lacks defense in depth. On the other hand, such families may gain strength after a disaster through short-run financial gains due to moratoriums on debts and grants from relief agencies. Lower-class families may also gain status in their communities after disaster, for they have nowhere to go but up, and in the wake of severe community disruption they are offered chances to gain respect and attention by heroism or hard work. At the very least, in rescue operations, they are able to rub shoulders with "the elite."

FAMILY DEFINITIONS OF SITUATION

The vulnerability of the lower-class family is, in theory, no greater than that of the middle-class family. Each has its Achilles' heel, as is illustrated by the depression studies. Although the lower classes have fewer resources, middle-class families are more prone to overestimate their hardships, as they imagine threats to their statuses and aspirations.

Hill and Boulding (1949), studying war separation and reunion crises, perceived three possible definitions of the crisis-precipitating event: an objective definition, formulated by an impartial observer; a cultural definition, formulated by the community; and a subjective definition, provided by the family. As the sensitivity of middle-class families illustrates, the most relevant definition in determining a family's crisis-proneness is the third.

Crawford (1957), adding a variable to the schema developed by Hill, suggests that the family will define a crisis on the basis of various influences, including the nature of the event or intrusive force; the degree of hardships or kinds of problems the stress creates; the resources available to the family, which may vary during the course of the crisis sequence; the family's past experience with other crises, particularly with those of similar nature; the evaluation of the situation which may be made by others outside the family unit.

Little investigation has been made of family definitions. It would perhaps be more accurate to talk of individual members' definitions, which may or may not arrange themselves into a family-shared definition. In our discussion, however, we will be served well by the fabricated "family definition." This concept, together with those of family resources and family hardships, allows us to examine the interplay of the most important variables in the adjustment of families to the stresses of disaster.

THE COURSE OF FAMILY ADJUSTMENT TO STRESS

It is useful to present a formula for the development of family crisis: A (the stressor and hardships) → interacting with B (the family's stress-meeting resources) → interacting with C (the definition the family makes of the hardships) → produces X (the crisis).

Though the B and C factors lie within the family itself, they are closely related to family structure and values. It should be quite clear that the B factor in the formula is a prime determinant of the C factor. We can combine deficiency in resources (the B factor) and the tendency to define hardships as crisis-producing (the C factor) into one concept of "family inadequacy." The major features of this concept can be presented in a polygon wheel of interacting forces which we reproduce in Figure 7-1 from the work of E. L. Koos and David Fulcomer (see Waller and Hill, 1951, p. 462). The wheel urges us to recognize that an initial disturbance in one area of family life tends to create tensions in other areas. These tensions in turn become conflicts in their own right. The wheel is only one suggested way to depict family adequacy, and it was offered over a decade ago. To date, little has been offered to replace it, although it was obviously intended to serve only a temporary expository function.

If carried another step, into the adjustment of the family to the crisis, Koos and Fulcomer's diagram reveals again an interplay of many of the same factors which originally make families prone to crisis. Causation is just as complex in adjustment as it is in the development of crisis.

Adjustment to a crisis depends upon the adequacy of role performance of family members. Each member is expected to act in certain ways; he has special roles to play. The family succeeds only if these roles mesh with one another without too much friction. A major effect of crisis is to create a need to change the alignment of these

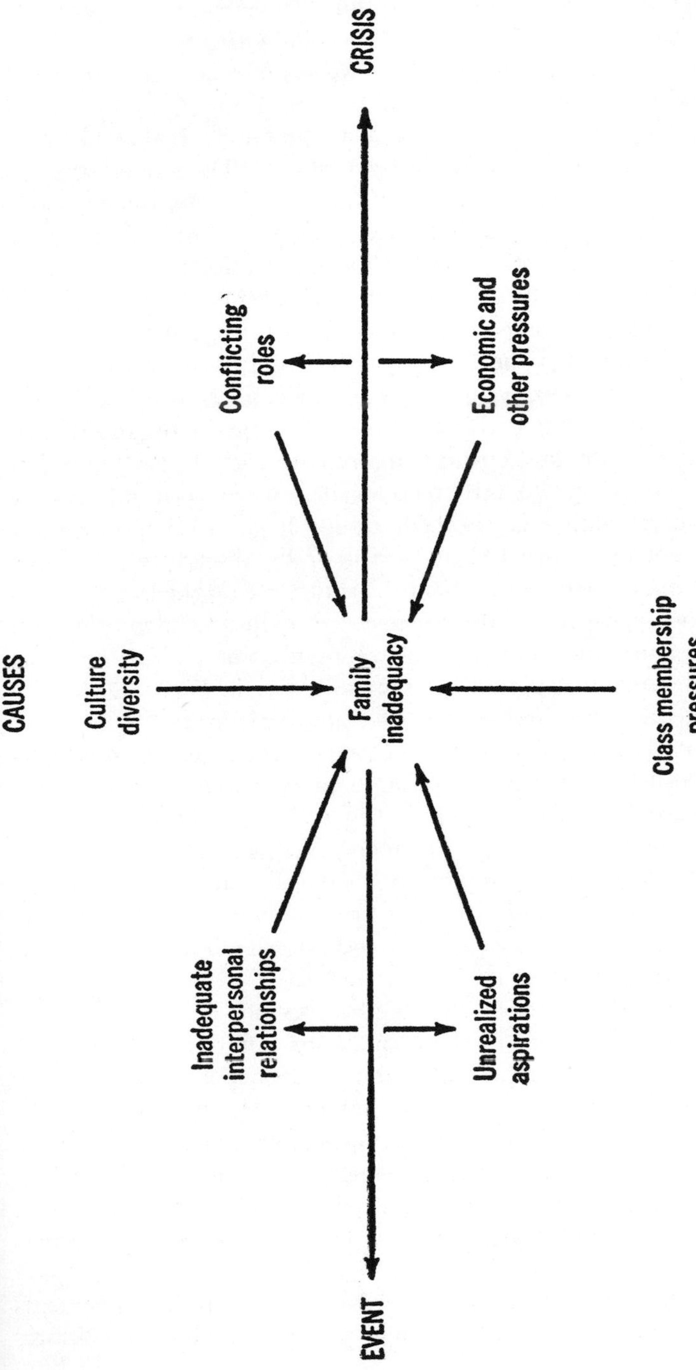

FIGURE 7-1. *A scheme for depicting the interplay of stressor event, contributing hardships, and family resources in producing a family crisis. (From Koos and Fulcomer, in Waller and Hill, 1951, p. 462.)*

roles; expectations shift, and the family finds it necessary to alter some roles and reassign others. This all takes time and energy, even if clashes and frictions are avoided. Yet physical needs cannot be denied, and the family is required to carry on business as usual during alterations. As a result, though physical needs may be met, the family is slowed up in its affectional and emotion-satisfying activity until the new patterns are worked out and avenues for expressing affection are opened once more. If roles were played well before the disaster, adjustment may be rapid; if poorly, adjustment may be slow and painful.

What can we say about the course of adjustment to crisis? It varies from family to family and from crisis to crisis, but the basic sequence may be charted in the form of an incomplete roller coaster. As the blow strikes them, family members are collectively numbed. Then, as the facts are assimilated, there follows a slump in organization—roles are played with less enthusiasm, resentments deepen, conflicts are expressed or converted into tensions that strain relations. As the depth of disorganization is reached, things begin to improve, new routines are arrived at by trial and error or by thoughtful planning, and some minimum agreements about the future are reached.

The component parts of the roller-coaster adjustment to crisis are: Crisis → disorganization → recovery → reorganization. This course of adjustment is crudely depicted by the solid line in Figure 7-2, with dotted lines representing only a few of many variations.

Reaction to community-wide disaster apparently causes modification of the roller-coaster pattern found in individual family crises. The roller-coaster pattern holds at the beginning of the disaster experience; but because the hardships are recognized, in the first days and weeks after the impact, as community-shared and accepted, recovery is marked by an almost euphoric increase in family solidarity (and in solidarity of the network of neighbors and friends). Thus we may expect the sort of pattern illustrated in Figure 7-3.

Immediately after impact, the family does not pull alone against hardships; for many persons in the community suffer, and all help one another adjust. But in families in which postponed hardships appear months and years after the impact, the family may not receive the support of others. Instead of aiding sufferers, the community may be only tolerant, indifferent, or outright hostile, and the family will be left with its own loss, demoralization, or shame. Thus we suspect that adjustment to *postponed* hardships will generally follow the pattern of Figure 7-2.

Combining the two profiles, Figure 7-4 depicts family adjustments to immediate and long-term hardships precipitated by the disaster agent.

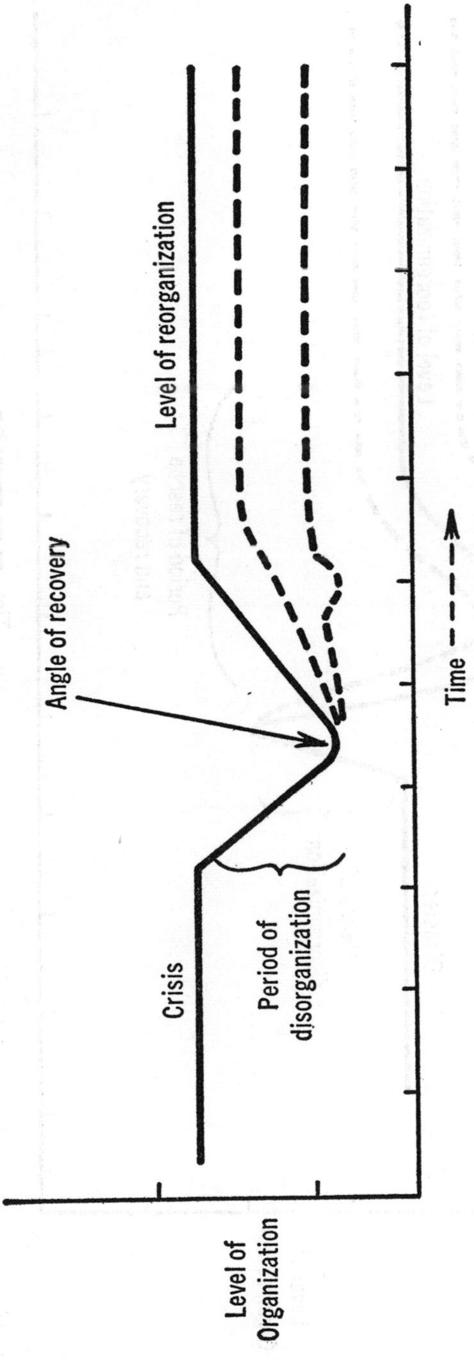

FIGURE 7-2. *Common patterns of family adjustment to crisis.*

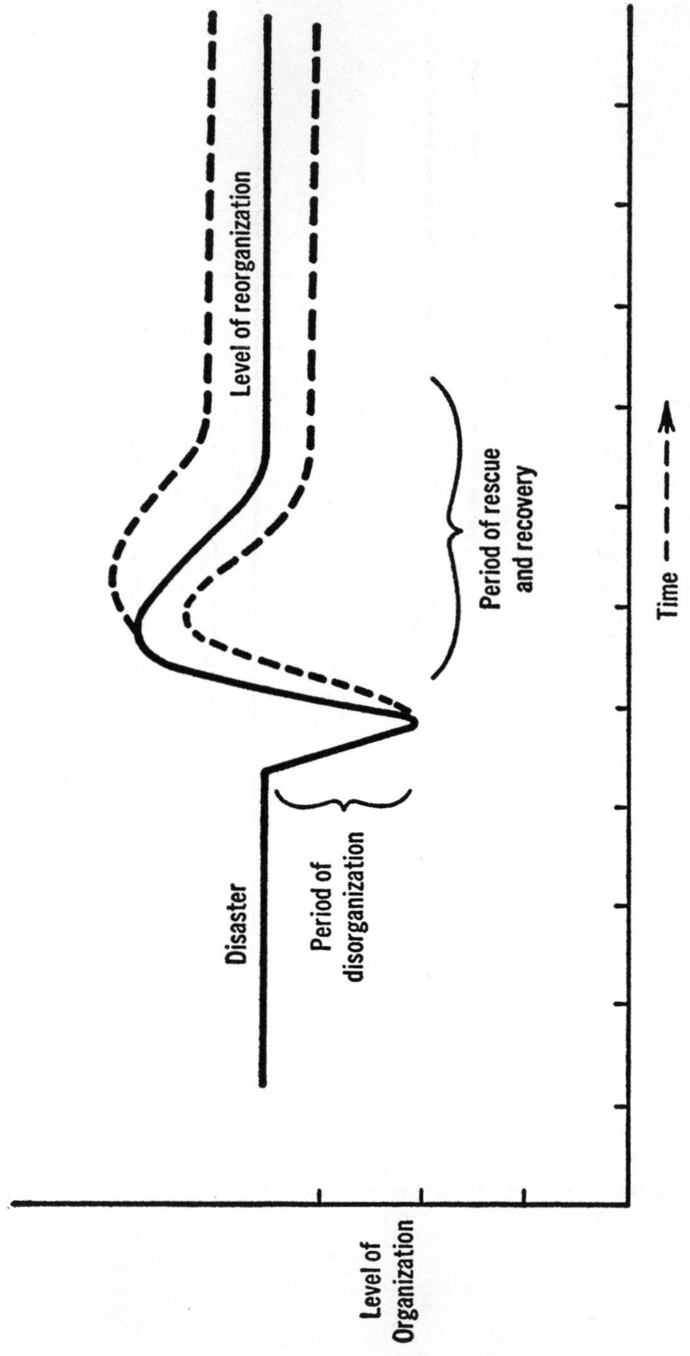

FIGURE 7-3. *Common patterns of family adjustment to community-wide disaster.*

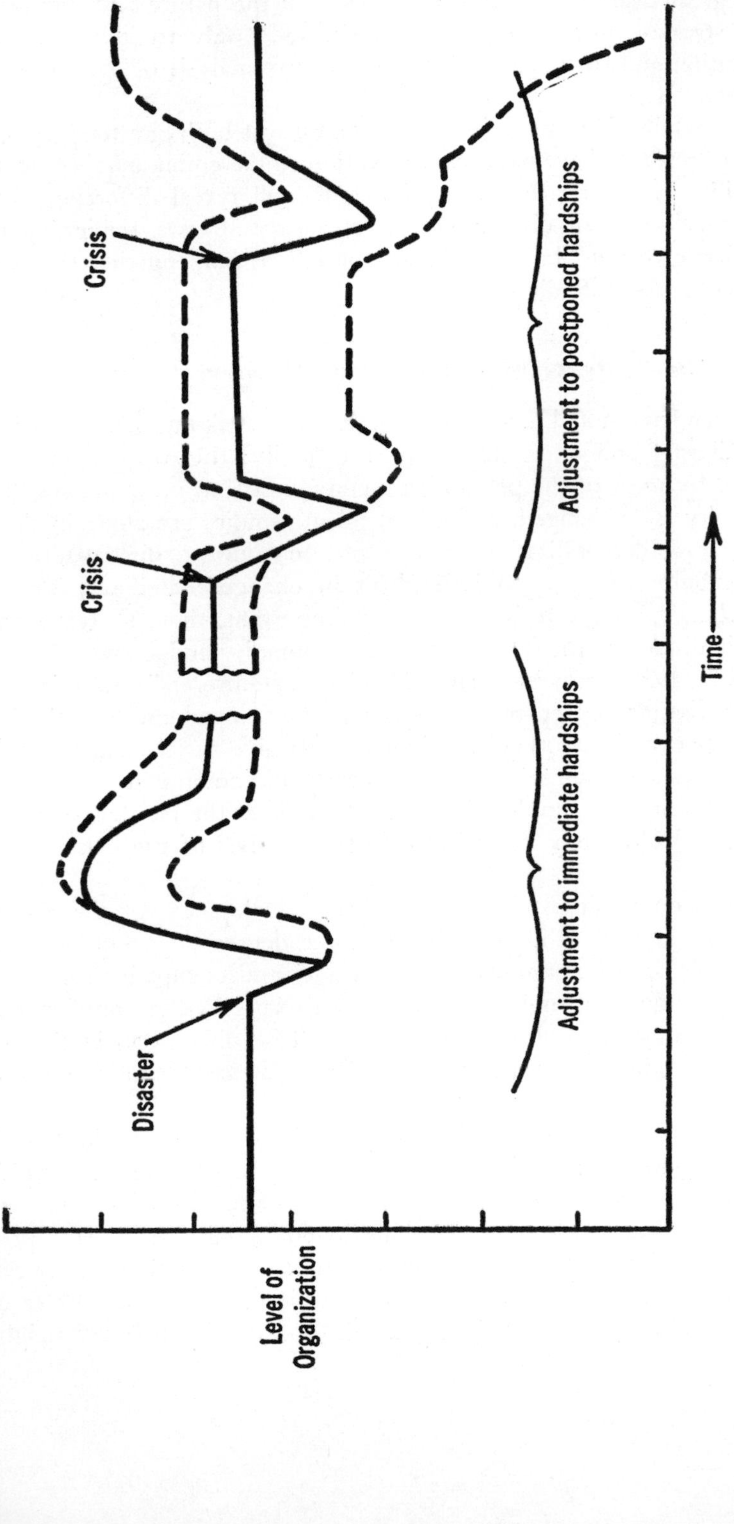

FIGURE 7-4. *Common patterns of family adjustment to disaster and subsequent crises.*

A great deal will depend, of course, on the nature and intensity of the stresses. These profiles should be used only to illustrate our presentation and to suggest a further tool for analysis of specific disaster data.

The family does not adjust in a vacuum, yet both disaster research and crisis research have paid scant attention to the community contexts of families in disaster. Even a quick look will reveal differences between the stresses of disaster and other family stresses, reminding us again that care must be taken in attempting to pull together the two streams of research findings.

Community Contexts of Families in Disaster

As we have noted, one fact alone leads to striking differences between disaster and other stresses on the family: the stress of disaster is shared by most of the persons in a community. In most stresses, the community is unchanged, and the stricken families are alone in their sense of loss, demoralization, and shame. In contrast, disaster creates the possibility of changed individuals in changed families *within a changed community*. It is particularly important, then, to relate the family in disaster to the framework of a community under stress.

Fritz (1958) suggests that "a society of sufferers" arises in the wake of disaster impact. Survivors rescue the trapped and help the injured, support one another emotionally, and give shelter and comfort to neighbors and even strangers. A "therapeutic community" develops and helps heal the wounds of individuals, adds to the family's own resources, and ultimately contributes to the survival of the community itself.

Does community structure affect the development of this therapeutic community? Will there be the same degree of group support, for example, in a community of mixed ages and occupations as there is in a community of mobile young professionals? We can only speculate, but scanty research suggests there will be differences in the reactions of families in rural compared with urban areas, and in zones of transition compared with suburban areas.

This difference can best be discussed through use of two "ideal" types of community: the *kinship-oriented* (or *kinship*) and the *individuated*. The distinction rests on the networks of relationships that connect kin to one another. In the kinship community there is a predominance of tightly meshed families with little activity between neighbors. In the individuated community, loosely knit, nuclear families predominate, and there is a great deal of activity between neighbors and friends. Many rural and mountain villages are of the first type, and most urban, industrial communities of the second.[2]

Following the impact of a disaster, individuated communities appear to adapt more quickly to the changed situation, for victims are more likely to seek and receive aid from many quarters. Neighbors help neighbors, and strangers offer ready support to sufferers, who are ready to accept aid wherever it can be found. In kinship communities, by contrast, individuals focus their attention on the suffering of their relatives and on the damaged possessions of their own kin group.

Because of its flexible helping patterns, the individuated community also might develop a more marked "therapeutic" atmosphere than might the kinship community. After impact, individuals see that they do not suffer alone and that the problem is shared widely. Often they seek satisfaction or expression of basic physical and emotional needs. In an individuated community, they can find satisfactions quickly and abundantly, for their small efforts to pull a neighbor from danger or for their smile at a friend or acquaintance. They find themselves in primary relationships which are satisfying and reassuring, yet strangely exciting after the trauma of impact and after years of comparatively contractual relations. There seems to arise a special pride in being survivors, in the knowledge that they are battle tested and have the scars to prove it.

Individuals in kinship communities are also caught up in this process. But the significant thing is that members of such communities tend to turn to their kinship groups rather than to neighbors and friends. Between families, there may be talk about the disaster and some cooperation and aid, but most effort goes to one's own immediate and extended family. In these kinship communities, we suspect, there is some increase in solidarity and informal activity between families, but the increase is probably far less than in the more loosely knit, individuated communities.

[2] The first type of families might be called "classical extended," and the second, "modified extended." The distinction between these types is Litwak's, and is more precisely drawn by him. He defines the "classical extended" family ". . . in terms of geographical propinquity, occupational dependence and nepotism, a sense that extended family relations are most important, and an hierarchical authority structure based on a semi-biological criterion, e.g., the eldest male" (Litwak, 1960b, p. 9). The modified extended family ". . . differs from past extended families in that it does not require geographical propinquity, occupational nepotism, or integration, and there are no strict authority relations, but equalitarian ones. Family relations differ from those of the isolated nuclear families, although aid has to do with standard of living (housing, illness, leisure pursuits), rather than occupational appointments or promotions" (Litwak, 1960a, p. 385).

Even before the disaster agent hits, the effect of community type can be seen. There are, of course, differences in the speed with which persons are warned of the danger and told what to do, but there are also differences in the readiness of residents to accept the information and in the range of activities that they will consider. What is accepted as true in an individuated community may be suspected in a kinship community, and the action that a person takes in an individuated community may not even be considered in another type of community.

When the Rio Grande threatened to flood, for instance, residents of a small Mexican kinship community were far less willing to believe the warnings of nonfamily members than were people in the individuated Texan community directly across the river. Furthermore, in preparing for the flood, Mexican townspeople were oriented so strongly toward the extended family that they almost completely neglected neighbors and friends when the disaster struck (Clifford, 1956).

In short, the individuated community seems to better arm its citizens for disaster and short-term recovery than does the kinship community. But in meeting the long-term effects of disaster, it is probable that the individuated community loses its advantage. People tire of helping others—physically, financially, and emotionally. In the wake of dramatic stress, neighbors may offer a roof and dry clothes, but a month later neighbors and friends may be sick and tired of helping the victims. Will the staying power of kin be greater? This question begs for research.

When the doors and kitchens of neighbors are open to almost everyone, the long-term stress brought by disaster may be absorbed. This is suggested by the Perrys' (Perry and Perry, 1959) comparison of two schoolhouse disasters with the Vicksburg tornado. The researchers, looking for children's emotional difficulties following disaster, found far less severe trouble in the schoolhouse communities, which were predominantly Negro and similar to the kinship type. Though there were many noticeable differences in the communities, the authors observed that in the schoolhouse communities "the family household systems were flexible enough so that the children were able, in most instances, to find some satisfactory substitute relations in case of the removal of the mothering figure by death or injury (p. 12). They held this difference to be a crucial determinant in the greater adaptiveness of the Negro community.

We do not suggest that relatives in individuated communities are unimportant in the adjustment of families after disaster. In both kinship and individuated communities, the usefulness of the extended family is apparent in short as well as long-term recovery (Quarantelli, 1960, p. 264). Although evacuated families living with relatives often report more open conflict than do families living with strangers, they remain with kin longer than with strangers or friends (Klausner and Kincaid, 1956, pp. 130-131). Expressed hostility, of course, is not necessarily undesirable, as the work of Coser (1956) should remind us. Research might profitably focus on the long-term satisfactions as well as the short-term tensions provided by extended families during and after disaster.

In any type of community, the extended family may offer more intense and lasting therapy to the family than other elements of the community. But kin become less and less helpful in a widespread disaster, especially when the impact is intense. For example, Young echoes the reports of Titmuss (1950), that during World War II small communities in England were less resilient than were large cities: when one family was hurt, chances were that all nearby relatives were also hurt. In a large city, families could move to an undamaged area, perhaps finding relatives there (Young, 1954). Young suggests: "What stands out is that the more scattered an extended family, the less effective it is for purposes of mutual aid in the process of recovery from a major disaster" (p. 389). On the other hand, if they are too closely grouped in a widespread disaster, all might suffer and none remain to aid.

Families in individuated communities may, of course, join distant kin if the disaster agent has not been too widespread and severe. But hurried removal of suffering families from the therapeutic community might retard recovery (Fritz, 1958). In the post-impact community, individuals not only find supportive relationships but also discover and help develop new roles, defined in the light of the changed community. These new roles can be the vehicles for rapid readjustment. Often suffering families in individuated communities face a hard choice: Should they suffer through recovery without kin, or leave their home and their "society of sufferers"?

Apparently, then, the individuated community is more adaptive in short-term recovery from disaster impact, and will give rise to a marked therapeutic community. But in long-term adjustment, unless the hardships are very severe, the extended family provides maximum therapy for a suffering family. In this respect, kinship communities are far better structured.

Does this mean that the kinship community is best adapted to withstand the stresses of disaster? For some disasters, perhaps. But the possibility of nuclear attack points up sharply the dangers of the inflexible relations and the highly structured authority patterns found in kinship communities. More will be said of this later.

Communities, of course, differ in far more ways than our two ideal types suggest. Hundreds of pages would not be enough to do justice to all the important aspects of community form that might influence the family in disaster. For example, we have not considered the influence of community norms, beliefs, and values, even though comparative studies illustrate their importance:

> In an Indian background, catastrophic events are often ascribed to supernatural causes and are traced to the accumulation of sin. . . . In this background it is legitimate to expect that the catastrophe will not always be met vigorously by appropriate reactions on the part of the stricken people, but by an attitude of resignation which though consoling is quite inadequate for the situation (Sinha, 1954, p. 55).

The island of Yap is threatened periodically by typhoons which, though terrifying, are not highly dangerous if they are prepared for. Strangely, there is little "intelligent" preparation, and damage and death roar through unprotected villages. Schneider (1957) found out why: the natives believed in a supernatural power that sends the typhoons as "punishment" at the request of their tribal chief. Their only hope, they believe, is to appease the powers through ritual and magic.

Disaster research, however, suggests little about the relation of disaster behavior to most other aspects of the community. We can only speculate on questions such as: How does the institutional structure of a community affect the family in disaster? Is a family crippled after a disaster if other organizations, through sources such as counseling and disaster relief, usurp the family's power over its members?

Can social institutions actually *prepare* the family and its members for stress, by providing roles and norms for post-impact behavior even before the disaster agent hits? There is some evidence that a community living under the continued stress of an ever-present danger (e.g., a mining town, ever wary of a cave-in) develops ideas and expectations that will help a family recover if the danger becomes reality. Perhaps, then, some degree of continuing stress may be "optimal" in preparing a family or community for possible disaster and recovery—for example, by predefining roles so they will better fit emergencies, or by developing institutionalized ways of coping with chronic uncertainty, or by creating very clear norms for bereavement and mourning after disaster. But the nation, community, or family that seeks to create a state of "optimal stress" walks the razor's edge, for constant alarm may produce so much anxiety that many persons are immobilized (Sinha, 1954, p. 57).

Rather than continue such speculation, we suggest that future research recognize that, for the individual family in stress, the community provides (1) a dynamic structure of status and power in which the position of any family may strongly affect either the range of behaviors actually possible or the range *thought* possible; (2) a reference framework—particularly of values and norms—in the definition the family will arrive at of its own stresses; (3) a source of verification or rejection of the family's definition of its situation and of the family's stress-meeting and role assignments; and (4) a possible source of aid to be incorporated into, or to usurp, the family's stress-meeting services.

Toward Research

HYPOTHESES AND CONCEPTUAL FRAMEWORKS FOR FAMILY-ORIENTED DISASTER RESEARCH

Hundred of disasters have been observed and carefully described, but without reference to family behavior. When the eye of the observer is on individual victims, on rescue operations, or on the recovery processes of a community, he does not seem to notice family activity.

If his gaze does fall on the family in some disaster, what will he see? Unless he is sensitive to the research complexities of family life, he will be able to do no more than describe, and his effort, in large part, will be wasted. To help him gain perception, then, we will try to fit him with crude lenses with which he can focus on families in a disaster-stricken community.

CONCEPTUAL FRAMEWORKS FOR STUDY OF FAMILIES IN DISASTERS

The technical term for "lenses" is "conceptual framework," which refers to the cluster of concepts with which an observer tries to describe and analyze his subject. Obviously no one framework is suitable for every subject; to study the family in disaster we need a framework that can cope with both the external and internal affairs of the family during the entire span of the disaster and its aftermath.

Such a framework has not yet developed in disaster research. If we turn to the general field of family study, however, we find several conceptual frameworks that hold some promise for study of families in disaster (See Table 7-1, p. 206).

The interactional framework Most generally, the interactional approach assumes that: (1) social conduct is a function of the social milieu; (2) a human being is an independent actor as well as a reactor to his situation; and (3) the basic autonomous unit is the individual in a social setting.

TABLE 7-1 *Current Approaches to the Study of the Family*

Conceptual framework	Developed in discipline of	Exemplified by
The interactional approach	Sociology and social psychology	R. C. Angell, E. W. Burgess, R. Cavan, L. S. Cottrell, T. D. Eliot, R. Hill, M. Komarovsky, E. T. Koos, E. T. Krueger, H. Mowrer, S. Stryker, W. Waller, P. Wallin
The structure-function approach	Sociology and social anthropology	K. Davis, W. Goode, C. McGuire, T. Parsons, L. Simmons, L. Warner, and others
The situational approach	Sociology	W. I. Thomas, L. J. Carr, J. H. S. Bossard and associates, R. Blood, E. Boulding
The institutional approach	Sociology and historical sociology	J. Sirjamaki, A. Truxal
The developmental approach	Sociology, borrowing from rural sociology, child psychology, and human development	Approximations seen in research of R. Faris, P. Glick, M. Sussman, L. Stott, and writings of E. M. Duvall, R. Foster, R. Hill, and L. D. Rockwood

Studies of nondisaster stress have usually been cast in this framework. The family is seen as a number of personalities interacting in an intricate arrangement of positions, norms, and roles; and the family is studied by analyzing the actions between its role-playing members. The framework focuses on family members when they are together, but not when they are with "outsiders."

Although this approach has developed useful propositions about stress, it fails to come to grips with the wide sweep of community and interfamily relations that are so important in the wake of disaster. The concepts necessary to a full community analysis can be gained, however, by combining the interactional framework with the independently developing actional approach (as used by Weber, Mills, and Martindale). The actional framework has not been applied extensively on a family level, though it seems that it could be used very profitably.

The actional approach does not deny, nor logically contradict, the emergence of a social system—indeed the "system analysis" of such authors as Caudill (1958) and Loomis (1958) appears quite compatible with actional theory.

The structure-function framework Very broadly, the assumptions of the structure-function framework are that (1) social conduct is best analyzed for its contribution to the maintenance of a social system, or for its nature under the structure of that system; (2) a social human being is basically a reacting part of the social system, and self-elicited (independent) action is rare and asocial (3) the basic autonomous unit is the social system itself, composed of interdependent subsystems (e.g., institutions, the family system); (4) it is possible and profitable to study any subunits of the basic system; and (5) the social system tends to homeostasis.

The structure-function approach may be viewed as one type of system analysis. In system analysis, the family is seen as an open system, linked to the personality systems of its members, to other small-group systems, and to the community system; what happens in any one system affects the others. Any of these systems may be made the focus of research attention, and system analysis seems, therefore, well adapted to the requirements of disaster research.

When system analysis emphasizes the self-regulatory nature of systems to the point of arguing that there is an over-all closed system (society) or that the entire system tends to homeostasis or equilibrium, it becomes contradictory to interactional approaches and begins to merge with traditional structure-functionalism. The structure-function framework, of course, continues to share many of the attributes of the less extreme system analysis to which it is related, but it has always tended to emphasize the statics of structure and to neglect change and dynamics. In these respects it is not useful for analysis and explanation of the rapid and extreme family and social changes following disaster.

The situational framework The situational approach assumes that (1) social conduct is a function of the situation (social, cultural, physical milieu); (2) behavior is purposive (i.e., directed to problem-solving, though not completely rational) in relation to the situation that elicits it; (3) the basic autonomous unit is the individual in a situation; and (4) situations and human groupings, as units of organization, have emergent realities.

Situationists would agree with interactionists that the family is a unity of interacting persons who experience relatively stable relationships. But rather than focusing on the interaction of these persons, the situationists turn to the study of the family as a social situation in which that interaction takes place. The framework thus centers on the family as a unit of stimuli acting toward a focal point (e.g., a child in the family), but it also allows for analysis of that focal point itself. It considers the family as open to outside influences, and does not hold that the family is the single source of stimuli for the contained individual.

Because of these properties, situational analysis is useful for disaster problems of limited scope. It has been successfully applied by Crawford (1957) to discern patterns of family readjustment to hardships following a tornado.

These frameworks are not the only ones that might develop for the study of families in disaster; indeed, researchers should realize the danger in allowing these to dictate choices of research subjects or methods. The frameworks should be taken only as guidelines, and to point out how important is the interrelation of concepts in research. This interrelation can commit the researcher to important assumptions; if he fails to understand his assumptions, his research and his theory may be distorted and misleading, since assumptions, together with verified propositions, generate theory. In disaster research almost nothing is verified as yet; indeed, we are still struggling to find out which propositions are most promising.

The following review of promising propositions is limited to disasters in which the impact does not incapacitate the entire community. Catastrophes of atomic magnitude, such as the Algiers earthquake of 1960, Hiroshima, and Nagasaki, are treated briefly later.

The propositions that follow have not been verified. In only a few instances is evidence solid enough to justify the ending of research efforts. We suggest, rather, that the propositions be treated as hypotheses to be tested in repeated researches on families in disaster.

PROPOSITIONS ABOUT FAMILY TRANSACTIONAL BEHAVIOR IN DISASTER

1. The post-impact community will differ from its pre-impact condition in structures, norms, and processes.

    a. Following impact, individuals and families will tend to define their situation with reference to the post-impact condition of the injured community.

    b. Class distinctions disappear in the wake of disaster but reemerge as recovery progresses.

    c. If a post-impact community is composed of a large group severely hit and another group undamaged, the social solidarity of the community may be endangered.

    1) In communities in which a large number of families are

forced to rely for some time on the resources of those in the peripheral impact areas, the community may divide into the "haves" and the "have-nots."

2) If a large group of families are evacuated to an undamaged community, there may arise over time a strong distinction between "refugee families" and "native families."

d. Pre-impact structures and norms will greatly determine the structures and norms in the post-impact community.

1) In urban middle-class America, the resources available in the family (see pp. 192-193) will be largely determined by the position(s) and roles the family and family members hold in the pre-impart community.

2) The pre-impact norms and values predominant in a community will influence the definitions families make of their disaster situation.

e. In the wake of disaster there arises a "community of sufferers" which provides therapy for injured families.

1) In a community, the scope of the society of sufferers is greatly influenced by the family types of the community.

a) In kin-oriented communities the community of sufferers is primarily within the circle of extended family members, with only modest support occurring between extended families.

b) In individuated communities the community of sufferers becomes a therapeutic community, encompassing most of the injured families.

2) The therapeutic community provides emotional support and release for the injured and ego-involved.

3) The therapeutic community arises from, and stimulates further, informal material and physical aid.

4) Material support and services of the community and other agencies may be resented or even rejected by those enjoying the informal aid of the therapeutic community.

5) Removal of individuals and families from the community of sufferers has a retarding effect on their adjustment to the hardships of disaster.

2. Recovery from the hardships of impact may be uneven, with some families recovering quickly and completely and others not at all.

a. Recovery will vary in accordance with the extent of personal loss, property destruction, and resources available to restore the losses.

b. With the return of some families to normality, other families will begin to define their losses and deprivations by predisaster standards and values.

3. There will be a great difference in actions and processes in communities characterized by different family types.

a. Kin-oriented communities will be less flexible, less well prepared, and less quickly adjusting than individuated communities (see pp. 200-203).

b. Individuated communities will be less able to aid individuals and families in long-term adjustment than will kin-oriented communities.

c. Even in individuated communities, kin relations become highly important to families in disaster. The more distant the kin, the less effective they are in meeting the needs of individuals and families in recovery and adjustment from disaster stresses.

4. An optimal amount of ever-present threat in the pre-impact community may help prepare families and individuals for post-impact behavior.

a. Optimal stress in the pre-impact community may alert persons to the danger of impact.

b. Optimal stress may lead to pre-impact prescription of roles for behavior in all phases of the disaster, including readjustment.

c. Optimal stress may precipitate the modification of community institutions in such a way that post-impact expectations are to some extent defined before the impact.

d. Optimal stress may stimulate physical preparation for the impact.

e. If the ever-present threat is too extreme, it may result in dysfunctional anxiety.

5. Individual family members will perform nonfamily disaster roles only under certain conditions.

a. Individuals will rarely perform nonfamily roles (including community rescue) if they do not know the fate of their loved ones.

b. Individuals will rarely perform nonfamily roles if their family is in any physical danger.

c. Individual family members will rarely perform roles in nonfamily organizations if they do not feel loyalty or obligation to the organization.

d. Individual family members will rarely perform roles in nonfamily organizations if they are not aware of well-defined roles which they consider as important in the emergency.

e. When none of the conditions a, b, c, and d hold, individual family members *may* perform disaster roles in nonfamily organizations.

f. Community-oriented tasks may be thwarted by the anxieties and searching of individuals separated from loved ones.

g. Individual family members who have well-defined and important disaster roles in the community will experience role conflict between family roles and community roles.

   1) If they doubt their family is beyond danger, individuals will choose in favor of family roles and neglect their community tasks.

   2) Even if their families are known safe, individuals who choose in favor of nonfamily roles may set off an array of disrupting reactions in the family, endangering its adjustive capacity.

NEGLECTED AREAS OF FAMILY TRANSACTIONAL BEHAVIOR IN DISASTER

In addition to these hypotheses, other areas of research need to be plumbed. We need to give further attention to the variable effect of the therapeutic community upon families in different social classes. Little has been done to control class variables or to determine the effect of different class statuses on a community. There is evidence from nondisaster situations that the lower classes are less able to cope with hardships but that the middle class tends to make more damaging definitions of the situation. We can only guess as to the effect of the therapeutic community on both classes.

The problem of agency aid in disaster situations raises the possibility that families of low adequacy will be stripped of functions. Authority and relief roles may be taken over by community or other agencies in the post-impact period and the family may never fully regain its power. For some families, of course, the reverse may be true; during a disaster they take on functions which they did not have before, and they find satisfactions in continuing to perform them after the crisis has passed. What effect will this have on long-term family adjustment?

Disaster, too, offers good opportunity to study phases of both delinquency and divorce when chronic conflict is splintering a family —what will be the effect of new hardships brought by disaster? We suspect that marital separations might decrease in the few months following disaster, as individuals set aside differences in order to rebuild. (Divorces very likely will decrease, but not only so that families may rebuild. Courts may be too crowded to handle divorce cases, or separating couples may not have the money needed for the court costs.) Again, the therapeutic community might have some influence in temporarily holding together a disintegrating family. There may be a slowing up of separation, but as time passes, original conflicts may revive and subsequent hardships may place even more stress on families. Then a "separation boom" may hit the community.

We have noted that irresponsible, rebellious teen-agers may be more active in community rescue and less active in family readjustment than will be youth more closely attached to family or to voluntary associations such as church and school. Following disaster, we suspect there will be a decrease in juvenile deviance as young people discover meaningful roles and duties offered them in rescue and recovery. Deviance will return to its previous level as recovery progresses or as the community becomes accustomed to disruption. In situations of continuing impact (such as bombings) the post-impact confusion may even be used as a mask for deviance.

PROPOSITIONS ABOUT INTERACTIONAL BEHAVIOR WITHIN FAMILIES IN DISASTER

Focusing on the internal working of families, we note these hypotheses:

1. The family group is extremely important to the individual throughout the disaster.
   - a. Even in violent impact, individuals continue to act toward other persons and objects.
     - 1) In danger, warning, and impact, the individual tends to act only toward persons and objects which he perceives as accessible to him in the available time.
     - 2) In danger, warning, and impact, the individual acts first toward the most intimate persons he perceives as accessible and subsequently toward less intimate persons and possessions.
   - b. In the post-impact period, the individual is oriented toward family members until he is certain they are out of danger.
   - c. In stress, family-assigned roles (e.g., mother as protector) will be more often played than will the more general community roles (e.g., men as protectors).
2. Compared to other social groups, the family is highly adaptive and protective in all stages of disaster.
   - a. The family's established authority and communication patterns will usually facilitate adaptive behavior.

b. The presence of loved and valued persons results in a heightened sensitivity to threat and motivation to act with respect to the threat.
c. Adaptive behavior is more likely in families that are intact and well integrated than in families that are not.
d. Adaptive behavior is more likely in families in which channels of communication are open.
e. Adaptive behavior is more likely in families in which the authority figure defines the situation as dangerous and is aware of ways to cope with it.
f. Adaptive behavior is more likely in families in which authority and status structures are flexible.
g. Adaptive behavior is more likely in families that have successfully met past disasters.

3. Families show a high degree of role complementarity in the first few days or weeks following disaster, but role conflict increases as recovery progresses.

a. Role complementarity in the family increases as the stability and organization of the community decreases.
b. Role complementarity increases in the face of a well-defined challenge.
c. Role complementarity increases as individuals find immediate and full return for their emotional and physical support to others.
d. Role conflict increases as the family is frustrated in efforts to meet the post-impact challenges.
e. Role conflict increases as family members recognize basic differences between themselves, especially in beliefs and assumptions.
f. Role complementarity or conflict may be increased by the exchange during impact of subtle cues of acceptance or rejection.

4. A disaster agent not only will bring immediate hardships to a family but also will precipitate development of other stresses which may not appear until months after impact.

a. If families are separated during impact, severe emotional hardships may result in following months.
b. Loss of a family member is defined as an extreme hardship by urban American families.
    1) The smaller the family, the greater the hardship resulting from loss of a member.
    2) The greater the degree of "closeness" in a family, the greater the hardship resulting from loss of a member.

3) The more crucial to the family the position and roles of the lost member, the greater the hardship.
4) The definition of death as a gateway to afterlife will decrease the hardships resulting from the loss of a member.

5. If disaster affects the family roles played by one member, other role relationships will have to be readjusted.

a. Derivative stress continues until a new role equilibrium within the family and with interacting agents is established.
b. The more autonomous the affected individual, the less the effect of his disturbance on the roles of other family members.
c. The more autonomous the unaffected individuals, the less avidly they will work for readjustment.

6. There is a limited amount of "emotional room" in a family, such that only a certain amount of affective disturbance can be shown at one time.

a. There is a sequential display of emotional ills following impact, in which family members take turns being disturbed.
b. Expression of an individual's emotional disturbance is a function of the post-disaster family structure and the roles being played by the family members.
    1) Expression of disturbance is related to the availability of an audience.
    2) Expression of disturbance is related to lack of post-disaster responsibilities.

NEGLECTED AREAS OF INTERACTIONAL BEHAVIOR OF FAMILIES IN DISASTER

Disaster research has neglected the effects of stages of family development on family vulnerability and recovery. There is some evidence that elderly "empty-nest" couples are reluctant to leave their homes in the face of danger; readers interested in the problems of the aged are referred to Friedsam's chapter (Chapter Six, this volume). However, other stages of family development await future research. These stages have been overlooked in the study of all phases of disaster, yet other areas of family research have found them to be a crucial variable.

Because so much research on family adjustment in disasters has yet to be accomplished, it is useful to set down explicitly some hypotheses for future testing that are strongly suggested by more general studies of the family. Stress literature confirms the following as important to good adjustment, particularly among urban, middle-class, American families: family adaptability, family integration, affectional relations among family members, good marital adjustment of husband and wife, companionable parent-child relationships, family-council type of contol in decision-making, social participation of wife, and previous successful experience with crisis.

The following generalizations are rather fully substantiated by past crisis research and may be used as sensitizers for disaster research: (1) Crisis-proneness, the tendency to define troubles as crises, is disproportionately frequent among families of low family adequacy. (2) Family reactions to crisis divide between short-time immediate reactions and secondary long-time adjustments. (3) Demoralization following a crisis usually stems from incipient demoralization before the crisis. (4) The length of time a family continues to be disorganized as a result of crisis is inversely related to how adequate its previous organization was. (5) Unadaptable and unintegrated families are most likely of all to be unpredictable deviants in adjusting to crisis. (6) Foreknowledge and preparation for a critical event mitigates the hardships and improves the chances for recovery. (7) The effects of crisis on families may be punitive or strengthening depending on the margin of health, wealth, and adequacy possessed by the family.

Wilson (Chapter Five, this volume) suggests the use of analogues to gain some insight into disaster processes. Some of these analogues (e.g., death and separation, disaster drills, normal life crises) have been discussed above. Their contribution to the understanding of family functioning, crisis formation, and crisis adjustment is great, and they offer further sensitizing theory for disaster research.

Some analogues, however, more closely approximate disaster situations than do others. Particularly useful, we feel, is the analogue of the burned-out family. Such a family is in a situation materially similar to that of hurricane and tornado victims who have suffered extensive property loss and possible injury and death within the family. The primary defect in this analogue, of course, is the absence of community-shared destruction, and hence the unlikelihood of a therapeutic community. Fritz (1958) suggests some differences that might be expected between disaster situations and other crisis situations; these offer some insights into necessary modification of crisis findings when they are used as sensitizers for disaster study.

Some Implications for the Family in Nuclear Attack

Moving from the implications of crisis literature for community-shared disaster, we postulate that extreme community destruction, such as might be expected in nuclear attack, will introduce further qualitative differences in contexts for behavior. Using disaster research as the analogue, we now ask: What are the implications for the family in nuclear attack?

Again we must urge readers to be critical of every statement, for the area is entirely without research evidence. But even speculation is important on some questions, and this is such a question.

To specify the problem and to guide our approach to it, we base our thinking on the following common assumptions about a nuclear attack. First, that the attack will come suddenly, with little warning. Second, that the impact will be highly intense and destructive of life and property. Third, that the destruction will be centered on large population and/or industrial areas, as well as on missile and other military bases. Fourth, that the destruction will be widespread over the entire country, i.e., will hit urban centers in all parts of the country at approximately the same time, and will continue for the duration of hostilities to present surviving families with danger and problems of shelter. Fifth, that the possibility of fallout will confront virtually every surviving family with danger and problems of shelter.

In the urban setting we further limit ourselves to middle-class families, not as a matter of sociological bias but because lower classes, cramped near the centers of urban targets, will suffer the most extensive fatalities, whether the warheads hit in the center of the city or to one side. The survivors will be predominantly middle class.

It seems likely that certain features of the impact of industrialization on the urban family would be sharpened by the sudden and unique stress of nuclear attack. The individual gets used to many and unimportant relationships with persons in mass society; the incessant flow of faces and voices allows a rapid turnover of friends, and discourages many intimacies of depth and durability. The industrialized man enjoys few intimate (primary) relationships, for the huge organization he works for demands his loyalty and time, and by emphasizing the importance of bowling and golf, of living "modern" and fashionably, seduces him away from his neighborhood companions and occasionally even rips him up by the roots and transplants him to strange communities. Neighbor, friendship, and (to a lesser extent) extended kinship ties grow increasingly contractual, as individuals and family groups relate to others for short-term gains, tending to offer and show affection only so long as they are sure a similar show will be returned.

The implications of this for nuclear attack appear highly important. Individuals accustomed to contractual relationships in the large-scale community will be able to act protectively and adaptively toward other persons and objects in their immediate surroundings during warning, impact, and extreme danger periods. In more traditional communities, characterized by elaborate family systems, individuals will use precious minutes in attempts to join their families, ignoring the needs of others with them at the time of warning. Warning time may be used in transportation rather than in preparation for the impact. In nuclear attack, then, we should expect the individuated community to be more flexible and better able to prepare for disaster in the short time available after warning. And in rescue and recovery following attack, the same flexibility might be expected in the individuated community.

The importance of the independence and mobility of the individuated community's families also enhances their ability to flee. In atomic attack, fire and fallout pose constant threats to survivors in the period following impact. In Nagasaki and Hiroshima it is attested that the survivors were those who could ignore the pleas of others around them as they sped from the dangers (Hersey, 1946; Nagai, 1951). The traditional, extended family with its intricate interlacings of loves and loyalties may well hold the individual or the intact nuclear family group in the danger areas until escape is impossible or flight is overly encumbered.

Also because of the democratization of family roles in the large-scale community, individuals as individuals may be able to behave more adaptively in all stages of the disaster. This means, for instance, that loss of a dominant authority figure may be less crippling in the recovery stage than it would be in a more traditional setting. The greater the internal cohesion of the family, the more will the family react to the loss of members; and the reaction may or may not follow trends present before the impact. Loss of one integrative person may bring dissolution of the family as already autonomous members strike out individually or in groups; loss of a cherished child may bring a companionate couple even closer together. On a community-wide basis, however, we would expect surviving members of the large-scale community to adapt more quickly to the loss of family members in the recovery period than would survivors in traditional communities.

Because the urban middle-class family is so typically involved in business, school, and other community organizations, there is a good possibility that family members will be widely scattered at the time of warning and impact. In nuclear attack, grave problems of transportation and communication may arise as survivors seek to discover the fate of their loved ones. The potential for community disruption is obvious.

In the individuated community, families more readily accept

warning and outside aid from both official and nonofficial sources. Before the disaster this may mean extra minutes for preparation as individuals accept the implications of warnings without having to seek verification from family authority figures. After the impact, individuals may be similarly less inclined to combat their hardships through family or friendship groups alone. We will thus expect government evacuation shelters and other service programs oriented toward national welfare (rather than toward the welfare of individual families) to be more successful and smoother in operation in individuated communities than in more traditional communities particularly if survivors of the nuclear family can be kept together.

For long-term recovery the advantages of the highly urbanized family disappear. Although in individuated communities immediately after impact neighbor may help neighbor and strangers may take in the homeless, the usefulness of such efforts is temporary. In prolonged stress there is nothing like the family to fall back on, and if the family—or at least part of it—is not available, recovery may be thwarted. The traditional family that survives the blast fairly intact is probably in the best condition to offer long-term recovery to its members; surviving families in large-scale communities have fewer resources for meeting the long-term stresses following nuclear attack.

Where, then, will urban families find the means for recovery? Disaster research shows that extended family relationships re-emerge in the recovery stage of disaster. Those who might have migrated from rural areas may return to intact branches of their families. But few persons migrate from city to country. The urban family without rural ties can look only to other urban-dwelling kin. The probability is therefore great that in nuclear attack there will be no therapeutic arms of the extended family available to most urban survivors; even when the arms are so widely separated that the same attack does not damage all of them, problems of communication and transportation over the separating distances will frustrate many possibilities of intrakinship aid. Long-range recovery from attack will necessarily be made by the surviving members of the nuclear family without great reliance on the extended family.

More markedly, shelter experience and long-term recovery will cast family differences in striking perspective. Although people act with reference to the altered situation following disasters, they do not necessarily change their assumptions and working principles. Nuclear attack, then, will bring to the fore the divergent tendencies and developed differences of urban family members. The impact of these differences in the event of nuclear war may be less severe than has been found in other disasters, if the family hardships and great destruction of the community prove to be mitigating variables. The assumption is, again, that the family is increasingly important in a chaotic world; the question is whether the increased importance is enough to offset the extreme differences developed in a large-scale community.

J. A. Vernon's (1959) "Hideaway" study of shelter life suggests that families can go through isolation without adverse effects and perhaps with benefit to their level of functioning. It is of course questionable whether all families would behave so well as this volunteer experimental group. What difference might different stages of family development make? Will teen-agers or old persons increase tensions? What would be the effect of knowing that there was nationwide destruction outside and the threat of invasion? We would expect that in families not marred by death the roller-coaster pattern might hold: a rise in complementarity in the first few days of isolation and increasing irritation and conflict as internment extended.

What of role conflict in the wake of attack? It is suspected that, in the warning, impact, and recovery periods, most pre-existing groups will have little influence over the individual, except to the degree to which they (1) command loyalty or subjection (most likely through power) of the individual, (2) have separated the individual, geographically and/or psychologically, from close primary ties, and (3) have provided and trained the individual in roles he defines as important to the emergency. Schools, especially after impact, will be almost totally unimportant, economic corporations important only when they can offer real material gain to workers who have no ties to damaged or threatened families; police and fire-fighting forces effective to the degree that their members have been indoctrinated as to their importance and special roles in emergencies.

Rescue work probably will not create much of the role conflict evident in limited disasters. In nuclear attack relatively few families will have escaped some loss of members or damage to property. Family members will have little doubt about their "proper places," and effective rescue work will have to be done by the uninvolved and by those with special protection against radiation hazards.

What of the therapeutic community in nuclear attack? Except in large shelters there may be little chance for it to develop until the shelter period passes; as long as persons are aware of the radiation threat, it seems likely they will stay in their small sheltered groups, actively seek refuge, or attempt to flee. Such conditions would hardly seem to encourage a therapeutic community. But areas in which large groups of persons seek refuge seem ideal for the development of a therapeutic community which includes all those within the shelter.

When the victims leave their shelter will a larger therapeutic community emerge to assist the family? We must remember that demoralization may overwhelm individuals as they emerge into a scene of chaotic destruction; and if destruction is too great, there may be no material aid to fall back on. Survivors will know they are not special in their suffering and that no one in particular is watching their community in its anguish, because the suffering covers the entire country. If there is also strong threat of another attack, it is possible that development of the therapeutic community could be greatly hindered.

Such obstructions could be severe, but limited experience indicates that a therapeutic community may arise nevertheless. It did even in Hiroshima and Nagasaki: individuals supported one another in death and suffering immediately after the impact; those removed from the cities for treatment felt like strangers, understood only by the fellow sufferers from whom they had been separated. Even more telling is the fact that reconstruction of the demolished cities began almost at once.

History and literature show that time and again man arises from his hells on earth to rebuild, and he gathers around him those he needs and can love. There is little doubt that if man lives through thermonuclear tragedy, the family, too, will survive.

Summary

We have attempted to highlight the importance of the family in disaster (1) by showing that general studies of communities in disaster evidence that the family affects disaster behavior and (2) by translating from studies of families under other types of stress those features particularly pertinent for families in natural disasters. In this attempt some dimensions of family behavior in disaster have been identified. Chief among them have been the stress agent, the community milieu, family organization resources, and family definitions of the event.

Every opportunity should be taken to test our many hypotheses, for it is difficult and expensive to maintain research teams in readiness to travel to the scene of catastrophic disasters. A fitting and easily available analogue for disaster family research is the study of burned-out families where extensive property loss and possible injury are accompanying hardships. The primary drawback of this quasi-disaster is the absence of community suffering. Nevertheless, the use of disaster analogues would be an important way to prepare for more extensive disaster studies and for anticipating the impact of nuclear attack on family organization.

The nuclear family deserves greater interest as a significant focus for disaster study, as an adaptive-protective unit in disaster through which rescue agencies will need to work, and as a training unit for preparing parents and children for the hazards of thermonuclear warfare. The thoughts of the late Ralph Linton offer appropriate conclusion:

> The ancient trinity of father, mother, and child has survived more vicissitudes than any other human relationship. It is the bedrock underlying all other structures. Although more elaborate patterns can be broken from without or may even collapse of their own weight, the rock remains. In the Gotterdammerung which over-wise science and over-foolish statesmanship are preparing for us, the last man will spend his last hours searching for his wife and child (Linton, 1949, p. 52).

► *eight*

THE EMERGENCY SOCIAL SYSTEM

Allen H. Barton

Introduction: The Problem of Social Organization in Disaster

A DISASTER can be defined as a sudden, large, unfavorable change in the inputs of a social system. The system affected may be anything from a small group to a national or world society. The change may be unexpected or expected, covering the entire system or only a segment. The inputs which change may be physical conditions, economic relationships, power relationships, or the belief systems of the population.

A large unfavorable change in inputs threatens and frustrates many members and disrupts the normal flow of activities in the system. Something has to be done to restore equilibrium, either by starting new activities or by adjusting activities and expectations to a lower standard of achievement. When such a change is sudden, it creates distinctive social processes of adaptation, which can be called an "emergency social system." The duration of this system may be a few hours, a few days, or longer, depending on how rapidly normal social processes can take over the adaptive task.

The emergency social system, like any other, has the problem of organizing human behavior to produce needed outputs. The problem of social organization has several levels. Individual behavior is normally regulated in part by social roles, which guide the behavior of individuals and make it predictable to others, and in part by personal emotions and preferences, which may be predictable in the aggregate but vary from individual to individual. The roles are organized into subsystems—informal groups like the family or friendship group, or formal organizations, like a work team, business firm, or government office. These subsystems in turn may be parts of larger formal organizations. "Individualized behavior" not regulated by social roles, and the behavior of small groups and organizations which are not part of larger formal organizations or informal arrangements, constitute "mass behavior" from the viewpoint of the system—that is, it is not predictable in detail, but it must be predicted or manipulated in the aggregate for the system to operate. The social system thus operates by organizing some behavior into roles, organizing roles into subsystems, organizing some subsystems into large organizations, and manipulating aggregates of individual and subsystem behaviors.

Thus a market economic system consists in part of formal organizations, with well-defined and well-organized roles for their members, and in part of unorganized masses of consumers, who may be either individuals, families, or organizations. The organizations and the masses act on one another through the mechanisms of the market and of mass persuasion. Democratic political systems consist of organized parties and interest groups competing for power, and of masses of individuals and primary groups. These organizations and masses act upon one another through the election system, mass propaganda, and other links.

Behavior in the emergency social system likewise consists of individualized behavior determined by personal emotions and preferences, role behavior in small independent groups such as families, and role behavior in formal organizations. The organization of behavior in the system may break down at the individual level, because members have inadequate role definitions, training, or motivation; at the small-group or organizational level, because roles are not adequately coordinated for disaster conditions; or at the community level, because organizations are not adequately coordinated with one another and because mass behavior is not adequately channeled.

The nature of the emergency social system, and the parts played in it by individualized behavior, small-group role behavior, and formal organization role behavior, depend on a number of factors. One is the scope of the impact: if disaster strikes only a small part of the system, formal organizations can be concentrated on it to perform needed services; if it is extensive relative to the capacity of the formal organizations, individualized and small-group role behaviors become very important. Another factor is time—how suddenly the needs arise, and the social costs of delay in meeting them, relative to the normal time-lags in formal organization and informal group processes. A third is the degree of preparedness of the formal and informal social organization. Fairly large-scale disasters can be organizationally handled if there is elaborate advance preparation, as for the air raids in Britain and Germany during World War II, or floods and hurricanes in areas where these recur. Other situations can be handled largely by mass action of family and friendship group members within their normal roles; this is how the population is fed, children are cared for, and minor illnesses are treated under nondisaster conditions; and in many disasters the victims' need for temporary shelter and food is met the same way. If neither formal organizations nor primary groups have established roles to guide behavior in a disaster, then behavior has to be individually improvised, with all the confusion and lack of coordination which this involves.

One preoccupation of recent disaster research has been the psychology of individual response to disaster; another has been the consequences of mass behavior, such as convergence or withdrawal; and a third has been the behavior of formal organizations in disaster. The present chapter is an effort to consider the operation of the community social system as a whole in the emergency period. It is concerned with the *distribution* of individual responses—how this affects the other parts of the system and is affected by them; with organizational response, the interrelation of organizations, and the relations between organizational and mass behavior.

The framework of analysis used here should be generally applicable to social systems in disaster; however, the particular findings presented are limited to the kinds of disasters for which we have a number of careful case studies. While individual and small-group responses immediately after any disaster may be similar, as long as the subjects are isolated from the larger social system, the organizational, mass, and community processes discussed here must differ greatly in disasters of different scope, speed, and degree of social preparedness. The most frequently studied type is the sudden disaster to a part of a relatively unprepared community. This paper will be mainly concerned with this type, although comparisons will be made wherever possible to more widespread and severe disasters such as regional floods and the World War II atom bombings.

I. The Emergency Social System in Sudden Community Disaster

When the disaster is sudden and on a large scale relative to the capacity of the normal system to cope with it, an "emergency social system" has to be created to quickly provide a large volume of disaster services. Existing organizations, primary groups, and masses of individuals must be mobilized to provide such services as rescue, transportation of the injured, medical care, food and shelter, reassurance and psychological support, and the restoration of damaged essential facilities. At the same time nonpostponable maintenance activities must be continued, including taking care of children and feeding families as well as keeping up public order and public utilities output. This improvised system must perform these services under conditions of damaged facilities and partly incapacitated personnel.

Research has pointed to a number of specific problems which influence the output of disaster services in the emergency social system. These are summarized in the following paragraphs.

Factors influencing the adequacy of the mass response

A. People exposed to severe threats to highly valued objects without adequate role definitions or equipment for dealing with them, or with conflicting role obligations, are put under great strain. This could conceivably lead to a high rate of nonadaptive behavior.

B. Normal primary-group ties provide quick help for many, but they do not provide for all victims. The entire group may be incapacitated or essential members may be away; and some victims may be socially isolated. Unless there is a norm requiring help to all community members in distress, or a general emotional response of sympathy for such people, many will go without aid.

C. Certain kinds of impacts cannot be handled by the mass response. They may require special skills and equipment which the general public does not have. Or they may saturate the primary groups with injuries and material losses so that many cannot help even their own members, and few can spare help for outsiders.

Factors influencing the adequacy of response of formal organizations

D. The mobilization of people to play family or general community-member roles competes with organizational mobilizations and may leave the formal organizations short of or entirely without personnel. This is the organizational consequence of the "role conflict" problem.

E. Organizations may have difficulty making decisions and directing their personnel under unexpected conditions and for unexpected tasks, due to inadequacies of the leadership or of previously worked out programs.

F. Organizations may not define the situation as one which requires them to act. Relieving suffering or helping the general community may not be "their business."

Problems of interorganizational relations

G. The separate formal organizations become highly dependent on one another in disaster, but they may lack experience, plans, and facilities for coordinating their activities under the unexpected conditions and needs of disaster, so that their joint output is far below what it should be.

Problems in the relations between organizations and masses

H. The uncoordinated mass response of individuals and small groups may overload facilities of all kinds, interfering with one another and with the formal organizations. One form of this has become known as the "convergence problem."

I. Organizations may need public support in supplies and personnel in a situation where there are no established expectations and channels, with the result that organizations may fail to take advantage of potential help, or the mass response may be too much or too little.

J. Organizations must find ways of getting their services to masses of people in a situation where there may be no established expectations and channels to guide the public and the organizations, or where normal expectations cause improper mass responses.

Some of the relationships involved in this set of problems can be summed up in Figure 8-1.

This scheme suggests the complex relations between the mass response and formal organization activities in producing the total output of disaster services. The mass response has certain unfavorable effects on the formal organization response, through its competition for personnel and the obstructive effects of mass convergence. The net balance of favorable and unfavorable effects cannot be known unless we have some quantitative estimate of the formal and the informal contribution to the output, and of the degree to which the one interferes with the other. The remainder of the paper will consider the system relationships outlined and diagrammed above and the social mechanisms by which output of the system might be increased.

II. The Output of the Mass Assault

Disaster studies have repeatedly shown the importance of the "informal mass assault" in providing disaster services quickly and on a large scale. This mass assault consists of the aggregate of primary-group activities to help their own members, and community-oriented

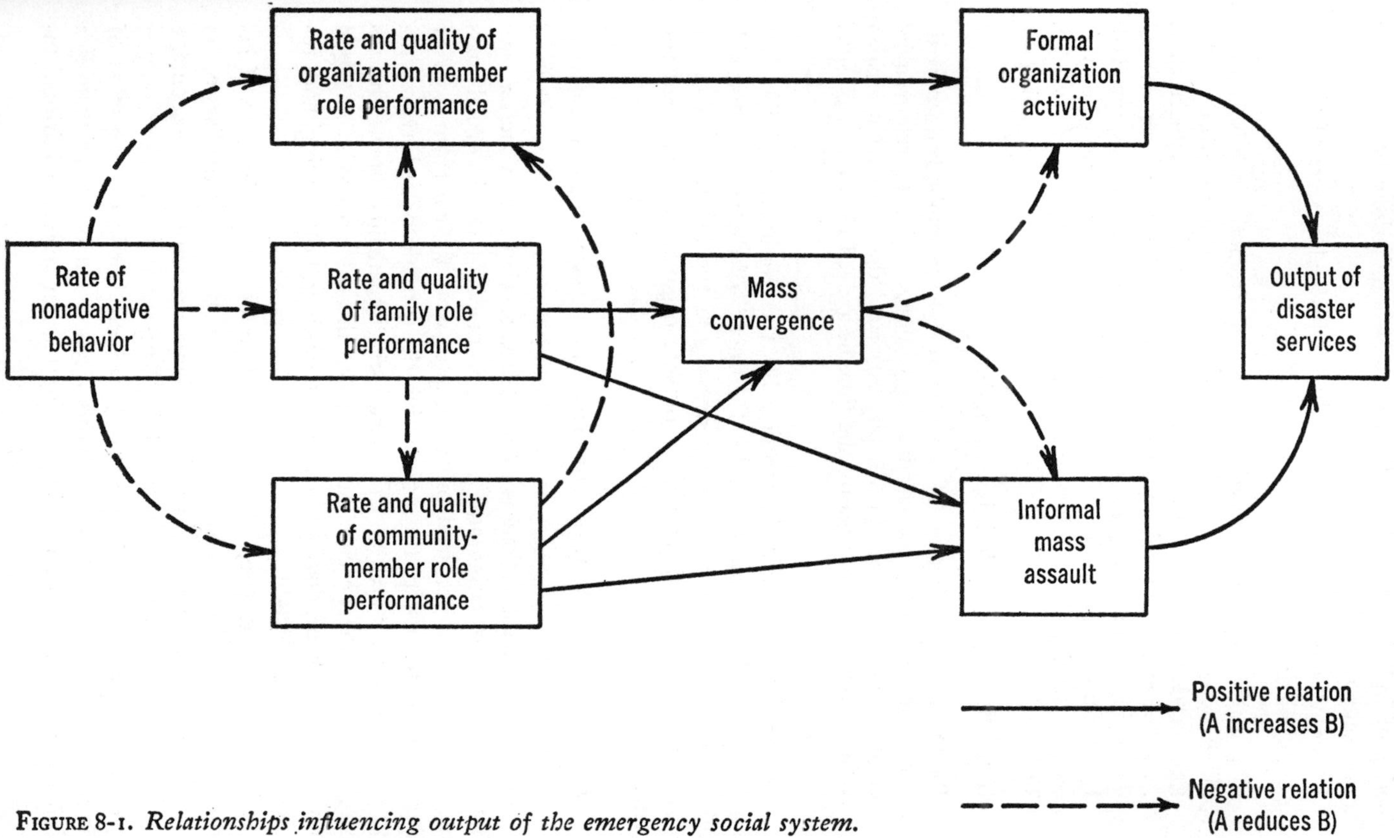

FIGURE 8-1. *Relationships influencing output of the emergency social system.*

behavior of individuals and small groups, although these two components are seldom distinguished.

In the Worcester tornado, a study of medical aspects of the disaster concluded:

> The major work of extrication of injured from the debris and the initial steps to get the injured to medical treatment have been functions carried out chiefly by volunteers who entered the impact zone. . . . The extrication and transportation of the injured has been carried out by intense individual effort which was at first largely disorganized. Later, partial organization characterized by activities of teams of volunteers developed . . . (Raker, Wallace, Rayner, & Eckert, 1956, p. 20).

In the Beecher tornado it is reported:

> By the time the emergency headquarters were established approximately three quarters of the dead and injured had been removed by civilian volunteers. Captain Murphy estimated that a thousand civilian volunteers were in the area by the time he arrived (Form and Nosow, 1958, p. 141).

In the Arkansas tornado studied by the National Opinion Research Center (Marks and Fritz, 1954), "most" of the rescue, first aid, and immediate relief was done by persons in the impact area or by individuals who went there before outside organizations reached the scene.

A QUANTITATIVE ANALYSIS OF THE MASS ASSAULT IN A TORNADO DISASTER

The study of the Arkansas tornado was carried out in such a way that a unique quantitative analysis can be made of the informal mass rescue and relief effort. Probability samples were drawn from a set of four adjoining townships through which the tornado passed, representing both the impact area and the relatively undamaged area. The researchers report the percentage of people in each area who engaged in various forms of disaster activity, including both giving and receiving help (Table 8-1).

These percentages tell us a good deal about the relative rate of involvement in the two areas and the effects of proximity to disaster on participation. The impact area residents have a much higher percentage giving rescue and relief, not only in the first half hour when only a tiny percentage of outsiders were able to help, but in every period of the first twelve hours. Only in giving medical aid by individuals is a higher proportion of the non-impact population active. Additional ta-

TABLE 8-1 *Rates of Various Disaster Activities in Impact and Non-impact Areas in the Arkansas Tornado*

	Performed service:		Received service:
	Impact area residents (per cent)	Non-impact area residents (per cent)	Impact area residents (per cent)
Rescue:			
First half hour	11	—	2
Next six hours	22	4	2
Second six hours (midnight-dawn)	6	1	—
At any time	27	5	5
Informal relief (shelter, food, etc.)			
First half hour	35	5	16
Next six hours	46	25	34
Second six hours	14	8	24
At any time	46	42	75+
Medical aid by individuals:			
First half hour	1	—	1
Next six hours	4	6	6
Second six hours	—	3	6
Search for friends, relatives, or victims generally:			
First half hour	32	7	
Next six hours	28	26	
Second six hours	4	5	
At any time	43	29	
Object of search not found in six hours	15	4	
Total sample:	139	158	139
Total population:	app. 1450	app. 11,000	
Adult population:	app. 850	app. 7,500	

SOURCE: Marks and Fritz, 1954, *1,* Tables 4-8, 4-9, 4-10, 4-16.

bles specify these rates for various social categories—men and women, skilled and unskilled, etc.

Here we are not concerned with the determinants of individual behavior, but with the operation of the community as a social system within which needs arise and resources must be found to meet them. Therefore we must look at the *total output* of services provided by each of the areas and its relation to the total needs of the victims. To obtain this information the percentages have to be projected into *absolute numbers* in the total population.

The crucial fact is that the undamaged sectors of the four townships studied had a population about eight times as large as the impact area; relatively few of the rural communities in the area were struck. Therefore, 1 per cent of the non-impact population amounts to as many people as 8 per cent of the impact population. The 22 per cent of the impact population engaged in rescue work from 6 P.M. to midnight amounted to 190 people; the 4 per cent of the non-impact population so engaged provided 300 people. Roughly the same proportion of both populations gave informal relief at some time; the numbers amount to about 400 impact area and 3,000 non-impact area residents. The proportion of the total number of helpers coming from each area is shown in part A of Table 8-2.

This table presents two sets of findings. Part A shows the relative contribution in manpower of the impact area and the much larger non-impact area of the four townships studied. (There are no data on contributions from still farther away, which became considerable in the later periods.) It shows that during the first half hour, rescue and medical aid were performed entirely by the impact area population. Even in this very early period, however, informal relief was being given by more outsiders than impact residents, and almost as many outsiders as impact area residents were searching for people they were concerned about. In the next six hours, the non-impact population contributed more to every category of helpers, from 61 per cent of the rescue workers to 83 per cent of relief givers and 93 per cent of individual givers of medical aid. This is apparently typical of "segmental" disasters where only a small part of a system is affected—here one-eighth of the four-township area.

We can also compare the absolute numbers of people performing disaster services to the numbers receiving such services. The smaller figures in part B cannot be taken too seriously; chance variations could make a great difference in these numbers, in samples of this size. But the figures do suggest that in the first half hour, there were scarcely more people engaged in rescue work than there were victims requiring rescue (of whom there were roughly seventy). This was a period of severe shortage of helpers relative to need. The next six hours add another 100 rescuers from the impact area, and 300 more from the outside; now the rescue workers outnumber those in need of rescue by about fifteen to one, and the area is probably saturated or oversaturated with rescue workers.

In the first half hour those giving relief are far fewer than the

TABLE 8-2 *Relative and Total Output of the Two Areas*

	A. Proportion of those performing various services who are:		B. Total numbers*		
	Impact area residents (per cent)	Non-impact area residents (per cent)	Engaged in activity	Receiving activity	Ratio of helpers to helped
Rescue:					
First half hour	100	0	94	35	3
Next six hours	39	61	490	35	14
Second six hours	40	60	125	—	—
At any time	38	62	600	70	8.5
Informal relief:					
First half hour	44	56	680	235	3
Next six hours	17	83	2,240	500	4.5
Second six hours	25	75	800	390	2
At any time	11	89	3,490	1,100+	3
Individual medical aid:					
First half hour	100	0	10	15	.6
Next six hours	7	93	485	70	7
Second six hours	0	100	225	70	3
Search for possible victims:					
First half hour	34	66	790		
Next six hours	11	89	2,190		
Second six hours	9	91	410		
At any time	14	86	2,565		

* "Total numbers" are projected from samples of 139 and 158 cases, and are subject to considerable sampling error; they are useful, however, in showing rough orders of magnitude.

number in need of it, judged by the total number who ultimately received relief. By the next six hours, however, the number of relief-givers had grown to exceed the total population of the impact area, largely through addition of 1,800 non-impact residents giving relief, and the output in terms of people receiving relief more than doubled.

The poverty of the impact area in people capable of giving medical aid is suggested by the figures. Other data indicate that about 115 people (8 per cent of the impact area population) had serious wounds or fractures, and another 485 (34 per cent) had other injuries. During the first six hours only 85 received any sort of medical aid from individuals, and this was mainly from individuals from the non-impact area. Those seriously injured eventually received treatment from the formally organized medical centers in a large town in the non-impact area.

A final point can be derived from the total numbers projected in the table: after the first half hour, a very large number of people were engaged in rescuing, relieving, and searching for victims. While some of these activities were carried on in adjacent areas (especially relief given to victims coming out of the impact area), it appears that several thousand people converged upon an area normally inhabited by about 1,400.

These figures are presented in detail because they illustrate the problems of total needs and supplies in the system: inside *versus* outside aid, total helpers *versus* total receiving or needing aid, and total people converging on the area relative to its normal population. They show the rapid mobilization and large output of the mass assault in this segmental type of disaster; they also suggest the problems created by mass convergence and the ineffectuality of the mass assault in performing certain specialized services such as medical care. It would be most useful to have similar data on the inputs and outputs of community systems in other disasters. This would require surveys using probability sampling.

THE RATE OF NONADAPTIVE BEHAVIOR

The Arkansas tornado study (Marks and Fritz, 1954) and most other systematic investigations of disaster indicate a rather low rate of nonadaptive behavior—panic, shock, hysteria, or other forms of personal disorganization. Given the strangeness of the situation and the severe threat to life, to loved ones, and to personal possessions, this is a surprising observation. It suggests that there must be social and psychological mechanisms which enable the population to cope with unexpected and frightening events.

One such factor, the N. O. R. C. researchers suggest, is the influence of primary-group role responsibilities: people are so strongly motivated to look after other family or group members that they do not engage in psychological withdrawal. Another factor is the borrowing of relevant skills from other roles. About one-third of the adult population (almost half of the men and one-sixth of the women) possessed some disaster-related skills from other roles—military experience, professional training, public utilities or construction work experience, or membership in government or disaster-related organizations.

The joint effects of these factors are not directly shown in the

N. O. R. C. report, but they are approximated in Table 8-3, which divides respondents by sex (which is highly correlated with skill) and dependency burden.

TABLE 8-3 *Per Cent "Uncontrolled or Shocked" by Household Status*

Household status	During impact (per cent)	First half hour (per cent)	Next six hours (per cent)	Number
Male head with dependents	6	9	9	(33)
Female head with dependents	4	40	14	(28)
Male head without dependents	15	4	8	(26)
Other nonresponsible roles (mainly females without dependents, plus some single and dependent males)	12	23	23	(52)

The number of cases is too small for the figures to be more than suggestive. It seems that those with family role responsibilities are less uncontrolled during the impact; but immediately thereafter the women with children (who are at the same time largely without disaster skills) show a quite high rate of nonadaptive behavior. Even in this group, however, such behavior is rather low after the first half hour.

The problem of "mass panic" and "shock" is discussed at length in the disaster literature. Janis (1951) examines the data from World War II air raids, and Quarantelli (1954) and others (Janis, Chapman, Gillin, and Spiegel, 1955) the evidence of many descriptions of natural disasters. These authors conclude that the rate of nonadaptive behavior in disaster is generally very low, even in impacts as intense as the Hiroshima atom bombing. Primary-group roles appear to provide people with strong motivation to act rationally; borrowed skills help many people to actually accomplish their goals, even if not very efficiently. Response to long-continued strains, such as unemployment, rural poverty, or prolonged racial oppression is another story; but this is a problem for the long-run restorative system rather than the emergency period.

THE RATE OF COMMUNITY-ORIENTED BEHAVIOR

It is not necessarily obvious that large numbers of people will be motivated to help other community members generally in a disaster. The normal relations between community members in urban societies involve few obligations and little emotional attachment. Mass suffering has existed in times of depression and it exists continually in urban and rural slums, poorly supported mental hospitals, prisons, and migrant labor camps, without calling forth a mass outpouring of sympathy and help.

There appear to be strongly internalized norms which require help to others in certain types of distress where the victims are manifestly blameless. Large-scale physical disasters are ideally suited to activate these norms, because the suffering cannot be blamed on the victims, and it is highly visible and well publicized. Physical disaster literally tears down the walls which divide people and exposes suffering to view; its dramatic and unusual nature activates both informal communications and the formal news media. The suffering of disaster victims has simple and understandable causes, and the remedies lie ready at hand. If people are injured, take them to a doctor; if they are homeless, shelter them; if they are hungry, feed them; if they are trapped in wreckage, free them. The problem is socially and ideologically much simpler than that of providing medical care for victims of "individual disasters" who cannot afford to pay, housing the slum dweller, feeding the chronically unemployed, or freeing the victim of mental illness from his psychic trap—to say nothing of the problem of recovery from a depression or prevention of a world war. Natural disaster is temporary, its causes lie outside the web of social institutions and vested interests, and its cures generally do not place a severe burden on social resources in modern societies. People can afford to be generous under these conditions.

Data from the Arkansas study (Marks and Fritz, 1954) show that almost half the adult population, both of the impact and the nonimpact area, was involved in rescue and relief activities, oriented toward community members generally, beyond the family and friends. About three-quarters of the rescuers were strangers or mere acquaintances of those they rescued. On the other hand, three-quarters of those receiving temporary shelter found it within the family or friendship group. Data from other disasters almost always emphasize the mass helpfulness of community members toward the victims. Either a norm of helping the blameless victims of disaster, or a very widespread individual emotional response of sympathy for them, appears to exist in Western societies generally and provides a major support for the mass response in the emergency social system. This is particularly vital in communities which are less closely knit by primary-group ties than rural Arkansas.

IMPACT VARIABLES LIMITING THE MASS ASSAULT

By the way of contrast with the ratios of helpers to victims found in the tornado disasters, it is worthwhile to examine two other cases in which quantitative data are available. A survey of evacuees from flooded communities in Holland reported that 29 per cent rescued themselves, 31 per cent were rescued by "fellow villagers or islanders," 6 per cent by fishermen, and 12 per cent by soldiers, police, or firemen; the other 23 per cent were unknown or "other" (Lammers, 1955, p. 190). This appears similar to the tornado disasters, in spite of the much wider and more prolonged impact. The Dutch analysts point out, however, that the picture would be drastically different if one concentrated on the most severely and suddenly flooded areas. Qualitative studies of three badly flooded communities report the complete inability of groups isolated on housetops and dykes to help themselves or others, and the inability of the rest of the community or nearby areas to aid them for a long period. In the deep and rough waters of the first day of flooding, boats were essential, and there were hardly any within the communities studied. A survey of villagers in one of these communities showed that only 4 per cent were rescued by fellow villagers and the same per cent rescued others. Of the total sample of evacuees, only 12 per cent were rescued during the first six hours, and 38 per cent spent more than twenty-four hours under the flood danger (Ellemers, 1955, p. 23).

In Hiroshima the A-bomb left 30 per cent of the population dead or dying and another 30 per cent seriously injured. Janis (1951) discusses the question of how much mutual help there was among victims in the first hours after the disaster. Some witnesses and some analysts suggest that the survivors behaved in an irrational and unhelpful manner:

> The people seemed stunned by the catastrophe and rushed around as jungle animals suddenly released from a cage. Some few apparently attempted to help others from the wreckage, particularly members of their family or friends. Others assisted those who were unable to walk alone. However, many injured were left trapped beneath collapsed buildings as people fled by them in the streets. Pandemonium reigned as the uninjured and slightly injured fled the city in fearful panic (U.S. Strategic Bombing Survey, quoted by Janis, 1951, p. 29).

Janis believes that these generalizations are incorrect and finds no evidence of mass panic in any primary source. On the contrary he finds many descriptions of efforts to help other victims, no complaints by respondents of not receiving aid when in need of it, and no one who admitted failing to give aid when it was possible to do so.

Quantitative data are unfortunately very sparse. Analysis of about fifty interviews with Hiroshima residents made by the bombing survey produced the following findings:

> Seventeen percent mentioned having received aid from strangers and 4 percent mentioned aid from family members or close friends. Furthermore, 17 percent mentioned giving help to strangers and 11 percent, to members of their own families or close friends. In general, a fairly sizeable proportion of the Hiroshima interviewees (over one-third) referred to rational, practical actions carried out in order to assist other people, whereas no one spoke of any form of neglect (Janis, 1951, p. 39).

This figure is less than the roughly 50 per cent of the Arkansas tornado impact area population who did rescue work or gave relief. If we compare the proportion giving aid with the proportion who needed such aid—the severely injured, including some who died for want of aid, and the dying whose sufferings might have been eased—the discrepancy is obvious. In the tornado, rescuers outnumbered the rescued by almost ten to one, and those who gave relief in the first few hours outnumbered those receiving it by three or four times. In Hiroshima the proportion of impact area residents giving any form of aid is about equal to the number who were severely injured but ultimately survived—to say nothing of the equal number dead, dying, or trapped. Furthermore, in Hiroshima, as in the Arkansas disaster, the general population was able to do little for the medical needs of victims. But in Hiroshima, unlike the Arkansas area, most of the doctors and nurses were killed or severely wounded and most of the hospitals destroyed, so that victims went without medical aid for long periods.

If we shift the analysis of the Hiroshima data from the question of "mass panic" to the problem of the relation of supply of help to demand, it appears that the mass assault, while still important as a source of rescue and relief, was grossly inadequate in relation to the need. The fact that "no one spoke of any form of neglect" seems to be weak evidence compared with the descriptions of many trapped without aid, dying without medical care, begging water from passers-by, and dragging their injured bodies out of the city.

The Dutch flood illustrates a disaster requiring special equipment and skills which could not be provided by the local population. The Hiroshima A-bombing illustrates an impact which produced so many victims that those capable of helping, even if they all were willing, were outnumbered by those in need. The public's self-help abilities, therefore, should not be taken for granted in every sort of disaster.

III. Organizational Mobilization in Community Disaster

If the mass assault is one arm of the community's response to disaster, the formal organizations are the other. Organizations can do many things beyond the power of unorganized groups, because they have coordination, special skills, and equipment. The problems of organizations in disaster are to gather their personnel together quickly, to get men and equipment into the disaster area, and to function as an organization, with internal communication, leadership, and division of labor, under difficult conditions. A prior condition is of course that the organization have men, equipment, and skills useful in disaster, and that it define its responsibilities as requiring action to help the community in the type of disaster which has occurred.

We will consider some of these problems of organizations in disaster and their remedies. The analysis of organizational responses to disaster is necessarily qualitative at present. While most case studies of disaster contain some information on the behavior of organizations, it is not standardized and detailed enough for systematic comparisons or statistical analysis. Details of how organizations mobilized, how they were managed, and how they cooperated are not always spelled out, and no "standard background data" are normally collected on organizations as there are on survey respondents.

The closest thing to a standardized description of organizations is found in Form and Nosow's (1958) study of the Flint-Beecher tornado. In that study, for each of seven organizational units, seven areas of performance are reported: (1) speed and completeness of mobilization, (2) degree of internal coordination, (3) relations with other organizations, (4) utilization of volunteers, (5) perception of tasks, (6) perception of organizational needs, and (7) self-evaluation of performance. In addition, "background information" is presented on their formal structure, strength of informal organization, social composition, training and commitment of personnel, experience with emergencies, and extent of planning for large-scale disaster. This makes their report much more useful.

If a "standard inventory of organizational background and activity" could be developed for future disaster studies, systematic comparisons and statistical analyses of the behavior of organizations would become possible. Here we will use a more traditional kind of "comparative analysis," in which we hunt through the case studies for facts bearing on a number of questions and try to draw conclusions from the resulting very crude "correlations" of organizational attributes and performance.

THE RATE OF ROLE COMPETITION

The choice between formal organization or professional roles, primary group roles, and informal community-oriented activities in a disaster may involve role conflict. The overload of demands created by the disaster breaks down the normal time-segregation of responsibilities. For individuals this may create psychological conflict and non-adaptive behavior. For organizations and groups, this must lead to failure to get participation of some or all of their members, with a resulting breakdown in group activities. From the viewpoint of the community system, many organizations are dispensable in preference to family or community-oriented behavior; but certain organizations and professions are essential if disaster services are to be provided and losses minimized.

Killian (1952), in his well-known study of the problem of role conflict in four disasters, gives examples of the failure of organization members to stick to their job, along with a few cases in which they did. Examples of the abandonment of organizational roles are also found in the Flint-Beecher tornado study (Form and Nosow, 1958), the Waco tornado study (H. E. Moore, 1958b), the Halifax explosion (Prince, 1920), and the N. O. R. C. disaster studies (Marks and Fritz, 1954). The tendency to abandon organization roles appears to be very general. The mechanism which solves the problem from the individual point of view—clear-cut role priorities which prevent doubt and confusion—generally favors the family role and contributes to the problem for the community system.

An examination of cases in which organizations did manage to function or to recover quickly suggests two kinds of mechanisms which support the needs of the organization. One set operates to give organizational roles the higher priority in case of conflict:

A. Training of essential organization members and professionals to give first priority to the job and not the family. The research reports contain practically no cases in which this has occurred. This may have influenced the orderly shut-down of the oil refineries in Texas City by workers whose families were in danger (Killian, 1952).

B. Visibility of organizational or professional personnel, so that clients and community members exert pressure on them to stay on the job. This clearly operated for the Texas City minister (Killian, 1952), the Flagler mortician (Marks and Fritz, 1954, *3*), and the Worcester bus driver (Wolfenstein, 1957, pp. 98-99).

C. Degree of primary-group loyalty among organization members. This also may have operated among the Texas City oil workers (Killian, 1952). Shils and Janowitz (1948) show the importance of this factor in a military organization in disaster.

A second set of mechanisms operates to avoid conflict between family and organizational responsibility.

D. Proportion of organization members recruited from outside the local area. In a disaster of limited scope such people will not be in conflict. Examples are state policemen and utilities workers.

E. Proportion of organization members without close family ties. This applies especially to the old-fashioned armed forces, and of course to the Catholic church (Prince, 1920).

F. Availability to organization members of information on the scope of the impact. In limited disasters this would eliminate family *versus* job conflict for the large number of organization members whose families were actually safe.

G. Availability of rapid communication with home, to reassure members whose families are actually safe (Form and Nosow, 1958, pp. 169-170). This is very difficult to arrange, due to limited capacity of communications systems and likelihood of damage to them; when organization members are actually at home at the time of impact, those whose families are safe know it and are less subject to conflict.

The extent to which organizations are inactivated or delayed in their mobilization by role competition will depend on these attributes of the organization, the community system, and the impact situation.

LEADERSHIP RECRUITMENT AND COMPETENCE

A second major problem in organizational mobilization is that of the competence and sense of duty of the organization leaders. This appears particularly in voluntary associations, but also where position in public agencies is obtained through general social status or particular social ties.

A striking example is presented by Form and Nosow's description of the Red Cross in a large city adjoining a tornado-struck suburb:

> The key committee chairmen in most cases either did not go directly to headquarters, or having gone there, did not remain there to organize activities. . . .
>
> As indicated, the disaster plan depended for its execution upon high status volunteers who occupied the key roles of committee chairmen. Only three of nine chairmen interviewed phoned others when they heard of the disaster. Three did not take action of any sort upon hearing of the disaster. . . .
>
> Rank-and-file members of these crucial committees . . . first responses were either to call the committee chairman or the Chapter House for orders or directions. In most cases, since orders were not forthcoming, the permanent volunteers went directly to the disaster area . . . (1958, pp. 190-194).

Those responsible for mobilizing the organization did not mobilize themselves, so that while there was a large input of individual activity, it was disorganized and inefficient. Why did this organization's leadership fail to play their assigned roles?

Form and Nosow explain the difficulty largely in terms of the problem of recruitment of personnel for a voluntary organization:

> Since it is difficult to get ideal personnel for each role, volunteers who lack competence must often be used. Hence, a situation often arises where the community status of the individual dominates the official evaluation of his competence. Consequently, high-status roles within the organization are often delegated to volunteers with high status in the community, rather than to persons who have more technical competence (1958, pp. 214-215).

However, it was not only these high-status "volunteers" who failed to do their job.

> After being alerted, the local members of the Red Cross exhibited a wide variety of behavior. Some responded immediately and acted in accord with the demands of their position, while others did not. One would anticipate that the former would be the professional workers and the paid staff. This was not entirely the case, for most of the professional personnel behaved almost randomly, and not in accord with the demands of their offices. Actually, those responsible for the *direction* of activities at headquarters, both paid and volunteer workers, went to the tornado area instead (1958, p. 193).

The behavior of these full-time employees is not explained by the "status-recruitment" hypothesis. We may speculate that they had never practiced their roles under stress, and were overwhelmed by the intense and confusing stimuli of the disaster situation.

By contrast we have in the same disaster the rapid and complete mobilization of the Salvation Army. All members interviewed had heard of the tornado within an hour. Officers with a corps of volunteers mobilized at the Social Hall, moved into the disaster area quickly, and set up rescue and relief teams. The secretary at the hall took telephone calls and directed incoming personnel to the field. Communications were maintained by messenger service in the absence of telephone lines.

The Salvation Army perhaps even more than the Red Cross appeared to have a formal bureaucratic structure; every member had a military "rank." However, it also had a very strongly developed informal structure:

> The dominant characteristic of the Army, actually, is its informal operation . . . the common bonds and sentiments of its members. . . . Its members comprise a religious congregation of close-knit families. The ties that bind them together are common religious, family, and

> class sentiments forged by constant personal association. . . . All members of the Army have an idea of what the organization is supposed to do in time of crisis: feed, clothe, and shelter people, and give them spiritual comfort (Form and Nosow, 1958, pp. 176-177).

The problem of leadership recruitment arises in several studies of peacetime civil defense organizations in the United States. These agencies appear to be something in between public bureaucracies and voluntary associations dependent on private support. In one city studied, the full-time professional head was a person without high status or political power, and lacked funds to build up his own organization. The basic activities were farmed out to committees headed by high-status volunteer chairmen who were capable of begging and borrowing resources from existing organizations. The rescue committee, for example, persuaded industrial firms to organize and equip rescue teams: "It is obvious that this could not be done by other than a high-status individual who can meet owners and managers of industrial firms on their own terms" (Friedsam, 1957b, p. 2). Similarly, the medical committee chairman had to obtain the cooperation of high-status leaders of the medical society and the hospitals to make medical preparations.

In this city the committee chairmen functioned actively both in planning and in actual disaster operation. However, the civil defense headquarters did not provide coordination. It had little influence on the planning, and when a disaster arose each committee chairman operated on his own, without even coming to the headquarters, which in any case had never been equipped with adequate communication lines. The effort to run a public agency largely through voluntary private support had resulted in recruitment of a leadership group representing various social constituencies, without allegiance to any central authority.

Two disaster studies from other countries provide further instances of "ascriptive" recruitment to public positions which resulted in poor disaster performance. In a Mexican city studied by Clifford, the mayor (*presidente*) was the product of a personalistic, one-party system dominated by the state governor, which selected candidates for the one-party local "elections" on the basis of: "(1) kinship ties to those in formal power positions and to other important prestige groups, (2) friendship ties, (3) repayment of past favors, and (4) evidences of personal loyalty and related characteristics" (Clifford, 1956, p. 23). The mayor's response to an early warning of possible flood danger was ineffectual.

> There were no attempts to check the warnings with federal agencies such as the meteorological and water resources office that might have had special access to accurate information. . . .

> Evaluation of warnings by personnel of the *presidencia* [mayor's office] seemed to rest on (1) trips to see the river, (2) a strong belief that the flood could not reach the city, and (3) least of all, on the increasingly urgent warnings that were being received from various authoritative sources (Clifford, 1956, p. 40).

The mobilization of community agencies was delayed for a whole day. The day after the warnings first came, an evacuation was carried out, using loudspeaker trucks to warn the population and trucks of various local agencies to carry the population; but by then, thousands were trapped by high water and well over a hundred were drowned. The evacuation having been completed, the *presidente's* office took no action to alleviate the problems of some 25,000 refugees in the hills until the arrival of the state governor and the army commander.

The performance of the local government in this Mexican city was in striking contrast to the effective warning, evacuation, and relief effort of the United States city of Eagle Pass across the river. There the city administration, headed by a professional city manager, responded rapidly and energetically to early warnings, with a high degree of cooperation between agencies. Repeated efforts were also made to pass on warnings to the Mexican city.

In Holland, control over the local dykes is under the authority of local polder boards. Polder boards are headed by a dyke-reeve; the dyke-reeves form the drainage area board for the locality.

> The main function of this "dyke-reeve" is organizational and administrative. The position carries with it a good deal of social prestige, and its bearer rarely knows much about tides or water levels (Nauta and van Strien, 1955, p. 13).

In a land below sea level, administration of the dykes might be thought a vital community task, and the technical incompetence of these officials comes as a shock, especially to foreigners brought up on legends of the Dutch boy and the dyke. However, the village studied had not had a serious flood since the sixteenth century.

The structure of the dyke-maintenance organization was fragmented and poorly adapted to coping with disaster: it was a patchwork of independent local authorities, rather like the government of an American metropolitan area.

> Resistance against a more centralized maintenance scheme must be viewed in the light of this form of organization, which acquired the character of a grouping of interests; expenses of the inner-polders were considerably less than those of the outer-polders, for they were not responsible for the maintenance of the sea-dykes (Nauta and van Strien, 1955, p. 10).

In 1953 a very rare combination of winds and tides raised the level of the North Sea. At low tide on the evening of January 31, the water stood at the high-water mark, but no one in authority paid attention to this warning; at high tide it rushed over the dykes. The situation in one town was described as follows:

> When various authorities received alarming news . . . they tried to put the people concerned—and themselves at the same time—at ease, without becoming alive to the seriousness of the danger. The members of the polder boards, too, paid little attention to the high level of the water. There were no overall alarm systems and there was little contact among the "dyke-reeves" who individually were autonomous, so that everything depended on the personal vigilance of the individuals concerned. . . . With the decentralized polder organization, there could be no question of the general mobilization of a "dyke-army." Any action was generally taken by the lower ranks. . . .
>
> It was quite a different stratum of the village community which turned out under the pressure of the growing danger. In the first place in [the village] it was those few in whose lives the water played a certain role—the truck driver, the municipal workman, the inn-keeper . . . and a few polder workers. Starting from them, a continuous line leads to a number of others . . . the personnel of the agricultural Cooperative Society, the two carpenters, and others (Nauta and van Strien, 1955, pp. 26-27).

Neither local government leaders nor the dyke officials were capable of organizing action to delay the flood waters or to give timely warning to the people.

EXISTENCE OF PRE-ESTABLISHED EMERGENCY PLANS

Some of the most effective responses to disaster come from public utilities corporations. Their networks of wires or pipes give them a direct "nervous system" throughout the community, and their normal operations require quick response to small-scale breakdowns or fairly large-scale weather damage; they have standard emergency plans which are recurrently put into practice. In recent years these have been supplemented by civil defense-oriented plans for large-scale disasters. These plans rely on the technical competence and initiative of local personnel to take quick action, backed up by a full mobilization of the organization's resources from a very wide area beyond the struck community.

These features are illustrated in several studies. Moore describes the electric company in the Waco tornado:

> The multi-community electric corporation supplying power to Waco, foreseeing the need for disaster planning, had drawn up a detailed plan

> to be used in case of a major calamity. This plan was put into operation immediately and seems to have worked excellently. For example, without any specific authorization from the company, one man quickly made a purchase of $4,000 worth of raincoats for linemen. This was one of the things he had been instructed to do when and if the emergency plan went into operation. Some persons immediately bought flashlights and other critical materials. Others placed emergency generators at strategic points to take care of such places as freezing and cold-storage plants and hospitals.
>
> The immediate task, of course, was to make sure that live wires were not exposed. Workmen traced the major lines throughout the affected areas . . . (H. E. Moore, 1958b, p. 42).

The Arkansas tornado study reported a like response:

> As soon as the power company discovered that its services were disrupted, it put its standard emergency plans into operation. This involved, first, locating the main sources of trouble, and, second, moving men and equipment into the area to deal with the problem spots . . . (Marks and Fritz, 1954, *1*, p. 291).

The gas company in Arkansas had not anticipated mass damage to its underground lines. However, its employees in the community acted promptly to cut off gas from the main valves—within twenty minutes in the village where they were, and forty-five minutes later in the next village, which they reached with difficulty through the darkness and wreckage.

> Despite the fact that no plans had previously been drawn for this type of disaster, the gas company was able to adapt its preexisting emergency plans to the situation. Individual servicemen and crews had been sufficiently trained to cope with this somewhat unusual situation (Marks and Fritz, 1954, *1*, p. 295).

Not all advance plans are put into effect. Notable failures are reported in the studies of hospitals in disaster (Raker *et al.*, 1956; Rosow, 1955, pp. 124-128) and in some of the civil defense organizations (Friedsam 1957b; H. E. Moore, 1958b; Rosow, 1955; Wallace, 1956). The cause of the failure in each case appeared to be the "paper" nature of the plan—the lack of careful rehearsal to make people learn their roles under the plan, and in some cases the failure to provide essential equipment to make the plan workable.

DEFINITION OF ORGANIZATIONAL GOALS IN COMMUNITY DISASTERS

There are some cases in which organizations, warned in advance of impending disaster to the community, have stood aside and done relatively little to help, at least in the early stages before mass suffering has arisen. A clear instance is the behavior of the army post in the Mexican city threatened by flooding. Word was received two days before the flood crest arrived. The post commander and his men made their own preparations, but aside from one visit to pass the warning on to the mayor, there were no attempts to coordinate warnings and early protective actions with other organizations of the community. Only after the flood had arrived did the army go into action to help the community; from this point on, fortunately, they provided a major source of rescue and evacuation assistance (Clifford, 1956, p. 43).

The police of this city, who were also responsible to an external hierarchy rather than the local government, showed even less concern with the community. The chief received warning from the American city across the river, but in the words of one official: "We didn't try to talk it over with anyone; we continued routine protection of the city." The off-duty half of the force was not called up. When the flood arrived, the only concern of the police force was to evacuate the prisoners from the jail and prevent them from escaping. The rest of the force "evidenced almost complete disintegration during the disaster" (Clifford, 1956, pp. 41-42).

This behavior of the army and police contrasts sharply with the community-service orientation shown by United States armed forces and state police units when nearby communities suffer disaster, as reported in many studies (Crane, 1960; Form and Nosow, 1958; Killian and Rayner, 1953; H. E. Moore, 1958b; Rosow, 1955).

In the United States disasters which have been studied, it is difficult to find a case of an available organization which did not try to play a part in the disaster effort; the problem is, indeed, that of competition to get into the act. Commercial organizations, whose formal, legal goal is to make profit for their owners, are regularly diverted to provide needed disaster services when human lives are in danger. In Waco (H. E. Moore, 1958b, p. 14), merchants made available their stocks of tools and work clothing to rescuers. A commercial laundry dried the rescue workers' clothing and gloves. In Flint (Rosow, 1955, pp. 338-342), industrial and contracting companies sent crews with heavy equipment to help with rescue and road clearance; one contractor took charge of mobilizing and dispatching equipment from those firms possessing it. In the Arkansas tornado (Marks and Fritz, 1954, *1*, p. 298), a contractor in a town thirty miles away brought in bulldozers and an electric generator within a few hours after impact; the next day government bodies and private firms for miles around sent in equipment, which was put in charge of one private contractor in town in order to coordinate street clearance. The strength of community identification and humanitarian motives is evident among leaders of every type of organization, in this obvious and "natural" kind of disaster. Almost the only reported examples of uncooperative behavior during the emergency phase are the refusals of some hospitals in Southern cities to admit Negro disaster victims. In other cases, segregation has been modified or temporarily abandoned to permit Negro victims to receive emergency care. The stronger the caste divisions in society, the less able it is to cope with unexpected situations which require a pooling of resources.

To answer the question of which organizations mobilize for action and which do not would require a more careful survey of organizations in the community and region of the disaster than has yet been carried out.

> In the case of the Flint-Beecher tornado, literally hundreds of organizations participated or claimed to have participated in the rescue and rehabilitation activities—to mention a few—lodges, churches, labor unions, Boy Scouts, businesses, volunteer police, hospitals, professional societies, Red Feather (Community Chest), and Civil Air Patrol. Many of them participated or claimed to have participated in all stages of the disaster—in warning, rescue, and rehabilitation (Form and Nosow, 1958, pp. 127-128).

It would be interesting to know which organizations regarded each phase of the disaster as "their business" and attempted to help as organizations, which suspended operations to permit members to function elsewhere, and which tried to continue normal operations regardless of the disaster.

IV. Coordination within and between Organizations

It is one thing for an organization to gather its members and send them into the disaster area; it is another to keep in touch with them, find out what problems they are encountering, and send them what is needed. The difficulty of coordinating activities under the time pressure and disruption of normal channels which characterize the emergency social system has been reported by many researchers. Some organizations serve simply as a source of manpower—training, mobilizing, and sending into the field competent individuals or small teams which thereafter function on their own; others try to act as organizations in the disaster area. The job of controlling the activities of personnel sent into the disaster area from many sources may be taken over by some single agency or improvised center, so that the various components become integrated in a "super-organization."

The problem of coordination has been studied comparatively in four tornado-struck communities by Rosow (1955) and for six organizations in one community by Form and Nosow (1958). H. B. Williams (1956) and Thompson and Hawkes (Chapter Nine, this volume) have summarized a large number of studies.

If organizations are to behave rationally, there must be communication between their leaders and the situation they are trying to deal with.

A good example of the problem of field communication is found in Rosow's (1955, pp. 324-329) analysis of the Flint-Beecher tornado data. At an early stage, the Michigan state police got a report that the center of the impact was a drive-in theater, which was in fact only on the periphery of the damaged area. Shortly thereafter a fire truck from a nearby town actually worked its way down the road past the drive-in, and found that there had not been a severe impact there. But what the firemen knew was not communicated to the state police. Assuming heavy casualties at the drive-in, and that the direct road there was blocked, the state police sent badly needed ambulances there on a two-hour drive over a roundabout route. Furthermore, when the state police found out the true situation, the Red Cross was not informed, and they sent a field radio station to the drive-in area. All three organizations had radio nets, but they had no shared communications center which could put all the information together (Figure 8-2).

A contrasting case is reported by Rosow (1955, pp. 173-178) in the Massachusetts town of "Shelby." Here the local police made an immediate survey of the area of destruction, making running reports to headquarters over the police radio; conditions in each area were noted on a master record in police headquarters and manpower and equipment were shifted according to needs revealed by this master chart. The police chief was even able to go into the field, with his field radio equipment, and continue coordinating the operation as he moved from point to point (Figure 8-3).

In the nearby town of "Harwood," the state police were making use of an open radio net between cars in the field and headquarters (Rosow, 1955, pp. 205-208, 211-222). As their cars moved into the disaster area they monitored the reports of the cars already there and directed themselves accordingly. Headquarters meanwhile mobilized equipment according to these same reports and dispatched it where it appeared most needed. This sharing of information made it possible for each unit to act rationally with a minimum of outside direction (Figure 8-4).

The centralized communications net (Figure 8-3) permits all information received from field units to be compared and recorded in the organizational "memory," so that instructions can be given to each

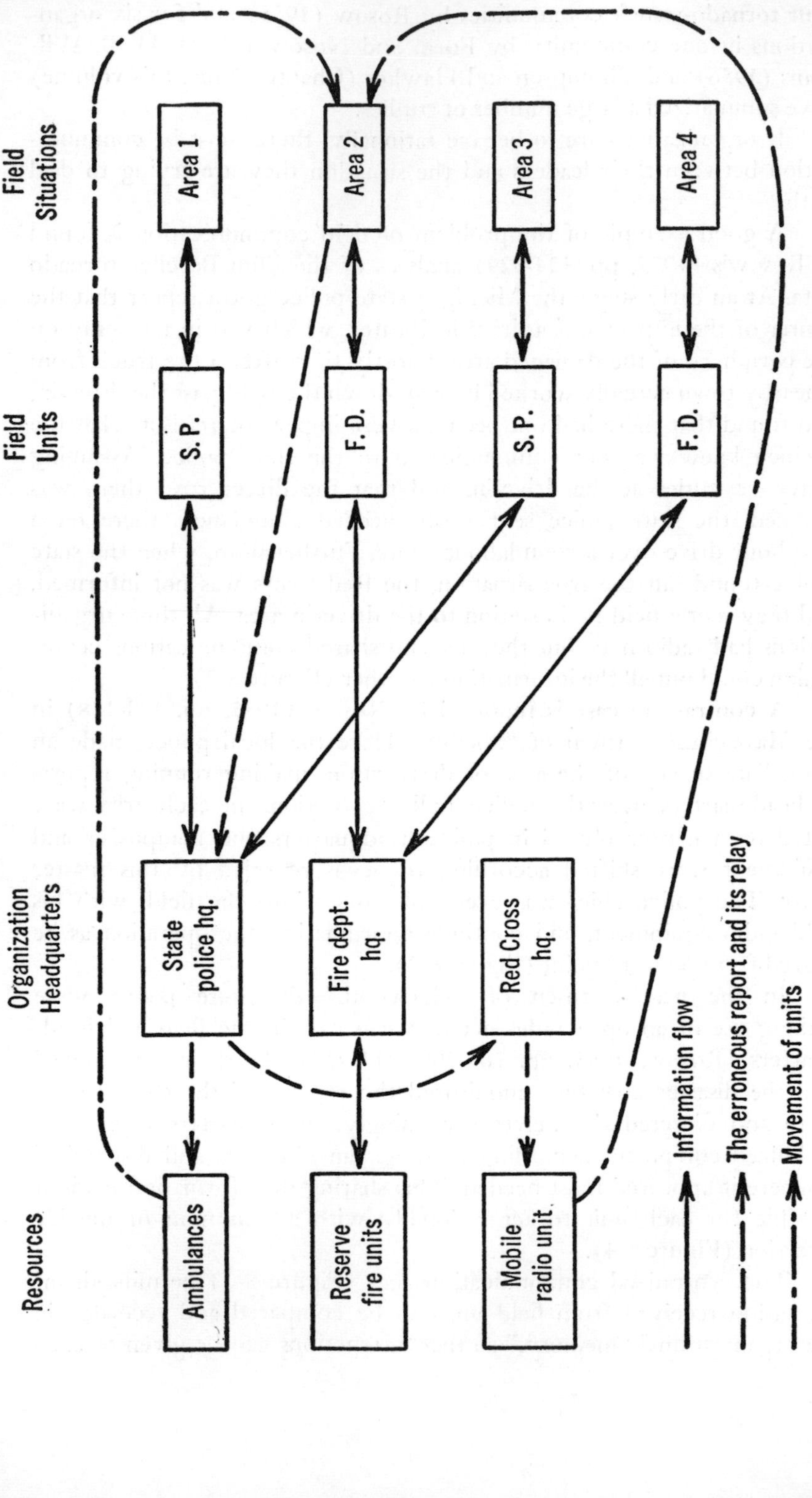

FIGURE 8-2. *Flint-Beecher: Communications about the drive-in incident.*

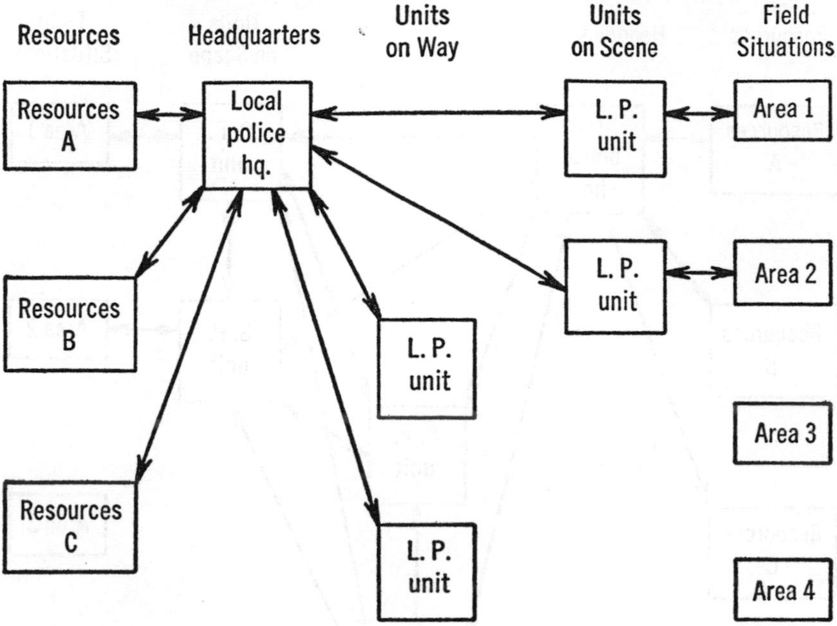

FIGURE 8-3. *Shelby: Centralized communications net of local police.*

field unit on the basis of what all other field units have found out. A centralized comparison of the reported "needs" of each area can be made, so that resources are allocated relatively rationally.

The "open communications net" (Figure 8-4) permits all this and more: each field unit is automatically possessor of the collective knowledge of the whole, and can adjust its actions accordingly without further messages from headquarters. However, such a system is limited in its total message capacity to what one channel can pass. If the number of field units were large, too many people would be trying to talk at once. But within the limits of its capacity, it has great advantages.

A seriously defective type of communications net arises if the field unit broadcasts its requests for help to many individuals and organizations which control resources, without any central coordination of the response. The result may not only be waste of resources but a harmful glut of supplies, personnel, and equipment in some areas. Examples are found in Moore's study of the Waco tornado, and in the Holland flood disaster. Moore notes:

> Civilian rescue "teams" were at first merely unorganized groups. Any member who lacked some article called out his need, and the request

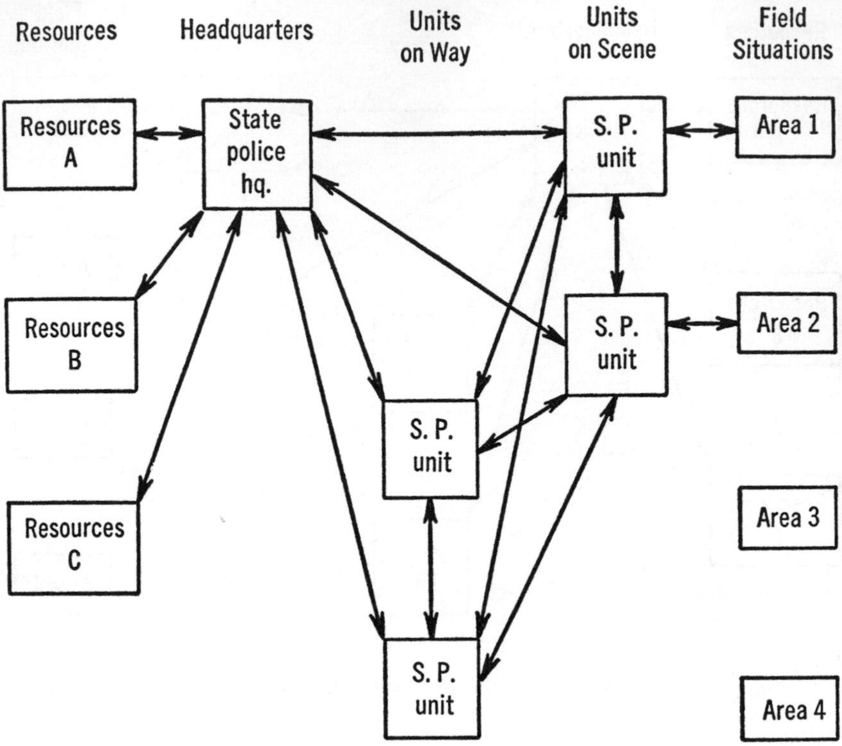

FIGURE 8-4. *Harwood: Open communications net of state police.*

was picked up and amplified by loud-speaker trucks. From here it often went out over radio, connected to a state-wide hookup. As a result, roads were choked with assorted public and private conveyances bringing assistance, some needed and some not. An officer in command of some 18,000 soldiers was told, when he asked what aid he could supply, to "send everything you've got." Fortunately, he did not take this demand literally and later discovered that no more than 200 of his men could actually be used to advantage (H. E. Moore, 1958b, p. 13).

Van Dijk and Pilger report this incident from the Dutch flood:

Via the military sender, [the village of] Haamstede asked for cattle fodder and a surgeon. The result of repeated broadcasts, which went over the whole of Holland, was seen next day. Six surgeons and ten tons of cattle food arrived. In the rest of the area, Haamstede was reproached for this. "Mr. Q (the burgomaster) lost his head," they said; "Mr. Q asked for more cattle cakes than he needed" (1955, p. 57).

In its simple form this type of communications net involves the one-way communication of needs from a single field unit to many unlinked sources of supply—an indiscriminate broadcast (Figure 8-5).

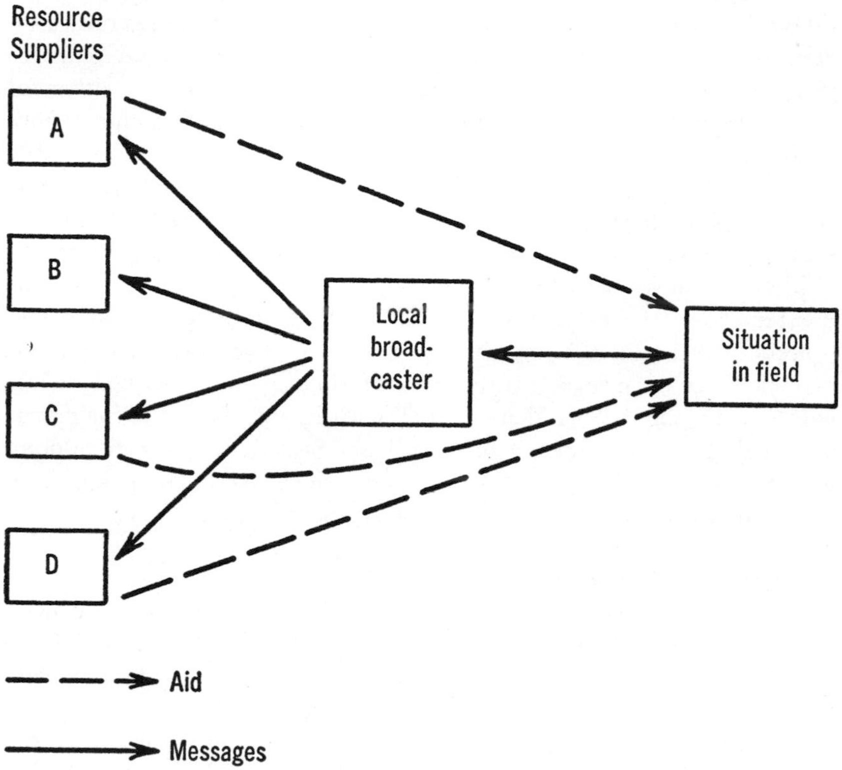

FIGURE 8-5. *Results of indiscriminate broadcasting from impact area.*

But note that, in both the examples given, the situation was still more confused. There was two-stage broadcast repetition—in Waco first by the loudspeaker on the scene and then by radio over the state, in Holland from the local broadcast to repetition by other stations over the country. A center is needed to coordinate messages from the field areas to the sources of supply and to assign particular resource units rationally among areas needing them.

The bad examples so far have been poorly *coordinated* communications systems; all of the units involved had the capacity to communicate, being equipped with two-way radio. Needless to say, this is not a universal condition for organizations and work groups. For most organizations, the loss of telephone service is literally disorganizing, although over limited areas foot or car messenger service may be used, as by the Salvation Army at Beecher (Form and Nosow, 1958, p. 178). This makes it especially important that organizations and individuals with radio communications facilities cooperate with other organizations which can provide disaster services. Such cooperation is not easily developed in the disaster situation, where each organization tends to give priority to its own communications. Prior planning, either of specific cooperative relationships or for a general local communications center, would be of great value.

The ability of modern societies to create an "emergency social system" of such scope, encompassing such wide areas and vast resources, is uniquely dependent on long-range instant communications. Without them the wave of information would spread slowly from the disaster scene; the emergency social system would be limited to resources available in the impact area itself. In underdeveloped areas it may be days or weeks before news of the fate of a remote village comes to the capital. Sudden disaster, with its urgent needs for rescue and medical care, requires a broadly based system which can respond in minutes to save lives; rapid communications make this possible, so long as disaster strikes a relatively small segment of the society.

THE GROWTH OF A COORDINATING CENTER

To be effective, the emergency social system requires a central coordinating headquarters which can pool information received from varied sources in the field, control appeals for outside aid, and allocate forces in the field and from the outside. Such a coordinating center was present, at least for the main search and rescue activities, in the Worcester, "Harwood," "Shelby," San Angelo, and Warner Robins tornadoes, and in the Eagle Pass flood. It was absent, at least for long hours after impact, in the Waco, Flint-Beecher, and Judsonia tornadoes, in the Brighton gas explosions, and the Lampasas flash flood. What determines the development of such a center?

Thompson and Hawkes (Chapter Nine, this volume) discuss the emergence of a coordinating center as part of their analysis of organizational processes in disaster. They note: "There are few clues as to where it is likely to emerge, but some evidence suggests that it is likely to emerge wherever knowledge of needs and resources overlap."

There is a hint here of a model which might account for the coalescence of such a center, in cases where it was not created by prior planning or authoritative decree. Organizations, subunits of organizations, and individuals become aware of their lack of information about where to get or where to give disaster services. They search for information at the same time as they spread the information which they possess. Out of this process of seeking and exchanging information, some "nodes" of great density of information arise, as proto-suns and planets emerge in the "dust-cloud" hypothesis of planetary formation. Once a concentration of information builds up, it attracts more communications from those with requests or offers; information "snowballs" in proportion to the amount already present. Those who wish to make decisions may then locate themselves at this center, or else the people who happen to be there may take over decision-making functions.

Such a concentration is most likely to arise where there is communication equipment, or a socially central location for interpersonal contact, which is known and accessible to the organizations and individuals interested in the disaster. Good technical facilities are not themselves enough; if access is denied to "outsiders," a potential center may remain limited to a single organization. An interorganizational center can develop only by participating in an "open" exchange process.

The problem of where "authority" is located was studied intensively by Rosow (1955) in four tornado-struck towns. A number of hypotheses about the growth of coordinating centers emerge from his analysis. In the town of "Shelby," the local police chief set up an effective radio communications net into the disaster area, as described earlier. He was also known by professional reputation throughout the region. These two factors induced the outside police, militia, and air force groups coming in to accept him as leader of the disaster effort in the community; and his office became linked into their communications system (Rosow, 1955, pp. 175-179, 190-192). Figure 8-6 shows the resulting system.

In the town of "Harwood" there was not much of a local police organization, but there was an energetic civil defense leader who had maps, blood-type lists, and a centrally located office at the town hall. This office became a center of local communications, especially for word-of-mouth, on-foot transmission. The civil defense director consulted with the mayor, laid out search and rescue sectors, and dispatched volunteers to these sectors as they arrived at the town hall. A central listing of casualties and damages was virtually complete twelve hours after impact and provided information for all those seeking residents of the impact area (Rosow, 1955, pp. 193-198, 208-210). Figure 8-7 shows this system.

The local civil defense headquarters had only limited telecommunications. It was linked to a civil defense mutual aid system with neighboring towns, but this system lacked a center to coordinate the dispatch of aid. Communications within the town were slow because of lack of local two-way radio cars. The state police provided most

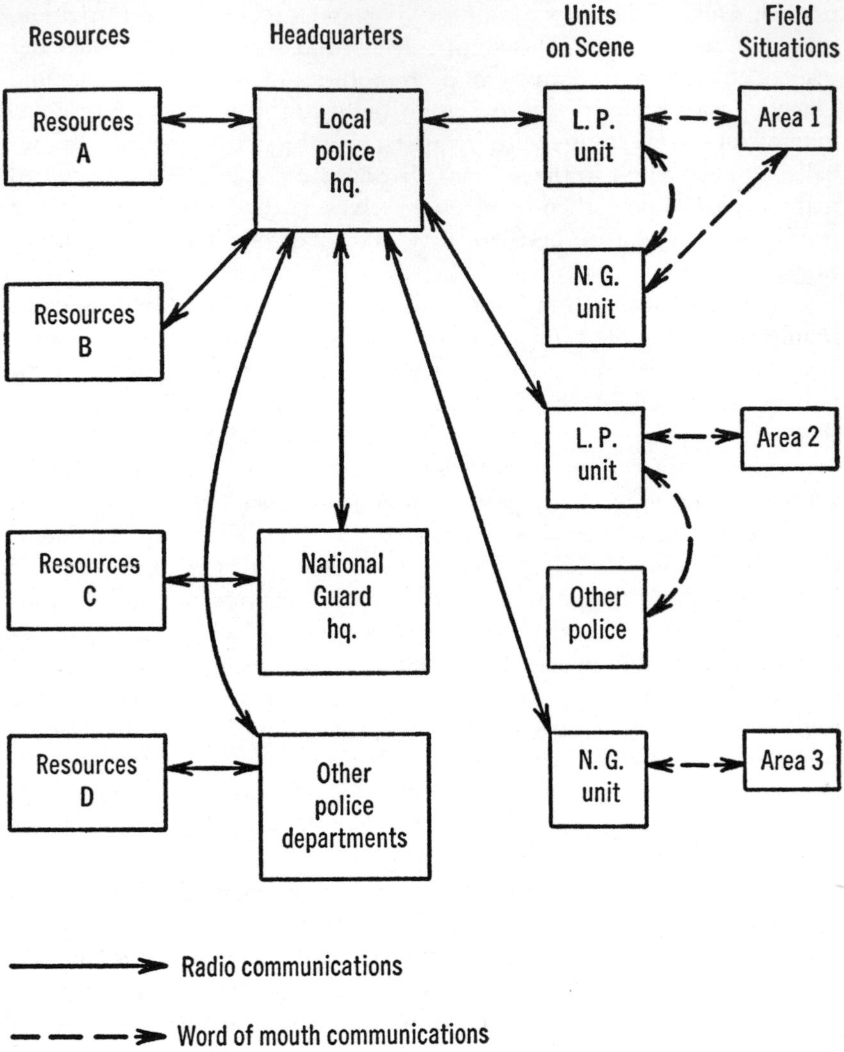

FIGURE 8-6. *Shelby: The local police serve as field headquarters for various outside organization units.*

radio communications in the "open net" between their Harwood post, their radio cars, and their headquarters some miles away. They coordinated the sending in of outside resources, and they provided mobile communications posts in the impact area (Rosow, 1955, pp. 206-208, 215-216).

The delay in creating a coordinating center in the Flint-Beecher

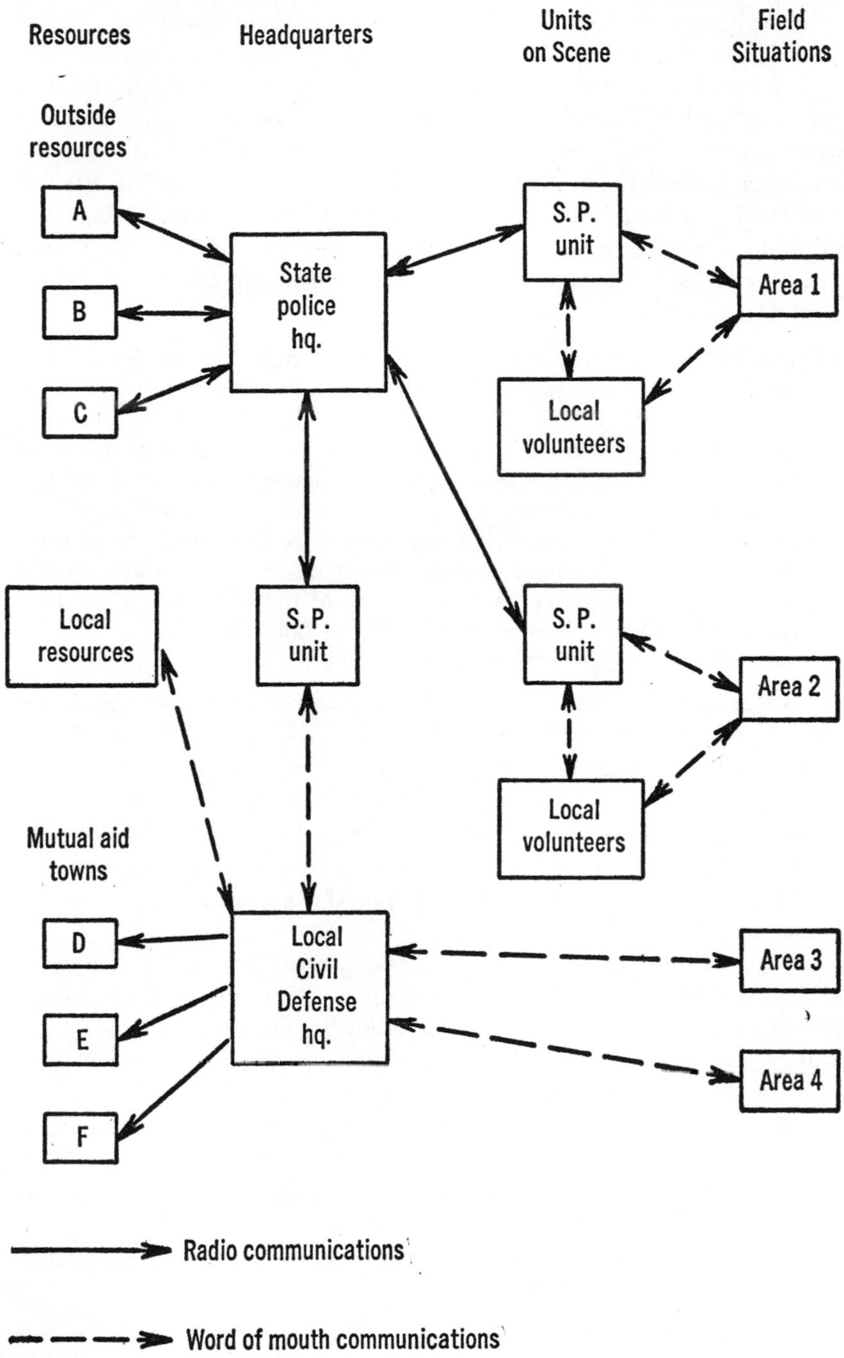

FIGURE 8-7. *Harwood: State police provide radio communications for local units.*

tornado is discussed both by Rosow (1955) and by Form and Nosow (1958). The local state police post did not realize for three-quarters of an hour that there was heavy damage nearby. The state headquarters was confused by fragmentary and erroneous reports, sending many cars to various places to check them; it was not until an hour and a half after impact that headquarters realized where the main damage lay.

During this period, approximately three-quarters of the dead and injured were being removed from the impact area by "civilian volunteers." The local state police post contributed manpower to this effort, but little coordination:

> An analysis of these actions indicates that members of the State Police at first did the very things that volunteers were already doing on the scene: digging for victims, carrying bodies, directing traffic, protecting property, and other tasks. . . . Only gradually did they begin to differentiate their activities and assume functions traditional to their work. . . .
>
> Although all troopers felt that they were functioning at all times as members of the organization, most of their actions were actually spontaneous and uncoordinated. Because of the confusion at the Flint post and field headquarters, and lack of walkie-talkies, communication to individual troops was poor (Form and Nosow, 1958, pp. 147-149).

Once state headquarters had located the impact area, its forces were rapidly mobilized and sent in. A field headquarters was established about midnight, three and a half hours after the impact; a systematic block by block search was instituted; by 1:30 A.M. control points were established on all roads leading to the impact area; by 3:00 A.M. the field headquarters had its own radio and telephone connections. By morning this headquarters had "become the communication channel for all agencies."

In creating a central disaster headquarters, the state police actually served three functions. First, they gave their own units a coordinating center so that they could function "as an organization" in the impact area. Second, they provided other agencies with communications between their headquarters and their field units, so that they could function more like organizations. Third, they provided for coordination between organizations, by creating a pool of knowledge of needs and resources on which each agency could draw, and by making certain allocation decisions.

The delay in creating a central headquarters was especially serious in Beecher because there was literally no local government.

> Beecher actually is the name of a water district that serves an area which encompasses parts of two townships. It is not a community in a formal sense but is a combination of neighborhoods amorphously tied

> together by the overlapping jurisdictions of Genesee County, the Genesee and Mt. Morris townships, the Beecher Water District, and the Beecher School District (Form and Nosow, 1958, p. 56).

When this anarchic patchwork was hit by the tornado, there was no local authority to which either insiders or outsiders could turn.

In this authority vacuum, the governor gave the state police overall coordinating authority. However, they did not exercise this authority to create an effective coordination center. Rosow (1955, pp. 352-362) attributes this to a conventional norm of respect for local authority and a rather limited view of its "police functions." They worked closely with other units of the "police cluster"—police of the adjacent city, National Guard, and private industrial police—but made little effort to coordinate the activity of civilian agencies—the Red Cross, the Civil Air Patrol, the contractors, the fire departments, and the nearby city governments. The state police were incapable of acting "governmentally" and broadly beyond their specialized functions.

V. *The Relationships of Organizations and Mass Behavior*

The collective behavior of the public and the activities of formal organizations meet at many points. The public may get in the way of organization members trying to reach their assigned place of work; they may contribute materials to the organizations or provide "volunteers" to the organizations; and they may seek services from the organizations. Most organizations have some normal relationship to the general public—as an electorate, a source of contributions, customers for services, or an audience. In the compressed time of the emergency social system, new relationships with the public have to be worked out. Therein lies much of the difficulty of rendering the emergency system effective.

THE PUBLIC AS AN OBSTACLE: MASS CONVERGENCE

The problems of public "convergence behavior" have by now been explored in many disaster studies and are summarized in the monograph by Fritz and Mathewson (1957). A vivid expression of the problem was given by a military man at the Waco tornado: "There were thousands of persons milling around; it looked like the storming of the French Bastille" (H. E. Moore, 1958b, p. 11). This seems to happen in every peacetime disaster studied except for floods which make travel impossible. The blocking of incoming rescue equipment and outgoing vehicles carrying wounded people to hospitals is reported in the Arkansas, Beecher, Waco, and Worcester tornadoes as a serious problem.

Efforts to control this influx have sometimes been effective after the immediate emergency was over, but the difficulty of setting up an almost instantaneous control of access routes makes it unlikely that it can be eliminated. Whether it would always be desirable to completely eliminate mass convergence may be doubted, in view of the many services quickly performed by the convergers and the relative slowness and limited resources of the formal organizations. On the other hand, once specialists and their equipment are available, it would be most useful to turn off the mass convergence and clear the roads for the organizations. This is typically done by setting up control points on the main access routes well back from the impact area, and screening traffic trying to enter; to do this effectively and without causing great delays is a major enterprise in itself.

Both convergence and the abandonment of organizational roles have a common origin: the desire of people to play family or community-member roles in the disaster situation. Fritz and Mathewson (1957), in their summary of the convergence problem, suggest that inaccurate and ambiguous broadcast news and the interpersonal flow of rumors outside the impact area arouse far more people to be anxious about family, friends, and relatives than need be. First "news flashes" are possibly more often inaccurate than accurate, because they are based on fragmentary and speculative reports and are put out without any check on their accuracy, to meet competitive standards which emphasize speed rather than correctness. They are likely to set many times as many people moving as actually need be concerned.

Finally there is a component in the converging mass—its proportion is controversial and we do not have even good estimates—of people motivated by idle curiosity rather than a desire to help—the "sightseers." These are the kind of people who respond to radio bulletins of fires, explosions, and possible airplane crashes, at which they could not possibly be of help, by jamming the highways and interfering with organized activities. Perhaps a greater public awareness of the extremely anti-social nature of this behavior would help to control it, as would a more responsible approach by the commercial news media.

THE PUBLIC AS SOURCE OF SUPPLIES TO ORGANIZATIONS

In a society as rich in material goods as ours, the general public can serve as a warehouse of supplies needed in disaster: flashlights, blankets, clothing, food, hand tools, power tools—even blood. The process of mobilizing these supplies, however, is full of difficulty, and has often created such convergence of people and materials that those who called for public aid wished they had not.

> In the Flint-Beecher, Michigan, tornado, for example, a public appeal for flashlights was made over the radio. Over 500 persons individually responded by driving their automobiles toward the stricken area to donate their flashlights, thus greatly aggravating the severe traffic congestion. . . . Just as one of the major hospitals was beginning to achieve order in the processing of disaster victims, it was suddenly confronted with about 2,000 unwanted blood donors, who appeared as a result of appeal broadcast over the local radio stations (Fritz and Mathewson, 1957, p. 26).

The influx of clothing to the relatively small Arkansas communities struck by the 1953 tornado was overwhelming, and itself constituted a serious problem for the local disaster authorities, since most buildings had been blown down.

Fritz and Mathewson write:

> The needs in disaster are strategic and selective needs. Equipment, supplies, and services are needed in particular quantities, types, times, and places. The mass media are not well adapted to serve this strategic supply purpose, since there is little control that can be exercised over the potential donors once the appeal is made. The central difficulty in the use of these media, in other words, is that they require institution of a screening function *after* the supplies begin arriving rather than *prior* to their solicitation (1957, p. 26).

These writers suggest that if mass appeals have to be used at all, or if mass contributions cannot be avoided, there be created a central supply clearinghouse outside the disaster area, and its location impressed upon the public mind. This clearinghouse would be connected to the central coordinating authority, which could screen all public appeals before they are issued and allocate resulting supplies rationally and efficiently to the disaster scene. Here H. B. Williams' (1956) emphasis on "feedback" and "control messages" corresponds very closely to reality; rapid "cease and desist" appeals could be broadcast if the rate of arrival of given items indicated too great an oversupply. For such control to be effective we would have to know the approximate time-lag and momentum of public response, and the "snowball" effects of interpersonal spreading of messages from the mass media. The leaflet-dropping experiments of the Washington Public Opinion Laboratory (De Fleur and Larsen, 1956) suggest the model for the study of these phenomena. By having the clearinghouse out of the way of the traffic into the impact area, it might also be possible to absorb most over-response to appeals without loss to the rescue-relief effort.

THE PUBLIC AS A SOURCE OF VOLUNTEER PERSONNEL TO ORGANIZATIONS

We have noted the enormous amount of emergency work done by the residents of the impact area and the early "convergers" from other areas as well as the serious problems of lack of skills, coordination, and equipment, which reduce the effectiveness of this great input of effort. Perhaps the most important single device for improving this effectiveness would be collaboration between the mass public's informal rescue-relief work and that of organizations. Organizations linked into a centrally coordinated system can direct this manpower to places where it is most needed and avoid overcrowding in other places. They can provide equipment and specialists to complement the mass of semi-skilled and unskilled rescue workers. And they can provide competent work-group leaders to compensate for this labor force's lack of disaster skills. The proper kind of organizational framework could have a "multiplier effect" on the output of mass activity. An improper attempt to control the mass assault might only strait-jacket it.

The normal protective agencies of the community are accustomed to thinking of the mass public as a nuisance, to be controlled and kept out of the way in normal, small-scale emergencies. Their monopolistic attitude toward emergency work is likely to persist even when the task is far beyond their capacity. The more rigid and authoritarian the organizations, presumably the less easily they can cope with the opportunity and the necessity of using public help. Form and Nosow report the response of several organizations to the use of "volunteers."

> There is no clear definition given by the Michigan State Police as to what a "volunteer" is. The only people who seem specifically exempt from this category of volunteer are members of the Michigan State Police. . . . The impression received is that the State Police in the field worked intermittently with the people around them, and that specific work groups composed of volunteers were not formed (1958, p. 151).

The Genesee county fire department was in one sense entirely composed of "volunteers," but they were trained and formally identified with their organization. They "did not spontaneously attach individuals in the disaster area to their work teams."

> Rather, their help was chiefly a group of auxiliary firemen selected from a standing list and from a group that volunteered at their firehouse in Geneseeville. This, in a sense, formalized the relationship between the Genesee firemen and their volunteers (1958, p. 173).

For the National Red Cross officials in this disaster, everyone in the local organization was defined as a "volunteer." The locals on the other hand tended to distinguish the "regulars" from the "transient volunteers." The local officials felt quite positive toward the use of all forms of volunteer; the rank-and-file "regular volunteers," however, "had some feelings of ambivalence toward the use of volunteers." Apparently "this loose and ambiguous definition of volunteers has the effect of breaking the bonds of identification so necessary for the persistence of the solidarity and morale of working groups." It is a wise leader who knows his own members. Cooperation with outsiders can perhaps best be achieved if everyone is clear about who is *inside*. The social heterogeneity and social distance within the Red Cross were a basic cause of this confusion (Form and Nosow, 1958, pp. 211-213).

None of these examples suggests a very effective use of nonmembers as temporary helpers by organizations. The Beecher study concludes, from its survey of 116 participants in informal rescue groups:

> Only 5 percent of the acts in the emergency stage were performed in conjunction with identified organizations operating in the impact area. Only 3 percent of the activities of individuals in their first phases were associated with organizations. In their third phase, one-tenth of the acts were so associated (Form and Nosow, 1958, p. 115).

Rosow's (1955, p. 312) description of the uncoordinated rescue teams in Beecher picking over piles of wreckage which some previous team has already searched, and hearing behind them other teams pushing the wreckage around which they have just finished searching, vividly illustrates the inefficient use of personnel in an unorganized mass assault. In the Waco tornado:

> The lack of control over volunteer workmen was often dangerous, the City Engineer pointed out: "We had a lot of people working around and sometimes they were working on each other. In one spot we were trying to get a valve uncovered, but we had a heck of a time keeping others from throwing lumber down on top of us!" (H. E. Moore, 1958b, p. 14).

Volunteer helpers who formed as a team before they arrived and who came from the same nondisaster organization were much more effective than random assortments made on the spot. Groups from the steel workers union and other local unions and student groups from the local university all formed effective teams. For those who were not organized in advance, leadership and communications equipment were eventually provided by the military organizations.

> Military workers brought organization to the rescue efforts by incorporating civilian workmen in their teams. By the second night these teams were commonly composed of 15 men under a leader and an assistant leader, with a walkie-talkie man to keep contact with headquarters and other nearby teams (H. E. Moore, 1958b, p. 14).

In another tornado-struck town, a minimal organization of volunteers was created by a police officer who formed the volunteers up into teams of five with one man in charge before they were sent into the impact area.

Further study of effective modes of relationships between disaster organizations and on-the-spot volunteer helpers should be of great practical value in disaster planning. The idea that everybody should be organized in advance is utopian. Organizations should plan and practice ways of exploiting the spontaneous mass response to disaster more effectively.

THE PUBLIC AS CONSUMERS OF ORGANIZATION SERVICES

An organization providing disaster services, like any other public service producer, cannot do its job unless it makes contact with those who need it.

When large numbers of the public find themselves in need of medical services, they generally know where to go—the hospital. In the Beecher, Worcester, and other tornadoes, "the" hospital was usually the largest, best known one in the area (Rosow, 1955, p. 153). The result of this mass definition of the appropriate place to go—apparently shared by such key personnel as ambulance drivers—was a great overload on certain large hospitals, while smaller institutions, including some much nearer the scene, were under-utilized (see Raker *et al.*, 1956, p. 28).

The situation was still more difficult for newly created hospitals and first-aid stations. We are told that "cars loaded with victims drove right by," that the services were under-utilized, that few people appeared until later when the rescue and rehabilitation workers used the facilities for care of minor injuries (see Form and Nosow, 1958, pp. 47-53). We do not know to what extent this happened because of public ignorance of the facility, and to what extent because of public definitions of what facilities are appropriate to the needs of injured people. The wide variation in the quality among places calling themselves "first-aid stations" may contribute to this problem of public definition.

In the case of first-aid stations, three things seem to be needed. There should be some way of grading and labeling them as to whether they have competent personnel and adequate supplies, so the customer can make a more rational decision. Their existence should be made widely known, especially to people transporting injured victims. And the public should be informed, preferably in advance, of the relative dangers of delaying all treatment until hospital facilities are reached and of delaying hospitalization to obtain first aid. We know little about how the public feels injured people should be handled; there is reason to believe that they are very badly informed about physiological shock, bleeding, extensive burns, or fractures. Unless they are better informed, they will continue to make irrational decisions. Similar problems arise with nonmedical services.

If sometimes the public goes to the wrong places, it is also true that the organizations sometimes provide the wrong services. The American Red Cross (1928, 1938) has a notable record of providing mass shelter for evacuated flood victims in the great river-valley floods. Tent cities built with army supplies and administered competently by the Red Cross sprang up in the Mississippi flood of 1927 and the Ohio floods of 1937. When tornado disasters struck Beecher, Worcester, and other areas (Rosow, 1955, pp. 89, 120, 150), the Red Cross tended to think of the evacuees as needing mass shelter. In the tornado disasters such mass shelter was invariably almost unused by victims, although it sometimes served later as quarters for imported rescue and cleanup workers. The surveys of the Arkansas tornado victims (Marks and Fritz, 1954, *1*, pp. 169, 258) and the Eagle Pass flood evacuees (Clifford, 1956, p. 118) showed that almost all found temporary shelter with friends or relatives. The difference between these cases and the river-valley floods lies in their ecology; these floods make whole communities and districts uninhabitable and knock out entire extended-family and friendship groups, while the tornado or limited flood does not upset a workable ratio of evacuees to untouched relatives and friends (Young, 1954).

VI. Methods for Increasing the Output of the Emergency System

If we go back to the scheme of relationships influencing output of the emergency system (at the beginning of this chapter), we can summarize and locate the main proposed methods for improving this output. One kind of improvement reduces the negative effects shown in the scheme; another kind increases the positive relationships between activity and output.

PRIOR TRAINING

Prior training, either of the general population or of a scattering of potential leaders in each neighborhood, may reduce the rate of non-adaptive individual behavior (panic, shock, etc.) at the same time that it increases the competence of disaster role performance. The panic-shock reaction itself does not seem to be quantitatively important in the disasters studied, but the efficiency of the mass response is clearly low due to lack of skills, and individual role incompetence in the face of strong motivation to help loved ones appears to create later emotional difficulties. It seems unlikely that training will overcome the tendency to abandon organizational for family roles among people who believe their families to be in danger. However, their number may be reduced by taking positive steps to insure their families' safety.

ACCURATE MASS COMMUNICATIONS

Accurate mass communications could have several important effects. By providing the mass public with trustworthy information on the scope of impact, it could reduce unnecessary convergence and abandonment of organizational roles. For each individual to go personally and look at his family is an extraordinarily inefficient system of communication; but our normal telecommunications simply cannot cope with the load of messages people want to send in a disaster. Broadcasting news of the precise areas of danger would of course arouse some people to leave organizational and other roles and converge on the scene; but as long as the area of *actual* impact is narrower than the area of *feared* impact there will be a net gain. Of course, complete and accurate registries of casualties and evacuees, made available through mass media or communications centers, would be still more effective; but this highly individualized information takes so much time and effort to put together that it is more feasible after the immediate emergency period than during it.

A COMMUNICATIONS CENTER

A communications center to receive all reports from field units would permit more rational allocation of organization units and of resources coming in from the outside. It would also be necessary if mass communications are to be made accurate. The increase in output due to more effective organization activity might be very great, especially during the period when rescue and medical care are the primary needs and time is of the essence. Such a center would permit organized activity by those agencies which do not have their own two-way radio system, and it would link those which do have such field communications into an information pool, multiplying many times the information available to each. Such a communications center would also permit a further step to be taken: *central planning and allocation of resources* by an over-all disaster authority.

ORGANIZATION

Organization of the informal mass assault and its integration with organizational activities is another way in which available resources can be rendered much more productive. Such a simple technique as the assignment of a leader to each informal work group and the assignment of areas with some means of marking off what has been done could greatly reduce wasted effort and uneven coverage. The linking of such semi-organized groups to organizations with specialized equipment, and to the communications center, would again multiply effectiveness. Such links are now sporadically improvised; if organizations in the field were trained to promote them, the "informal mass" might become more of an organized body. The art of quickly organizing a large body of "volunteers" could be developed if organizations were willing to admit their legitimate function in large-scale disaster.

The *direct* effects of the four proposed policies on the emergency social system can be shown in a simplified scheme of variables (see Figure 8-8). By referring to the earlier scheme (Figure 8-1), it is possible to trace out a number of indirect effects, both positive and negative. Convergence might be reduced by withholding information from the mass media or by concentrating police efforts on sealing off approach routes; but this entails a *cost* in reduced output of the "informal mass assault," which has to be roughly weighed against the possible gain. We have assumed that some desirable measures are impossible—for instance, making every organization member stay on his job regardless of the plight of his family. The problem is to maximize output within the (crudely indicated) system of constraining relationships.

Training any significant number of citizens, training organizations to assist and work with informal volunteer groups, preparing for accurate mass media coverage, and creating a centralized disaster communications system all require community planning and organization in advance of the disaster. Skills and coordination do indeed eventually emerge in unprepared communities as the disaster goes on, but at the cost of great inefficiency and loss in the early phases. Whether the investment in such community disaster preparation is considered worthwhile depends on the amount by which it would reduce losses in various types of disasters, relative to the probability of those types of disaster. Areas subject to frequent threat of tornadoes and hurricanes have already begun to develop such systems—notably Texas and Flor-

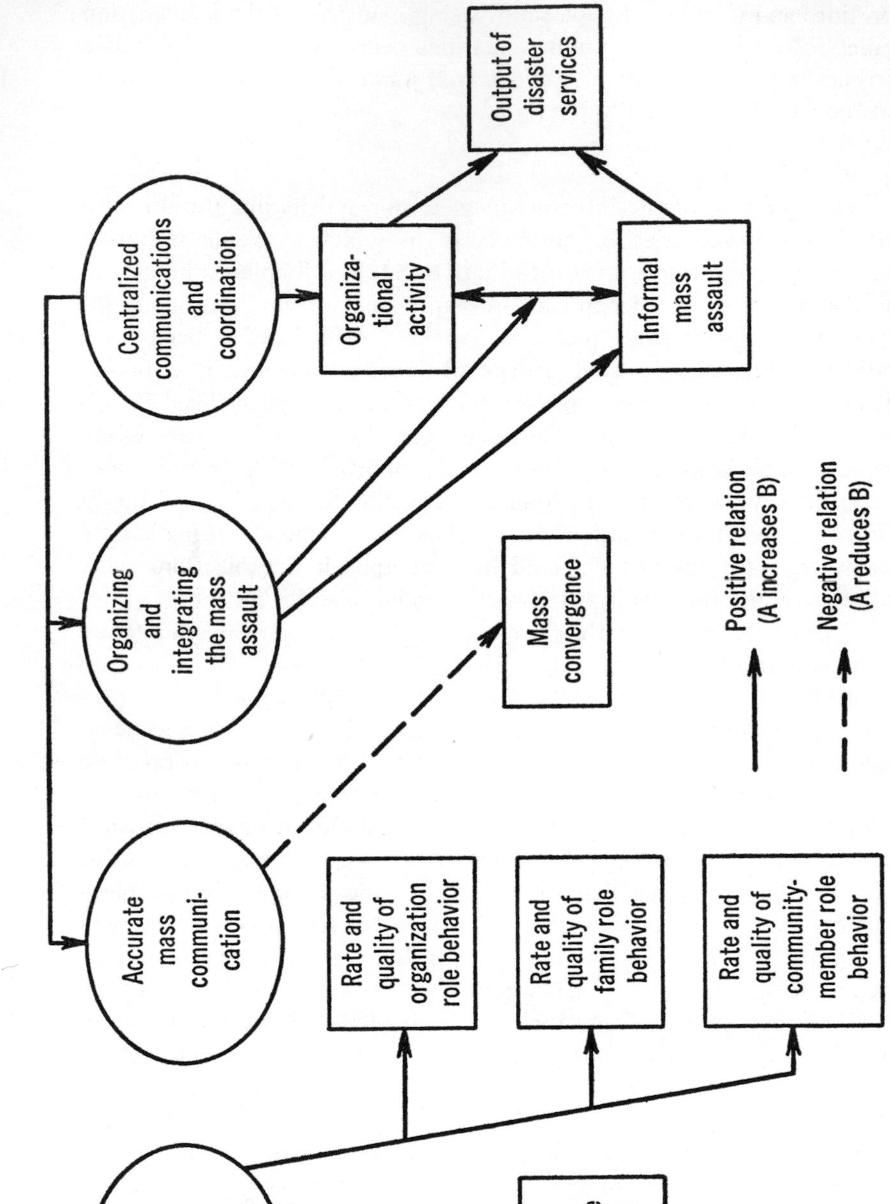

... Direct effects of four policy variables on the emergency system.

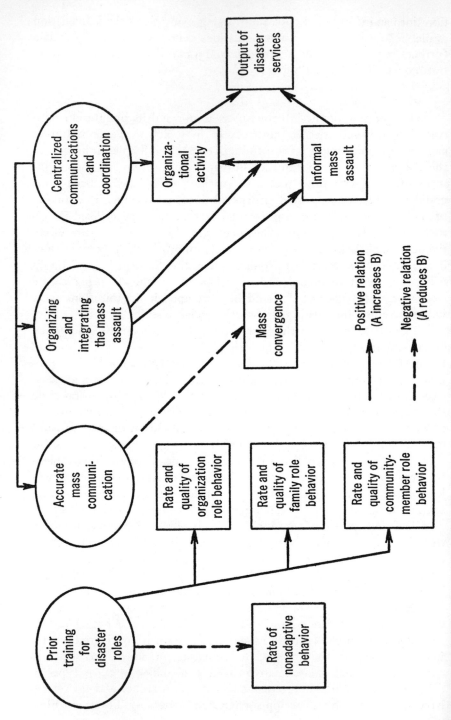

ida. The creation of such systems to cope with tornadoes, hurricanes, floods, earthquakes, and accidental explosions in other parts of the country is largely a question of cost.

Whether the kind of emergency social system studied in one-community disasters has any relevance to the problems of regional or nation-wide destruction, as in major floods, earthquakes, or massive nuclear attack, is not easily answered. We have tried to suggest some limiting conditions by making comparisons with the flood and atom-bombing situations which have been studied. The breakdown of organized civil defense in the major fire-raids on German and Japanese cities and in the atom bombings of Hiroshima and Nagasaki suggest that systems adapted to one scale and type of impact may be quite ineffective in disasters of a different order of magnitude. The question cannot be answered by simple extrapolation from smaller-scale disasters.

Rather it requires two kinds of extension of the analysis. One would have to try to estimate the probable response of community systems to much more devastating, and technically different, types of impacts, and second, to estimate the extent to which the national social system could contribute to these community efforts. If this is done, it will become possible to guess at the consequences of large-scale disasters and the extent to which various types of preparation would reduce losses.

▶ *nine*

DISASTER, COMMUNITY ORGANIZATION, AND ADMINISTRATIVE PROCESS

James D. Thompson and Robert W. Hawkes

TWO FUNDAMENTAL CHARACTERISTICS of any system are (1) that it has differentiated parts and (2) that its parts are interdependent. In focusing on the community as a type of social system we must therefore attempt to identify its parts, determine how they are differentiated, and examine their interdependence. But by watching the system as it changes we gain understanding not only of the distribution of parts and their interrelationships but also of the *processes* by which the system *allocates* its elements and *integrates* them. Sudden, severe shocks to the system are particularly revealing, for they tend to highlight allocation and integration processes that may go unnoted in communities under more normal conditions.

Our focus will be on the processes by which communities allocate and integrate their parts in responding to such disasters as tornadoes, floods, explosions, and hurricanes. The gradual decline of a community's economic base is outside the scope of this paper; so is capture of a community by an enemy. Our reference to "disaster" is to sudden and disruptive events that overtax the community's resources and abilities to respond, so that outside aid is required.

Our reference to "community" is geographic. The community has a place in time and space, it may be identified on maps, and it can be located by longitude and latitude. Thus the "community of schol-

Throughout this project we have had the valuable consultation of Dr. Robert W. Avery. His notions of "synthetic organization" and of the importance of institutional patterns were major contributions. We also are indebted to our other colleagues in the Administrative Science Center, especially Dr. Carl Beck, for valuable criticisms.

ars" is excluded, and we concentrate on what in everyday terms are referred to as towns, cities, or urban areas. For purposes of convenience we do not consider such metropolitan complexes as London, Tokyo, New York, or the crossroads settlement of a dozen families.

This chapter is organized into five sections. In Section I we sketch out our conception of the community as a social system in its normal state. We present in Section II a set of propositions about the phases through which the system moves in response to a disastrous event. In Section III we outline a model composed of variables and changes in their relationships which we believe describes the passage of the system through the several phases. We examine relevant descriptions of community disasters in Section IV, attempting to illustrate the model in action. Finally, in Section V, we summarize and discuss some implications of this exercise for social system analysis and administrative theory.

I

System Problems in the Community

A community in contemporary American society has many facets in its normal state. It can be viewed economically, as an arena for commercial, industrial, or fiscal transactions. It can be viewed politically, as the place where collections of individuals govern themselves, using the government as a vehicle for obtaining things that individuals alone cannot provide—such as streets, schools, sewer systems, and police protection. From the health and welfare standpoint the community is a place where "the helping skills" and resources beyond the scope available to most individuals are collected and dispensed to members of the community. The community can also be viewed as the arena in which children are nurtured into adulthood and where families obtain needed shelter, food and clothing, and religious expression.

In the communities under consideration all of these things—and more—are normal and are going on simultaneously. This means that the community is a *multi-purpose* system, and one of its problems is to allocate and integrate its resources so as to attain its several purposes, virtually simultaneously, subject only to ebb and flow in tempo between night and day, weekdays and weekends, or seasonal fluctuations.

The community is also an *open* system; it is not self-sufficient but exchanges materials, energy, and information with its environment. In order to maintain the necessary environmental exchanges, some parts of the community must play dual roles—one within the community as a component part of the community system, and one as a link in a larger system. These parts of the community receive resources from and must be integrated into two systems, which means that the community's allocative and integrative processes to these parts must leave room for adjustment.[1]

The community must somehow manage its resources not only to serve its several purposes simultaneously but also to meet the conditions posed by its physical and social environment. The resources it has to allocate and integrate may be grouped under four headings: (1) tasks, or social roles; (2) personnel, or role players; (3) physical facilities; and (4) money.

Basically these resources are allocated into families, the *primary parts* of the social system. Historically, American communities usually developed around collections of families and the larger, *secondary parts* (such as firms, associations, and agencies) were later developed to solve problems beyond the capacities of families as individual units. Even where large-scale enterprises are installed "in the middle of nowhere," families must be lured and communities built up. In part, secondary units are created to handle problems stemming from the simple concentration of families in a geographic area, but in large part the secondary units are developed to handle technological processes which have grown too complex to be operated by even an extended family.

Varieties of tasks and facilities have been allocated to secondary units in the community, but the family remains the ultimate source of personnel, the ultimate consuming unit of the products of secondary units, and the ultimate investing unit (as the source of corporate shareholders, taxpayers, and voluntary contributors).

Community Decision Processes

As primary units of the social system, families are interrelated in several ways. Some of these are family-to-family relationships, as neighbors and friends, but significantly families experience much of

[1] The boundaries of the system are not only penetrated through these linkages but are also kept somewhat vague and unstable by the multi-purpose aspect of the community. For political purposes the community may be segmented into a central city and autonomous suburbs; for economic purposes no such distinction is made. The difficulties of determining, operationally, the boundaries of a community are not merely inadequacies on the part of social scientists but are very real problems for the communities themselves. Inability to maintain precise, stable boundaries does not rule the community out of consideration as a social system; it merely means that the community belongs to that class of system whose boundaries are somewhat fluid.

the interdependence through the larger, secondary units. Families whose interdependence occurs through secondary units may not even be aware of one another's existence, yet somehow their independent behaviors and decisions must more often than not fit into a larger pattern serving the purposes of the system. To a large extent the necessary patterning is accomplished by bureaucratic secondary units. A distinctive characteristic of bureaucratic organizations is their ability to emphasize *computational decision processes*. These processes involve a previously-established goal and orderly, synchronized activity to achieve the goal with a minimum of confusion about who is to do what and when he is to do it. Computational decision processes result in programs locking many tasks into long-linked technologies and assuring, within limits, that the necessary resources are at the right place at the right time. Thus, for example, men at two places in a production line need not be aware of one another as persons; so long as the programs have been properly computed, their behaviors mesh.

In the typical community much allocation and integration is accomplished through computational decision processes in large, bureaucratic organizations. This holds true not only for economic and governmental organizations but also for educational, medical, and welfare organizations. But computational decision processes are appropriate only so long as goals are not called into question, that is, only so long as the question is one of means toward known ends.

Hence when we shift our focus to the allocation of resources *among* organizations, and between families and organizations, we find that the community relies primarily on *pluralistic decision processes*. This involves not only a lack of prior agreement with respect to specific goals but also, as a consequence, a lack of agreement with respect to who should do what, and when. These processes are accomplished through negotiation among a plurality of groups,[2] and provide the give-and-take which permits multiple, simultaneous adjustments among primary and secondary units in the community, and between them and the environment.

Since the community is both a multi-purpose system and an open system, it is constantly in the process of reallocating and reintegrating, never achieving the fully integrated state. From the standpoint of the system, there is always a certain amount of misallocation and maladjustment among its parts.

Yet under normal conditions the underlying order within the

[2] Computational and pluralistic classifications of decision processes are derived from a typology developed elsewhere (see Thompson and Tuden, 1959). For an extended discussion of the necessity for pluralistic processes among organizations, see Thompson and McEwen (1960).

community is remarkable. There are patterns in the community which both members and nonmembers can and do take for granted. If we select a family at random, the chances are high that it depends on other primary or secondary units for provision of public sanitation and health protection, for personal safety and protection of property, for the formal education of its children, for supplies of food, clothing, and shelter, for economic income, and so on. Not only does the family expect such things to be provided, but its expectations are satisfied daily and routinely.[3]

Institutionalized Constraints

This underlying order in the community, in spite of the large number of decision-making units operating simultaneously, comes about primarily because resource allocations are channeled and constrained by a number of *institutionalized patterns*. As "rules of the game" which are understood and sanctioned by virtually all members of the community, institutional patterns regulate the allocative and integrative processes. Since all members of the community are constrained to observe institutional patterns, they permit each member to meet certain expectations held by others, and at the same time they permit each member to hold reliable expectations of others.

Three such institutional patterns appear particularly significant for our purposes: *property*, *contract*, and *authority*.[4]

At least in Western societies one of the important behavioral constraints contributing to the independence and integrity of community members and organizations is the institution of *property*, which defines rights to exercise discretion over the use of physical and symbolic resources. It also grants to those who possess property the right to leave such resources unused and to deny their use to others.[5] Thus the institution of property permits relatively permanent allocations, makes

[3] This is not to say that every family in the community is adequately provided for by existing standards. Nor is it to say that families are necessarily satisfied with the quality of the services. Market and legislative arenas, for example, often are scenes of negotiation among those who want fewer resources allocated to public works or education and those who want larger shares of the community's resources so allocated.

[4] For a more extensive discussion of the relations of institutional patterns to purposive behavior of collectivities, see Parsons (1960, Chapter 4).

[5] This and the other institutions we will discuss have certain limitations placed on them. Property rights are restricted under certain conditions by governmental power to exercise eminent domain, to condemn property, and to prevent the use of property for illegal purposes. The exact limits of the several patterns are not important for this study.

possible the identification of who has discretion over the use of such resources, and thereby provides a basis for order in the system.

A second important institution providing behavioral constraints under normal conditions is *contract*. Generally speaking, contract provides the rules which enable two or more parties to arrange binding expectations of each toward the other. This frequently takes the form of expected behavior now, by one party, in exchange for expected behavior later, by the other. In other words, contract permits prearranged agreement. This may come through prolonged bargaining or it may be arrived at very quickly, but we suspect that when it is quickly determined it rests on prior knowledge or assumptions of each party about the other.

A third important institution providing behavioral constraints under normal conditions is *authority*. We are referring not to the particular ways in which authority is exercised but to the complex of norms which recognize the necessity of authority relationships and limits to authority and spell out the conditions under which authority may be exercised. As Max Weber (1947) pointed out, the institution of authority may take different forms in various cultures, and without the particular form he labeled "rational-legal," the long-linked technologies requiring complex, large-scale organizations would be unlikely.

Institutions and Decision Processes

The underlying order of the community under normal conditions —which channels tasks, personnel, facilities, and money to the several purposes of the community and constrains their employment in those channels—is achieved through a combination of pluralistic and computational decision processes. These are made by a large number of both primary and secondary units of the community. *Within* any one unit, these decisions may be made through *computational* processes, which are supported primarily by the institutional patterns of authority. So long as members of the unit recognize the authority of the decision maker, the allocation and integration of resources as decided by him will generally obtain. Although primary units (families) frequently use computational decision processes for arriving at programs, it is in the larger, secondary units that we find authority most explicit, for the operation of long-linked technologies makes programed allocation and integration indispensable, and hence requires primary reliance on computational decision processes. When it comes to allocation of resources *among* units, both primary and secondary, computational decisions are no longer appropriate. Here pluralistic processes are required, and the institutions of property and contract are indispensable.

In summary, the contemporary American community normally relies on pluralistic processes for allocating resources among its parts and for attaining integration of those parts. This makes possible the simultaneous mutual adjustment of many parts, many purposes, and many conditions posed by the environment. This give-and-take is never complete, however; the community never is a *totally* integrated system. We can describe the community, under normal conditions, as being in a *pluralistic phase.*

II

Because we believe the normal state of the system is the pluralistic phase we have just sketched, we expect the community to respond to severe stress by taking actions that will restore it to a pluralistic phase. This is not to say that the parts of the community will be restored to their former condition. Streets, buildings, and bridges may or may not be rebuilt or repaired. Families may or may not survive. Organizations may or may not be revived. What we are predicting is that the *processes* of allocation and integration, which under normal conditions permit the community to maintain itself as an on-going system, will be restored.

We believe that the business of restoring normal processes is not the simple one of plugging holes or gaps, or "propping up" the system. Instead, the system goes through several phases in order to re-establish a new equilibrium. In this section we will present several formal propositions, and sketch the kinds of behavior to which they refer.

Proposition 1 By endangering families and organizations, disaster interrupts normal relationships among these units, requiring them to operate more autonomously than before. Hence the system's processes of allocation and integration are *fragmented;* the system is less well knit.

If we leave the community in its normal state and return to it an hour or two after it has been struck by disaster, the picture is quite different.[6] The panic popularly linked with disaster is not present, but neither does there appear to be order in the system. Within the impact area, activity is frenzied and may be inefficient; persons are behaving alone or in very small groups. If there is coordinated effort, it is likely

[6] Descriptions in this section are composites of aspects described in the empirical studies of disasters. For purposes of illustration we are overlooking important variations. We are assuming, for example, that the disaster strikes without warning, during "working hours," and that its main force is in a residential area. A somewhat different but equally predictable pattern could be described if the disaster were to strike in the early hours of the morning or hit an industrial area, or if the downtown commercial center were leveled.

to be of two men lifting a beam to reach an injured person, a woman caring for two or three children, or a doctor and a volunteer carrying a victim to a safe area.

But behavior within the impact area is not random. It is *purposive* and *direct*, in the sense that the means at hand are employed for immediate purposes, and long-linked technologies are not in operation. The rationality in the system is organized only in the coordinated efforts of groups of two, three, or four. The large secondary organizations held in readiness for occasions of this type—the Red Cross, the Salvation Army, state police, ambulance services, and so on—have not yet arrived on the scene. The few representatives of such organizations who may be in the impact area are not likely to be in contact with their organization and are, instead, taking part in direct rescue efforts as members of small teams.

Outside the impact area, disaster-ready organizations such as police and fire departments are under partial mobilization or still demobilized. They are in doubt over the allocation of those resources immediately available. The extent of the impact area is unknown, and resources dispatched under these conditions can easily be sent to places that turn out to be nonstrategic. Moreover, the independent actions of two or more disaster-ready organizations may duplicate one another, resulting in an overconcentration of resources in one part of the impact area and underdeployment in another. Inaccurate and contradictory messages have been issued, both within the community and from it to elements of its environment. Assistance in various forms is expected, but when and where it will arrive is unknown.

As in the impact area, behavior elsewhere in the community is not random, but it is much less coordinated and less coherent than under normal conditions. Secondary organizations with no clear roles in disaster are partially or completely deactivated.

From the standpoint of the social system, it appears that resources are being allocated on the basis of family and geography, and behavior is that of many individuals and small groups doing similar things, rather than *designed* behavior reflecting specialized division of labor. The community in this phase is a fragmenting community—a collection of independent parts loosely related only by similar goals. This is not to say that there is no order in the system, but rather that the degree of order is considerably less than existed in the system in its normal state.

Proposition 2 In reaction to fragmentation, the community takes on a more than normal amount of interdependence, allocating resources into a *synthetic organization* which can employ computational decision processes.

Now we are returning to the community at a later point. In absolute time it may be six hours or six days following impact, depending on a number of variables, but our concern is not with absolute time.[7]

Evidence of physical destruction is clear, but something is being done about it. The impact area has been divided into zones, and crews are systematically going through the wreckage to make sure no victims remain and to identify and remove hazards. Following them, other crews are using bulldozers, trucks, cranes, and tractors to remove debris.

Communication centers have been established within the impact area, and between it and "headquarters." The area has been sealed off and restricted to those who have recovery-relevant business. Nearby churches, dance halls, and school auditoriums have been converted into temporary hospitals, dormitories, or supply stations. Lists of the injured and those in dormitories are being prepared and submitted to "headquarters," so that family members may locate one another. Facilities have been established to care for children whose families are unable to do so.

Outside the impact area, traffic is controlled so that vehicles with recovery errands can move rapidly. Commercial transactions, building projects, and manufacturing activities are at a standstill or are sharply curtailed, while some of the resources on which they depend are diverted to recovery purposes. "Headquarters" has established dispatch and control procedures, so that it knows what recovery activities are under way, where, and by whom. Teams and organizations have been informed of the scope of their jurisdiction and responsibility, and each knows approximately what to expect from related units. Duplication of effort has been virtually eliminated, and gaps have been filled. Inventories of useful resources have been made and aid from the environment is being routed to the appropriate location as it arrives.

The community appears as a super-organization, synthesized from parts that have been taken out of normal contexts and reallocated and integrated in new ways. Its social units—especially its large-scale secondary organizations—no longer behave as autonomous units. Their roles in the community during this phase are not being determined by pluralistic decision processes. Instead they are subordinated to a central headquarters which is allocating resources and integrating them through a "master plan" or program derived through computational decision processes. While it is true that many social units in the community have no active part in the recovery process at this phase, they

[7] Assertions made in the following paragraphs are intended to indicate the types of activities and arrangements present during this phase of recovery, and are not to be interpreted as statements about the quality of activities and arrangements.

remain parts of the system, subordinate to headquarters, in latent capacities.

Proposition 3 As the bases for normal relationships gradually are restored, the system withdraws resources from the synthetic organization and gradually returns to pluralistic processes for allocation and integration decisions.

Now we are returning to the community several weeks later. The injured are recuperating or have been released from hospitals, rubble has disappeared, and restoration is well under way. Field hospitals and makeshift dormitories have been cleared out. Firms which had lost their autonomy during the synthesizing phase have regained it and are extremely active. Building contractors, banks, construction supply firms, and transportation companies are working overtime, and manufacturers are busy trying to catch up with backlogs. Welfare agencies are inundated. Public works agencies and public utilities are working overtime to replace temporary facilities with permanent ones. Traffic is flowing freely throughout the community, and environmental units have withdrawn their policing forces.

From the standpoint of the system, essential roles have been restored and in many respects normal interaction and relationships are in operation. The synthetic organization still exists and continues to program important aspects of recovery, but organizations subordinated to the programs of central headquarters are demanding adjustments of the roles and resources allocated to them. Factions and cliques have developed within the synthetic organization, and informal agreements have been worked out among some organizations in the synthetic organization to modify their assigned roles.

Other organizations deactivated or allowed to operate under restrictions now are seeking more autonomy as they are pressed by other social units within and outside the community to re-establish normal relationships. Now that the most obviously pressing aspects of rescue and relief have been satisfied, various social units within the community have differing conceptions of proper priorities for allocation of resources, and they are pressing the synthetic organization to modify decisions and programs.

The synthetic organization no longer has unilateral control over its constituent organizations. Internally, pluralistic processes of decision are competing with computational processes. Outside the synthetic organization, such social structures as markets and governmental councils have been fully reactivated to facilitate negotiations. These compete with one another and also with the synthetic organization for control over the allocation and integration of resources. The system certainly has not returned to its normal state, however. The synthetic organization is an element which had not existed in the normal state, and this makes interrelationships in the community more complex than normal.

Scarcity of resources, urgency on the part of the various social units, and competing arenas and processes for establishing priorities and allocating resources all combine to yield more widespread and deeper conflicts among the parts than existed in the normal state. Scarcity and competition not only generate more conflict than existed normally but they also intensify interaction rates and hence interdependence. Therefore the system has a greater degree of integration than under normal conditions, at the same time that its component units are emphasizing their integrity and independence.

III

The implication in the above propositions is that the community as a social system has properties which tend to restore it to equilibrium after it has been disturbed. Equilibrium has been a central concept in social system and organization theory, just as in theories of biological and physical systems, but the equilibrium mechanisms are not nearly so well identified for social systems as for the other types. In this section we will attempt to set forth a model identifying some variables and relationships that enable the system to proceed through several phases until equilibrium is re-established.

It must be emphasized that the model is tentative and hypothetical. In fact, each of the variables identified and relationships stated constitutes a separate proposition. Some of these, for which we have evidence that can be interpreted as consistent, we hold more confidently than others. Even if the variables and relationships turn out eventually to be significant ones, we may not have identified all of those necessary to account for phase movement from equilibrium through impact to equilibrium. We cannot be precise about the sequence, but in a rather close order the following occur after impact:

Primary values underscored Perceived serious threat focuses attention on the values of life, health, emotional support, and general well-being. When these are endangered, less fundamental values such as wealth, status, and comfort lose whatever saliency they may have had.

Time perspectives shortened Sudden threat focuses attention on the present realization of primary values. There is a sense of urgency, and complicated means-ends plans toward long-range goals are set aside.

Behavior oriented toward family The social locus of primary values is the family, and when those values are threatened family roles take priority. Strong social norms require the individual to set aside all other obligations so long as the family is in danger. Thus individuals are withdrawn from all but family-oriented communication nets, rendering most normal communication channels inoperative.

Direct action predominates The sense of urgency rules out the use of long-linked technologies. Obstacles between the individual and his family are attacked with whatever means are at hand; there is no digression to search for more appropriate means.

Institutional patterns relaxed Normal constraints over the allocation of role-players and other resources are ignored. Individuals whose families are threatened set aside the authority of secondary organizations to which they normally belong, and such organizations usually waive normal authority. Normal rights over property are ignored if that property is seen as useful in direct, family-oriented action. Contractual obligations are set aside.

From the system's point of view, these, in effect, are conditions arising "spontaneously" as an immediate result of the impact, and they are conditions over which the system has no control. They result in the system "instinctively" rushing personnel to the impact area, relaxing the normal constraints which might interfere with personnel allocation, and empowering those personnel to appropriate whatever resources seem necessary.

There is considerable uncertainty within the impact area, and this radiates into other parts of the system and beyond the system into the environment. How?

Integrity of secondary organizations damaged As personnel are withdrawn from secondary organizations, and thereby removed from normal communication nets, the effective boundaries of those organizations shift and the extent of their authority is uncertain.

Interrelations of secondary organizations damaged The simultaneous shifting of the boundaries of many secondary organizations means that none is clear about what to expect from others, or what others expect of it. Thus, contract as an institutional pattern is inoperative from secondary organizations outside the impact area as well as for primary groups within the impact area.

Environmental relationships severed With authority and contract inoperative in the community, secondary organizations are able to make neither contributions to the larger systems into which they normally are linked nor use of the inputs they receive from the larger environmental systems.

"Instinctive" reaction of the system to disaster impact, then, has not only allocated resources to the "wound" but has also deactivated long-linked technologies, either by demobilizing the organizations operating such technologies or by removing the institutional foundations of such organizations. Resources that appear directly and immediately usable have been allocated to primary groups. All other resources and organizations are, for the moment, in storage. Power to decide the allocation of active resources has been decentralized to a large number of primary groups, each under pressure to act quickly and directly, and little or no attention is given to the linking of these resources by spanning the boundaries of primary groups.

The system is fragmented.

What puts the brakes on this fragmentation? Why does it not simply disintegrate? Several conditions occur to account for this. They may occur simultaneously or in temporal order which varies from community to community.

Direct action defines disaster situation As family members determine the conditions of their families and accomplish whatever direct action they are capable of, some are freed to join disaster-ready organizations, and others recognize the need to link the family with the longer technologies operated by disaster-ready organizations.

Environment sends disaster-ready organizations Groups especially trained and equipped for disaster roles, and without the role conflict generated by concern over their own families, arrive on the scene. Environment is motivated to send them by mutual aid agreements with local disaster-ready organizations, and desire to restore the community as a reliable part of a larger system.

Local disaster-ready units activated Members whose families were not threatened are joined by those who have satisfied family obligations, and relatively long-linked programs are put into effect, allocating tasks, personnel, and facilities in support of primary groups.

These events call a halt to fragmentation, and set the stage for a new pattern of integration. The presence of groups larger than families means that technologies beyond the capacity of the family can now be operated and resources allocated according to broader programs. These larger groups are met by families seeking access to the same longer technologies. This contributes to, but is not alone sufficient for, the reintegration of the system as a totality. Each disaster-ready organization has a delimited capacity or geographic area of operations. Allocation of resources within each organization according to an integrated program does not prevent gaps or duplication of functions. Efficient operation by each of the several organizations independently is not integrated behavior so far as the system is concerned.

We have hypothesized that as fragmentation is halted a new synthesis begins, and that it gains momentum as it goes along. How does this occur?

Disaster-ready units search for new linkage To increase reliability of their programs, disaster-ready units seek additional information about the activities of other organizations, both earlier and later in the longer-linked technologies.

Secondary organizations search for new roles Unable to perform normal roles, secondary organizations seek new roles related to recovery from disaster by spreading information about their resources and abilities.

Information and authority coalesce Information pumped into the system by disaster-ready units identifies needs for resource allocation and integration; information spread by secondary organizations seeking to be integrated identifies resources available. Both types of organization seek authoritative information, and impute authority to whatever individual or group can perform the brokerage function.[8]

Boundaries are spanned The interrelating of families, disaster-ready organizations, and supporting secondary organizations makes possible the operation of even longer technologies which flow through the several kinds of organizations.

Programs are elaborated Recognition of a central headquarters, to which the several organizations attribute authority, results in the funneling of additional information to that headquarters. The disaster gradually is defined more precisely, the roles of the several organizations are more clearly delineated, and their interrelationships are refined.

A new super-organization has been synthesized out of old parts.

Broadly speaking, the new organization has a single purpose and is built on the institutional pattern of rational authority, with little or no regard for normal institutional patterns of property and contract. It has emerged gradually through the increasing accrual of authority. Why does it not continue to accrue authority and become a new and permanent center of the total system? Several things halt the synthesizing process.

Time perspectives expand As programed activities proceed, further threat to primary values is eliminated, the sense of urgency disappears, and it becomes apparent that the full realization of primary values requires complicated means-ends plans extending into the future.

[8] A more extensive treatment of this concept of the executive's role is contained in Hawkes (1961).

Intermediate goals and secondary values become salient As the future becomes salient, families consider intermediate goals which will contribute to the long-run realization of primary values and also give thought to such secondary values as wealth, status, and comfort.

Secondary organizations are pressed to resume normal roles In part, this pressure is applied by members who temporarily withdrew but now seek to resume normal roles. In part, it is applied by nonmembers whose recovery depends on the output of secondary organizations. And in part, this pressure is applied by other secondary organizations both within and outside the community, who want reliable relationships restored.

Institutions are reinforced Whatever uncertainty remains in the system now is centered around secondary values and secondary organizations. Organizations are therefore pressed not only to reassert normal authority but also to reinstate patterns of property and contract, so that uncertainty in relationships may be reduced.

There is competition for resources The pressures operating on the several primary and secondary organizations to resume normal expectations lead them to seek resources. While there may be oversupply of some, there is relative scarcity of others. Hence allocation priorities assigned by the synthetic organization are disputed.

Authority is withdrawn from synthetic organization The pulls on organizations to resume normal roles outside the program of the synthetic organization, together with conflict among organizations within the synthetic organization, lead these organizations to withdraw the authority they have attributed to it.

The synthetic organization has now been desynthesized.

Its components have been reallocated to the several relatively autonomous parts of the community, and mutual adjustment and reallocation are again handled by pluralistic decision processes.

IV

We are now ready, in the light of the propositions advanced above, to examine reported research into disasters. Understandable difficulties in disaster research provide certain limitations, especially in determining how typical or unusual reported events and behavior are, and how far we can generalize from them. The frames of reference which the several researchers took into disaster-struck communities varied widely, so that they reported certain phenomena of interest to us but ignored other phenomena which would have been useful for our purposes. We will be forced at many points to make inferences, filling in gaps from other evidence or from "common sense," and to supply interpretations which researchers have not made. The following examination of the evidence therefore does not constitute a test of our propositions, but we hope it indicates that they have empirical support.

From Equilibrium to Fragmentation

Here we are looking for evidence that primary values are underscored, time perspectives shortened, behavior oriented toward the family, and that direct action predominates.

A tendency to disregard property loss when life is at stake is well known (Fritz and Mathewson, 1957, p. 31; Wolfenstein, 1957, pp. 173, 175). The sense of urgency so frequently noted in disasters seems closely related to the primacy given to human welfare. Raker, Wallace, Rayner, and Eckert (1956, p. 27) note that both victims and volunteers are impressed with the need for speed, with the result that further injury to the victims may occur. Even those highly trained for emergency roles, such as physicians and hospital personnel, may feel this pressure for immediate action with respect to human life, to the point where performance may be regressive (Raker *et al.*, 1956, p. 8). In the Flint-Beecher and Waco tornadoes, police and firemen at first did the very things that volunteers were already doing on the scene, and only gradually did they begin to differentiate their activities and assume functions more traditional to their work (Form and Nosow, 1958, pp. 147, 193; Moore, 1958b, p. 9). Even when attempting to proceed to their emergency posts, many found the immediate demands of the situation so strong that they joined with volunteers in direct rescue activities (Form and Nosow, 1958, p. 162). In the Flint-Beecher case, Red Cross personnel, both paid and volunteer, who were responsible for the direction of headquarters activities went to the tornado areas instead (p. 147).

The saliency of primary values is most strikingly illustrated, however, in the immediate focus of attention and behavior on the family by those in the impact area and those whose families are believed to be in them. This fact is so widely reported that it requires little comment here, except the note that if and when families are found to be safe, attention is likely to be turned to relatives, friends, and neighbors, all of whom are normally linked directly to families. If behavior of those in the impact area is focused on victims in general, it is usually after those other obligations have been met.

The pull of the family on its members is dramatically highlighted when those members are also members of disaster-ready organizations. The result is role conflict as the individual is forced to choose between strong and mutually exclusive alternatives. How such conflicts will be resolved is, on the basis of present knowledge, problematic. Evidence from the Texas City explosion indicated that the "great majority of persons . . . involved in such dilemmas resolved them in favor of loyalty to the family . . . or friendship groups" (Killian, 1952, p. 311). Volunteer firemen in the Flint-Beecher area saw to their families first if their families were in danger (Form and Nosow, 1958, p. 162).

In two reported cases, however, groups trained for disaster roles shifted into those roles despite concern for their families. In Texas City, most of the refinery workers stayed on the job until their units were safely shut down, as they had been trained to do (Killian, 1952, p. 311). And following a San Angelo tornado, telephone company employees were reported to have stayed at their jobs even though many had homes in the area hardest hit (Moore, 1958b, p. 186). In both of these cases, the individuals were at the appropriate post before the disaster struck.

This brings us to an examination of evidence related to our proposition that institutional patterns of authority, property, and contract are relaxed.

We suggest that the role conflict experienced by those who are at the same time members of families in danger and members of disaster-ready organizations illustrates the strong challenge primary values pose to institutional patterns of *authority*. It appears that the conflict will be resolved in favor of the family and primary values—unless the individuals are, at the moment of perceived threat, already active in disaster-ready roles and in the physical presence of others in similar roles. Under these latter conditions, the authority of the disaster-ready organization is not only active but is reinforced by the fact that the most immediate action a member can take toward disaster recovery is in his active role. When members of disaster-ready organizations must be assembled after impact, however, they are more likely to decide role conflict in favor of family obligations. Moreover, when disaster-ready units must assemble their members, even those who have no concern about their families may experience conflict between direct action and reporting to disaster-ready positions, as has been indicated earlier.

Relaxation of institutional patterns of *contract* is more clearly documented, particularly where medical care has been rendered on the basis of need and reckoning of cost delayed until later (Raker *et al.*, 1956, p. 42) or services provided by medical personnel and hospitals with no intention of seeking reimbursement (Wallace, 1956, p. 92; Moore, 1958b, p. 171). These actions were bolstered by the medical ethic of service on the basis of need rather than ability to pay; hence the waiver of institutional patterns of contract is not surprising. But the use of *property* without regard to ownership, designed purpose, or contract is also reported. Vehicles of all sorts are pressed into service or eagerly offered by their drivers (Raker *et al.*, 1956, p. 27) and the commandeering of boats is reported from flood areas (Grieve, 1959, p. 321).

These materials describe for us an "instinctive" reaction of the community to disaster, consisting for the most part of purposive behavior, but behavior which has not been planned and for which permission is not sought. It is organized around family or family-related groups, augmented by volunteers. In and around the impact area, at this early stage, authority, property rights, and contractual procedures are not apparent. In most cases, even the disaster-ready organizations have not been able to mobilize their members to make authority operative, and if their members are active, it is likely to be outside the chain of command of the disaster-ready organization.

It is worth noting that the rescue activities usually are accomplished through this improvised action of many small groups, coordinated with one another only "spontaneously" if at all, before larger organizations are effectively mobilized. (Form and Nosow, 1958, p. 156; Raker *et al.*, 1956, pp. 20-21).

We now turn to an examination of the propositions that the integrity of secondary organizations is damaged, that their interrelationships are damaged, and that their environmental relationships are severed.

Within the impact area, then, it seems reasonably clear that the restoration of order is initially accomplished through unrehearsed, unplanned allocation of tasks, personnel, and facilities. The literature is much less clear about what is going on in the system outside of the impact area, but we can make some inferences from the reports.

We know, from examples cited above, that secondary organizations can sometimes put emergency procedures into operation immediately, as in the Texas City refinery and the San Angelo telephone company. Where this will occur, and indeed whether it will occur at all in the early phase of disaster, seems unpredictable, depending on many factors such as the nature of the impact, the time of day, and the types of facilities damaged. But it seems rather safe to suggest that those secondary organizations which have emergency programs will activate them as soon as possible, and that many of the same variables discussed above will operate in the same fashion, although perhaps in different degree.

Killian (1952, p. 313) reports that after the Texas City explosions in which several oil firm executives were killed and others injured or missing, men found themselves suddenly "promoted" to the position of being in charge of the firm's damaged property, and that the common reaction was to think of the men first and of the plant later. It is a reasonable inference that still less important goals, such as production and shipment quotas, were ignored.

The pre-planned relaxation of contractual constraints is demonstrated in Waco, where the electric corporation supplying power to the community immediately activated an emergency program which permitted local agents to purchase emergency equipment without specific authorization or the usual corporate controls on procedures (Moore, 1958b, p. 42).

We thus have some indications of what may be going on in the community outside of the impact area while immediate rescue proceeds inside it; disaster-ready organizations are attempting to mobilize, and secondary organizations with emergency experience are also attempting to implement emergency procedures.

The disaster literature is for the most part silent about what is happening to *other* secondary organizations at this time. We believe it inevitable that many of the persons who converge on an impact area have left roles in secondary organizations, but research has focused primarily on their behavior in the impact area, not on what they have left behind. Killian (1952, p. 313) does note that in four disasters, merchants and clerks rushed from stores to aid in rescue work, leaving goods and cash on the counters untended. This is an example of the demobilization which we believe must occur, at least in some degree, in secondary organizations, but which is seldom mentioned in the literature. Moreover, we can only infer that normal relationships *among* such secondary organizations have been damaged.

There is some mention in the literature of the disruption of relationships between the community's secondary organization and the environmental systems to which they normally are linked. Ellemers (1955, p. 26) concludes from the Holland flood experiences that many nongovernmental as well as governmental organizations, accustomed to receiving orders and assignments from higher headquarters, went through a phase of "helplessness" when cut off from those echelons before they made new contacts at their own levels in the community. A similar situation is reflected in the analysis of reactions to the Piedras Negras flood (Clifford, 1956).

In summary, the initial reaction to community disaster does indeed appear to be one of fragmentation. It is as if the multi-purpose community has suddenly set aside all but one goal. Those groups which have obvious roles with respect to the single purpose begin to mobilize immediately, and since in a period of community uncertainty the most obvious role obligations for most individuals are family obligations, family groups are generally the first to mobilize. Disaster-ready organizations follow, often rather closely. But other secondary organizations, for whom roles related to the single purpose are not clear, mark time or demobilize, cut off from reliable relationships with one another and with the outside environment. We think, therefore, that while the physical destruction and uncertainty may be confined to the impact area, social chaos has rapidly spread into other parts of the community. Lacking reliable relationships with other groups and organizations, the various social units both within and outside the impact area are forced to make their own decisions regarding allocation and integration of resources left to them. Allocation and integration are going on, but in many separate islands unrelated to one another.

The Halting of Fragmentation

The evidence we wish to cite here is related to the propositions that direct action results in definition of the disaster situation, and that disaster-ready units are activated, both locally and by the environment.

While confusion and inefficiency are inevitably noted during this period of direct action by primary groups, the collective result seems to lay the basis for more organized effort, for direct action produces a grass-roots identification of needs. In Beecher (Form and Nosow, 1958, p. 150), where state police operated spontaneously, their needs at first "were limited to equipment such as chain saws, portable lights, phones, and bulldozers." In Waco (Moore, 1958b, p. 13) "Civilian rescue 'teams' were at first merely unorganized groups. Any member who lacked some article called out his need and the request was picked up and amplified by loud-speaker trucks."

Direct action by those in the impact area also results in some initial definition of the situation for disaster-ready units. Hospitals most closely located to disaster areas often are warned of the event only by the appearance of ambulatory injured who have maneuvered their way out of the rubble (Raker *et al.*, 1956, pp. 16, 22). This direct action of the injured or their rescuers, however, permits the nearby hospital to alert others more remotely located.

Direct immediate action also sets the stage for mobilization of members of disaster-ready organizations. As was indicated above, the role conflict experienced by those whose families are believed endangered but who are also members of disaster-ready organizations usually is resolved in favor of the family. But many of these learn that their families are safe and *then* assume other roles. The suggestion is that they are pulled away from the family by obligations to the disaster-ready organization, but that en route they may be diverted into rescue teams as volunteers. In either event, the direct action of assigning themselves to the family results in a definition of the disaster as excluding the family, and permits their reassignment to other units.

While local disaster-ready organizations are learning something of the existence and extent of the disaster and mobilizing their members, similar organizations from other communities may be coming into action. The fact that they are outside the area of destruction permits them to congregate at the proper places, act according to organizational plans, and respond to the orders of those in authority within the organizational hierarchy (Form and Nosow, 1958, pp. 168-169).

Private utilities as well as governmental and voluntary agencies from the environment can likewise be effective in reversing the fragmenting process. Often gas, electricity, transportation, and communication firms are linked with systems that supply the same services to many communities within the region, and Moore (1958b, p. 41) notes that this multi-community character provides a ready supply of workmen from other communities because the work is so highly standardized within the corporation.

Utility crews and others with highly specialized emergency roles, so long as their families are not involved in the disaster, can add organized rationality to the picture because they are likely to be disciplined against the direct action of assistance to victims. Killian (1952, pp. 312-313) reports that

> these (utility) workers reported no awareness of a conflict of roles, regarding it as a matter of course that they concentrated on their often quite dangerous jobs. Some indicated that preoccupation with the job was so intense that they were scarcely aware of what went on around them.

What motivates outside organizations to enter the stricken community is not clear from the disaster reports. Private corporations may, in part, respond to protect their property and employees. It is common knowledge that such emergency agencies as police and fire departments often have formal or informal mutual aid understandings. In many situations, we believe, utility systems depend on local branches for relays, and may be motivated to restore missing links in their systems. At this point, however, these must be speculations. One additional motivating factor has been reported from Holland, where leaders of at least two organizations saw the disaster as an opportunity to give their organizations the acknowledgment and reputation which had been denied them previously (Ellemers, 1955, p. 25).

Whatever the motivations, environmental organizations rather rapidly dispatch teams which are not subject to the distractions of family and friendship role obligations, and which frequently can focus their efforts on restoring vital, but nonhuman, resources. For members of these organizations, like those of hospitals, the discipline of long-linked technology can constrain behavior. But while these organizations do introduce into the disaster situation programs of greater scope than family-oriented rescue teams can manage, we suspect they are acting independently of one another at this early stage. Fragmentation has been halted, but not eliminated.

Toward a New Synthesis

Now we are looking for evidence that disaster-ready units search for new linkages, while secondary organizations search for new roles.

Terms such as "chaos" appear frequently in descriptions of behavior even after disaster-ready units appear on the scene. But the "chaos" described at this later stage is the situation as seen by those at various headquarters and refers apparently to the lack of coordination among several large organizations. Little coordination exists among the many headquarters at first, or as the Waco chief of police put it (Moore, 1958b, p. 11): "For the first twenty-four hours we went around in circles in one direction; for the next twenty-four, we went around in circles in another direction."

It seems clear that interorganization chaos or lack of coordination is experienced by members of the organizations both in the field and in headquarters, and that the demand for such coordination mounts as immediate rescue efforts diminish (Form and Nosow, 1958, pp. 150, 163, 178; Moore, 1958b, p. 11; Ellemers, 1955, p. 27).

The search for new linkages within the community is not restricted to disaster-ready organizations. There are many reports of secondary organizations seeking new roles related to disaster activities. Merchants have remained in their stores or reopened them to distribute materials needed by rescue workers (Moore, 1958b, p. 43; Ellemers and in't Veld-Langeveld, 1955, p. 108; Fogleman and Parenton, 1959, p. 132). Summer camps, churches, the "Y's," and clubs have found active relief roles (Wallace, 1956, p. 94). Such service industries as laundries (Moore, 1958b, p. 14) and restaurants (Grieve, 1959, p. 337; Raker *et al.*, 1956, p. 53) have performed active relief roles.

In addition to those organizations which quickly find new roles which they can perform themselves, there are secondary organizations which seek roles as suppliers. In Worcester, funeral directors and industrial plants volunteered ambulances (Wallace, 1956, p. 74). In Waco (Moore, 1958b, pp. 12, 45), "civilian contractors who owned needed machinery had brought it and had joined the military in operations on a voluntary basis," and "volunteer workmen, using equipment largely supplied by the military or other outside organizations, donated well over 20,000 man-days of labor. Much of this was aided by heavy equipment loaned to the community and operated by persons not residents of the city."

It seems clear to us that the relatively direct behaviors of those groups first into action do arrive at a "frustration point" where they want to know what others are doing and want to make their needs known to others who might be helpful. How quickly this occurs is not at all clear from available evidence. Meanwhile, some of the individuals and secondary organizations elsewhere in the community are motivated to be useful toward the single goal of the community. Even though many of these desires to be useful are being expressed, we can only guess about the channels employed.

We can now turn to an examination of the evidence with respect to the propositions that information and authority coalesce, that boundaries are spanned, and that over-all programs are developed.

As primary groups and disaster-ready organizations determine their needs and seek contacts with others, and as volunteers and secondary organizations seek new roles related to disaster, it is not surprising that the swamping of communication channels is reported of virtually every disaster. Fritz and Mathewson (1957, p. 15) also conclude that "there is an informational convergence on communication centers, in the form of inquiries, offers of assistance, and other messages."

When adequate warnings have been acted upon, as in Eagle Pass, Texas, a center for communication and authority may exist to coordinate various subcenters for communication and authority, and in such cases, the main center is likely to be manned by governmental officials.[9] When disaster comes unexpectedly, however, or when governmental officials cannot or will not act, the emergence of a communication and authority center is problematic.[10]

[9] In Eagle Pass, Clifford (1956, p. 64) reports a "constant emphasis upon coordination of efforts through conferences of officials; immediate and continuing agreement upon placing decision-making power in the hands of a central agency —the city manager—even though the city mayor, the county judge, and the county sheriff each was independent of or in 'higher' official positions than the city manager." This is an interesting example of the relaxation of normal patterns of authority.

[10] There are a number of cases of officials refusing to act because they would be exceeding their "legal authority." We interpret this as failure to recognize that in disasters, the institutional patterns governing authority are relaxed. For examples, see Spiegel, 1957; Clifford, 1956; Ellemers, 1955, p. 10; and Moore, 1958b, p. 15.

It is likely to emerge wherever knowledge of needs and of resources overlap and an individual is able or willing to act on such knowledge. In some cases, spontaneous leadership occurs (Spiegel, 1957, pp. 4-5; Fogleman and Parrenton, 1959, p. 132); in other cases individuals in several agencies form *ad hoc* organizations (Moore, 1958b, pp. 14-16; Form and Nosow, 1958, pp. 141-142, 156).

For the most part the evidence is not enlightening about the supporting activities of secondary organizations during the rescue and relief period. For example, the Red Cross and Salvation Army are inevitably cited as having distributed vast amounts of food and clothing which converge on disaster-struck communities, but little is said about the organized activities which bring such supplies to those distribution agencies. Fritz and Mathewson suggest (1957, p. 45) that voluntary associations and business organizations play important roles in the collection and transport of supplies dispersed by relief agencies.

Who "assigns" such roles, and to which organizations, we cannot determine from the available evidence. Moore (1958b, p. 101) points out that since various Waco welfare and relief organizations placed their facilities and personnel at the services of the Red Cross and Salvation Army, they "did not appear to be as active in disaster work as they actually were."

Some of the necessary connections with the environment are, of course, accomplished by the component units of the synthetic organization, without being considered by central headquarters. Hospitals, for example, have received spontaneous assistance from drug suppliers (Raker *et al.*, 1956, pp. 49-50). But other connections with the environment cannot be so decentralized. In San Angelo (Moore, 1958b, p. 30), donations began to pour into the city and a committee was set up to receive them and to solicit others. Just who "set up" the committee, and at what stage, is not clear, but we can speculate that if it was not established by the synthetic organization it later became part of the larger coordinated pattern. This leads to the further suggestion that the center of information and authority may shift from one group to another or that two or more such centers may be amalgamated, as the synthesis of the community develops. This was illustrated in the initial phase of synthesis in Cameron Parish, where an individual emerged as leader before officials could arrive on the scene and later remained active, together with those officials, in the direction of affairs (Fogleman and Parenton, 1959, p. 132).

This case suggests to us that the synthetic organization can fan out as contact is established between two or more centers of limited scope, and that there may be transfer of authority within the synthetic organization as recovery progresses. We have no direct evidence for the further point that as additional links are activated in what ultimately are long-linked technologies, the synthetic organization may co-opt individuals with knowledge of or access to those technologies. As effort turns to rehabilitation, for example, and financial processes again become important, we would expect the synthetic organization to co-opt officials of organizations which specialize in such matters.

In virtually every report of American community disasters, some over-all headquarters appears, to which the several active organizations attribute authority. It seems clear that whatever its base (local government, state police, or spontaneous leadership), this headquarters gradually comes to coordinate authoritatively the efforts of local governmental agencies, private utilities, voluntary organizations, and representatives of state and national organizations. How far this extends beyond relief into rehabilitation is not revealed by available evidence.

Desynthesis to Equilibrium

The propositions that, following disaster, time perspectives expand, and intermediate and secondary values become salient, require no documentation.[11] *Here, however, we want to examine the evidence that these factors cause pressure on secondary organizations to resume normal roles, and bring about reinforcement of institutional patterns.*

During the rehabilitation of Waco and San Angelo, economic activity was considerably stimulated, with bank loans increased, real estate sales stimulated, and a boom in construction (Moore, 1958b, pp. 65-66). Especially in Waco, where manufacturing plants and retail establishments were in the tornado path, we believe the economic stimulation reflects pressure on such firms to get back into business.

While the most frequently used sources of funds for reconstruction were personal funds, the Red Cross and the local disaster-relief committees, the fact that banks, savings and loan associations, federal agencies, construction firms, and individuals were also active in making funds available indicates considerable energy devoted to the restoration of physical property (Moore, 1958b, p. 44).

At least for some of those whose families were not involved in the disaster, the concern over secondary values and restoration of institutional patterns was not long in coming.[12]

[11] They are supported by several well-known summaries of disaster research. See Fritz and Williams, 1957, pp. 48-49; Fritz and Mathewson, 1957, pp. 30-31; and Wolfenstein, 1957.

[12] It should be remembered that most of our evidence comes from Waco,

In Waco (Moore, 1958b, pp. 81-82) businessmen were immediately concerned with discovering what had happened to their merchandise, and they resented the police cordon thrown up to prevent anyone not engaged in rescue operations from entering; within two days business leaders began to demand access to the area to salvage merchandise. There followed, within the synthetic organization, a hassle over the restoration of normal property rights, which expanded into what borders on questions of contract.

> City officials became convinced that they ran a serious risk of incurring liability for further destruction of buildings and merchandise. No thought had been given this question of liability in the first days of the emergency when rescue of the injured and the removal of corpses were paramount (Moore, 1958b, p. 82).

In Waco, also, city engineers at first placed signs on all buildings deemed unsafe for occupancy. Later, however, damage suits were feared from owners who could obtain engineering opinions that the buildings were safe, so most signs were removed and the city adopted a "hands off" policy.

Fragmentary evidence suggests to us that as time perspectives expand and the sense of urgency is removed, some individuals and organizations believe that their urgent actions earlier had contained by implication contractual elements. "One merchant in the heart of the disaster section (who had supplied materials needed by rescue workers) later presented a claim to the Waco Disaster Fund Committee for some $4,000 worth of work clothing he had handed out during the rescue period" (Moore, 1958b, p. 43).

Tendencies toward the *controlled* activation of institutional patterns, rather than full immediate restoration, are reflected in disaster literature. Regarding rehabilitation of Worcester, where insurance did not nearly cover the total amount of damage, there were compromise settlements between victims and institutions holding mortgages on their homes (Wallace, 1956, pp. 98-99). In Waco, a problem arose over disposal of materials taken from damaged buildings to the city dump, some of which was salvageable merchandise, raising questions of ownership and salvage rights (Moore, 1958b, p. 85).

While we cannot say much about the rate of reactivation, it appears to us that as time perspectives expand and secondary values again become salient, pressures are generated within the system for reacti-

---

where the commercial section rather than the residential section was struck. Merchants' families, therefore, were more likely to be threatened by the financial effects of disaster than in terms of human life. The concern of merchants for their businesses is understandable.

vation of secondary organizations, and, on a controlled basis, of institutional patterns.

We now turn to the evidence related to our final two propositions —that there is competition for resources, and that authority is withdrawn from the synthetic organization.

The task of rehabilitation ultimately requires many long-linked technologies, and this in turn requires the participation either directly or indirectly of many of the secondary organizations available locally plus some secondary organizations from the environment. Moore (1958b) gives perhaps the most complete account available of the activities of federal, state, and local governmental agencies, voluntary organizations, and private corporations.

But these many organizations become active in community recovery at different stages, perform their disaster roles, and withdraw to other roles at different stages. For those which have completed their disaster tasks, we suggest, "normalcy" appears imminent; having done what they can, they now wish to take up normal roles and relationships. If this occurs at different times for different organizations, we would expect the synthetic organization to be subjected to strains—on the one hand to maintain controls over institutional patterns because normal conditions have not been established, and on the other hand to restore normal institutional patterns as the last obstacle toward normal conditions.

In particular we expected to find these strains exhibited in conflicts over priorities assigned to the services of building contractors, suppliers, etc. The disaster literature is strangely silent on this topic. Intensification of construction and related industries frequently is noted, without elaboration. Where the literature is voluminous, during rehabilitation, is with regard to conflict about *restitution,* i.e., priorities, amount, and procedures for the allocation of disaster-recovery funds.

The criteria of need and ability to pay seem clearly to lie behind the antagonisms frequently reported toward the Red Cross. In the relief and rescue stage of recovery, the Red Cross like the Salvation Army dispenses its services without asking questions, largely on the basis of apparent need (Moore, 1958b, p. 101). But the predominant share of its assistance, in dollar terms, comes later in recovery, in connection with rehabilitation. And for this purpose it demands that the applicant "demonstrate his need and his inability to meet that need from his own resources," which often is interpreted as "putting a penalty on thrift and foresight" (Moore, 1958b, p. 180).

We can suggest hypothetically that some members of the community expect relief funds to restore their pre-disaster positions in terms of wealth, status, and so on, whereas welfare agencies may attempt to restore the victim's ability to compete for such positions. Difference in the criteria of "loss" and "need" as the basis for allocating funds may help account for the appearance of independent relief funds. Raker and associates (1956, p. 43) note the establishment of independent temporary committees to receive and distribute relief funds in four major disasters. Conflict between these temporary agencies and the Red Cross generally ensued.

There appears to be a strong tendency for various disaster-ready organizations to compete for "social credit" for their roles. Raker and associates (1956, p. 8) assert that hospital administrators "are apt to haggle unduly over 'ownership of the disaster' and regard unemotional out-of-town representatives of national agencies like the Red Cross as competitors rather than colleagues."

Whether relief necessities or political gain motivated certain actions seemed to be the issue in a conflict in Worcester, which involved the Federal Civil Defense Administration, the Worcester Housing Authority, and the Red Cross (Wallace, 1956, pp. 97-98). And Williams (1956, p. 380) also reports an incident in which the local welfare agencies began to compete for credit after the national headquarters of one started releasing publicity.

For the disaster-ready organization, "social credit" for its role in disaster would seem to be indispensable. Generally speaking, these organizations gain their support indirectly, rather than by direct exchange through explicit contract. Rather, there is an implied contract that, in exchange for tax payments or voluntary contributions, the disaster-ready organization will act if necessary. If these organizations are to obtain support in the future, then, it becomes vital for them to make clear to the community that they did perform as promised. Hence we would expect competition for social credit to be almost inevitable among disaster-ready organizations.

But there are other factors leading to conflict about restitution. One of the most significant appears to be the problem of interpreting governmental policies. As Moore (1958b, Chapter 3) documents, various laws designed to help offset losses caused by the disaster raise questions about conditions just prior to impact and whether the disaster was the "last straw" or was alone responsible for the damage suffered. Especially where laws provide for federal, state, and local sharing of the burden, there is apt to be confusion, uncertainty, and frustration.

If our interpretations are correct, once disaster-ready organizations are committed to rehabilitation activities they must remain active until their tasks are completed, no matter how unpleasant their relations with other organizations. But the frictions that seem certain to arise, coupled with the need for social credit, probably encourage such organizations to re-emphasize their identification and reassert their independence. If this is true, it weakens the synthetic organization. We find little direct evidence of actual withdrawal of authority from synthetic organizations, however; our question seldom is treated, one way or the other, in disaster research reports.

A few cases in which the synthetic organization rejected parts of its authority are reported by Moore (1958b, p. 83), however. In Waco, when merchants demanded control of their damaged buildings and stocks, "the city authorities placed on the property-owners the responsibility for continued search for bodies . . . emphasized that the property-owners would be held responsible for clearing away any danger to health or property of others . . ." A similar problem arose in the interpretation and enforcement of the building code, adopted a year before the tornado. The city adopted an ordinance setting up a Building Safety Committee, with power to hold hearings and make recommendations to the City Commission. Moore concludes:

> The creation of the Building Safety Committee and the manner in which businessmen and property-owners were given control of their damaged buildings at the termination of rescue work seem to indicate that the city government preferred to use quasi-legal procedures and instrumentalities rather than to rely on its own authority (1958b, p. 86).

In summary, the evidence is disappointingly sketchy regarding competition for resources and withdrawal of authority from the synthetic organization. Competitive factors clearly appear as rehabilitation proceeds, but the reports barely hint at the effects of competition on the synthetic organization.

V

Implications for Administrative Theory

Ultimately, administrative theory must deal with processes of growth and decline of organizations, as well as with the on-going nature of such organizations. We believe that what we have called *synthesizing* embodies a number of processes necessary to the development of any complex, special purpose organization. Admittedly we have not proved the existence in disaster-struck communities of a single, all-encompassing synthetic organization, but the evidence points to the emergence of something approximating it and illuminates some of the variables making it possible.

Undoubtedly growth and decline of organizations vary with such factors as organizational purpose and the nature of the context out of which organizations grow. Disaster is perhaps a very special case, but we suggest that it is a special case of a more general pattern which is not yet well understood. To that extent the community in disaster has provided a useful laboratory in which to study general processes. Some of the same problems and processes, for example, seem to occur when rapidly developing nations attempt to synthesize complex organizations to operate long-linked technologies, using national resources which have typically been allocated and integrated into very different patterns. By considering disaster as one type of system stress, and community as one type of social system, we can begin to identify parallels in the processes by which nations or firms respond to such stresses as nationalistic competition or economic decline.

This points to a need for a typology of stresses. We cannot offer one at this time, but as an initial clue we can suggest that distinctions need to be drawn among various types of disaster. From the point of view of the larger society, for example, the tornado which levels an isolated village is not the same thing as one which cuts a path through a large community. A factor in the distinction probably is the degree of interdependence between the site of impact and the larger society; the response of the larger society probably will be more vigorous if it has numerous and important linkages with the community.[13] A second factor is the suddenness with which stress occurs. If the larger society has time to make gradual adjustments by shifting its interaction to other communities, as in economic decline, its response is likely to be less vigorous than if the stress occurs suddenly.

Available evidence has increased our confidence in the general framework advanced earlier, by indicating that there are identifiable properties of the community as a social system which make it self-regulating, i.e., which move it from a relatively fragmented state to a relatively integrated state before re-establishing equilibrium. At the same time, this exercise has emphasized that, just as the degree of im-

[13] The degree of interdependence suggests a fundamental difference between the community disaster and a nation-wide disaster. When the disaster site is part of a large complex community, it may be assumed that the community will rush assistance to the disaster site in order to participate in setting up a synthetic organization to restore effectively the damaged physical and social relationships. When, however, the disaster site encompasses most of the nation, then the undamaged rest of the nation may be inadequate to supply the resources necessary to establish the long-linked technology required of a synthetic organization. Tenuous international relationships, lacking the interdependencies of a cohesive community, are dubious sources of such assistance. Thus a return to pluralistic normalcy in the case of a nation-wide disaster becomes problematic.

pact is a variable, the degrees of fragmentation and integration and the rapidity of movement through these phases are variables.

Some perspective seems to emerge on the role of leadership or administration in recovery from community disaster. In the first place, the self-regulating phase movement of the community as a system appears "inevitable," whether or not the community has a disaster plan or a weak or strong governmental executive. Regardless of this, primary groups are going to be most important in halting fragmentation, secondary groups are going to be temporarily demobilized, and institutional constraints are going to be relaxed. Leadership variables may make important differences in how rapidly, smoothly, or efficiently these things occur, but they are going to occur one way or another.

Perhaps one of the most important leadership variables is the ability or willingness to accept or assume authority that is "rational" but not "legal" and to exercise this authority to redefine such institutional patterns as contract and property. This may not be an easy assignment for individuals who have had these constraints deeply ingrained in them, as we suspect public officials in Western nations are likely to have had.

A second important leadership variable may lie in co-opting additional leaders, thus enabling the synthetic organization to "fan out" as additional long-linked technologies are activated and focused on recovery. Co-optation enables the incorporation of new elements into the computational decision-making structure, allowing allocation and integration to follow a unified priority schedule; absence of co-optation during recovery may leave roles of newly activated groups to be determined by the slower, pluralistic processes.

Finally, we believe this study has more direct implications for administration of such special-purpose systems as governmental agencies, business firms, and so on. Computational decision processes seem most appropriate when the system is a single-purpose system, whereas pluralistic decision processes appear more appropriate for a multiple-purpose system. We would expect, therefore, that the corporation or agency which expands from one "industry" into several would find it necessary to redefine the role and structure of its headquarters from one making computational decisions to one negotiating pluralistic decisions, with computational decision responsibility "decentralized" to lower levels.

Implications for Social System Analysis

The scientific utility of a critical experiment or incident is that criticalness is associated with "essence." A critical incident should help us identify what normally is not clear or is taken for granted, and it was our hope that this would result from a review of research into community disasters. Although neither the evidence nor our review of it is as complete as we would like, we believe the exercise has had the desired utility.

It has pointed up the importance of institutional patterns as norms linking social values to role behavior.[14] Behavior in social roles enables individuals and collectivities to realize certain values, in greater or lesser degree. Under some circumstances certain values are activated and "behaved toward"; under other circumstances a quite different set of values may be activated, evoking correspondingly different behavior. A disaster, as we have shown, is followed immediately by two alterations: (1) primary values are activated, and (2) institutional patterns are relaxed and redirected. It is as if the activation of primary values brings consequences in two directions. It impels individuals to move directly to the locus of these values, the family, and to engage in what we have called "direct action." Simultaneously it alters institutional constraints so that "direct actors" can disengage themselves from almost any other activity and be assured that direct action is both legitimate and profoundly necessary.

We have glimpsed some of the ways in which behavior, directed by a sudden change in values and regulated by a simultaneous revision in institutional constraints, is able to reduce the threat to primary values and to restore the social relationships which exemplify them. The realization of primary values via these direct behaviors is a gradual and uneven matter, but, just as gradually, intermediate and secondary values are successively activated, calling for institutional patterns which are appropriate to formally organized activity and "bureaucratic behavior." We have characterized this phase by superimposing upon the

[14] In summarizing the system framework we have used throughout this paper, we refer the reader to the source of our categories. Parsons has delineated this "general classification of the structural components of social systems. The first, least differentiated level, which can be taken as an analytic point of reference for structural analysis as a whole, is the system of values which, relative to the other elements, must be formulated on a high level of generality. . . . The second level is that of institutions. Institutions are still normative patterns, but on a less general level; they are differentiated relative to the situational exigencies and structural subdivisions of the system. . . . The third level . . . is what I call that of collectivities. A collectivity is a concrete system of interacting human individuals, of persons in roles" (Parsons, 1960, p. 171).

activities of separate crisis-ready organizations, of segments of other organizations, and of volunteers the notion of a synthetic organization. Step by step, as the values activated by disaster are one by one realized and the threats to them allayed, the synthetic organization surrenders functions to the organizations and groups within the community which "normally" serve those functions. We believe these functions are transferred approximately as fast as the "normal" institutional patterns associated with them can be shown to have reacquired their previous power to constrain and channel behavior.

We are not ready for precise theorizing, but we believe that in the *interaction* among values, institutional patterns, and role behavior can be found some of the self-regulating properties implied in the concept "social system."

Part Four

METHODOLOGY AND THEORY: OTHER VIEWS

THIS FINAL SECTION is concerned with a number of matters that are more comprehensive than those to which the previous chapters are devoted. We turn here to some large questions of theory and methodology that are highly relevant to the conduct of research on disaster behavior and are also of general concern to the behavioral sciences. This section examines the findings of research on disaster not only to understand disaster but, even more important, to discern what these findings may suggest as governing concepts and procedures in social science research at large.

The point of any scientific activity is to devise and sharpen theoretical models that will lend clarity to the events of interest. And although it is questionable whether a comprehensive but unified model of man and society in disaster is yet—or even ultimately—possible, the number of partial models being constructed to fit aspects of that enormous phenomenon is relatively great. These models are quite heterogeneous. Chapter Ten, therefore, analyzes what appear to be the major dimensions along which alternative models can differ. Such dimensions are by no means peculiar to the conceptual formulations of disaster research; they characterize social science models generally. For the purposes of disaster research, however, models within certain ranges of these fundamental dimensions may well be the most useful and the most feasible for testing.

When it comes to the methods by which models are put to empirical test, we always hope to be able to isolate for study precisely those variables in which we are interested at the moment. The locale in which this hope has most often been fulfilled is of course the laboratory; and both social psychologists and experimental sociologists have been turning with considerable success to the simulation of social situations in miniature, under conditions that permit crucial variables to be manipulated and observations to be recorded unambiguously. But there remain many social phenomena for which simulation in the laboratory has not yet succeeded or even been attempted. Chapter Eleven explores the possibilities of applying laboratory methods to the study of phenomena in the field of disaster behavior, where the difficulties of miniaturization are notably great. It examines also the most efficient strategies for field research in the interests of applying to that kind of study the most laboratory-like controls that can be devised.

Chapters Twelve and Thirteen both are concerned with the relation between disasters and the theory of broad, enduring changes in societies and cultures. Although the temporary consequences of disaster in a community have been much studied, the more profound alterations which truly deserve the name of social change have received far less attention. Chapter Twelve inquires into social changes which might be expected to occur when a sociocultural system accommodates to profound disruptions induced by disaster. Chapter Thirteen finally directs attention to the ultimate disaster, the actual collapse of a society and its culture. What, it asks, are conditions under which a social system would not merely become somewhat different in response to disaster but would actually become incapable of furnishing for its members the satisfactions that make it viable? It would be difficult to think of a more urgent question than this one at a time when the Western world is living in painful awareness that its claims of indestructibility are under determined attack.

▶ ten

DIMENSIONS OF MODELS IN DISASTER BEHAVIOR

Dwight W. Chapman

THIS CHAPTER WILL EXAMINE properties of theoretical models in relation to research on the human and social phenomena that occur in and around disasters. More particularly, we shall consider some important dimensions along which such models can vary, and form some judgments about what characteristics make a model particularly useful in disaster research. To do this, we must be aware that disaster research has two goals: to advance knowledge in those social sciences pertinent to understanding disasters, and to draw conclusions useful for controlling behavior in times of emergency and for mitigating the harm wrought by disasters. To bring our analysis to bear critically on some actual theorizing, we shall then look at two examples of models that have influenced present thinking.

During recent years the term *model* has enjoyed increasing popularity in the social and behavioral sciences, and has come to be applied to a variety of concepts. Hence, we begin by defining our term.

Anyone interested in explaining human behavior under certain circumstances will think about the characteristics a human being must have that lead him to behave in the ways that he is found, empirically, to behave under the given circumstances. The inventor of the model may think of the human being as responding to certain stimuli (*inputs*) and as a result emitting certain kinds of behavior (*outputs*). To this extent he constructs a model of the human being; he asserts that this conceptualized human being has the stated properties, these properties being relations between inputs and outputs. In this form his theorizing may be said to treat the individual as a "black box." That is to say, he thinks of an entity without begging any questions about what things are inside it; he specifies only that the entity functions in such a way as to produce the crucial relations between inputs and outputs.

This is a minimal model. It is successful if in any conceptual description of a situation the relationships (inputs, outputs) between the model and the total situation correspond with empirical reality. Later this black-box model may begin to get filled with conceptual insides to "explain" why it works.

The Principal Dimensions of Models

Models of the general nature described above may differ markedly in respect to a number of characteristics, which we represent by the following nine scales. The adjectives at the ends of each scale define its extremes.

1. *Implication*
   Descriptive (and hollow) ⟷ Implicated (and filled)
2. *Situational Reference*
   Individual ⟷ Situational
3. *Level of Abstraction*
   Low-Level ⟷ High-Level
4. *Systematic Unity*
   Eclectic ⟷ Systematically Unified
5. *Comprehensiveness*
   Segmental ⟷ Comprehensive
6. *Temporal Extension*
   Contemporary-Field ⟷ Time-Extended
7. *Spatial Extension*
   Local ⟷ Space-Extended
8. *Manipulability of Independent Variables*
   Nonmanipulable ⟷ Manipulable
9. *Evolutionism*
   Static ⟷ Developmental, Evolutionary

These dimensions are elaborated upon and discussed in the following sections.

IMPLICATION

We use the term *implicative* to mean that the model displays laws and regularities which relate its input variables to its output variables.

In the fully developed and most useful sense, *implication* carries with it the assertion of such laws in quantitative form—that is, laws that connect degrees or values of input variables with degrees or values of output variables. The more this is true of a model, the more we can say that the model is actually implicative. It is clear that not all models are by any means fully implicative in this meaning of the term. The original discovery, for instance, of the occurrence in disaster situations of the passive and benumbed behavior of many individuals—which has been called the disaster syndrome—is an elementary model of disaster behavior: it predicts certain kinds of behavior under the specified conditions of disaster. This prediction, however, is gross and non-quantitative. It is as if we were to say that bodies in the presence of another body will be affected by the gravitational field attached to the latter. Such a statement is a useful and orderly conceptualization, but it has nowhere near the implicative power of an exact statement of quantitative laws of gravitational attraction. Even fairly crude statements of the interpretation of disaster behavior in terms of game theory (Nicholson and Blackwell, 1954) are somewhat more implicative than our elementary model. These statements have the virtue of asserting that if cognized conditions of the situation vary in a certain way, the behavior (for example, the probability of fleeing or remaining) can be predicted from the values of the cognitive variables. Fully developed laws connecting the conditions of learning with the learned behavior itself (such as laws connecting the likelihood of responses with previous values of reinforcement, or of reinforcement-scheduling) are cases of relatively precise implicative models for human behavior.

Models may be looked upon as occupying different positions along this dimension, which runs from full implication to very low degrees of implication; models at this latter end are properly called descriptive. It is probably true that there is no real case of a purely descriptive model. All statements of any association between input variables and output variables are statements which imply at least a gross relationship, or a condition in which the more there is of A the more likely one is to find B. We think of an ideal dimension with its ends labeled "implicative" and "descriptive," but with the descriptive end of the scale unoccupied by any actual model.

The distinction implied by this continuum is an important one for scientific progress. Much effort at constructing improved models is directed toward making them more precisely implicative than they are, and the progress of any science or field of study has to be looked upon in part as progress along this continuum.

Another dimension, while it can be distinguished from the first, is for practical and logical reasons so tied to it that it is better treated as simply another aspect of it. This is the matter of whether a model is *filled* or *hollow*—whether it exhibits a fully developed set of internal concepts explaining the relation of its input variables to its output variables (its internal machinery, so to speak) or whether it is a black-box model which simply states the lawful relationships between inputs and outputs without trying to account for the relationships by the device of any intervening concepts or, so to speak, internal mechanism. In the early stages of thinking out any theory, one begins essentially with such a black box; this primitive model arises as a result of regularities noted in the observation of empirical cases, when these regularities are felt to be strong enough for theoretical reliance. Further research usually tries to discern why the facts stated in the original model should be true, and the theory about why they are true usually gives rise to an idea of some internal mechanism in the locus about which one is theorizing, the action of which accounts for the observed relationships.

Now it is clear that no purely descriptive model can be also a filled model. The presence of intervening variables or internal conceptual mechanisms would bring the model closer to the other end of the implicative-descriptive continuum. For this reason, therefore, the variation from "hollow" to "filled" models is linked with the variation from "descriptive" to "implicative" and cannot be considered separately.

We realize that some scientists take the methodological position that essentially hollow models are perfectly sufficient for the ultimate purposes of the sciences in which they are interested. The psychologist B. F. Skinner (1953) holds a strong preference for the hollow model, or black box, both because of his legitimate fear that some of the hypothetical machinery with which models tend to get filled may be taken too seriously and because of his interest in the sheer enterprise of building a science parsimoniously, with as few concepts as possible.

In terms of scientific practice, however, there is a strong tendency for models to get filled as the science progresses. This does not relieve scientists of the obligation to be parsimonious or to regard the internal cogs and gear wheels of the model as entirely conceptual until they are demonstrated to have observational validity. But in the long run, models will indeed move toward being "filled" as they progress from the more descriptive to the more implicative.

SITUATIONAL REFERENCE

It is typical of many models for disaster research—as of many models in social psychological research in general—that they are intended to be workable constructs of the *situation* in which people find themselves at the critical time. Other models, equally serviceable for different purposes in disaster research, are essentially interpretations of the behavior of an *individual* or of a group of individuals within these given situations. Another of the principal dimensions along which models vary, therefore, must be one which runs between social and physical situations at the one end and the individual within these situations at the other.

There are models in disaster research exemplifying nearly every position along this continuum. In part, this reflects the fact that disaster research is necessarily interdisciplinary. Historically, it began as a study of the awesome physical conditions which would be imposed by a disaster such as an atomic bombing. Consequently, some models in disaster research are almost completely physical. They state, for example, the nature of tornadoes and the important physical effects of destruction and injury to be expected under the circumstances. The main notion behind the study of available natural disasters in order better to understand atomic disasters is that many of the physical effects of more common disasters are not unlike the physical effects we might expect from an atomic bombing—for example, the disruption of physical channels of communication, widespread death and injury, the destruction of material goods.

For the pure sociologist, such surrounding physical conditions become the input variables for the models in which he is interested. That is to say, the outputs of the physical model of the striking force in any disaster become input variables for models of the ways in which communities, institutions, families, and other aggregations of human beings respond to the physical impact of floods, tornadoes, and fires.

For the pure psychologist and even the social psychologist, both the physical impact and the social consequences of disasters may become inputs for the main models with which he is concerned. His models represent the behavior of individual human beings under the impact of both the physical attack of the disaster and the new social situation which is caused thereby. The psychologist may be interested in how people react to direct personal injury; or he may be interested in how individuals react to the social changes that occur during a disaster, in which case the outputs of the social model are the inputs for the psychologist's model of the behaving individual.

Two aspects of this theoretical situation are patently clear. The first is that disaster research, being thoroughly interdisciplinary, may generate models anywhere along this continuum, even at the very ends. The second is that a complete model of a disaster—if one were to exist—would be one of which these various disciplinary models formed the internal mechanism. They would be the meat with which the conceptual pie was filled.

The importance of recognizing this dimension is not merely theoretical. It has considerable practical consequence for the understanding and manipulation of human behavior under disaster conditions. One consequence is that any particular piece of research can be assessed for practical purposes in part by considering where its model lies along this situational-individual dimension. If the model lies at one place, it may help to explain certain phases of a disaster and to devise means for controlling or predicting these phases. If, however, the model lies at one point but practical interest concerns another point, this may serve to rule out research governed by that model as essentially irrelevant. A complication here is the lack of connection between two models at different points on the continuum. For example, a leader in a disaster situation has the job of controlling individual behavior in some respect. But if he uses a model of the behaving individual that permits him to predict the input conditions under which this behavior may take place, this model may still be inadequate for pragmatic purposes, simply because in order to control the input into this model, the output from a model of a higher order of social generality must itself be known and controllable. This in turn demands some model of the social situation in question. In short, for practical purposes it may be necessary to have a good acquaintance with at least two models, each at a different position along this situational dimension, but connected in an input-output fashion.

It is clear, in the light of some research, that a complete understanding of disaster phenomena is not available largely because most of our models do not exhibit an output-input connection. At the time of the first serious research on disaster we had very good models of the physical nature of the disaster-engendering forces, and we had considerable psychological knowledge about the reaction of individuals to particular features in their social situation; but these two were not automatically connected. The output of one did not feed directly into the input of the second. This situation leads one to hope for a third model intervening between these two; this must be a model of the social situation induced by the output of the physical model, which in turn has stimulus effects upon the individual such that his behavior can be understood as a function of that social situation. Given all three models, an almost complete account of the corresponding phase of disasters would result and one could work back and forth among these three in an implicative fashion. But all three models are not always available, and it must be admitted that today our general model of the disaster has some empty places in it where intervening models are not yet available or discernible.

We must note, in passing, another more general difficulty. It is that one science tends to furnish the input variables for another science. It follows from this that progress in the one science may wait upon progress in the other. For example, it is true of experimental psychology—particularly of the area of psychophysics—that a great deal of knowledge from the fields of physics and physiology provided useful, measurable, and well-understood input variables against which the output variables of the individual could be investigated; the physics of simple sensory stimuli was already well developed. The field of social psychology has not been helped in this way; it can be argued that much further progress in social psychology depends upon the success of psychology in defining those outputs of a social situation which become the principal stimuli bearing upon the behavior of the individual. This is to say, we require a *sociology of social psychology* in the same sense that psychophysics required and found a *physics of psychology*. It may indeed be hoped of disaster research that the interdisciplinary interest that has gone into it may give rise to clearer and more urgently regarded decisions about the stimulus variables for the individual which the social mechanism does in fact provide. No doubt many of these important stimuli lie in the area of communication; perhaps the advancing science of communication which disaster research requires may be one pathway to a more productive relationship between the end products of sociology and those stimulus conditions with which the psychologist, by the nature of his science, must begin.

In thinking of the situational-individual dimension, we should be alert to the possibility that, as with other dimensions, there are regions along the continuum at which models for disaster behavior may be more productive and useful than at some other points. For example, models too close to the individual extreme of this continuum are not likely to be of great pragmatic value in the control of disasters. This is because the problem, practically, is not to understand the behavior of a single individual—or indeed of a class of individuals if this class is defined psychologically, or in terms of highly personal variables or previous conditions. The problem is, rather, to make a prediction that persons who have been exposed to certain previous circumstances (which must be open to fairly rapid and succinct determination) will behave in such and such a way under given conditions. This means, in turn, that the best model of the individual for this purpose is the one that places him within a class of persons separated from other classes by individual differences which are common in our culture and which are relatively easily measured or identified through observation of behavior. In this region the model becomes powerful indeed for practical purposes.

This is not to say that these "class-behavior" models are the easiest ones to construct, on the basis of the research we have had so far. This is partly because most of our psychological knowledge is tied to highly personal variables which form grand models of the individual that are tied to basic theoretical orientations—that of psychoanalysis, for example. Perhaps the psychoanalytic explanations of human behavior in disasters, true and theoretically sound as they may be, offer models which are constructed a little too close to the individual end of the scale. That is, they require for their conclusions a close knowledge of the internal workings of particular individuals. But for the purposes of disaster research, the behavior predicted on these grounds is either not the central concern in disaster control (e.g., "private" emotional reactions) or is based on causes which could seldom be verified in actual field observation (e.g., the childhood family relations of present adults).

These considerations relate also to another dimension we discuss later—differences among models with respect to manipulability of the variables to which they refer. This further dimension overlaps the present one, partly in meaning and partly in some of the implications it has for the practical consequences of theorizing about disaster behavior.

LEVEL OF ABSTRACTION

Another dimension along which models vary is that from extreme generality to extreme specificity of their terms and relations.

In models of the highest level the terms are general and the relations universal. Such models are often referred to as "basic," because they specify truths that permeate large areas of phenomena and because they offer fundamental propositions from which many special corollaries may be logically derived for empirical testing.

The models which serve as the bases of contemporary learning theory are excellent examples. They come from a prolonged and careful distillation of many empirical facts. Their terms are constructed with the utmost parsimony. The relations among these terms are an effort to assert all the important relations from which the intricate facts of learning can be deduced, and to do so in highly explicit and quantitative form. Finally, most learning theorists have attempted to provide fundamental laws of such scope that the field of human behavior which these theories elucidate is by no means limited to the classical division of "learning" but may be extended practically without limit. Much contemporary theory of learning, for instance, pretends really to a general theory of behavior.

It may or may not mean the same thing to say that (1) a theory or model is of broad scope, fundamental, and potentially capable of yielding corollaries of an enormous range, and to say that (2) it is fruitfully applicable to many practical problems. One difficulty, surely, in regarding these two statements as the same is that, although the theory may be entirely relevant to the problem at hand, it may not be discriminate with respect to that problem.

When we say that a theory is not *discriminate* with respect to a problem, we mean that although the terms of the theory correspond to terms in which the problem may be conceptualized, they correspond also to the terms in which rather different problems may be conceptualized. In such a case it is plain that the theory no more predicts the existence of the problem at hand from known previous conditions than it does several other alternative problems which it says might also have occurred.

Suppose, for example, that we rely upon a theory of "defense-against-anxiety" to explain some of the behavior that occurs under the threat of disaster. The behavior in response to threat, the theory asserts, may be (1) denial of threat, (2) exaggeration of threat, (3) personalization of the source of threat, etc. If, then, in a given disaster situation we find denial of threat to have been the principal phenomenon in the period of actual threat, the finding is indeed consistent with the theory; but so would have been several other phenomena which did not occur. In such a case, it is certainly hard to say that the theory explains the facts within any profitable meaning of the verb *explain*. This very difficulty has often been remarked as embarrassing empirical tests of those psychoanalytic theories which predict several possible, but highly different, reactions. Such theories are nearly impossible to test. Under the conditions specified by the theory, the expected reaction may occur; but if it does not occur, the results may still be in keeping with the theory, since the theory also predicts the possibility of a strong suppression of that reaction.

It is a tendency of all theories or models to become less and less discriminate with respect to empirical problems as they reach higher and higher levels of abstraction. This is particularly so of all general theories which come close to being fundamental for every sort of behavior—for example, general theories of learning or the basic theories of perceptual organization. Since the model *is* global, it tends to be evidenced in every specific case that practical work encounters, and it therefore exerts very little or no explanatory force on the particularities of the case in hand. For example, it states a great deal systematically, but very little specifically, to say that in all disaster behavior there occur learned responses, and that these responses must have been pretty frequently and consistently rewarded in the past—for this, on learning theory, will be true of *every* case of behavior.

SYSTEMATIC UNITY

Any model which purports to interpret a considerable segment of some large social phenomenon, such as disaster and its accompanying behavior, may be measured by its position on another continuum. On the one hand, the model may be highly systematic, in that it uses a strongly integrated system of variables to fill its model space. In this way it refers to all the facts which it proposes to explain to a single dominant theory, however simple or complicated. On the other hand, perhaps more commonly in our time, a model may contain a number of submodels, each explaining a different aspect of the whole. It may, for example, draw strongly on learning theory for one aspect, on cognitive theory for another, on motivation theory or psychoanalysis for additional facts. In this case the model is really a collection of models chosen for their individual suitability to the events they are used to explain.

It is quite natural that disaster research today should more frequently use the eclectic type of model than the systematic. A unified and systematic theory or model of disaster would be possible only late in the course of research. Thus, for example, contemporary accounts of disasters draw on theoretical models which range all the way from sociological theories of organization and disorganization or psychophysiological theories of stress and regression to psychoanalytic theories of child development and children's reaction to trauma. The temporary advantages of such a composite model as a working tool are quite plain. It does indeed relate the phenomena that we wish to explain to theories which have some standing in their respective social sciences. For each of the submodels it is possible to point to empirical research, independent of disaster research, which has tended to verify it.

At the same time, just as with very low-level theory, recourse to eclectic models must be considered a temporary device and less satisfactory in the long run than a unified theory of disaster behavior. Just as in low-level models, so with an eclectic model: the submodels within it are chosen, we must often believe, because of the particular preference or familiarity of the research worker. He has a penchant in his ordinary work, let us say, for Gestalt psychological formations; that part of his general model which deals with the cognitive aspects of disaster behavior tends to reflect this. Or he may be very biased for or against psychoanalytic theory; the submodel by which he chooses to explain the dynamic aspects of human activity in a disaster, or more particularly the unconscious determinants of this activity, will reflect his bias.

This is not to say that in practical terms a disaster situation may not be much better understood with an eclectic model than with no model at all. Nor is it to say that the practical man studying disasters in the light of such a model may not find a great deal of guidance as he moves from one of the submodels to another, in spite of their theoretical diversity. Certainly two jobs in the management of human behavior during a disaster are to give useful information and to restrain emotionally motivated human behavior; the first can be done better by reference to any reasonably well-demonstrated theory of cognition, and the second by reference to any reasonably well-supported theory of motivation. For such practical purposes, it does not matter that these two theories have little or nothing in common with respect to the vocabulary of their concepts or that they make rival claims for centrality in a theory of the human being.

Nevertheless, after general eclectic models of disaster have been developed, it is doubtful that further refinement of the various parts would be as profitable as the unifying of the concepts and dynamisms which are used to explain human behavior in these situations. This kind of progress is, of course, by no means the duty solely of disaster research. It is a desideratum for all of social science or at least, certainly, for sociology and psychology. It goes without saying that disaster research will not achieve unified models much faster than the relevant sciences themselves achieve them.

Since, however, disaster research requires the explanation of a great many facets of human behavior and employs people of widely different theoretical persuasions, it is not unreasonable to hope that it may serve as a spur toward unified theory, wherever this is desirable and possible, in the social sciences concerned.

COMPREHENSIVENESS

The systematic-eclectic dimension we have just discussed is related to another dimension: a model may be of the *total* event or of some quite *restricted part* of the event. In disaster research, the model may attempt to explain a great deal of what happens, or it may restrict its explanation to some particular facet of the situation which is nevertheless in itself important. Wolfenstein's (1957, Chapter 3) treatment of the rejection of threat is a tightly knit model which intends to do no more than explain why it is that people who are given some advance information that a disaster may occur can reject this information and its implications. It is not a model that makes any attempt to explain, for example, social disorganization or convergence behavior or the many phenomena of recuperation that set in after a disaster. Withey, on the other hand, has constructed a somewhat eclectic model of disaster behavior, which pretends to the explanation of the many phases of a disaster and the many behaviors that occur in these phases (Chapter Four, this volume).

It is clear that a systematic model may be either total or partial in its intent, and to this degree these two dimensions—comprehensiveness and degree of systematic unity—are independent of each other. But it is clear also that, in general, an eclectic model arises because it has many things to explain and seizes upon likely theory for each of them. An eclectic model is usually one which attempts to explain more than one phase of human behavior; this eclecticism disappears as a model becomes less comprehensive in intent.

TEMPORAL EXTENSION

There is a dimension of causal-extendedness which also can be applied to models. We do not refer simply to the total time embraced by the model. We refer rather to the pattern of causes for the outputs of the model—whether or not they must be traced and identified back through an extended chain. This would be true of any conceptual system in which present behavior can be predicted only in the light of processes which are historical for a community or biographical for an individual. In those models of disaster behavior, for instance, which owe a good deal to psychoanalytic theory, one begins with certain facts about the early development of individuals. These facts of development and family life lead to certain kinds of social phenomena which further condition the behavior to be expected in response to disaster. The ultimate behavior explained by the model may indeed be separated from its essential causes by a great many years.

The difference between theoretical systems which depend largely on historical explanations and theoretical systems which draw upon the forces operating in a given situation at a given moment—which are contemporary and field-theoretical—has been sharply pointed out by Kurt Lewin (1951). His preference for the latter type of theoretical formulation rests on two important arguments. First is the fact that, of course, history can operate upon the present only through present forces which are indeed there to be discovered and described. This argument leads to the second one, which is that when we depend upon historical explanations, we probably reveal our ignorance about some feature of the present field operating in a given situation. If we can do away with our ignorance, we can do away with historical explanations. We are then in a position to make predictions out of present facts, which are much more easily observed and measured than historical facts, which may be incomplete or difficult to obtain.

We must certainly grant that the contemporary-field explanation of an event is the most advanced for any science. However, it requires a fairly complete knowledge of the phenomena in question, and for this reason it offers a considerable test of the maturity of the science to which it belongs. But some question arises as to whether field-theoretical models, if they are too instantaneously contemporary, are as serviceable or enlightening as is supposed. One might suspect that something analogous to the Heisenberg principle of indeterminacy may operate in the social sciences. That is, it is conceivable that the more precise our knowledge about the present state of a process, the less may we be aware that the present state is indeed in process. For example, no study of contemporary opinions on some social issue can, by simply making its descriptions or measurements more precise, give us any idea of how these opinions have arisen or in what direction they are tending over time. In turn, however, this may be merely a difficulty with some incompleteness of the model. There ought to be ways of detecting at the present moment whether social processes are in a state of change, or whether, say, the opinions of an individual are in a state of change. But the ways of finding this out are not clearly known.

Lewin's argument in favor of the contemporary-field model neglects a very practical point. However true it is in principle that the past acts through the present—a point difficult to contradict because it is so embedded in our implicit definitions of past and present—it nevertheless remains that for practical purposes some of the important processes may conveniently reveal themselves only at certain periods in time. This is not to say that they are by their nature undetectable at any given instant, but only that some points in time are more propitious than others for observation, and that some of the manifestations of these processes are more simple than others to observe and record. For example, if people in a given disaster have been through a previous disaster of much the same sort, this knowledge would lead one to make different predictions about their present behavior than one would make if these people were innocent of any previous experience. This prediction must be different, because at present there are residues of the past experience which make these individuals different from what they would be had these experiences not occurred. In principle, it would seem possible to get people to verbalize about these previous experiences at the present time. But it would also have to be granted that the original experiences might well have left residues that are essentially unverbalizable and yet are potent for present behavior. In such a case a simple knowledge of previous events in this community would lead to a far better prediction than would any data gathered at a cross-section in time or during those phases of a disaster when it was inconvenient or impossible to get people to provide any verbal account of their previous experience.

For this reason a serviceable model of disaster will probably be somewhat retrospective. It will seek out dependencies upon previous experiences and historical trends which on the one hand have been demonstrated (clinically or experimentally) to yield differential predictions of behavior and which on the other hand are feasible to identify and study. However, as we have pointed out, extremely remote previous causes can sometimes be identified only through inference from present behavior. When the model has the job of predicting present behavior as an inference from past causes, and where this function of the model is really based on a previous backward inference, the logic of the model becomes circular. In short, there appears to be a middle ground of extended causation that makes a model especially useful for disaster research.

SPATIAL EXTENSION

While it is perfectly clear that any disaster by its nature covers some extent of space—often a very large area—it is nevertheless true that models of disaster vary along a dimension which may be referred to as that of spatial extension.

An example may well illustrate what we mean. A disaster model which concentrates upon the regressive behavior of the individual under the impact of sudden emotional stress we would regard as essentially spatially restricted. Its input variables are variables just outside the skin of the individual, so to speak, and its output variables are similarly close to the individual. The whole realm of events which the model undertakes to explain is contained within a very small circle which goes only a little beyond the behaving person.

This is not equivalent to saying simply that spatially-restricted models are always models of individual behavior. They are not necessarily. Even a model of disaster events and behavior which is derived from a considerable portion of a community, and which therefore covers many people, may be relatively restricted spatially. In contrast, a spatially-extended model would be one which considered (as do models of communication networks or of the operation of constituted authority in disaster) the utmost spatial limits within which can be found events relevant to the disaster or products of it.

There are in fact models which go so far beyond the disaster itself as to be considered models of the society within which a disaster takes place. A disaster is generally regarded as an event that produces severe disruption of the social organization; it is clear then that disaster in a given community may have effects, and may depend upon events, far outside that community. Moreover, these events are (in the areas in which they are located) by no means principally "disaster" events; they may constitute relatively normal problems for the operation of government or other authorities. For example, such groups as the American Red Cross play a considerable part in the organizational activities connected with most disasters. The effects of the disaster upon the Red Cross specifically can hardly be called disruptive. They are part of its normal course of business. Nevertheless, we cannot fully understand the disaster in its primary locale without considering the role of those organizations affected by it or ready to affect it—what they are prepared to do, how they go about doing it, and what impact their activities have upon the disaster-stricken community.

To some extent, but by no means perfectly, the dimension of spatial extension is related to the dimension of comprehensiveness of the model—the extent of the disaster phenomena which it attempts to explain. In part only, this dimension is also related to the difference between models which concentrate mainly upon explaining individual behavior and models which have a broader scope. But these relations, we stress again, are imperfect; the sheer geographical or social space which a disaster research model undertakes to systematize is a distinguishable feature in itself.

We have given the opinion that temporally-extended models become unwieldy when they begin to invoke causes too remote historically. It might be thought by analogy that spatially-extended models might suffer the same practical defect. But one great difference must be noted. No matter how extended it is spatially, a model can nevertheless be roughly contemporaneous. It can be made to approach a field theory with any degree of approximation desired; therefore, in spite of its spatial extendedness, its variables are now presently available to study. The difficulties, however great these may be, are only difficulties of tracking essential data down over wide physical areas, or difficulties of the complexity of the model itself. These difficulties can in the long run be overcome by reasonable effort.

Therefore, we would take the position that ideal models for disaster research are probably highly extended in space. They should and can include a broad geographic area of influences and consequences. Indeed, only if they are broadly inclusive are models ultimately suitable for the most pressing national problems connected with the preparation for disasters and with human management when they occur. Consider, for instance, the striking fact that virtually all disasters in the United States have happened in a "cornucopia society" —that is, one so rich in goods and services that the consequence of most disasters is to evoke an over-abundance of help. The question immediately raised is, what would be the effect of a nationwide disaster such as an all-out atomic bombing of the United States? Obviously, we cannot answer such a question unless the model of the disaster is one large enough geographically to include the essential differences between these two situations.

MANIPULABILITY OF INDEPENDENT VARIABLES

Models also differ in the degree to which their variables can be manipulated. The input conditions of some models can, in practical situations, be manipulated to a considerable extent. The input conditions of other models have to remain, in any practical situation, the givens of the situation, whether their values are known or unknown. Examples of the latter kind are the several studies of disaster behavior which lead to models whose main input conditions are the existing attitudes toward one or another aspect of the disaster—attitudes of rejection or acceptance of the idea of danger, or favorable versus unfavorable attitudes toward the constituted authority in the community about to be struck by disaster. Such variables are demonstrable predictors of some kinds of behavior under disaster conditions, but they are not very easily open to change at the hands of those who have the job of influencing disaster behavior. At the other extreme are variables like those of the character of the leadership which is exerted during a disaster situation. The variables involved in this sort of input can to some extent be manipulated at the time of disaster by those who are ready to exert their influence—by constituted authority, by persons at the disaster scene who have some training or some understanding of leadership roles, or by some of the physical conditions arranged for communication in case of disaster.

This variable of manipulability is, of course, a pragmatic one. It matters relatively little for theory itself; it matters a great deal for the uses of theory in social engineering.

It would be absurd if this distinction led us to urge that all of the input conditions of disaster models be readily manipulable. If this prescription were followed slavishly, it would undoubtedly put distinct limitations upon the scientific achievements of disaster research.

It is probably wise, however, to keep in mind that models with input variables expressed in one vocabulary may need ultimately to be translated or transformed into models with other, correlated inputs which are themselves more open to pragmatic manipulation. We do not mean that this is all merely a matter of vocabulary and of translating technical matters into terms which are understood by administrators and agency personnel. A model, for example, which depends largely upon attitudes as its independent variables is not the same as (and perhaps cannot be wholly translated into) a model which depends largely upon characteristics of leadership. Nevertheless, wherever it is possible to point to some correlation between the behavior stemming from given attitudes and the kinds of leadership that may be exerted in the situation, this represents a kind of practical transformation of the first model into an approximate model-in-parallel which may be much more useful for administrative purposes. The reason we include this dimension in our listing of the important dimensions of models for disaster research is that much of this translation has to be done by those persons who have built the original models. If they do not do it, the translation will be performed by people less qualified to do so, with a consequent probability of error. Put briefly, we are urging that the expert translation of models into practical terms is an important matter, and that some of this had better be done, in the case of any model, by those persons who have been most concerned with the building of that model itself.

EVOLUTIONISM

The concept of equilibrium is usually a feature of comprehensive models of the human being or his society. In models that embody this concept, the effects of stimulation or of social events may be thought of as impacts upon a system which tend to disrupt a state of poise. Consequent activities—that is to say, the outputs of the system—are then regarded, at least in part, as processes directed toward bringing the system back to some state of equilibrium.

It is an important point, and one which has been stressed by developmental psychologists, among others, that the equilibrium to which the organism, individual or social, finally adapts itself is not always the original equilibrium. From this fact there emerges an evolutionary concept, which goes beyond that of the return to equilibrium to study those equilibrium states which are successively preferred by the organic system. This progression of normal states of equilibrium with increasing age and experience in the individual is, of course, the central phenomenon in any psychological system which calls itself developmental. Such an approach recognizes that the individual passes from stage to stage and that these stages are, to a considerable extent, irreversible. They are progressive because each set of experiences produces something new in the system which prevents it from ever again coming to equilibrium under the conditions which formerly balanced it.

The pertinence of this idea to much of disaster research is quite evident. Many disaster studies note the fact that the impact of disaster upon a community, for example, is not simply to disrupt this community's original state of equilibrium and to initiate processes which return it to a state of equilibrium, but is also sometimes to induce lasting social changes in the community. The consequence of a disaster may, therefore, be that from one system a new system is produced with its own quite different normal state.

It is, therefore, desirable that any model of disaster events and behavior, particularly at the level of the community affected, should recognize and account for development within the community as a result of disaster circumstances. The extent to which any reasonably comprehensive model of disaster phenomena does this may place it on a continuum between, on the one hand, quite static models, which attempt to explain through mechanisms that bring the behaving system back to original states of equilibrium, and, on the other hand, developmental models, which embody some scheme of the succession of events as producing new dynamic situations with their own new equilibrium state.

A different way of putting this matter, which emphasizes much the same idea, is whether the model regards the social or individual system as essentially "closed" or "open." If the system is treated as a closed one, in which the forces at work are all intrinsic to it, then the model that emerges is likely to be comparatively static. If the system is regarded as open to important exchanges with more embracing systems, then the model is more likely to have a developmental character, which takes account of the new relations and impacts from outside the system and the relative permanence of the results of these.

However, it would be an inaccurate representation of developmental thinking in social science to put the whole emphasis upon the open-ness or closed-ness of systems. The psychoanalytic system of the individual, for example, considers the individual as essentially more nearly closed than open; yet developmental stages emerging from interior dynamics and solidified by them are a very prominent and essential feature of the system.

It is worth noting also that the failure to account for developmental features of an evolving social or psychological situation often happens when very high level theory is applied to such special phenomena as disaster behavior. On the one hand, it is true that disaster behavior does accord with the basic principles of learning, motivation, perception, etc. But the more precise model of the disaster will have to include specific information about specific situations, in order that more precise predictions of behavior may be made than simply the predictions that learned and motivated behaviors will emerge under the usual lawful guidance of perception and cognition.

It is true also that a sufficiently developmental model must be somewhat extended in time. This overlap between the two dimensions is quite clear. However, the two dimensions are not entirely the same. A quite time-extended model may nevertheless fail to be really dynamically developmental; and a developmental model which is extremely useful and enlightening may nevertheless not have to be greatly extended historically. For this reason the two dimensions remain substantially independent.

Dimensional Analysis of Two Models

The foregoing general analysis of the dimensions of models should be useful in assessing specific theories of disaster behavior. We turn now to two available models, which we will examine in these terms in order to draw some conclusions about their theoretical and pragmatic adequacy for problems of disaster.

WOLFENSTEIN'S MODEL

Martha Wolfenstein (1957) proposes a number of explanations of individual behavior in disaster and its aftermath. These explanations are well enough related, through the fundamental kinds of psychological process which they invoke and through the unitary sequence of external disaster events to which they are addressed, to serve as one example of conceptual model-building in the field of disaster. Wolfenstein introduces her contribution with a candid warning that the ideas she proposes are not carefully tested and are rather the tentative implications of already developed theory, illustrated by examples from the empirical literature.

The model begins with a description of external conditions of threat, and then seeks to account for varying personal attitudes toward dangers not yet become real. When the threat is highly remote, the theory notes that predispositions to worry about it may arise from fear that one cannot control one's hostility under adverse conditions, or from feelings of deserving punishment and a subconscious interest in the punitive symbolism of a catastrophe let loose on mankind. As the threat becomes more imminent, the needs to deny it may arise from infantile motives to defy the warnings of parent-like authorities, or from the defensive sense of immunity as a refuge from impending danger which one feels helpless to cope with. Deeply interiorized

American cultural norms also support our popular repudiation of anxiety and worry. Actual precautions taken against the threatened danger may be valued as symbols of obedience to a harsh parental authority whom one seeks to propitiate; or precautions may be ignored altogether if one feels that one has already accumulated enough obedience to this authority to forestall retribution. Rehearsal of preparations may reduce the anxiety of anticipation. The threat, in all these cases, may be interpreted as the threat of abandonment, which, to the child, is presumed to be primally intense; for this reason, the presence of others who share the threat may allay anxiety about being forsaken, and may for this reason even act as a deterrent to the most active planning.

Moving to the period of impact of disaster, the theory notes the common finding that the victim at first believes that only he has been hit. This is often a plausible feeling, from past experience with accidents, and may be bolstered by a defensive unwillingness to recognize a disaster so widespread as to seem to express one's feelings of general hostility toward others. It may also be due to pre-disaster feelings that, "if it hits me, it will be a punishment of me alone." The sense of abandonment that follows the first impact recalls the infant's fear that he will be deserted; this in turn explains much of the overflowing gratitude with which disaster victims at first welcome those who come to help them. Even people who go through a disaster unharmed may be expected to be shaken by the nearness of the "judgment" that might have chosen them for its victims. Those with greater initial anxiety may be predicted to be disturbed by even remote "misses," whereas the less anxious will be similarly threatened by a near miss. Defense against the anxiety aroused by the disaster is also displayed in dazed and immobilized postures, which shut out sensory stimuli until the victim can begin to assimilate the post-disaster situation. (This is, of course, the well-known "disaster syndrome.") Anxiety may also be allayed by an intense concern to protect others and by suppression of anxious behavior in favor of objectively helpful activity.

After the disaster, the main personal problem becomes the working-through of the traumatic experience and its emotional residues. Frequent recall and discussion would afford a way of gradually accustoming oneself to intense emotions which had arisen too rapidly to be well assimilated; the taboos on recall exerted by some families and communities would lead more often to prolonged emotional difficulties. Fears of recurrence of the disaster are nourished by the experience of having lost, or almost lost, one's omnipotence and by the feeling that the retributive animism behind the disaster cannot fail to hit one on a second try.

Some general community phenomena that follow disaster, and which this model interprets are: the low level of complaint about loss of property, due to its being viewed as the price of remaining alive or due to deep conflicts between the materialistic and spiritual components in the prevalent protestant ethic; emphasis on the good fortune of survival, with its relation to previous guilt feelings and expectation of punishment; prevalence of warm attitudes toward other survivors, which counteract shameful feelings of abandonment and feelings of hostility aroused by the disaster. This post-disaster warmth may also reflect the opportunity for the expression of positive feelings inhibited by social convention in the normal state of a community.

It should be said that the theoretical model governing such assertions as those summarized here is not explicitly developed as a unitary structure, even in Wolfenstein's book. The more explicit model is, of course, the familiar body of depth-psychological theory, which the book does not repeat in full, but from which it draws its specific interpretive hypotheses. This basic theory would include such propositions as the following, familiar in psychoanalytic interpretation and in its modern developments:

1. Human beings are motivated in directions which may involve conflict.

2. Where conflict arises between motivations of which some are strongly connected with maintenance of self-regard (ideals, superego prohibitions, socially approved actions), anxiety results.

3. Many such conflicts stem from anxiety-laden childhood conflicts and they continue to be expressed in symbols which derive from the early child-parent relationships. There is, consequently, a lasting sensitivity to stress situations which in some respects duplicate those infantile situations (e.g., conflict with authority figures, dangers of abandonment, instigations to forbidden hostility, etc.).

4. In the effort to allay intolerable anxiety under such conflict, ego-defensive mechanisms come into play: repression, rationalization, perceptual distortions and defense, and the numerous others familiar from psychological theory.

5. Human behavior in such situations is therefore to be understood as a mixture of rational problem solving and irrational defense; the proportion of the latter may in some cases be very large.

6. Specifically, then, if we can recognize in the conditions of disaster the replicas of more infantile situations which initiated conflicts unresolved by the individual, we can predict aspects of his behavior by reference to the basic theory.

LOCATION OF WOLFENSTEIN'S MODEL ON OUR DIMENSIONS

Let us now attempt to locate this theoretical model on each of the nine dimensions we discussed earlier.

1. Implication Wolfenstein's model falls quite clearly at the implicative end of this dimension. It states causal relations between stimulus situations and consequent behavior. Far from claiming comprehensive classification, it selects aspects of behavior for which it can adduce explanatory principles. Thus, for example, it does not try to account for all problem-solving in critical situations, but only for what is presumably due to the more or less unconscious response to aspects of the situation that reflect infantile and neurotic emotional problems.

On the related scale, the model is nearer the filled than the empty extreme. It sees many intervening mechanisms as mediating between situation and response—for example, all the ego-defense mechanisms which psychoanalytic theory has conceptualized.

2. Situational reference This model is highly individual. It explains how a single person reacts to situational stress, and not how these stresses arise in the social milieu. It may also be said to define the stress of disaster from the point of view of the emotional economy of the individual. In all respects it is thoroughly psychological and unsociological.

3. Level of abstraction The model does not use, directly, the psychological concepts which are regarded as basic in contemporary theory-building (such as those in learning theory). It uses, rather, concepts presumably deducible from such ultimate variables as "contiguity," "reinforcement," "drive reduction," etc., and which specify particular mechanisms which can form and persist as the results of human learning, basic motivation, and cognition. Thus, for instance, the model is concerned with a number of features of behavior which center about efforts to minimize anxiety. It does not try to furnish an account of anxiety-reduction in terms of still more basic processes —say, a more general class of tension-reducing mechanisms. Nor, again, does it make explicit application of basic laws of learning to describe the conditions under which the individual might be expected to develop repressive tendencies.

It begins, rather, with a set of concepts presumably derivable from more basic ones, but does not carry out this derivation. Perhaps a useful term for the level of the model is "clinically basic"—that is, a level below the utmost generality of the basic concepts found in experimental psychology and yet considerably above the specificity of types of reaction to disaster. The model thus gains some predictive precision from the fact that its concepts can be applied with some particularity to such general features of situations as "threat of destruction" or "being narrowly missed by disaster" or "the warnings of authorities,"—aspects which more basic principles of learning, motivation, and perception could not deal with differentially. On the other hand, the model retains a level of generality which enables it to tie together the interpretation of substantially different patterns of behavior by reference to a limited set of principles. A typical example is embodied in the following excerpt:

> Anticipation of danger may be affected in a number of ways by the fact of having undergone a disastrous experience. . . . A frequent reaction to a disaster is the anxious expectation of an imminent repetition of the event. This attitude, while manifestly forward-looking, may be in effect directed more towards the emotional mastery of the past trauma. . . .
>
> Sometimes following a disaster previous habits of denial of danger become re-established in what seems to be very slightly modified form. . . . However, one may perhaps see a difference in emphasis in the post-disaster attitude in that there is more conscious effort to avoid becoming aware of danger signals. Denial has become more difficult, less automatic, more a matter of policy. Intentional avoidance of alarming stimuli is observed as a defense against anxiety, and even as a magical means of warding off the external threat (Wolfenstein, 1957, pp. 39-40).

That is, a need to deal with personal anxiety is the principle referred to for the explanation of both patterns of behavior; and motivation directed toward reducing anxiety is typical of the level of concepts which are made basic to the system. Further, the same concept unites genotypically two phenotypically very different behavioral outcomes: alert expectation of further danger on the one hand and denial of danger on the other. Indeed, from the point of view of predicting which of these two outcomes will dominate in a given individual, the theoretical model is at this point still too "high-level." It requires, but does not provide, some further principles intermediate between anxiety-reduction and the specific behaviors of anticipation or denial.

Throughout the related treatment of disaster phenomena, the model frequently suffers from this defect. It is a lack of lower-order principles which would permit actual differential prediction among pairs or groups of phenomena, all of which occur and all of which are generally consistent with the model. This is to say that the model is too high-level to discriminate predictively behaviors which must be discriminated if responses to disaster are to be predicted. This does not overlook the fact that, in the example given, the conjunction of anxiety-reduction *plus perceptual defense* as principles would indeed lead more readily to the prediction of denial of danger than to the prediction that danger signals would be overanxiously interpreted. But the model leaves us with no way of predicting whether, in a given individual, perceptual defense would be a consequence of anxiety. We should not be surprised, theoretically, by cases in which it is a consequence or by cases in which it is not.

4. Systematic unity With respect to this dimension, the model is difficult to classify. On the one hand, the fundamental theory it uses is the quite closely woven network of concepts and relations composing broadly psychoanalytic theory; from this point of view, the basis of the model is strongly systematic. On the other hand, the model itself selects those elements of psychoanalytic theory most appropriate to the facts of disaster behavior.

5. Comprehensiveness This unity of reference does not, however, lead to any claim that the model accounts for all of disaster behavior. Large areas of behavior are left uninterpreted—for example, leadership behavior, ordinary rational problem-solving, and many of the routine phenomena accounted for in social psychology and group dynamics. From the point of view of the whole range of disaster activity, then, the model is eclectic; it says, "For such-and-such phenomena, the systematic concepts of this theory are to be preferred; for other phenomena, other concepts (which we are not here exploring) might be chosen." One is left with the impression that Wolfenstein would agree that a comprehensive interpretation of disaster behavior might be quite eclectic.

6. Temporal extension Much of classical psychoanalytic theory holds that present behavior is to be understood as the latest event in a time-connected series of developments, without a knowledge of which the present event remains somewhat ambiguous. As we have suggested, this is not so much to say that the event cannot be understood in terms of the present conditions created by that long causal chain, but rather that the present conditions may be so obscured by repression and symbolic distortion that it may be more easily inferred from a reconstruction of more patent past history. Thus knowledge of the childhood of a person may give a better clue to his present difficulties than any verbalized account that he can easily render.

Wolfenstein's model is distinctly time-extended, in that sense. While it occasionally illustrates the congruence of present behavior with present cues, its most usual explanations and predictions draw upon the presumptive personal history of development of phobias, areas of anxiety, habitual defense mechanisms, and the like.

Assuming that such predictions of individual behavior are accurate, the model would nevertheless require for practical predictions a formidable amount of information. While in individual clinical practice such information can be painstakingly developed, it cannot be rapidly developed about an individual in a short time, let alone about whole groups and populations. Even if we have the greatest assurance that individuals with persistent feelings of guilt will show extreme reactions to the impact of disaster, there are simply no data to tell us what proportion of any given community is made up of such individuals. And while the model might in the long run be richly verified by elaborate retrospective studies, its utility for predicting the incidence of the behaviors it explains would always be sharply limited. The model says in advance what range of behavior may be expected, but it cannot very well specify the likely frequencies within that range.

7. *Spatial extension* Because this model is of the type that interprets individual behavior rather than the events of total social structures, it can hardly be located on this seventh dimension. Its adequacy is claimed for individuals in and around a disaster—or, really, for individuals who feel themselves affected or threatened by the catastrophic events. Geographically, the model is therefore without precise limits, though it covers the areas (social or geographical, within whatever limits) in punctate fashion rather than treating human behavior as a supra-individual pattern.

8. *Manipulability of independent variables* The independent variables of this model—hidden emotional and symbolic human predispositions (or, alternatively, the remote events of personal histories that give rise to these predispositions)—are not easily open to practical control. Many of the problems of preparing for human efficiency in disaster therefore become problems in the general field of mental health. If survival chances are enhanced, as must be concluded from the model, by personal psychic health and self-awareness, the job of prophylaxis against disaster extends into the mental hygiene of family living and child rearing. No doubt it does. But the practical necessity of preparing people for disaster can hardly wait on the success of any program extended enough to produce significant changes in general mental health. This is not to say, however, that the model might not be of significance for some of the tasks of rehabilitation—for example, for differential assistance to segments of the population that had revealed sufficiently distinctive reactions to an already-suffered catastrophe.

9. *Evolutionism* It is unlikely that a model of individual disaster behavior will be to any degree developmental unless it takes as its unit of analysis the individual in relation to explicit developments in the

social structure of groups or of the community. Wolfenstein's model hardly does, since its attention is focused upon the reaction of personal dynamic systems already developed in the individual. The nearest approach to what we have termed developmental point of view lies in the model's analysis of the individual sources of the widespread friendliness and mutual helpfulness that characterize the post-disaster period. But this period is viewed as temporary; the social system gradually moves back toward normal social stratification, inhibition of informal social relations, and the other marks of ordinary community organization that prevailed before the disaster. The model is, therefore, generally static, in the meaning that we have used for this term. Presumably it would not be inadequate to predicting the kinds of behavior in which it is interested under the conditions of the emergence of new and irreversible forms of social structure in a disaster-affected community; it is simply that the model does not undertake to examine whether such changes take place, since it is so highly individual-centered.

Summary The Wolfenstein model can be characterized in terms of our dimensions as *implicative; individual;* moderately *high-level; systematic* in its limited theoretical reference, but *eclectic* in that it would require other theories and concepts to explain disaster behavior beyond its range; *time-extended* in respect to its independent variables; neither *space-restricted* nor *space-extended;* relatively *non-manipulable;* and *static.*

The principal advantage of the model, as assessed on these dimensions, appears to be its potential for explaining behavior which would not be readily understood as a simple function of the immediate stimulus situation in disaster—for example, degrees of apprehension or apathy which appear to be out of proportion to the instigating circumstances, behavior which is mediated by symbolic cognition of the disaster situation, and, in general, behavior which depends in considerable part on dispositions acquired by individuals early in their personal development. The time-extendedness of the model and its emphasis on systematic understanding of "neurotic" determinants contribute to this potential.

On the other hand, the subtlety and the remoteness in time of the independent variables make tests of the theory under the limitations of disaster research quite difficult. It has the further drawback of offering systematic explanations of selected forms of behavior only.

WITHEY'S MODEL

In his monograph, "Reaction to Uncertain Threat" (Chapter Four, this volume), Withey has developed a model to account for typical individual behavior at successive stages of the approach and impact of disasters. Briefly outlined, this scheme is as follows:

1. Cues for threat at some degree of intensity and structure produce recognition of the threat, affected of course by individual dispositions and sensitivities toward recognition or denial.

2. Recognition sets off a state of personal vigilance characterized by heightened sensitivity to further external cues and to internal apprehension and anxiety. There are aroused strong needs to organize all this information into a meaningful cognition, including an estimate of the nature of the impending event, who is involved, and the likely outcome.

3. Affecting this estimate, there will be self-defensive processes (a second line of defense following preliminary vigilance) which operate to minimize the threat.

4. A third line of individual defense is the formulation and evaluation of plans for escape or self-protection. Attention is increasingly directed toward any stimuli which offer means for these.

5. As both the threat itself and the recruitment of psychological resources proceed, there is increasing involvement of the individual and commitment to the forming line of action.

6. Decision is made on a tactical plan, which is brought into action.

7. If this plan fails to produce the anticipated relief from threat, there will result increased anxiety and the formulation of new tactics, including tactics against the anxiety and conflict aroused by failure.

8. At some critical point of frustration, the whole process may move suddenly to a new plane of anxiety, direction of attention, type of response, or other variable. This step-function represents a discontinuity which may be extremely important in understanding stressful behavior and in predicting its course.

9. With repeated failures of this defensive cycle, we may expect behavior to regress through a hierarchy of defensive maneuvers in the following order:

   a. exaggeration of normal defensive and vigilant functions;
   b. partial detachment from reality;
   c. hostile discharge against substitute symbols;
   d. displacement of hostility to the self;
   e. transitory ego-rupture with violence;
   f. psychotic confusion and severe isolation from reality;
   g. self-destruction ego-disintegration.

It is possible, however, that this hierarchy may take the form of a *lattice*, in which regression may take one of several alternative lines of behavior at various points.

10. The condition for regression in this series (or, otherwise put, discontinuities of behavior over the course of time) may be basically the value of the ratio:

$$\frac{\text{Degree of (experienced) threat}}{\text{Degree of (experienced) potency to deal with threat}}$$

We may expect reasonably effective behavior at values of this ratio of less than 1, and perhaps even a sense of pleasure and mastery. As the ratio increases above unity, we should expect an accelerated regression from mere hyperactivity to the more psychotically desperate forms of behavior.

LOCATION OF WITHEY'S MODEL ON OUR DIMENSIONS

1. Implication This model lies well toward the implicative end of the scale. It assumes a series of events that is causally sequential and, therefore, a function (though not necessarily a linear function) of time. Each event in the chain is considered a necessary and sufficient condition for the next event; and this conditionality rests upon well-known principles relating problem-solving, probability-reckoning, selective attention, motivation, frustration, regression, etc., to one another.

For this same reason, the model is distinctly a filled one, packed with the intervening variables common in the psychology of such behavior and essentially without conceptual gaps.

The model therefore is, at least in principle, analytic and testable at each of its points.

2. Situational reference Although the model seems on first consideration to make assertions only about probable individual behavior, the fact that it analyzes this behavior as a causal sequence and, consequently, as a function of time, makes the model partly applicable to the course of mass behavior. That is, the probability that any behavior in this chain will occur is in a general way heightened by the duration of exposure to the stress situation; thus the incidence of the behaviors predicted should statistically increase with the duration and the intensity of the disaster.

The model is not, however, designed to predict patterns of stress at the level of social organization, nor to predict changes in social organization to accommodate these. In this sense, then, it is not social-situational. Indeed, it suggests that a complementary model of sequential events in social breakdown which occur—partly as a result of the hypothesized personal sequence of events—would contribute to a complete model of disaster. Would it, for example, be possible to suppose that a similar ratio of threat/resource might be investigated for a community viewed as a social unit, and that discontinuities leading to typical progressive disintegration phenomena could be related to increasing values of this measure?

3. Level of abstraction The model appears to fall in the range of middle-level theorizing. It does not assert relationships between concepts so pervasive and global that no stress or disaster situation could shed critical light on its validity. On the other hand, it is not an *ad-hoc* formulation only of behavior in disaster, but is rooted in a wide range of research on continued stress under varying conditions of the ability to cope with stress. Nor, again, is the theory highly specific with respect to the behavior predicted; it hypothesizes classes of behavior under given conditions but without specificity within such classes. That is, for example, it predicts displaced aggression under certain conditions but without specifying the form it would take. The model therefore has distinct limits of particularity of prediction, but also few of the faults of theories that rest on very general principles—like those of learning, motivation, unconscious determination, etc.—which apply to nearly all behavioral situations.

4. Systematic unity The degree of systematic unity that marks this model appears to be about the same as that of general psychology as a whole. No one doubts, we may suppose, that psychology at some future time will be able to assert theories that more nearly unify its still somewhat separated fields than do the prevailing treatments. There is not much, for example, that unifies present theories of attention and present theories of regression; one suspects that these concepts are somewhat isolated by history and special research interests and that they will one day be replaced by more general concepts. Withey's model shares this immaturity.

On the other hand, it makes a notable attempt to unify its structure through the sequentiality of its predicted events. It uses those aspects of perceptual theory, regression theory, frustration theory, etc., which can be stated roughly as functions of time or of increasing stress over time. In this respect, a single continuous independent variable unites the parts of the model. This variable is, of course, only a general determinant of behavior; what the model does not predict are the dependencies of behavior upon specific kinds of social situations or situational stimuli which may arise somewhat independently of the progress of time and the disaster. But it is not so eclectic as those models that turn for independent variables now to a feature of social organization, now to a known effect of anxiety, and now to the facts of individual childhoods.

5. Comprehensiveness This model is reasonably comprehensive in the scope of human reactions that it is designed to systematize. It does not, however, try to order social phenomena at the level of groups and institutions.

6. Temporal extension This model is a particularly explicit example of the contemporary-field type. The independent variables (immediately antecedent conditions) and the dependent variables (present behaviors) are joined by minimal time intervals. Even those independent variables which are undoubtedly linked through various theories (e.g., through psychoanalytic time-extended mechanisms) to remote past experiences of the individual appear in the model as contemporaneous with the disaster events to which they apply, in the form of present attitudes, present residues of learning, personality predispositions, etc. Provided these can be specified in a given case (and there is of course some difficulty in this), the model requires no data beyond what can be gathered from the individual in the present field of stress-stimuli.

7. *Spatial extension* Withey's model, like Wolfenstein's, is difficult to locate on this dimension, and for the same reasons. It is essentially a model of individual behavior. Its spatial extension is therefore simply the spatial distribution of persons who experience threat in the event of disaster. This extension is not governed by any geographical dimensions, by any spread of pertinent social structure, or by any formal relationship between spatial areas and the immediate area of disaster. That is, no such variables appear as such in the model.

There seems little doubt that the model could be improved by taking cognizance of some such factors. For example, the chain of individual behavior is strongly dependent, in this theory, upon the relationship between threat and the resources for coping with it; the second of these two crucial variables must, even subjectively, be influenced by the perceived availability of assistance from others in the vicinity. Such perception is going to differ greatly according to individual situations. Even the mere presence of others is known to be a condition that helps in resisting stress. It appears, therefore, that extensions of the theory could be made which would in no way alter its basic logic but which might provide additional specificity of prediction.

8. Manipulability of independent variables The model falls near the manipulable end of this continuum. Not only are the independent variables present in time; they also depend upon actually manipulable events such as perception, information-gathering, decision-making, frustration, and the like. Although it would be difficult to control such variables at the height of actual disaster, some advance control over them is not out of the question. Perceptions can be prepared, anxieties can be worked through in advance, information can be supplied, some forms of frustration can be made less likely by sheer preparation of physical means for problem-solving, escape, and rescue. The model offers many implications for preparation for foreseeable disasters (for example, fires, tornadoes, floods) and for evaluating different sorts of preparation for their likely utility.

9. Evolutionism A concept central to this model—namely, that of behavior changing at critical points to new forms and to new dependencies on surrounding conditions—makes it rather more developmental than are most models. One implication of this is, of course, that the theory envisages a sequence of behavior that in many respects must be irreversible: efforts by an individual to relieve stress will derive their character in large part from immediately preceding efforts. Panic, for example, would not occur as a simple function of general disaster conditions, but at a late stage, after the individual's exhaustion of available psychological resources under progressive frustration. It is true that a seriously exhausting sequence of frustrations might occur within a brief length of time, particularly if circumstances were so restricting and urgent as to give the individual little scope for a variety of responses. Therefore the emergence of behavior that is characteristic of the failure of all resources is not a simple function of the duration of disaster stress. This notion of the successive unfolding of types of behavior throws some considerable difficulties in the way of prediction, since the behavior to be predicted is so dependent on a precise sequence of problem-solving efforts. Despite this difficulty, the model should be testable in principle; retrospective accounts of survivors should be useful for verifying it in a general way, and it would be both interesting and valuable to find whether the degree of breakdown in coping with disaster is, for any individual, well related to the number of escapes attempted and frustrated, his cognition of available directions of escape, and, indeed, his estimate of his own resourcefulness.

Summary In terms of our dimensions, Withey's model is *implicative* and *filled;* mainly, but not completely, *individual; middle-level;* fairly *systematic;* psychologically *comprehensive; contemporary-field;* neither truly *space-extended* nor *space-restricted;* pragmatically *manipulable;* and more *developmental* than most.

Several of these features offer distinct advantages, both for the development and verification of disaster theory and for the solution of practical problems of disaster control. That the model is implicative at a middle level, is of the contemporary-field type, and is systematic in its basic reference, makes it testable at many points. These characteristics plus the manipulability of its independent variables make it practically useful.

Its weaknesses are probably the connected ones of inadequacy for the task of understanding social processes (since it is individual) and for dealing with the structure of disaster as related to space.

► *eleven*

JOINING FIELD AND LABORATORY WORK IN DISASTER RESEARCH

Harold Guetzkow

DOES THE LITERATURE of disaster research tell us whether experimental methods might now be fruitfully attempted? When and how might it be strategic to use the contrived laboratory experiment or the controlled field situation for the study of disaster? This essay attempts to answer these questions with full awareness that, as of today, with but a philosophy of science rather than a science of our social sciences (Guetzkow, 1958), conclusions will be most uncertain.

We will note first the general trend in the social sciences toward increased use of experimental contrivance in investigations, both in the laboratory and in the field. We then will analyze the limitations and advantages of field and laboratory for the study of disaster behavior. Finally, we will consider a proposal, deriving partly from that analysis, for joining disaster and nondisaster research and which may benefit both the basic and the applied researcher.

Increasing Use of Contrived Experiments in the Social Sciences

In nature, human behavior comes with complications, one incident seldom duplicating another. There is a plentitude of natural "experiments" which serve many useful purposes. But scientific investigation demands the isolation of variables, and contemporary statistical methods require replication. Experimental techniques devised and proliferated for the study of the individual (Boring, 1929) were adapted subsequently for the study of group behavior in the second and third decades of the twentieth century (Allport, 1954).

They came into wider use in research on the face-to-face group after World War II (Cartwright and Zander, 1960). Only a few of the more venturesome have endeavored to contrive large social systems (Chapman, Kennedy, Newell, and Biel, 1959) and to induce cultural transmission (Rose and Felton, 1955) in laboratory settings. One sociological laboratory has now developed a man-less simulation of social conflict for the computer (Coleman, 1960).

In its classical use the laboratory simplifies phenomena so that the canons of *ceteris paribus* may be realized. By varying only one attribute at a time in the experimental situation, consequences may be explored with thoroughness. As our realization of the potential importance of interaction among variables has grown, more complicated statistical designs have been introduced, so that the effects of one variable may be studied while other variables are held successively at several different levels.

In recent years statistical methods capable of handling multi-variate analyses have relieved pressures to reduce the number of variables studied simultaneously. Complicated statistical treatments given to experimental data now emphasize the importance of replication, so that adequate numbers of cases will be available for cross-tabular and other more intricate comparisons.

Thus the advantages found by social science experimenters in their increasing use of contrived situations are two: (1) more adequate penetration of complex phenomena by the reduction and manipulation of variables and (2) easier generation of replicated data to which multi-variate techniques of analysis may be applied. These advantageous techniques now are well established. Are they, then, applicable to the needs of those concerned with disaster phenomena? An examination of the state of disaster research may help us to estimate whether an experimental approach would be useful.

Characteristics of Disaster Research

The research literature on disaster focuses on the behavior of individuals and groups under conditions of stress. Researchers apply contemporary psychological and sociological concepts to explain behavior in situations which injure and disrupt individuals and their social institutions. As yet there is no inventory in disaster research comparable in scope or formality to our effort at explicit enumeration of propositions in the literature on organizations (March and Simon, 1958). A prototype for such, however, may be found in the miniature inventory of some fifteen propositions developed by Mack and Baker

(1961, Chapter 6) on the dependence of the warning system upon elements of social structure.

Massoti and the writer have listed all the conceptual terms used in a set of ten articles from the literature of disaster research (Massoti, 1960). About half of the articles are summaries of important subsections of the disaster literature. Of the 150 concepts we found some eighteen are especially related to disaster as such (e.g., "strain," "threat," "panic," "evacuation"). The remaining concepts may be divided into seventy-six that characterize ordinary individual behaviors (e.g., "aggression," "intelligence," "involvement") and fifty-six that focus on groups and their normal processes (e.g., "morale," "rumor," "power"). In the main, furthermore, the eighteen disaster concepts are related analytically to the nondisaster concepts. For example, Wallace's (1956) description of the "disaster syndrome" involves such concepts as "withdrawal," "passivity," and "suggestibility," which are common in the nondisaster literature of behavioral science, however unique the whole syndrome as a concurrence may be.

The first important characteristic of present disaster research may be said to be: *Fundamental variables in the study of disaster are almost entirely those used in common with ordinary, nondisaster psychology and sociology*. As Janis predicted almost a decade ago, "we must expect the theoretical developments in disaster research to grow directly out of the current theoretical concepts and hypotheses with which research workers in each of the various disciplines are preoccupied" (Janis, 1954, p. 16). The foregoing, however, does not mean that as our understanding of disaster phenomena deepens we will not discover new processes, unencountered in nonstress situations. It is just that to date such has not been the case.

The limits of intensity of variables commonly studied in psychology and sociology restrict applicability of the findings of nondisaster research to disaster. Torrance (1961) argues that one must take into consideration the intensity and duration of stressful conditions if one is to explain the apparently contradictory results of some stress research. A second characteristic of disaster research may therefore be put in this way: *The values of the variables in disaster research are often outside the range of those commonly explored in the ordinary, nondisaster research of psychology and sociology*. Nature's laboratory of accident and catastrophe fabricates treatments of great severity. Could the extreme situations contrived by the experimenter in his laboratory compete at all in intensity or scale with the havocs of nature?

A marked scarcity of empirical tests of theory has so far, also, limited disaster research. The literature enumerates a multitude of overlapping variables, usually annotating their operation by descriptions of occurrences in actual disasters. There are case studies of particular disasters, some of which include systematic interviewing of survivors. There are also theoretical efforts presenting frameworks within which disaster phenomena may be analyzed. But, as Killian has pointed out, "disaster research is usually entirely post hoc" (1956b, p. 4). This leads, then, to the third and last fundamental characteristic of the present state of disaster research: *The soundness of the formulations of disaster research has not yet been subjected to the basic scientific test—the prediction of behavior in disaster.* There has been no systematic effort to forecast behavior and then actually to check these forecasts when disaster hits. The plethora of extant hypotheses must be accompanied by explicit, detailed statements of their consequences under a variety of conditioning circumstances so that they may be in fact tested and not merely illustrated.

Some years ago Killian warned that "disaster researchers should not undervalue descriptive case studies, nor should they neglect the need for exploratory studies" (1956b, p. 6). This advice has been well heeded. But perhaps now the time has come to join laboratory work and controlled field work as a supplement to disaster study, so that the applicability of contemporary social science theories to disaster phenomena may be subjected to the test of prediction.

Laboratory Study of Disaster-Related Behavior

Can the lack of empirical tests in disaster research as it stands today be remedied through laboratory studies? There have been a number of studies of disaster-related behavior undertaken during the past twenty years, many of which are listed in the special bibliography at the end of this chapter. Particularly relevant to disaster research is work in which the behavioral processes operate within the special context of stress and rapid change, as well as of exposure to new and strange situations. The pertinence of this work may be immediate, as in the case of the psychological stress literature (Horvath, 1959).

An example of the potential value of the laboratory experiment in extending more general psychological findings to disaster-like situations is found in Hudson's (1954a) work on anxiety in response to the unfamiliar. By contriving two experimental situations—one in which a sequence of sounds related to a simulated nuclear attack was presented over a twenty-five-minute period to groups attending lectures or meetings, and another in which the observed behavior was in response to strange combinations of familiar stimuli—Hudson was able to demonstrate anxiety arousals which parallel those obtained by Hebb and others in animals and humans in nondisaster but stressful experimental situations. The phenomena produced by these experiments closely resembled phenomena described in the disaster literature.

An example of the usefulness of the laboratory experiment in the area of group behavior is found in the work of French (1944), in which he contrasted the reactions of organized and unorganized groups in their response to a simulated fire. Mechanisms of group conformity proved to be operative in the disaster situation in a way identical to their operation in nondisaster circumstances.

If the phenomena observed and the concepts found useful in the experimental study of disaster are essentially identical to those in the study of nondisaster behavior, then laboratory checks of important extrapolations of nondisaster findings should provide the basis needed for more confident use of contemporary psychological and sociological knowledge in understanding disaster behavior. But this conclusion may be in error because of the loose and *post hoc* way in which researchers have handled disaster data. Hence, the critical question for the laboratory is: Does disaster produce behavior that is unique or fundamentally unlike that encountered in nondisaster situations? This question can be answered only by vigorous and parallel pursuit of the unique in the field and then in the laboratory.

A Priori Limitations of the Laboratory

There would seem to be two ways in which the potential of the laboratory may be examined for its possible usefulness in the study of disaster. (1) Because disaster usually involves behaviors not only in new and rapidly changing situations but also in "extreme" situations, it is critically important to insure that the *range of the values of the variables* involved in laboratory work be extended into the extremes apparently present in natural disaster situations—or even beyond. Will it be possible to do this in the laboratory? (2) Further, it is of moment to introduce controls on the potential "artificiality" of the laboratory experiment. Because the scientific laboratory in contemporary American culture is seen as an experimental, exploratory site, to what extent do the protections and skepticisms aroused by contrivance produce disturbing *side-effects?* Let us examine these two problems in the use of the laboratory for the study of disaster behavior.

1. RANGE OF VARIABLES

Most research underlying the concepts in psychology and sociology has been done within nonstressful situations. Because disaster phenomena are concerned with extremes, experimental situations must be contrived so as to induce extremes of the variables being studied if one wishes to extrapolate from the laboratory to field conditions.

The advantages of the laboratory for disaster research rest precisely on its potential ability to produce the intensity and duration of variables hypothesized to be of importance in stressful situations but usually not encountered in ordinary behavior. However, because of the mores of a humanitarian, democratic society, it is impossible to fulfill in the laboratory for disaster research one condition whose cruciality is as yet unknown—that of involuntary physical and emotional insults. In the laboratory one cannot injure or kill the subjects themselves, or their relatives and friends. Nor could one destroy personal possessions and property without the voluntary agreement of the subject, which might negate the similarity of the experiment to reality.

What role does the absence of severe and intense involuntary deprivations play in limiting the validity of experimental work in the laboratory? By and large, laboratory stresses have been moderate, consisting of reactions to delayed aural feedback, electric shock, and social pressures (such as harassment and time-pressures). Even the Human Resources Research Office (HumRRO) in its Task-FIGHTER studies has been unable to develop situations as extreme as those encountered in the crises of mortal conflict (Berkun *et al.*, 1959).

There appear to be three ways in which the extrapolation of results from experiments in mildly stressful situations might fail to generalize to extreme situations: (1) It may be that the functional relation between two variables is of a more complex form than had been previously realized, so that at extreme values of either variable the function takes a special nonlinear form, one factor being much more or much less sensitively related to the other than in moderate situations. (2) The model provided by the experiment may be an oversimplification; in extreme situations important new conditioning variables appear. Or (3) a relationship may be found to be discontinuous at extreme ranges. This last state of affairs is argued by Fritz (1961, pp. 685-692), who sees step-function changes in innovative social adaptations to disaster, with the development of a "community of sufferers" in which "values and norms are emergent."

Of consequence, then, is whether nonlinearities, new conditioning variables, or generic changes of relationship are evoked by conditions of stressful extremity. Should there be no such discontinuities or radical alterations of the relation of variables to each other in extreme situations—and the present disaster literature gives little evidence of such—then the laboratory will be most useful. But how will one know until the extremities are explored?

2. SIDE-EFFECTS

Experimenters are becoming much more aware of their laboratory side-effects or "unwanted variances which may be introduced by the way in which experimenter-subject relations and tasks are structured within the culture of the experimental laboratory" (Riecken, 1958).

What happens when the participant responds with skepticism, because of suspicions that the contrivance is not reality but simply a hoax? Sherif argues that an important methodological consideration in the use of experimental technique is "that the subjects be kept unaware of the fact that they are participating in an experiment on group relations. . . . The presence of a personage ever observing, ever recording our words and deeds in a situation in which our status and concerns are at stake cannot help coming in as an important factor in the total frame of reference" (Sherif, 1954, p. 764).

Yet, what are the consequences of such deceit? And have we not now created around the American laboratory a culture in which we automatically generate suspicion by our very invitation to participate, after generations of students have been duped by researchers? This would seem especially true since our professional ethics demand eventual revelation of deliberate deceits perpetuated during the course of experiments to which the subjects have given at least their implicit consent. The induction of emergency behavior by the radio program "reporting" an "invasion from Mars" before World War II suggests that the variable of credulity is amenable to study (Cantril, 1940, pp. 128-139). It is not only a concept of importance to substantive theory about disaster; it is of critical importance in assessing reactions in laboratory situations.

The tendency of experimenters to avoid engaging career-related and life-embedded motivations in the experimental situation is another difficulty that plagues laboratory work. The contrived experiment is, from the subject's point of view, a transient experience whose consequences are usually insulated from the enduring patterns of his life. It was exactly this that induced Kennedy (1955) and his associates at the RAND Corporation to embed their simulation of the Air Defense Direction Center within a natural military organization. Because natural disasters often involve such important and long-run consequences—even of life and death—for their victims, it is crucial to test the transferability of our concepts by completely engaging motivations in the laboratory.

Recently members of the U.S. Army Leadership Human Research Unit of HumRRO ingeniously contrived five quasi-laboratory "emergency" situations in which the subject was fed information that "forces him to believe that some unforeseen accident, mixup, or mistake has occurred," creating a disaster-like situation in which "subjects are not aware that they are subjects being tested" (Berkun *et al.*, 1959, p. 39). Four of the experiments—a need to crash-land an aircraft, threat from a forest fire, artillery rounds no longer remaining in their designated impact area, unexpected radiation hazards due to wind changes—are thought by the subject to be potentially productive of bodily harm to himself. In the fifth, the experimental subject believes he has caused injury to another soldier in an explosion for which he may be held responsible. In addition (1) to being judged as stressful by the observers, the situations (2) are reported subsequently as of more stress by the subjects than they are by persons in control groups. The subjective responses are accompanied both by (3) "alterations in objectively measured behavior" and by (4) "transitory physiological responses." In the findings reported to date, however, there was no evidence that the subjective, behavioral, or physiological reactions of the subjects to these disasters were different in any fundamental way from those obtained by other researchers in laboratory experiments in which volunteer subjects are aware of both the contrived nature of the stress and of the measurements which are being taken—as for example in the work of Funkenstein, King, and Drolette (1957).

Might a potential solution to the possible limitations of the laboratory be found in the use of hypnosis as a means for the induction of disaster reactions? In his work on hypnotic arousal of conflict, Luria claims that he and his associates "succeeded in producing models of complexes, which almost entirely reconstruct all the symptoms characteristic for the natural affective traces in the personality" (Luria, 1932, p. 136). The immediate relevance of Luria's work for disaster research is in the fact that he was able to produce "external trauma" as effectively as he was able to induce "affective complex." In using hypnotic techniques, Luria exercised much care to avoid suggesting the nature of the symptoms which should result from the conflict-stress situation in which the subject is placed.

More recently, using quite similar techniques, Rosenberg (1960) has secured attitudinal change through hypnosis. Rosenberg also avoided suggesting the change directly, but merely induced an affective state which in turn forced cognitive reorganization of the attitudinal response. Presaging Rosenberg's work are Orne's results in distinguishing "fake" from "real" hypnotic phenomena: "The major difference appears to be a tolerance by the 'real' subject of logical inconsistencies" in the bona fide hypnotic state (Orne, 1959, p. 298).

Would the hypnotic induction of bereavement and traumatic shock be feasible as a way of creating an engagement of the total personality of the individual in the laboratory situation? Despite the impressive success of Luria, Orne, and Rosenberg, the interpretation of the results from such a disaster experiment would be controversial until there were more understanding of the nature of hypnotic phenomena in general.

Would it be useful to employ role-playing in experiments with disaster problems, especially those in which the experiments would need to transcend the bounds imposed by humanitarian considerations or by the inability of the experimenter to bring natural or man-made forces to bear in his experimental situation? Pepitone, Diggory, and Wallace (1955) explored hypothetical reactions to different levels of hypothetical threat of gas warfare. Although they found "a close parallel between such hypothetical responses and behavior observed in real-life disaster," their results may merely assess the extent to which their subjects were acquainted with widespread folklore about reactions to disaster. In his short-term experiment with hypnosis, Rosenberg employed a group of subjects who were to "role-play" a change in their affective response, as a control for the hypnotic induction. The attitudinal changes were stronger and more general in the role-playing than in the hypnotized subjects. As in the Pepitone, Diggory, and Wallace experiment, the changes during role-playing reflected the preconceptions of the subjects about how attitudes should change rather than exhibiting the smaller, more narrow cognitive reorganizations in attitudinal response which are typical of "natural" inconsistency reductions.

CONCLUSION

Given the present state of the disaster literature, it is critical to check whether understandings of a social science that is rooted largely in nonstress behavior may be extrapolated for the prediction of behavior in natural disasters. At first glance, the laboratory would seem an ideal situation in which to pursue extreme ranges of variation in a factor, given its leverage for the study of variables in isolation. In addition, it permits sufficient replication to allow application of statistical methodologies. But further analysis reveals that the disaster situations simulated in the laboratory and conducted within the bounds of professional ethics may fail to engage the life-and-death motivations of the subjects. Further, the laboratory situation is susceptive to unwanted interpretations as a hoax. Hypnosis and role-playing do not hold immediate promise for surmounting these basic limitations of laboratory work.

The Simulation of Disaster

Considerable effort has been devoted by those involved in civil defense to the use of exercises and "dry runs," simulating conditions of disaster to various degrees of consonance with natural events. Such studies are listed in *Field Studies of Disaster Behavior: An Inventory* (Disaster Research Group, 1961). A simulation involving both human beings and computers seems to fall halfway between the laboratory and the field experiment (Malcolm, 1958). By attempting to elicit full engagement of individuals in a rich, all-encompassing situation, a striking resemblance to nature may be produced.

There are as many and as formidable difficulties, however, in the use of simulations for research purposes as in the use of the laboratory (Guetzkow, 1962). The great costs involved would hardly be justified if these contrivances were to be used for research purposes at the present stage of our understanding of disaster phenomena. No doubt the usefulness of simulations for instruction and practice will continue to be attractive to operating agencies; but on the whole such uses do not make for the kind of experimental design that would much advance research. While the researcher will often have access to such exercises, they cannot be expected to serve his purposes primarily, and he should entertain only modest expectations of getting much of his work done by such means.

Quasi-Experimental Research in Field Situations

Granted that an integral characteristic of disaster—its elicitation of life-and-death-related behaviors under conditions of extreme stress—may limit the potential usefulness of the laboratory and of simulation as research sites, is the field situation susceptible to controlled experimentation? An impressive array of post-disaster studies has been completed in the field on some 103 events (Disaster Research Group, 1961). Could use be made of a controlled approach in the field for checking alternative theories of behavior in disaster, thereby avoiding the limitations of the laboratory but gaining some of its classical advantages?

It is not difficult to understand why this has not been done. Even research after disaster has occurred is expensive. The resources allotted to the study of alleviation and recovery measures after disaster have been meager, especially when contrasted with the resources devoted to research on ways of bringing disaster to an enemy by means of nuclear weaponry. And in addition to inadequate resources, rigorous researchers view field work as inadmissible because the standards of design applicable in the laboratory are impossible to achieve in the field (Killian, 1956b, pp. 5-13). But instead of relapsing into *post hoc* studies, would it not be better to press toward the utilization of quasi-experimental, partially controlled designs?

Campbell (1957, 1960) has written insightfully with respect to "quasi-experimental" designs, in which a partial, but still useful, compliance with rigorous scientific standards is possible. By making more explicit the sources of invalidity in analyses of data, Campbell has provided a means by which the strengths and weaknesses of quasi-experimental designs may be assessed.

The quasi-experiments to be prescribed below would need (1) field sites in which the occurrence of disasters might be predicted as having a much greater than average occurrence, and (2) a mobile research unit, to capitalize upon disaster warnings so that observations might be made of disaster in its various stages, including the critical junctures from warning to impact, and from impact to short-run aftermath. The unit would have at hand special techniques for rapid assessment under disaster conditions. It also might tailor its standing research plans to the practicalities of the immediate situation, as has been sketched by Killian (1956b, pp. 10-15). The magnificent work of Pace and his associates (1956) in carrying through physiological and psychological studies of randomly sampled infantrymen in combat in sites of intense local military action in Korea indicates that it is possible to work in intimate contact with intense stress situations should the courage of the scientists be adequate and the need for the observations be imperative.

Building upon Campbell's analysis and using his terminology, consider the following types of observations which might be conducted in the field, taking advantage of naturally occurring disasters.

1. SINGLE AND MULTIPLE TIME SERIES (CAMPBELL'S DESIGNS 7 AND 13)

Because the literature demonstrates that there is much variation in reactions to disaster (Marks and Fritz, 1954) it is imperative that pre-disaster studies be undertaken, so that the existence of conditioning variables may be used to explain why, for example, certain leadership patterns develop in one community and quite different ones in another after both have been hit by a similar disaster.

Would it be useful to obtain periodic observations at a randomly chosen site drawn from a population of communities having high disaster probability? By working with a small team of local individuals, the mobile disaster research unit might obtain base lines for testing its major hypotheses should disaster later occur. These "pre-measures" then could be used for understanding better the observations of the course of reaction made to the disaster by the observer-victims and by the mobile disaster research unit after it arrives.

Further, it would be important to augment the "single time series" quasi-experimental design by simultaneous studies, say of ten sites chosen randomly from the already established population of disaster-prone communities. Each of the nine unstricken communities then might serve as a control for various aspects of the disaster reactions of an unfortunate tenth community. Over a series of years, as another and then even a different site is struck by disaster, the untouched and recovered communities again could serve as controls.

The results of such longitudinal studies would become even more valuable were the research sites checked as to their representativeness of the total universe of national communities. Conclusions reached on the basis of the disaster-potential sample might be generalized to a wider population of communities less often hit by disaster. One way in which this question of the nonuniqueness of the disaster-prone sample might be resolved would be to examine whether its various social processes are in any way different from those in a larger, randomly selected set. An illustration of such research is to be found in Project Revere, in which Dodd and his associates (1958-1959) determined the characteristics of opinion-spreading in cities of various sizes. Using those data as normative, one might replicate their experiments on leaflet distribution in the disaster-liable communities, thereby estimating whether communication processes in the special sample differ from those in the universe of communities represented in Dodd's studies.

Using Campbell's method of schematization, in which *X* represents exposure to the "experimental" or nature-imposed event (in this case, disaster) and *O* represents the process of observation or measurement, it is possible to make graphic presentation of this "multiple time series" design, as is done in Table 11-1. The left-to-right dimension indicates temporal order, from time 1 to time 10. Parallel rows represent units (u_j, u_k, u_l) of some degree of equivalence—individuals, families, work groups, municipal governments, or whole communities. Reference to Campbell's "check-off" tables (1960, Tables 1 and 3) indicates that many of the sources of internal and external invalidity in experiments are removed through the use of such a time-series.

TABLE 11-1 *Schematization of Time Series, Using Campbell's Notation*

$Unit_j$	O_1	O_2	O_3	O_4	X_i	O_6	O_7	O_8	O_9	O_{10}
$Unit_k$	O_1	O_2	O_3	O_4	O_5	O_6	O_7	X_i	O_9	O_{10}
$Unit_l$	O_1	X_i	O_3	O_4	O_5	O_6	O_7	X_{ii}	O_9	O_{10}

2. SEPARATE-SAMPLE PRE-TEST–POST-TEST, WITH OR WITHOUT CONTROL GROUP (CAMPBELL'S DESIGNS 11 AND 12)

Even though one may be forced to forego the benefits accruing from the time-series designs treated above, one need not become entirely *post hoc* in the study of disaster, as has been the case in extant field work. One might at a minimum do "before" and "after" studies on "interchangeable" units, as is suggested by Selltiz and her colleagues (1959, p. 110). This design, with and without controls, is represented in Table 11-2. By describing a population of disaster-liable communities in terms of relevant social variables, it would be possible to make periodic observations on a sample of these which were interchangeable with one another. One of these communities could then become the "before" unit against which the usual "after" study in a disaster-struck community, interchangeable with it, could be checked. This technique would avoid six of the eleven sources of invalidity that Campbell has distinguished (1960, Table 2). The addition of controls, in which "before" and "after" measures are made on disaster-free communities interchangeable with one another and with the disaster-liable communities, eliminates another four of Campbell's sources of invalidity. The "before" research and the research on disaster-free communities might well be carried out by the mobile research team while it was on "stand-by" awaiting disaster. These separate pre-test–post-test techniques would be considerably less costly than a multi-time-series design.

TABLE 11-2 *Schematization of Separate-Sample Pre-test–Post-test Designs, Using Campbell's Notation*

Separate-Sample Pre-test–Post-test Groups	$Unit_j$	O_1		
	$Unit_k$		X_i	O_3
Control Groups	$Unit_l$	O_1		
	$Unit_m$			O_3

If one were interested in less than total communities, it would be easier to engage in pre-studies preparatory for the study of disaster in neighborhoods during hurricanes and tornadoes, reactions to explosions or fires in factories, or behavior during death and subsequent bereavement in homes. With the increasing accuracy in prediction of hurricanes, it should be possible to work with local authorities to make systematic observations of behaviors in matched neighborhoods for tests of predicted outcomes. By securing the cooperation of the community's fire department, one might study group flight reactions to limited disaster over a protracted period, in which different theories of response might be checked out. In this case the mobile research unit might trail after the fire-fighting apparatus, alongside the familiar underwriters' property protection vehicle. Or, similarly to the way in which Janis (1958b) used the opportunity for before-and-after study of stress in some thirty surgical cases, one might work with medical practitioners or social service agencies in the location and observation of families in which there is possibility of death—for example, because of the hazardous nature of the husband's occupation.

There has been awakening interest in the utilization of prediction techniques in field situations. In large-scale phenomena, Miller (1957) has developed a technique for predicting the outcome of substantive decisions in communities and has applied it to a community decision. Two years later, Hanson (1959) used the Miller-Form theory, with some further explication, to predict a state-wide decision. It would seem entirely feasible to develop comparable specific predictions with respect to disaster, which then might be tested in a separate-sample pre-test–post-test control group design in the field. By the utilization of such techniques, researchers might obtain grounds for improvement of our theories of disaster behavior.

CONCLUSION

Given the present state of the disaster literature and formidable barriers to confident use of the laboratory or of simulations as research sites, it is imperative that quasi-experimental designs be used in field situations for the study of disaster behaviors. It would be possible to enlarge the single-case post-test investigation now traditional within disaster research to include pre-tests, controls, and time-series, thereby obviating important sources of invalidity. The extension would demand definition of a universe of community units which would be interchangeable with disaster-struck units. In addition, it would be necessary to develop mobile research teams which might be dispatched for pre-tests to scenes of predicted disaster.

Articulated Research through Field and Laboratory Experimentation

Because of high costs and inconvenience in awaiting the occurrence of natural disasters, it would seem advantageous to organize field work so it may be linked directly to experimental endeavor in the laboratory. The activity of the Institute for Social Research at Michigan, with its experimentally toned Research Center for Group Dynamics and its field-oriented Survey Research Center, is an example of the successful integration of field and laboratory work, as Likert (1959) illustrates in a report on an aspect of their studies in the area of organization and management. The researches of Ancel Keys and his associates (1950) at the University of Minnesota in the area of semi-starvation included comparison laboratory work with clinical findings from the field. The studies were remarkable in having induced by physiological means—dietary deprivation of volunteers—phenomena which were once thought more a consequence of the adverse socio-psychological environment which usually accompanies the physical conditions of "natural" human starvation than of the physiological deprivation itself. In both of these instances, again, there seem to be no phenomena found in the field which could not be produced in the laboratory, and vice-versa.

Yet in these examples, the coordination of field and laboratory research has not been as rigorous and close-knit as would seem desirable. A miniature example of more precise articulation of the two techniques is found in the work of Funkenstein, King, and Drolette (1957), in which the laboratory production of stress behaviors through hazing during problem solving and through delayed aural feedback is coordinated in the same subjects with reactions to naturally occurring stress. By asking roommates to rate everyday emotional reactions of the same subjects who were put in experimental stress situations, a comparison of the extent to which the same fundamental reactions occurred in the laboratory and in the life situation was obtained (Funkenstein *et al.*, 1957, Table 4, p. 70). "The roommates interviewed were selected at random. Neither they nor their interviewers knew how the subjects reacted in the laboratory" (p. 71). Although data were obtained only for the acute emergency phase of stress responses, the agreement reported is remarkable. It would be feasible to extend such a technique to persons who had endured severe stress in disaster situations, so that they might later be tested in laboratory experiments. Conversely, it would be feasible to attempt to predict reactions in natural stress situations by studying reactions in the laboratory before the cooperating persons were subjected to analogous stress in the field.

If the conclusions of the Social Science Research Council's Inter-university Summer Research Seminar on Field and Laboratory Studies are correct, the principal gap between the two kinds of studies rests only in the difference in orientation to theory of the researchers who use field or laboratory techniques. "Field workers tend to talk a different dialect from that used in the laboratory, and field and laboratory results are less often contradictory than incommensurable" (Riecken,

1954, p. 38). The outstanding work of Torrance (1961) in utilizing field simulation and laboratory techniques simultaneously in the study of group leadership behavior under stress is the closest embodiment of commensurability this writer has encountered. Torrance observes, ". . . we have obtained essentially the same types of phenomena in the realistically simulated survival situations and in the laboratory as these described by survivors of actual emergencies and extreme conditions. Panic and group disorganization occurring in the laboratory and in simulated survival situations are as clearly identifiable as in actual situations. Likewise, subjects in these simulated situations discontinue adaptive behavior and resort to behavior analogous to the loss of will-to-survive found in actual emergency or extreme situations" (1957, p. 213).

An experiment allows the researcher who is attempting to interpret natural phenomena to be more confident of his results when he has been able to reproduce the same phenomena in a laboratory situation. For example, the narrowing of the range of behavior of survivors reported in the disaster literature becomes more adequately established when Ericksen and Wechsler (1955, p. 461) induce sharp reductions in variability in response alternatives in their laboratory through the use of electric shock. Sherif's experimental production of intergroup conflict in contrived groups again gives confidence to observations after disaster about reactions of in-groups to out-groups (Sherif and Sherif, 1953).

There are a variety of maneuvers which can be used to incorporate reality into the laboratory experiment through both persons and groups. The researcher inadvertently introduces personality characteristics into the laboratory, as subjects cannot help but bring their past experiences and styles of behavior to bear upon the responses they make in the experimental situation. In fact, one must guard against bias in the very methods one uses for recruitment of subjects, in that personality differences between volunteers and nonvolunteers have already been demonstrated (Riggs and Kaess, 1955). Snyder (1960) argues that it may be possible to use in laboratory situations crisis-prone individuals who tend to live in self-induced extreme situations. Were it possible to pre-select subjects who readily engage themselves wholeheartedly in any task—including laboratory tasks—the experimenter might then find his less-than-extreme stressors capable of producing drastic and marked effects because of the proclivity of the subjects to engage deeply. Although it has not yet been tried, the suggestion has been made of linking long-term life success motivation patterns into experimental work on risk and stakes in decision-making by rewarding or punishing the subjects through life annuity income policies.

As the group laboratory is used conventionally, it is a short-term experiment in which participants who are strangers to each other assume a posture as subordinates to the higher-status experimenter. Yet, one can utilize subjects who have spent many years in establishing their structures of interaction, as when Strodtbeck (1951) employed husband and wife pairs in his study of decision-making in Navaho, Mormon, and Texan cultures. In a study of intergroup conflict, Sherif (Sherif and Sherif, 1953) conducted his experiments over so long a time-span that the participants became thoroughly acquainted with each other, developing strong in-group feelings. It would be possible to link the experiment to very fundamental life patterns by importing individuals and groups with previous histories appropriate for the special purposes of the research. Thus, for example, if one is interested in the processes of leadership succession from noncrisis to crisis, it would seem possible to use community groups with long histories of stable leadership patterns in crisis situations in the laboratory.

Closely articulated research in field and laboratory, then, possesses important advantages over proceeding either through field or laboratory work alone. The laboratory needs confirmation of the extrapolability of its results by coordinate studies in the field in which the range and depth of engagement of the variables are tested. The field needs release from its complexity and from its inability to go beyond "nature" by coordinate, more rigorous studies in the laboratory in which "nonnatural" situations may be explored.

The urgent need is to induce the whole body of laboratory and field researchers, oriented largely to noncrisis behavior, to include disaster substudies as part of their on-going research designs. Consequently, disaster researchers should work in tandem with those engaged in noncrisis research rather than in isolation.

Adjunct experiments would seem an economical way to increase our understanding of the extent to which noncrisis behavior extends into crisis situations. Once there is a body of relatively tight theory in that area, it should be possible to decide which on-going experiments and field studies in noncrisis conditions might be tapped to check the extrapolability of their results to disaster conditions. Experimenters might be induced through auxiliary research contracts to add "crisis" explorations. For example, French's (1944) work on frustration in unorganized and organized groups contained a most useful addendum on the reactions of these two groups to disaster, in the form of a simulated fire in the laboratory building. Would it not be possible to encourage experimenters who are working in areas of their own special interest and competence to add another variation—this time "disaster"—to their experimental runs? Many researchers would welcome another opportunity to assess the fundamental quality of their formulations by submitting their hypotheses about behavior mechanisms to tests in stress situations. Certainly, their nonstress data would be enriched by comparisons with stress data. The collateral effects of the induction of rapid change and intense anxiety would be an important addition to many field projects.

Strategic collaboration with field researchers implies monitoring of on-going projects. Just as the Department of Defense maintains pilot operations for the manufacture of war materials on a miniature scale even in time of peace, so a headquarters responsible for disaster research might maintain a "disaster research readiness" within on-going research projects located in disaster-liable sites. Projects might be prepared to assist the disaster mobile research unit personnel in the event of disaster. On the other side, the mobile researchers would need to develop means whereby their observations during and after disaster could be coordinated with the pre-disaster measurements obtained by the noncrisis project researchers.

There are a multitude of factors which determine the location of field projects, many of which are related to the convenience of the researchers rather than to intrinsic requirements of research design. It might be possible to encourage location of particularly critical field projects in disaster-liable sites, so that the chances of securing disaster data are maximized.

An adequate understanding of disaster behavior certainly will necessitate further studies of stress itself, as, for example, in the work of Holtzman and Bitterman (1956), whose abortive attempt to obtain common factors for use in the prediction of adjustment to stress indicates how difficult are the research problems that lie ahead. But precisely because the knowledge sought is so broad in scope and so full of complications, the task is hopeless unless the strategy is changed to emphasize a more adequate articulation of disaster research with the great bulk of on-going laboratory and field research in noncrisis situations.

Special Bibliography of Laboratory Studies of Disaster-Related Behavior

Chapman, R. L., Kennedy, J. L., Newell, A., & Biel, W. C. The Systems Research Laboratory's air defense experiments. *Mgmt. Sci.*, 1959, *5*, 250-269.

Cline, V. B. The assessment of good and poor judges of personality using a stress interview and sound film technique. Unpublished doctoral dissertation, University of California, Berkeley, 1953.

Cowen, E. L. The influence of varying degrees of psychological stress on problem-solving rigidity. *J. abnorm. soc. Psychol.*, 1952, *47*, 512-519.

ERIKSEN, C. W., & WECHSLER, H. Some effects of experimentally induced anxiety upon discrimination behavior. *J. abnorm. soc. Psychol.*, 1955, *51*, 458-463.

FRENCH, J. R. P. Organized and unorganized groups under fear and frustration. *Univ. Iowa Stud. child Welf.*, 1944, *20*, 229-308.

HAMBLIN, R. L. Leadership and crises. *Sociometry*, 1958, *21*, 322-335.

HUDSON, B. B. Anxiety in response to the unfamiliar. *J. soc. Issues*, 1954, *10* (3), 53-60.

LANZETTA, J. T. An investigation of group behavior under stress. Annual status report, University of Rochester, 1953.

———, HAEFNER, D., LANGHAM, P., & AXELROD, H. Some effects of situational threat on group behavior. *J. Abnorm. soc. Psychol.*, 1954, *49*, 445-453.

MEIER, N. C., MENNENGA, G. H., & STOLTZ, H. F. An experimental approach to the study of mob behavior. *J. abnorm. soc. Psychol.*, 1941, *36*, 506-524.

MILLER, K. S., & WORCHEL, P. The effects of need-achievement and self-ideal discrepancy on performance under stress. *J. Pers.*, 1956, *25*, 176-190.

MINTZ, A. Non-adaptive group behavior. *J. abnorm. soc. Psychol.*, 1951, *46*, 150-159.

OSLER, W. F. Intellectual performance as a function of two types of psychological stress. *J. exp. Psychol.*, 1954, *47*, 115-121.

OSTLAND, L. H. Group functioning under negative conditions. *J. educ. Psychol.*, 1956, *47*, 32-39.

PALERMO, D. S. Proactive interference and facilitation as a function of amount of training and stress. *J. exp. Psychol.*, 1957, *53*, 293-296.

PEPITONE, A., DIGGORY, J. C., & WALLACE, W. H. Some reactions to a hypothetical disaster. *J. abnorm. soc. Psychol.*, 1955, *5*, 706-708.

POSTMAN, L., & BRUNNER, J. S. Perception under stress. *Psychol. Rev.*, 1948, *55*, 314-323.

PRONKO, W. H., & LEITH, W. R. Behavior under stress: a study of its disintegration. *Psychol. Rep. monogr. Suppl.*, 1956, *5*.

SMITH, E. E. Choice of own versus group attainment under threat and reduced threat and in overt and covert situations. *Amer. Psychol.*, 1957, *12*, 366 (abstract).

SWANSON, G. E. A preliminary laboratory study of the acting crowd. *Amer. sociol. Rev.*, 1953, *18*, 522-533.

VOGEL, W., BAKER, R. W., & LAZARUS, R. S. The role of motivation in psychological stress. *J. abnorm. soc. Psychol.*, 1958, *56*, 105-112.

ZILLER, R. C. Four techniques of group decision under uncertainty. *J. appl. Psychol.*, 1957, *41*, 384-388.

► *twelve*

DISASTERS AND SOCIAL CHANGE

Gideon Sjoberg

OUR PRIME CONTENTION is that disasters are a key variable in altering the social structures of industrial-urban societies. But to support this hypothesis we must examine the social impact of disasters in comparative perspective—in pre-industrial *versus* industrial societies.

An understanding of how and why social systems and their component structures undergo change is a vital, albeit neglected, facet of contemporary social science. Not the least of this neglect has been the failure to explore—both in the modern world and through the purview of history—the interrelationships of disasters and social change. A disaster is, almost by definition, a trigger for alteration of the social landscape. And because disasters are often succeeded by spectacular social transformations, they are of considerable methodological moment. For here certain social processes unnoticed in more normal circumstances appear in exaggerated or highly accelerated form.

As a prelude to our investigation, we must comment upon some theoretical issues implied in our use of the concepts "disaster" and "social change." In the second portion of this essay, which considers disasters in comparative perspective, we contend that disparate systems respond to disasters quite differently. The third and fourth sections, bearing directly upon our main hypothesis, consider the impact of disasters—both their short-run and long-run consequences—in modern industrial orders. Then, drawing upon some of our observations, we

Although I alone am responsible for the final product, I want to thank George Baker, John Gillin, Roger Nett, Jeannette Rayner, and John Rohrer for their critical comments on a prospectus of this essay, and to gratefully acknowledge the research assistance of Patricia Straiton.

speculate on the possible fate of an industrial-urban society in the event of atomic war, and conclude with a discussion of needed research in the realm of disaster and social change.

I. Theoretical Orientation

Recent writings on disasters commonly stress the need for more satisfactory theories on both the macroscopic and the microscopic levels; we have elected to stress the macroscopic approach, because social scientists have more frequently confined their research on disasters to the local community level.

DISASTER AS A CONCEPT

The term *disaster* is utilized in diverse fashions, reflecting in part the differing requirements of research, in part the confused thinking on this subject. We define *disaster* as a severe, relatively sudden, and frequently unexpected disruption of normal structural arrangements within a social system, or subsystem, resulting from a force, "natural" or "social," "internal" to a system or "external" to it, over which the system has no firm "control."[1] For us the term *catastrophe* is synonymous with *disaster*.

Our definition recognizes that disasters arise from either natural or social forces: by extension, then, we refer to natural or social disasters. Not a few writers have tended to limit the concept *disaster* to violent social disruptions caused by natural forces or by bombing attacks.[2] But once we admit of war or its derivatives as disaster-inducing mechanisms, we are logically driven to label as disasters certain other man-made upheavals as well. But our definition of disaster does not ignore the distinction between natural and social disasters. In point of fact, some of the long-run consequences of depressions, military defeat, or the purposive destruction of one social group by another differ considerably—particularly in certain types of social systems—from the consequences of floods, hurricanes, tornadoes, and other natural disasters.

Further, although natural catastrophes are by definition extra-societal in origin, socially derived disasters may arise from within or without the social system: contrast a revolution with an attack by hostile outsiders. And at times it is theoretically useful to distinguish between socially produced disasters that are not purposively initiated

[1] The term *disaster*, for us, refers to situations in which groups are affected, *accident* to situations in which individuals alone suffer loss.

[2] Authors who use the term in this more restricted sense include Form and Loomis (1956, p. 180) and Tiryakian (1959, p. 292).

—for example, certain economic depressions—and those that are "planned," notably the extermination of countless Jews by the Nazis.

What we have been saying is that the nature of the disaster-producing force can be a significant variable for understanding the disaster itself. In addition the question arises: "Disaster for whom?" [3] For one man's misfortune is often another's gain; what is catastrophic for one system, or elements thereof, may be viewed as nondeleterious, even as advantageous, for another. The catastrophes suffered by the Jews were not such, at least at the time, for the Nazis who engineered them. So in war, one side profits from the other's losses, although the victor's spoils may be reduced, or his gain offset somewhat, by his own expenditure of resources. Then too, what is a disaster for a small group may not be such for the broader society, and vice versa. If we take as our reference group the numerous families in the United States every year who suffer the loss of one of their members in automobile collisions and the like, we perceive an endless succession of small-scale disasters for the families involved. Despite the widely advertised efforts to reduce the traffic toll, the high rate of fatalities has nonetheless come to be accepted as a matter of course by sizable segments of the society and only the more bizarre situations receive publicity outside the local community context. When law-enforcement agencies do take firm steps to reduce these highway disasters, some citizens are sure to protest this encroachment on their "freedom." One writer has gone so far as to contend in a nation-wide publication that these traffic disasters are simply one of the prices our society must pay for the social gains it reaps from the "automobile culture" (J. D. Williams, 1958).

Time is another variable complicating our analysis of disasters. A given set of events may at the specific moment of its occurrence be viewed by many elements of the populace as a veritable catastrophe, only to be adjudged in later years as a positive contribution to the society's advance (Hoffer, 1951). Thus an abortive revolution is a tragedy for the defeated, but it may be reinterpreted by later generations as advantageous to the social order, as having exercised a "revitalizing" effect upon the social system. Depressions, once seen by many persons as beneficial to the social order (e.g., by ridding the business world of inefficient workers or entire enterprises), are today more generally viewed as disastrous (see Burns, 1960, p. 12).

ELABORATION OF FRAME OF REFERENCE

But social change involves more than mere passage of time. It implies alteration of the social structure and/or its components. We are

[3] For a discussion of the implications of reference group behavior for sociological research, see Merton (1957, Chapter 8).

concerned, then, first and foremost with the structural dimension and only secondarily with the social-psychological one, although the latter cannot be disregarded. And if we are to "measure" or understand the extent of the transformation of a system, or various elements thereof, we must determine the "starting point" in the alteration process. We must ask ourselves: "Change from what to what?" Nor do we underestimate the difficulties of clearly distinguishing "statics" from "change" (see Machlup, 1959). Although we cannot delve into the issues surrounding these concepts, we seek to avoid some of the more obvious pitfalls involved in their usage.

As to our more fundamental theoretical orientation, we utilize a modified form of structural-functional analysis. We attempt to reformulate the traditional structural-functional schema by recognizing the presence not only of "dysfunctions" but of "contradictory social structures" as well. From the latter we impute certain contradictory functional requirements (Sjoberg, 1960a). No social system is ever perfectly integrated; strains and stresses inhere in all, for some contradictory arrangements appear to be essential for the maintenance of almost any social system. Even so, a system does seek to sustain some kind of working equilibrium among its component parts and/or with respect to its external environment, which includes other systems. And actors in the system generally share some notion of what is normality for it. Yet considerable empirical evidence supports the proposition that both scientists and actors in a system find it exceedingly difficult, often impossible, to discern precisely when and if the system is in equilibrium. Only in extreme situations, when a disaster leads to dramatic deviations from the traditional patterns, will the consensus among actors be that the system is clearly out of kilter. This may in part explain Leach's argument that the notion of equilibrium is best treated as an "as if" concept (Leach, 1954, pp. 284-285).

Implicit in most structural-functional analysis is a theory of action: ultimately it is the actors who sustain the system's normative structure. Regarding action theory, we pay special heed to the manner in which actors orient themselves, through both positive and negative values, to the system's norms, means, and ends. Negative values, especially, come to the fore as mechanisms for re-establishment of equilibrium in the wake of the system's breakdown or disintegration.

II. Disasters in Comparative Perspective

We could, when viewing disasters cross-culturally, assume one of several worthwhile theoretical stances. We might examine the manner in which selected "disaster-producing" occurrences are handled by social systems displaying divergent value-orientations or distinctive social or power structures. The available evidence indicates that value-orientations do shape the manner in which, and the extent to which, a disaster induces social change. So too, the power structure—either across cultures or within them—is a variable that influences the way disasters effect revisions in the social structure of communities or societies. Although we de-emphasize these variables in our analysis, we do not disregard them. But our prime focus, as we contrast the differing impact of disasters upon pre-industrial civilized (or feudal) orders and upon industrial-urban ones, is the technological variable.

Such a comparison concentrates upon civilized orders rather than upon pre-literate or folk societies. However, many of our generalizations concerning disasters in pre-industrial civilized societies seem to hold for pre-literate ones as well, although various significant differences, into which we cannot delve here, are nonetheless present.

The pre-industrial civilized society, like the pre-literate one, functions upon a technological base that utilizes almost exclusively animate—i.e., human and animal—sources of energy and that has, relative to the industrial-urban order, scanty technological know-how. (The knowledge of how to use tools is an essential ingredient of our definition of technology.[4]) But the civilized pre-industrial system, in contrast to the pre-literate pre-industrial type, has advanced technologically to the point that it can support urban centers wherein resides the literate elite that commands the key positions in the complex political, religious, and educational bureaucracies and that thus dominates the society. Still, the vast bulk of the population is made up of a relatively powerless and disadvantaged peasantry and a somewhat smaller body of lower class and outcaste urbanites.

The major features of this societal type—exemplified in traditional China, Tibet, India, and numerous other social orders—have been delineated elsewhere by the author (Sjoberg, 1960b). For present purposes we need only observe that the society's elite generally disparages practical pursuits—those involving manual work, experimental "scientific" knowledge, and commercial activity—in favor of nonmanual pursuits: politics and administration, perpetuation of the traditional learning, and matters spiritual. The upper class scorn for work with the hands and utilitarian knowledge is associated with the marginal, or near-marginal, subsistence that is the lot of most persons in the social order.

[4] *Technology* refers to the sources of energy, the tools, and the know-how connected with the use of both tools and sources of energy for the production of goods and services. Industrialism is that type of technology that utilizes inanimate sources of energy for driving its tools.

So, too, the poorly developed technological base is functionally related to, and is a reflection of, the pre-industrial society's purview of the natural and/or divine order—the belief that it is essentially immune from control or revision by man. Practical and "scientific" knowledge, we noted, is considered of little worth, and the search for it is often viewed as a presumptive attempt to tamper with the natural or the divine. But although the elite justifies its existence through this *Weltanschauung*, contradictory requirements do operate: some practical activity, in the realms of commerce and manufacture, must be tolerated, indeed encouraged, if the system is to survive.

It is our thesis that pre-industrial civilized societies everywhere evince some significant structural similarities, even though the value-orientations of certain cultures induce variations from our constructed type. More specifically, these social orders exhibit marked similarities in the manner in which they respond to disasters.

That disasters have been commonplace in pre-industrial civilized (or feudal) societies like medieval Europe or traditional China or India is hardly open to question. Famines, floods, epidemics, earthquakes, and wars have all exacted a heavy toll of human life and wreaked incalculable property losses. For example, Ho (1959, Chapter 10) has amassed materials on traditional China that would indicate the loss of life by the millions in the periodic rampages of the elements or of man himself. Pre-industrial man, be he urbanite or rural villager, has ever dwelt in the menacing shadow of nature, which might at any moment unleash its forces for destruction. And he has stood by almost as helplessly as his leaders have embroiled him in war and its often disastrous consequences.

As to change in these pre-industrial civilized orders, we submit that most disasters—catastrophic though they be for countless persons and family groups—seem, over the long haul, to have had relatively minor effects upon the society's dominant structural arrangements, especially when these are contrasted with the industrial society's patterns. In a sense the pre-industrial society's structure is an accommodation to, or a product of, a more or less continual "reign of terror."

Of course, if we compare one historic phase of a given pre-industrial civilized society with another, or contrast the specific content (rather than the form) of these societies over time, we do perceive significant modifications. One involves the extinction or near-extinction of subsystems or total systems. The eruption of Mount Vesuvius forever changed the destiny of Pompeii by snuffing out its life in a shower of lava and debris. Military defeat has laid waste the cities in many thriving social systems. Also, it has been seriously argued that the power structure of a number of ancient societies, including Athens and Rome, was undermined by the scourge of epidemics, which set the stage for conquest by alien peoples.[5] And the eventual demise of the traditional order in Europe may have been hastened by the plagues, which, by decimating a large portion of the labor force, opened up to the disadvantaged groups possibilities for social mobility.

Some of the most visible and far-reaching consequences of disaster have been the upheavals in the demographic structure that in one way or another affect the societal organization. Many of the great migrations of history have had their origins in disaster. We need only cite the great famines in Ireland (at the time still largely pre-industrial) that impelled thousands of persons to cross the Atlantic in search of a new life, exerting a social impact upon both the homeland and the American society to which they came (see, for example, Edwards and Williams, 1956).

Other demographic shifts within a society—say, the abandonment of a city by its inhabitants—are attributable to disasters ranging all the way from droughts and floods and epidemics to social catastrophes such as military defeat. The manner in which disasters leave their mark upon a society's rural-urban composition, affecting especially the rise and fall of cities, has been documented in some detail (given the limited nature of the sources) for both medieval Europe (Mols, 1955) and traditional Japan (Taeuber, 1958).

Disasters, we earlier intimated, may also reshuffle the status position of persons or groups within pre-industrial civilized societies. Disasters are unlikely to heap their destruction in a manner proportionate to the existing status system; some persons will profit or lose more than others. The result: some upward and some downward social mobility. In spite of this, the over-all social structure—compared to the industrial-urban form—remains largely unchanged over time.

But what are the specific adjustments to disasters in pre-industrial civilized orders? In these societies most disasters, whether of natural or of social derivation, are typically attributed to the actions of a deity (or deities) or the caprices of malevolent spirits. Undeniably, some naturalistic interpretations of disasters are intermixed with the spiritual; yet, famine, epidemics, earthquakes, even military defeat, are interpreted primarily as punishments from God or the whims of hostile genii. For many persons the ravages of the Black Death in Europe were clear evidence of God's displeasure with sinful mankind, and/or visitations from the Devil and his aides. Still more recently in Europe, this reasoning was employed by the victims of the great Lisbon earthquake. Such thinking persists in numerous societies that are only now under-

[5] For a popularized account of this view, see Zinsser (1945).

going transition from the pre-industrial to the industrial form (see, for example, Sinha, 1952).[6]

Significantly, this orientation to disaster—wherein "supernatural" interpretations overshadow the "natural" ones—holds for nearly all pre-industrial-urban societies (and pre-literate ones). And from this conception of disaster certain patterns of behavior seem to emerge.

1. A typical adaptation is resignation to one's fate. When catastrophe is thought to be engendered primarily by spiritual forces, man can himself do little to alter the course of events apart from recourse to religious and/or magical practices. Recall that he assumes the immutability of the natural-divine order, which includes also the social arrangements about him. Add to this the meagerness of technological know-how of the sort that would be useful in disaster rehabilitation and we see that mute acceptance of one's lot is the logical result.

2. As intimated above, the strongly religious orientation of the pre-industrial civilized society shapes people's reactions to disaster; the populace comes to pay special heed to religious matters. Kendrick's remarks concerning the response of victims of the Lisbon earthquake of 1755 are pertinent in this regard.

> If this were a deliberate chastisement by God of a sinful people, as was generally asserted by the clergy, the mechanical task of recovery was of little importance compared with a first and pressing duty of making peace with God and imploring Him not to punish further His now penitent people. It is understandable that in a deeply religious land this should quickly become a dominant thought, and to sustain it there came from all sides abundant evidence of miraculous happenings that attested the supernatural character of the earthquake; moreover, it was not long before elaborate public acts of contrition gave open expression to this feeling and acknowledged the wickedness of a population thus humbled beneath the scourge of a still wrathful God (1957, pp. 113-114).

Here, as in other pre-industrial civilized societies, accommodation to disaster through supplication and atonement to appease an angry deity is in part a reflection of people's greater concern with the "hereafter" than with the "here and now."

3. Recourse to magic is another common response to disaster. Admittedly the empirical distinction, or the theoretical one for that matter, between magic and religion is fuzzy. Like certain other sociologists, we define religion as concern with "ultimate" values and goals; magic on the other hand involves the use of "spiritual" means to achieve immediate "empirical" ends.

[6] Of course, these patterns of thought have by no means disappeared from industrial-urban societies, but they are no longer dominant.

Manipulative magic—as contrasted with the preventive and predictive types discussed below—is widely employed in pre-industrial societies as a means of alleviating the consequences of disaster. Such manipulative efforts as calling upon the good spirits to battle the malevolent ones that cause disasters, thus restoring normalcy, have been widely employed in these societies. We have detailed accounts of how the Chinese resorted to magic in the face of epidemics, of how in traditional Tibet the chief shaman, a state official, performed complex magical rites to halt the droughts that were impoverishing the land (Hsu, 1952; Harrer, 1953, p. 172), and so on in numerous other pre-industrial societies.

4. A special response to disaster, involving magico-religious features, is found in the various forms of "collective behavior." Activities of this type occurred on a grand scale in traditional Europe, as an aftermath of the great plagues. Among these were the self-flagellation movements. People would roam from community to community engaging in this self-torture as atonement to God for man's wickedness, in the hope that the catastrophes they could not control would come to an end (Backman, 1952; Cohn, 1957, Chapter 6).

The so-called dancing manias in medieval Europe also followed on the heels of some of the most devastating epidemics. Sociologists have by and large failed to explain, or have erroneously interpreted, this kind of collective behavior to which they so often make allusion. Some writers have gone so far as to class it with the dancing following, for instance, a victory in war—as on V-J day in America at the culmination of World War II. But such an analogy taxes one's credulity. The dancing manias in Europe were a compulsive, almost "involuntary," reaction to the profound despair of many persons who had seen disaster strike again and again, quite a different proposition than some jubilant celebration.

Our own interpretation of the dancing manias—one that finds support in recent writings on the subject (Backman, 1952)[7]—is that they were primarily "magical rites" through which the plague-ridden populace was seeking to exorcise the evil spirits responsible for the fearful disturbances in the natural order. The populace was not attempting to remake an otherwise chaotic world through its own direct intervention but rather was seeking to influence the supernatural itself to re-establish equilibrium. The dramatic and compulsive collective behavior that characterized the dancing manias was largely an expression of people's intense frustration and feeling of helplessness before the many disasters that had struck medieval Europe in close succession.

[7] Although sociologists may quarrel with some of Backman's interpretations, this is a valuable study.

5. Still another response to disaster is "scapegoating" as a means of restoring order. In this instance, specific groups or persons are singled out as perpetrators of the disaster (usually because of their alleged use of magic). So in medieval Europe various large-scale pogroms against the Jews were initiated in the hope that these would rid the social order of the plagues that ravaged the land. And the burning of thousands of "witches" at the stake was, indirectly at least, a result of the disasters that beset fifteenth to seventeenth century European society (Robbins, 1959; Nohl, 1960). Similar phenomena occur in other pre-industrial civilized orders.

6. A final response to disasters in these societies is an essentially practical one. Up to now we have focused upon certain nonempirical mechanisms, religious and magical, that the pre-industrialite utilizes in an effort to adjust to, or dispel, disaster. But although magico-religious practices loom paramount in these societies, actors must, to survive, employ some empirical, "scientific," or practical devices. Theoretically, the pre-industrial society displays an ideology and a technological know-how which presume that man himself cannot and must not remake the natural and/or divine order. Yet some empirical means must be employed to restore balance in the post-disaster period, even if the underlying ideology and status systems are threatened thereby. In other words, contradictory functional requirements come into play.

By way of illustration, we could point to efforts to rebuild damaged areas after a flood or earthquake. Or we could cite the exodus from the cities during the great plagues in Europe. By the time of the London plague of 1655, the citizenry had taken purposive steps to segregate the victims and often also their families (Defoe, 1884).

Moreover, pre-industrial man relies heavily upon his kin group in troublous times. The low level of technology, and the consequent difficulties of capital formation, permit few large-scale agencies to care for the needy during a disaster or to rehabilitate the social order in the wake of devastation. Under these circumstances, dependency upon one's kinship system—which, incidentally, is far more widely ramified in the upper than in the lower class—is essential for survival when disaster strikes.

But apart from these more immediate accommodations to disaster, what are the longer-range effects—the measures taken to avert, or facilitate adjustment to, future crises? To this end, both empirical and nonempirical measures are employed. Here again, religious and magical practices loom large in the pre-industrial civilized order. Protective magic is widespread. In many societies, actors regularly perform rites that are geared to warding off the demoniacal spirits that bring disaster. Predictive magic is commonplace as well. Ordinary people, even the society's rulers, regularly consult astrologers and the like to avoid actions that might lead to catastrophe. In Japan and China, for instance, homes, businesses, even cities, were located according to the advice of geomancers, who would single out those sites where a particular structure or city could be built without disturbing the spirits.

Then too, there are some practical, empirical methods to prevent or to reduce the impact of catastrophes. Dikes and dams, at least of a simple sort, have been developed in pre-industrial civilized societies to control rivers and streams and thus diminish the possibility of devastating floods. And pre-industrialites have commonly constructed walls about their urban communities. Without these minimal social and technological controls over disaster-producing forces, these societies could not have sustained cities and the elite therein but would have reverted to the pre-civilized level. Significant structural changes did occur over time, laying the basis, in fact, for the Industrial Revolution.

On many counts industrial-urban systems stand in sharp contrast to pre-industrial civilized orders. The typical industrial-urbanite assumes by and large that man can remake and control the natural and social orders—which he separates sharply from the divine—not just in the immediate post-disaster situation but through preventive means over the long haul as well. Passive acceptance of calamity is not the credo of industrial man. Yet, despite the progress that has been made, many problems are still to be resolved and others continually emerge. An understanding of the tie between disasters and the industrial order is therefore both theoretically and pragmatically significant.

III. Short-run Consequences of Disasters in Industrial Societies

Social scientists during the past two decades have focused their sights on the shorter-run consequences of disasters, from the research during World War II, through the post-war studies in Germany and Japan, up to and embracing the wide gamut of empirical investigations of disasters in the United States (and elsewhere), supported primarily by the National Academy of Science's Disaster Research Group. Many of our propositions relative to the short-run impact of disasters are based upon these investigations.

Yet this research has been narrowly focused upon special kinds of disaster—those resulting from natural forces such as tornadoes, floods, etc., or those produced by the bombings in World War II. Sound propositions concerning disaster demand that we also examine such other destructive forces as economic depressions, military defeat, and revolutions.

Nor must we forget that much disaster research in the past two decades has been community oriented; researchers have been concerned primarily with the ways communities (not whole societies) cope with, or adjust to, natural disasters. This is an eminently worthwhile approach and an understandable one, given the fact that the community-wide disaster has been the most common type during the past decade and a half in the United States. Nonetheless, such community-level analyses have only limited generality. The total society, largely unscathed by these catastrophes, has been a bounteous source of assistance to the community in its hour of crisis and in the aftermath of disaster. We hypothesize that when a subsystem can draw extensively upon a broader society for succour in the disaster situation, the results are likely to diverge perceptibly from instances where the community has to bear the full brunt of destruction and rehabilitate itself without external aid. Thus, the knowledge gleaned from these various community studies must be used cautiously; they tell us little about the problems a nation would face in, say, an atomic war, when it would probably have to undertake its own rehabilitation. Iklé suggests that the effects of the plagues of medieval Europe, striking as they did total social orders, are a more realistic analogy to the problems that would face modern communities and nations in the event of an atomic holocaust (1954, p. 185). That large-scale disasters in the modern world are in many respects of a different order than those suffered by one or a few communities is empirically indisputable.

With these qualifications in mind, we can now set forth a number of propositions with respect to thc short-run impact of disasters on industrial systems or their subsystems. Although we could trace out the modifications in specific institutions—governmental, religious, educational, and so on—we have elected to sustain our more macroscopic orientation. We begin with the following proposition set forth by Form and Loomis:

> Almost immediately after the impact of the destructive agent, a disaster system arises spontaneously to meet the human problems created and to restore a social equilibrium. Far from having a condition of social *anomie*, social systems continue to operate through *all* of the disaster stages, new systems emerge, and continuity is found between the old and the emergent social systems (1956, p. 181).

This suggests one of the major theoretical and practical findings of the recent social science research—i.e., negation of the "panic myth" (Janis, Chapman, Gillin, and Spiegel, 1955). Contrary to the time-honored views of scholars and laymen, men generally do not behave in wild, disordered fashion when disasters strike. Janis, after surveying the reactions of persons in Nagasaki and Hiroshima, observed that ". . . the meager, fragmentary evidence available on overt behavior does not provide substantial support for claims that overt panic, disorganized activity, or anti-social behavior occurred on a mass scale during the two A-bomb disasters" (1951, p. 43). And Galbraith has dispelled the notion that mass panic behavior in the form of suicide succeeded the stock market crash of 1929 (1955, pp. 133-135).

But we should not confuse panic behavior with withdrawal. The latter does occur during (or prior to) the disaster's impact, at times on a massive scale. Still we must seek to explain the seemingly inconsistent evidence. In certain instances people cling to traditional patterns, by, for example, refusing to abandon their homes and familiar surroundings. In other situations there may be a general exodus from the disaster scene. After the Nazi invasion of France, thousands fled before the German armies, clogging the highways and accentuating the general confusion and disorganization (Freeman and Cooper, 1940). Perhaps past experience with enemy invaders had provided the French people with a strong foreboding of what was to come, whereas in the case of certain recent natural disasters in the United States, many people did not perceive the extent of the potential danger and steadfastly refused to abandon their homes. It seems, then, that people must be convinced that the disaster threat looms larger than the lesser upheaval of withdrawal if they are to take leave of their old surroundings.

Reverting to our main thesis, the data indicate that very soon after the initial shock of the disaster, some form of social organization emerges as people recognize the need for cooperative effort. And in their efforts to cope with new situations actors necessarily draw upon their past experiences. In most cases the emerging social organization, whether formal or informal in nature, is constructed upon a base somewhat familiar to all. As Form, Loomis, and others suggest, there is some continuity between the social forms of the pre- and the post-disaster periods.

Disasters of the especially virulent kind, however, may force a sharper break with the past than do more moderate ones. The emergent social structures of tornado- or flood-ravaged communities are more apt to be closely linked with the traditional forms than are the social structures that develop after such a thorough-going and intensive catastrophe as the Nazi extermination of the Jews. Nonetheless, the patterns of accommodation even in the concentration camps were linked to the past knowledge, values, and social structure of the Jewish subsystem.

Another facet of the aforementioned proposition of Form and Loomis (1956) is that quite soon after the disaster, actors strive to reinstate the disrupted patterns—to recover the state of normalcy or equilibrium. Earlier we indicated that the notion of equilibrium is a fuzzy one, from the standpoint of both sociologists and actors in the system. Nevertheless in the post-disaster situation actors do agree that the system is out of kilter and that something must be done to readjust it. This point has been stressed by students of the Holland flood (Instituut voor Sociaal Onderzoek, 1955, especially Vol. 4), by Form and Loomis (1956) in their researches, by H. E. Moore (1958b) in his Waco-San Angelo studies, and so on. Thus the writings on the Holland flood speak of the participants having a "wished-for former state." Such a pattern holds not only for natural disasters but for social ones as well. In the wake of the Great Depression, actors longed for a return to the normalcy of the 1920's. Here the government at first assumed that the system would right itself without outside intervention, a supposition that proved to be incorrect. In modern industrial-urban societies it is in fact increasingly presumed that the citizenry can and must intervene to re-establish equilibrium. Indeed this lies at the very heart of much recent disaster research. Social scientists are seeking to discover more effective means of restoring the system to normalcy, and much attention is being paid to the stumbling blocks to such rehabilitation.

A second proposition, much interwoven with the first, appears in various guises in the literature. One version holds that on the heels of a disaster a heightened degree of cooperation and unity develops within the affected system. Demerath, on the basis of his review of various disaster studies, concludes: "Previous inter-group differences are lessened, co-operation and social solidarity are heightened in the first post-impact period" (1957, p. 29). H. E. Moore (1958b, pp. 313-314) [8] had earlier arrived at a similar conclusion from his researches on the Waco-San Angelo disasters.

According to this view, persons of sharply divergent groupings —based upon age, class, etc.—who otherwise maintain fairly strict social distance, do submerge their differences and cooperate closely in the immediate post-disaster period. Although this proposition has considerable generality, it does require some qualification.

The actual degree of heightened cooperation seems to vary among sociocultural systems as well as according to the kind of disaster involved. Above all, it is essential that "hope for the future" remain

[8] Compare his theoretical discussion with ours.

high. Apparently only where people believe they can control in considerable measure the course of events following upon the disaster does a large measure of cooperation come into play.

Interpersonal cooperation and heightened morale do not emerge when a social order is shaken to its very roots by disaster. Quite the contrary. Take, for example, a nation that experiences defeat in war. After the German invasion of France in World War II, the French people were close to a state of collapse as the columns of the German military might swept over the land. Large segments of communities, in a desperate effort to flee the enemy, reportedly abandoned their homes and clogged the highways (Freeman and Cooper, 1940). Their disorganized behavior, their failure to unite against the aggressor, reflect, it seems to me, their hopelessness. Certainly Germany just after its defeat in World War II displayed little evidence of heightened cooperation or morale. Everyone (or almost everyone) seems to have recognized the finality of the defeat and the futility of any cooperative efforts against the disaster-producing force. Restating our position for clarity's sake: heightened integration and morale emerge only where the populace has confidence in the eventual restitution of the *status quo*. When such cannot be envisioned, integration and unity are unlikely to be displayed.

A third proposition, one which is implicit if not explicit in some of the literature on disasters, assumes that stable primary-group affiliations aid immeasurably in restoring disaster-stricken individuals (and social systems as well) to a state of normalcy. The studies of the bombings in England, for instance, lend support to this conclusion (Titmuss, 1950, pp. 345-346; Young, 1954); the data suggest that, in general, individuals preferred staying with their families in the bombed areas to removal to the relative safety of the countryside. Living with family members in the city provided persons not only with continuing knowledge of the fate of loved ones, but also with a sense of security even in the face of continuing danger.

Still, sociologists tend to exaggerate the role of primary-group ties. Disasters at times wreak havoc upon primary groups themselves. During the Great Depression of the 1930's in the United States the chief wage-earner's loss of employment—and thereby of status—had calamitous effects upon the stability of the family (see Komarovsky, 1940). Then, too, close primary-group ties may actually lead to an individual's destruction. Look at the adjustment of the Jews in Nazi concentration camps. Often it seems to have been the individuals who lost their identification with any primary group and with their ethnic subculture who survived. And some data suggest that certain Jews who survived had linked themselves with the Nazi superstructure, taking on positions in the lower echelons (Poliakov, 1954, p. 218). The harsh facts are that in this situation, where the Nazis were hell-bent upon destruction of the Jewish people, little could be gained in terms of sheer survival from close primary-group ties within this subculture.

A point of considerable theoretical interest is that some of the best adjusted persons in the Nazi concentration camps or in, say, the Warsaw ghetto were those whose chief reference groups were on the "outside." Those who had strong reference group attachments with professional or intellectual roles were apparently best able to accommodate to the loss of primary-group ties and the collapse of their everyday world.[9] Social scientists must more carefully detail the conditions under which primary-group ties are functional to, or dysfunctional to, adjustment and survival in disaster situations.

Another proposition regarding the accommodation to disasters has been advanced by Sorokin—namely, that formal organizational activity and control (especially by the government) increases in the post-disaster period, relative to the pre-disaster situation (1942, pp. 122ff). The evidence from industrial-urban orders supports this conclusion. For industrial systems rely upon formal organizations to re-establish equilibrium not only for individuals but also for the society's constituent structural elements as well.

Sorokin's generalization is not as pertinent for pre-industrial civilized orders. Indeed it is only in the modern industrialized and urbanized context that a vast roster of agencies can arise (see below) to effectively assist the victims of disaster. Thus in England during World War II it was after various highly organized agencies had come into existence that cities and their inhabitants were really able to adjust to the bombings (Idle, 1943).[10] Extensive and efficient police, fire-fighting, ambulance, and rescue corps were all essential to reduce the impact of the recurrent disasters.

We do not mean to imply that these formal organizations do not work through informal social arrangements. But it is the formal ones that take priority. As a matter of fact, a careful examination of the research studies on disaster reveals that many of these are geared to probing for more effective means to allow the formal organizations to

[9] This is my interpretation of the observations of Bettelheim (1943). Bettelheim himself seems to have maintained a sense of sanity by playing out the role of an intellectual observer whose reference group was outside the prison. There are a number of other impressive case studies of men who retained their perspective by recording their observations while in this extreme crisis situation. See Biderman (1960) for other data bearing on this problem.

[10] Even such a study as Form and Nosow (1958) tends to point to the heightened role of formal organizations after a disaster.

operate through (and control) the informal ones, and in the end to hasten the re-establishment of normality.

Up to now we have considered selected facets of the disaster-stricken populace's efforts to regain a state of normalcy. But we have in a sense jumped ahead of ourselves. We must pause to ask: Why are people so disturbed by disasters, even where loss of life or personal physical harm is not involved? The prime reason seems to be that the disaster upsets the normal status system. For instance, the destruction of property is of concern largely to the extent that it brings about the owner's loss of status.

Clearly disasters exact a heavy toll when they rearrange the status patterns of persons in the system (even where they do not destroy the structure itself). Disasters, particularly large-scale ones, open up avenues of mobility for some, channels that in normal times might be considered nonlegitimate. Or they induce sudden downward drops in status for others. One reason the Great Depression was viewed as such a violent cataclysm is that many traditionally upper status persons—e.g., stockholders—found themselves impoverished almost "overnight" in the crash of 1929 and in the economic disorder that followed (see Shannon, 1960). Something similar happens when a nation is defeated in war. Many persons, at least those in the traditional positions of power, slide downward in the social scale, while others experience for the first time the opportunity to ascend. Even strictly community disasters are apt to create some upheaval in the status relationships.

Still another proposition emerges from the foregoing. Where the traditional status arrangements are violated in the rehabilitation process, tension is likely to ensue. There is some evidence to indicate that in American communities agencies which do not act in terms of the traditional status hierarchy are subject to criticism. At times the universalistic policies of national, extra-community agencies run counter to the particularistic status arrangements on the community level (Crawford, 1955). For instance, some agencies have built or rebuilt homes for disaster victims with few or no savings, doing little or nothing for the more provident persons, who had perhaps lost a good deal more but who still had some funds available. Here is generated a state of "relative deprivation" for the thrifty, while those lower in the social scale experience a heightening of status. Tension and perhaps conflict are the inevitable result (Merton, 1957, pp. 227-236).

If the status system continues in a state of disequilibrium long after the disaster, tensions and strains are likely to multiply, with the emergence of what H. E. Moore refers to as the "brickbat" stage (Moore, 1958b, pp. 315-316). This leads us to a consideration of the longer-range implications of disaster for social change.

IV. *Long-run Consequences of Disasters in Industrial Societies*

Although the prime focus of most recent studies has, understandably, been the short-run changes initiated by disasters, some of the longer-range modifications are just as significant (or more so) sociologically. The long-run changes generated by the disaster itself and the efforts of the social system to prevent (or to curb the destructive effects of) future disasters are topics we single out for special attention.

LONG-RUN CHANGES INITIATED BY DISASTERS

Wherever possible, people strive for equilibrium in the social order. And to a considerable extent this can be achieved even after a major catastrophe of societal dimensions. Several studies have suggested, for example, that the post-World War II family in Germany was reconstituted in a form much like that of the pre-war era (Iklé, 1958, p. 228). Moreover, if we compare the industrial-urban forms to those in pre-industrial civilized societies, in many cases the changes resulting from disasters seem relatively minor. On the other hand, using a different standard of comparison, we observe that the new arrangements of the post-rehabilitation period are never quite like those predating the disaster—not just in the relationships among persons in the structure, but in the structure itself. Unfortunately, detailed research, on either the community or the societal level, into a disaster's impact over several decades is notably lacking.

Yet, present evidence indicates that disasters induce changes wherein the resultant social structure differs considerably from the pre-disaster forms. We can safely argue that when a nation experiences a major military defeat, the system hardly ever reverts to its former state, least of all in its political structure. Or when a social system is hit by a major economic recession, many of its features will never be the same again. Economic, political, and demographic structures are the most obvious candidates for change. Thus, in the United States the Great Depression was a major factor in reducing the birth rate, a change that has been felt in the past two decades—notably in the shortage of labor. In turn this has influenced many facets of American social organization. But we cannot review all of the many long-range effects of disasters. We must restrict ourselves to some general propositions concerning them.

One proposition that emerges from some disaster studies is that disaster brings to the surface changes in the system that actually were underway prior to the catastrophe. Iklé, for one, suggests that some of the practices employed in the rehabilitation of German cities after

World War II were actually extensions of patterns that had been initiated prior to the war (1958, p. 223). On another level, some writers (e.g., Eisenberg and Lazarsfeld, 1938) contend that many of the opinions, attitudes, and values of individuals of the crisis or post-crisis era are crystallizations of those toward which persons were moving before the disaster struck.

Of greater import are the various propositions as to the changes that ensue when equilibrium is not, or cannot be, restored within a "reasonable" length of time. One proposition we would suggest, in line with the thinking of Eric Hoffer (1951), is: Actors will struggle to re-establish equilibrium in the system if they see hope for its attainment within a reasonable period. But when they hold little confidence in the utility of their efforts, people will passively accept the disaster's consequences, distasteful though this may be.

The reaction of the Jews under the Nazis serves as one confirmatory case study of this hypothesis. Going back over various of the writings on this profound human tragedy, we discover some inconsistencies in the interpretations of the end result (e.g., Friedman, 1957; Iwańska, 1957; Kalmanovitch, 1953, especially the editor's introductory note; Poliakov, 1954). Some writers stress the firm resistance of the Jews, even through the dire days in the concentration camps in Germany and eastern Europe. Yet other observers suggest that unified resistance was the exception rather than the rule, particularly in Germany and eastern Europe. The vast bulk of the Jews, subjected to a kind of suffering unimaginable to most industrialites (although, ironically, the advanced industrial technology provided the efficient tools for mass murder), almost passively accepted their fate. A minority held out, a few cooperated with the Nazis, but most simply drifted with the tide into oblivion.

Concerning the issue of Jewish resistance, Poliakov writes:

> . . . How was it that several million men let themselves be led to the slaughterhouse without joining together in a final furious battle with their oppressors?—since their death warrant had been sealed, why did they not choose to die fighting?
>
> This is certainly a rankling question for the Jewish people, who are ready either to overestimate and generalize legendary but isolated feats of arms, or to point resignedly to the impotence of the disarmed ghetto population (1954, p. 224).

Ringelblum (1958), in one of the most remarkable documents ever published, details the life of the Jews in the Warsaw ghetto and, at least as we interpret the evidence, shows that as time elapsed and hope for "salvation" increasingly dimmed, the Jews lost the will to resist and came to accept their lot. (Interestingly, we have no persistent evidence of any strong resurgence of religion in either the ghettos or the concentration camps.)

In explaining these patterns, Poliakov (1954), for one, brings up the historical background of the Jews—their continued isolation and submergence in a ghetto system and their lack of any military tradition. Although something more than these cultural variables was involved, it appears nevertheless that the technological efficiency of the Nazi war machine, combined with the paltry assistance offered by the outside world, led to utter frustration and hopelessness, which in turn obviated any possibility of effective resistance, at least in Germany and eastern Europe where the Nazi might was strongest. Not only do subsystems sometimes lose the will to resist, but whole nations may exhibit this reaction. For example, the Germans and the Japanese mutely accepted their countries' defeats, for they saw little avail in continued resistance against overwhelming odds.

Contrast this with the attitudes of the populace in the bombed cities of England, or even in Germany and Japan while they were still winning major battles. The early bombing in Germany, devastating as this was, had relatively little effect upon those persons most committed to the Nazi cause—those displaying the greatest confidence in their country's ultimate victory (Form and Loomis, 1956). Apparently the enemy bombings became more effective as morale destroyers as the hopes for victory waned.

Although we can cite instances in modern industrial-urban societies where disaster-stricken persons have drifted into apathy, these are far from typical. What about the many situations where the actors view the system as out of balance, where status disequilibria generate all manner of "relative deprivations," yet where men sustain confidence in their ability to set the system right?

This leads to the following proposition: Where hope for a "normal" state of affairs remains, and where persons are permitted access (either directly or indirectly) to the mechanisms of social and political power, definite efforts are made, often in the form of "mass movements," to reconstitute the social order. Here, the dissatisfied, particularly those who occupy unstable status positions, strongly negate the existing order and seek either reform or revolution. The leaders of the existing order, as well as their policies, become the objects of extreme negation. For we contend that people can agree more readily on the evils of the social order, immediately perceptible to them, than on any positive program to remedy the system's ills (Sjoberg and Cain, 1959).[11]

[11] Our remarks do need some qualification to avoid misunderstanding. Not all persons involved in crisis situations (e.g., those resulting from disaster) resort

To be sure, people talk about "returning to the good old days." For, paradoxically, all great movements take some idealized concept of the past as their vision of a brighter future. Even so, the stress is on negation of existing "devils," not upon a firm, positive program for future action. Again, the objects of negation are much more tangible and serve as the pivots around which persons of highly divergent social backgrounds and statuses can unite.

Social movements arise on both the local community and the societal levels, the latter type being by far the more significant. By way of illustration we might note the Great Depression, which engendered the New Deal movement. At first it was assumed that the economic system would eventually correct itself, but when the situation gradually worsened and more and more persons suffered loss of employment and of status, the way was open for "radical" change through direct action by man himself (not through the magical devices of the pre-industrialite).

Franklin D. Roosevelt, in the election of 1932, rode the tidal wave of the negation against the chaos generated by the Depression. More emphasis was placed upon criticizing the incumbent leadership than in formulating a positive program. Around this negation a hodgepodge of ethnic and status groups rallied. People longed for a return to normality—i.e., prosperity—yet these same persons would probably not have agreed on a given program of action. Actually, as a firm set of policies did evolve after Roosevelt's election, some of his supporters became disillusioned and drifted away.

One final comment on this movement. Roosevelt, at least in his early campaigns, both sought to sustain and, in a sense, reflected people's belief in a rosier future. He continued to reassure them that prosperity could be regained, with a better life for all. This was, then, one positive goal among the many negatively stated rallying points of his campaign.

Some of the same principles were in operation in Germany after its defeat in World War I, itself a kind of disaster, but one which induced further cataclysms such as inflation and unemployment during the 1920's. Inasmuch as normalcy and stability apparently could not be restored after more than a decade had passed, the system was ripe for an extremist movement such as Nazism. And Hitler was a master at negation. The older order and the Jews were only some of the objects of his venomous attacks. Through wide use of negative symbols he rallied supporters from many diverse groups, especially those who

---

to negation. Some may become apathetic (see, for example, Zawadzki and Lazarsfeld, 1935, especially p. 247).

had experienced status instabilities of one kind or another.[12] Although Hitler spoke glowingly of restoring Germany's past glory (here again a conception of the past was used to form an image of the future), much of his program took shape only after his actual accession to power.

But by way of qualification: we must not assume that all social movements originate in disasters, as did the New Deal and, at least indirectly, the Nazi movement. But a goodly number of them do. And to the extent that disasters engender social movements—particularly of the revolutionary, as contrasted with the reform, type—the society's basic structural arrangements will undergo considerable revision. Without question, some of the dramatic social changes in industrial societies have had their origin in movements that represent the system's response to catastrophe. Who can doubt, for instance, that the New Deal has left its mark upon almost every facet of the modern social scene in America? For although instigators of social movements utilize a concept of the past as their model for the future, the end result is usually quite different from what even the leadership originally took to be its goal.

ATTEMPTS AT DISASTER PREVENTION AND CONTROL

One of the most impressive consequences of disaster in industrial societies, relative to pre-industrial orders, is the proliferation and extension of a host of organizations that have as their primary goal the handling of the periodic upheavals to which society is subject. Nowhere is belief in the scientific method, with its concept of control and manipulation of the natural and social orders (viewed as sharply separate from the "divine"), more transparent than in this facet of the social structure. Not that some members of industrial societies do not question this orientation; they do. However, science and the technology it fosters are overwhelmingly accepted as legitimate means by which to stave off disaster or greatly reduce its disruptive effects.

Moreover, it is the new science and its technology that permit man to resist disaster more effectively. Thus the ravages of infectious disease have been largely nullified in industrial-urban societies through advancements in sanitation and preventive medicine. So, too, industrial systems are in the main exempt from periodic famines, not only because more food is produced, but because storage and transport facilities, permitting food surpluses to be rushed to threatened areas, are highly developed. One of the prime causes of famine in pre-industrial

12 That Hitler rallied the disenchanted seems to be a conclusion of some writers (e.g., Kornhauser, 1959).

civilized societies has been the inability of the populace to shift food surpluses from one region to another.

Furthermore, the advances in technology and scientific know-how enable industrial societies to amass the capital required to support the complex and large-scale social organizations designed to fight disasters.[13] These may function only part of the year, yet they must be continually sustained.

In a somewhat different vein, we advance the proposition that relative stability and order over time is a functional imperative for a complex industrial-urban social system. The advent of a large-scale disaster means that capital that might be channeled into more productive enterprises must be siphoned off into sheer reconstruction.[14] This is hardly in keeping with the "rational" utilization of labor and capital. Then too, disasters are not necessarily respecters of people's skills and status positions. Theoretically, a disaster could wipe out the most crucial specialists upon which the industrial order rests. All in all, an industrial-urban society must perpetually guard against large-scale disasters. A democratically oriented one like the United States, emphasizing as it does the worth of the individual, is even more committed to protecting citizens from unexpected and violent upheavals of natural and social origin.

The agencies that have developed in modern industrial societies for control of or protection against disaster are legion. And they embody some truly new structural forms, distinct from anything in the pre-industrial civilized order. As indicated above, these structural apparatuses are of two kinds: (1) those that seek to prevent disasters, and (2) those designed to reduce the effects of the disasters that cannot be averted.

Included in the first of these types is a long roster of organizations that have come close to eliminating many natural disasters. In America there exist on the local and national levels numerous agencies geared to the prevention of epidemics. Food inspection, mass inoculations, mosquito control, and so on, are only a few of the measures employed. Dams and sea walls are built to contain floods, and the Coast Guard has as one of its prime functions the prevention of disasters at sea. Moreover, an industrial society exercises vigilance against possible socially produced disasters, particularly economic recessions. In the United States, currency and interest-rate controls, unemployment insurance, and the like are mechanisms whose purpose is the prevention of another major economic catastrophe (Burns, 1960).

[13] Note, for example, the growth of the Red Cross with expanding industrial urbanization (Dulles, 1950).

[14] For the cost of natural disasters in American society, see Lemons (1957).

Even on the international scene steps of a sort have been taken to counteract disasters. For example, the United Nations organization was intended as a means for discouraging the use of armed might among nations, as a counter-agent to a possible major calamity or calamities.

The second approach to disaster assumes that some kinds of disruption cannot be avoided, but that the blow can be softened through careful planning. Thus have evolved complex warning systems along the Atlantic and Gulf coasts which have as their prime objectives tracking hurricanes and advising the populace when a storm is imminent. Science has not yet conquered this natural force, but it can assist the populace in avoiding some of the more dire consequences of it. People can board up their homes, flee the threatened area, or take other protective measures.

Once a disaster strikes, a series of agencies like the Red Cross and Civil Defense stands ready to act. Their goal is to supply immediate aid to disaster victims and assist the community in its reconstruction efforts. And we must not overlook the numerous other programs geared to alleviating the effects of disaster, such as the multifarious insurance plans, income-tax deductions for losses suffered, and so on. And such measures as drought relief suggest the extent to which an industrial society like the United States goes in order to protect its citizenry. More and more, the total society is assuming responsibility for assisting the victims of disaster, be they individuals or whole communities.

With this introduction behind us, we can now offer some propositions, admittedly of a tentative nature, concerning the efforts at disaster prevention and control. Unfortunately we have often had to rely upon semi-popular commentaries, for lamentably little systematic social research on these problems has been accomplished.

Our main proposition is that organizations designed to handle relatively predictable kinds of disaster, generally the naturally induced as opposed to the socially induced ones, are more likely to achieve "success" than those attempting to cope with disaster-producing agents of an unfamiliar or erratic nature. Moreover, it is easier to create and sustain organizations that are geared to the more predictable disaster-producing phenomena than those concerned with more ephemeral ones. Thus organizations that combat communicable diseases or track hurricanes or tornadoes can more readily justify their essentiality to the appropriate legislative or decision-making bodies, and to the public, than can those seeking to avert some potentially far more devastating catastrophes such as would be occasioned by nuclear warfare. Hurricanes and tornadoes are generally foreseeable annual occurrences; even epidemics may evince some regularities in their patterning; but no one is sure when, where, and if a thermonuclear war will be launched. Lacking any adequate knowledge of the full dimensions of such an eventuality, scientists themselves cannot agree as to the proper steps to be taken to avoid the chaos that would ensue. Under these circumstances, decision-makers are hard put to justify to their constituencies the expenditure of millions, indeed billions, of dollars on programs of disaster prevention in the realm of thermonuclear warfare, seemingly so far removed from the work-a-day world of the man on the street.

We implied that organizations designed to meet the more predictable sorts of disaster are not only easier to justify (and create) but are more "efficient" in meeting their assigned tasks. For one thing, their techniques, periodically put on trial, can be steadily refined. But consider the complex sets of controls that have been devised to avert a serious economic recession in the United States. Some specialists remind us that these instruments have not been subjected to rigid tests. And who would want to create the necessary conditions to achieve this end? As matters now stand, we simply do not know just how effective these measures would be. If they did prove ineffective, what about people's reactions to the government that had assured them that the economy was operating within a margin of safety? The repercussions within the system would be forcibly felt.

Implicit in the foregoing discourse is the notion that the industrial-urban system is plagued by contradictory functional requirements of sorts. Should a nation—the American society, especially—spend many millions to provide bomb shelters for its citizens and to support various agencies for disaster prevention and control in the event of an atomic disaster that may never occur? Some would contend that, given the overwhelming destructive effects of an atomic war, any shelters that were constructed would have scanty value for the majority of the people and that, in these circumstances, the large-scale investment of capital would constitute sheer waste (see "Meyner Doubtful . . .", 1960; for a contrary view, see "Civil Defense . . .", 1958). The money and labor could be better spent for other purposes, such as firming up the American industrial base, etc. Others see an atomic holocaust as distinctly possible and argue that even the most elementary precautions would prove invaluable in saving lives and property. The danger of nonpreparedness, they contend, looms too large, the society's very survival being at stake. People's standard of living may be temporarily lowered, but the vast expenditures required for defense against a thermonuclear attack are eminently worthwhile. Contradictions of this sort, although perhaps less dramatic, plague modern social orders seeking to construct preventive mechanisms against other types of disasters—for instance, economic recessions.

Our final proposition—that the intense demands upon disaster-preventive organization and techniques (which are both required and made possible by the industrial-urban system) will not diminish over time—deserves elaboration. For although the industrial-urban order, in lively contrast to the pre-industrial civilized society, has made giant strides in removing the populace from the grip of many kinds of disaster, the industrialization process itself increases man's vulnerability to catastrophe on other counts. For one thing, with the achievement of an all-time high in its standard of living, the citizenry now has much more to lose: it has become more vulnerable to disaster. Given the greater expectations, people's suffering in a disaster could well become social-psychologically more intense than in the past. A severe economic recession would create great hardships and in all probability generate all manner of animosity toward the existing government. Then, too, the grander and more complex our cities become, the more susceptible are they to malfunctioning under adverse conditions or to near or complete collapse in the case of nuclear attack. It seems that the further industrial-urban society "progresses," the greater leaps forward it must make just to protect and sustain these advances. We can, therefore, expect continued expansion of the organizational apparatus designed to prevent and control natural and social disasters.

This brings us once again to the greatest disaster threat of modern times—the possibility of an atomic war. We comment briefly on some of the issues that would plague an industrial-urban society if such event occurred; we draw mainly upon principles discussed earlier.

V. Social Change and a Thermonuclear Attack

We have recently been subjected to a barrage of stories in the mass media conjecturing what the last days on earth will be like if an atomic war is unleashed. The problem merits some serious speculation. And speculation it must be, for except for the experiences in Nagasaki and Hiroshima, there is little basis for sound prediction as to what the aftermath of such a holocaust might be. Still, we can make some reasoned, scholarly guesses as to what lies in the offing.

We begin with two assumptions: (1) that some persons will survive the thermonuclear attack and (2) that the country will not be accupied by the enemy after the bombing.

The magnitude of the task of physical reconstruction after a severe atom bomb assault, to say nothing of the sheer struggle for survival on the part of the living who must now face the danger of radiation, staggers the imagination. The estimates given before Congressional committees indicate the potential casuality rate, even in a "moderate" attack, to be towering (U.S. Congress, 1959, especially pp. 846-855). And the matter of how survivors are to obtain an adequate supply of uncontaminated food and water has hardly been probed. But let us turn our attention from the physical-biological factors in rehabilitation to concentrate upon the question of social organization, on which the whole reconstruction operation rests.

If we can judge by other disasters, some kind of social system will emerge soon after the attack: most probably this will be reconstituted along pre-disaster lines, or, at the very least, people will adjust to the new situation largely in terms of their past experiences.[15] The most pressing matter will be to set up an authority system that the populace will accept as "legitimate." And this can be achieved only in terms of familiar symbols. We can expect the amount of formal governmental controls exerted in the post-disaster period to be considerably greater than in the pre-disaster situation, for the monumental tasks of distributing the "scarce" supplies to the needy and rebuilding the social order will require the firm hand of authority.

A crucial problem facing the existing governmental organization and its satellite agencies will be reconstitution of the lines of communication. Only thereby can the governmental leaders fulfill the populace's pressing demand for meaningful and understandable goals. Without this the reconstruction process could not proceed effectively. Various large-scale disaster experiences in industrial-urban societies clearly demonstrate the need for confidence in the future. However, recent writings on social organization in the post-nuclear attack context overlook the ideological component that will provide the survivors with the values "worth living for." The monumental tasks of reconstruction, calling forth every ounce of energy from an already exhausted citizenry, will not seem worthwhile without the vision of a better future. But to induce hope under these dire circumstances will tax even the most ingenious leadership. Some forethought must be given to a program of action in this area if survival is to be maximized.

Closely related to the matter of morale is the need for formulating a workable program by which people can be assured of an equitable post-disaster "reimbursement" for their losses. The bombing in all likelihood will destroy much of the old status structure; some persons will slide down the social scale while others ascend. But somehow this new distribution of "wealth" must be rationalized for the duration of the emergency and a program calling for "equitable" sharing of losses promised for the post-emergency period. Unless this can be accom-

[15] For other views on this problem, see Hirshleifer (1956), Iklé (1954), and Tiryakian (1959).

plished, the status instabilities will result in intense strains and conflict and further demoralization of the populace.

Finally, we stand with those who contend that unless all the key centers are reduced to fine atomic dust, or unless continued waves of bombings sweep over the land, an industrial society, given the populace's firm determination to exist, should recover relatively rapidly from the devastation, certainly more rapidly than the most ardent pessimists assume (compare, for example, the views of Herman Kahn in U.S. Congress, 1959, p. 909). As long as technical know-how survives, either in the hands of specialists or in our libraries, the industrial system should be able to right itself in due time, even though restoration to full bloom might take generations.

These admittedly fleeting observations on the probable nature of the social structure after an atomic attack serve, we hope, to suggest some implications of our earlier stated propositions on the matter of disasters.

VI. Conclusions

Our avowed purpose has been to point to some of the relationships between disasters and social change from a macroscopic perspective. We argued, first, that in pre-industrial civilized orders the technology, viewed broadly, and the society's precise orientation toward the natural and social order, lead to special kinds of adjustment to disaster and, consequently, particular forms of social change. That the response to disaster is in part determined by the sociocultural context should come as no surprise to students of disaster. At the same time, no one has used the pre-industrial civilized society as a point of reference for understanding the impact of disasters on industrial-urban orders. Writers generally compare the pre- with the post-disaster period within industrial societies (which we have also done), but taking the pre-industrial civilized order as a base against which to contrast various changes in industrial societies adds a meaningful dimension to our analysis of social change.

In discussing industrial systems, we began by pointing out various facets of the short-run changes wrought by disasters. Admittedly we have not considered all the many issues involved—many of the specific problems with respect to, say, communication did not come under scrutiny. Yet, within the original definition of the problem, we sought to set forth the main issues.

But the long-range consequences of disasters are those most slighted by social scientists. The proper study of these effects should assess the development of anti-disaster agencies and the problems they face in an industrial-urban society (even during the periods when they are not fighting disasters). We need to know why some kinds of disaster command more interest than others—such not always being in proportion to the toll of human life exacted. And what about the instabilities of organizations created to handle disasters that may not appear for generations, if ever? How do these agencies manage to sustain themselves, to garner the necessary support? These and a host of other vital issues—all bearing, directly or indirectly, on the problem of disasters and social change—await attention.

Thus, although industrial societies have made great strides in conquering disasters on the order of famines, hurricanes, or epidemics, modern technology has created the potential for much more devastating holocausts (like thermonuclear war), and this technology has made modern man, now luxuriating on a plane of existence never before imagined, more susceptible to catastrophe, in that he has far more to lose than ever before. The result is that modern industrial society must be prepared to invest capital in disaster prevention of various types—although the extent of this prevention and control will always pose a dilemma. Should the society invest in preserving what it has, or should it live dangerously but forge ahead to technologically higher levels of attainment? Only one thing is certain—the study of disasters will remain a key aspect of modern society. The task of the social scientist in this realm has only begun.

▶ *thirteen*

THEORETICAL POSSIBILITIES OF INDUCED SOCIOCULTURAL COLLAPSE

John P. Gillin

IN GIVING SOME CONSIDERATION to the possibilities in national disaster or collapse I hope that I shall not be accused of pessimism. On the contrary, I believe that if we devote more attention to these matters and understand more comprehensively the possibilities, we shall then be in a position to take appropriate measures to protect our own sociocultural system and those of our friends in the perilous days we do and shall face. Once we achieve such understanding and implementation, we shall be in a much more optimistic situation than we are today. Pessimism and hopelessness often arise from ignorance and confusion. Even if no danger faced us, a thorough-going analysis of the possibilities of disintegration of complex sociocultural systems would deepen our knowledge of the principles of social and cultural integration. The negative approach often sheds light on the positive side.

The cause for present concern is, of course, the fact that the United States, its allies, and most of the emerging nations of the underdeveloped regions find themselves under attack from Russia and the Soviet bloc, in a species of conflict that has been variously described as Cold War or Peaceful Warfare. In this type of contest the Soviets seek every possibility, short of nuclear warfare, for weakening target nations and alliances to the point where they collapse or become nonfunctional. On our side, both policy-makers and the thinking public seem not to have realized the complexity of the problem and often oversimplify it. This sort of conflict is not merely economic competition, not only a propaganda war, not simply a contest in development and diffusion of technologies. It involves these and many other possibilities the range of which we must take into consideration and understand as a whole. Otherwise, we shall continue to be constantly surprised and unprepared as the Soviets pull one unexpected "trick" after another. And it is by no means beyond the bounds of possibility that they could bring about our collapse before we fully realized what is going on.

The present discussion can be but a sketchy outline of these problems, in which I use a few rather obvious illustrations to indicate the need for intensive and systematic research and thinking. One thing should be clear: I am not dealing with the cycle type of theories, such as those of Spengler and Toynbee, which for diverse reasons see each civilization as inevitably declining and falling at a certain stage in its historical course. I seek the principles upon which the strategy and tactics of Peaceful Warfare may be developed. In other words, I am interested in the theoretical bases upon which one complex sociocultural system may plan to bring about the malfunction or collapse of another such system without resort to all-out warfare.

In my attempt to suggest the major categories of possibilities, I shall at the same time try to relate them ultimately to the area of cultural values in what might be called a values theory of disaster or calamity.

Cultural Values and Disaster

To say that "disasters or calamities exist in the minds of men" is not to deny that they are real, but is meant to assert that what may be one people's disaster may be something quite different for people of another society, time, or place. This point came home forcibly to me recently as my wife and I stood in the ruins of Herculaneum, trying with some effort of imagination to picture the state of mind of its inhabitants on that day nearly two thousand years ago when Vesuvius burst and an ocean of hot mud rolled over their city. Our guide, an ancient Italian who had learned idiomatic English during long years in America, cackled, "It probably looked like the end of the world to them, all right. But for us people who live around here now, it's a gold mine." And I recalled the paragraph in the guidebook which explained that "a fortunate combination of circumstances" had resulted in the preservation of many of the houses and their contents almost intact, so that "scholars have been able to study the details of ancient life in a way that would otherwise have been impossible." Poor Herculanians! Happy tourist guides! Fortunate archaeologists!

Turning to more recent times, one remembers Hitler's liquidation of some six million Jews. There is no doubt that the proceedings were a series of unmitigated calamities for the victims. Yet the evidence collected since World War II reveals that very few of the Nazis who participated in the tortures, poisonings, rapes, burnings, and shootings felt that they themselves were involved in disaster. On the other hand, the Germans who lived in Cologne, Dusseldorf, Hamburg, and other target areas, after German air cover and antiaircraft defense had been effectively destroyed, could not but view the results of the pulverizing allied bombing raids as calamity. Conversely, to the allied airmen and the allied public in general the same series of events appeared as glorious victory. As the old saying has it, what is one man's meat is another man's poison. If this is true for individuals, it also seems to hold for social groups, communities, and whole societies.

All of this is by way of introduction to what I call a values theory of disaster or sociocultural collapse. I am concerned here primarily with disaster or catastrophe on the sociocultural level as it may affect social groups and whole societies. From this point of view a disaster is any event, series of events, or situation which renders highly valued goals of a group or society unattainable to the degree customarily considered essential by the members.

People everywhere organize together and participate in sociocultural systems, and they share their evaluation of goals with other members of their system. A sociocultural system consists of a socially organized population and its culture; its general purpose is to attain certain positively valued goals (desirable states of affairs) while avoiding certain negatively valued goals (undesirable states of affairs). Such goals are formulated and defined within the system and they are (or are believed to be), respectively, unattainable or unavoidable by individuals without certain patterned types of cooperation from fellow members of the system. A disaster for any such system is obviously the *most* undesirable state of affairs, one which renders the system totally or in large measure incapable of attaining its positively valued goals. My basic assumption, then, is that any sociocultural system's functioning is to be judged in terms of its positively valued goals. The basic question is: What events or situations may spontaneously occur or *be produced* by human agency that will bring such a system to the state of disaster?

For some people the words "disaster" and "calamity" suggest end results of a rapid process. Disasters *may* come rapidly, but they may also come slowly—in which case "slow disintegration and final collapse" may be a more appropriate phrase.

First, we note that "desirable states of affairs" fall into two categories: (1) those thought to be attainable, according to the belief patterns of a given system, and (2) those thought to be desirable but not fully realizable. The former may be called realistic goals; the latter, idealistic goals. For example, "an end to war forever" has been a highly valued goal in Western society, at least for the past forty years, but there still is much skepticism as to its realism. Within a system people feel they "have a right" to expect the achievement of realistic goals at once or in the foreseeable future. Actual attainment of idealistic goals, on the other hand, while desirable, is not among the "rights" which the system owes to its members. For present purposes I shall focus primarily upon goals believed within any system to be realizable, and I shall refer to them merely as "goals." To simplify the presentation I shall no longer use the phrases "undesirable states of affairs" or "negatively valued goals," but shall refer to "malfunctions." (Malrather than dysfunction is used because of the emphasis placed upon value orientation in the present analysis; malfunction carries a pejorative connotation.) Extreme malfunctions or combinations thereof I shall call "disaster."

Materialistic Support of Goals

To reach its goals, a sociocultural system requires *energy*, for which there are, in the last analysis, two general sources: natural and human. We are here speaking of physical energy, which at least theoretically can be measured in foot-pounds, horsepower, watts, or other similar units. "Psychic energy" is another matter, which, in the present theory, I shall discuss in connection with communication, influence, and the cathecting or attracting power of goals. Modern systems are distinguished by the fact that by far the greatest proportion of the physical energy generated for the production of goods and services is derived from natural sources, with only a small fraction of the total developed from human muscles or human metabolic processes.

In any sociocultural system, the first energy requirement is obviously that necessary for keeping its human membership alive, if not in perfect health—in other words, it must provide food for its population. Life of the population is a basic goal of all viable human systems. Beyond this, energy may be generated to be used for attaining other goals.

Inadequate Knowledge of Nature

The success of a system in finding and developing nonhuman sources from which to generate energy depends upon the *knowledge of nature* at its disposal. In modern systems there has been an increasing trend to rely upon scientific knowledge, although so-called knowledge of nature based on intuition or revelation from supernatural sources is still operative. The body of native knowledge patterns in a selective way the perceptions of the specialists and, to a varying extent, of the general population. To take a well-known example, white experts viewing the Mesabi Range in Minnesota perceived it as a source of iron ore, whereas the Chippewa Indians who had roamed the area aboriginally saw the same formation mainly as a source for wild game. Whether knowledge be scientific or of some other type, it also involves a system of beliefs and explanations—which may or may not be rationally or logically organized. In scientific systems, such beliefs and their consequences are supposed to be empirically verifiable; this is not demanded of beliefs based upon intuition or revelation, or at least "empirical" receives a different, nonscientific definition.

The "knowledge" at the disposal of a sociocultural system covers the entire universe of experience within the purview of the system, of which energy sources are but one aspect. In modern systems we find a tendency for knowledge to be predominantly scientific when concerned with "nature," less so when concerned with human relations and matters of the "spirit." Inconsistency as between certain segments of the total belief system may lead to malfunction. For example, the tendency of Americans to rely upon common sense, hunches, incomplete revelations, and inadequate science when dealing with other peoples of the world contrasts strongly with their insistence upon a completely scientific approach when dealing with nuclear warfare or space travel.

Lack of Natural Energy Resources

The energy potential of a system depends not only upon "knowing" where to find sources of it but also upon the *availability* of such sources. Ample materials may exist within the boundaries of a modern nation, although such a situation is rare in recent times. In order to secure an ample supply of raw materials, modern nations have relied upon peaceful patterns of international trade or exchange. They have also resorted to wars of conquest against either underdeveloped areas or other nations in order to "make secure" their sources of supply. It is clear that any serious blockage of energy resources will lead to major malfunction, perhaps disaster, in a modern system. It is conceivable that science will one day discover means of supplying all energy requirements from the atmosphere or from radiations from outer space. Currently, however, the primary energy resources are found on the surface of the earth (soils suitable for crops, pastures, or forests); in seas and other bodies of water containing edible life and useful minerals; or in the earth itself (coal, petroleum, ores amenable to atomic fission and fusion, and other useful minerals). Consequently, there is a constant preoccupation with land and sea surface boundaries.

Faulty Technology

The exploitation of energy resources rests upon a system's *technology*, which is an application of knowledge and skill involving not only the discovery and invention of ways and means of manipulating the potentialities inherent in natural resources but also the *training* and *organization* of human beings. In modern systems, technology has given rise to a very complex subdivision of the population into specialized groups and categories, each with something of a distinct subculture, often called the division of labor or function. Each subculture embodies goals. During the past hundred years the goals of certain subcultures have been at least ostensibly in opposition to those of other subcultures; the conflict between labor and owners is one example. One of the great debates of the contemporary world revolves around the question of whether the various subgoals of a modern technological production system can be brought into consistency with each other in support of the major goals of a national system. Classical Marxism maintains that under capitalism such values are by their nature incompatible and therefore lead to inevitable conflict within the system. One version of current American theory, on the other hand, maintains that labor, management, and ownership all subscribe to the common value of increasing production in which each segment shares, and that they can be coordinated on this basis to the mutual satisfaction of all.

Other solutions have been proposed. These matters are mentioned here merely to remind us that reliability of basic knowledge and efficiency of technique are not alone sufficient to guarantee a system against malfunction or even disaster. Goals and the values associated with them are still fundamental. This leads us to another important aspect of sociocultural systems: namely, *social organization and the patterning of human interactions.*

Weakness in Social Organization

All sociocultural systems are subdivided and show some range of variation. Modern systems, as compared with primitive or folk systems, are distinguished by the vastly greater number of their constituent subdivisions and the complexity of the relations between these. First, no two individuals in the population are exactly alike. They show differences in aptitudes and talents, in interests developed through variations in experience and training, and in patterns of action and attitude associated with status. In any system a basic problem is to determine at what point a balance should be established between conformity to general pattern and freedom for individual spontaneity. Complete individualism is by definition the negation of the sociocultural system and, if permitted in a modern nation, would result in its collapse—but it would also result in the death of most of the individuals. Human beings cannot live entirely from their individual resources without any kind of interaction with their fellows; by their nature they will always make common cause with some of their fellows. The question is: Will they work together with the other members of a certain group within the society, showing opposition to others? A modern nation requires a certain minimum sense of common cause among its members if it is not to disintegrate. At the same time it needs to recognize originality and spontaneity in those individuals who can help to reach goals or who can refine or redefine the understanding of the goals themselves. The totalitarian type of modern system has emphasized conformity; the democratic type has at least claimed to promote realization of the individual's full potentialities within the framework of the general welfare.

It must be noted also that "conformity," "spontaneity," "realization of human potentialities," and "general welfare" are cultural values translatable into goals. Current national systems differ with respect to the rating given to each.

Social groups consist of individuals in social contact with each other as persons. And in social groups the contacts or patterns of interaction are to some extent organized, either formally or informally. In societies the world over we find kin groups (including nuclear families), sex groups, age groups, and groups focused upon culturally generated interests. There are, however, two distinctive characteristics of modern complex societies as compared with other types: the much greater reliance they place upon instrumental rather than face-to-face contacts, and the proliferation of interest groups in proportion to other groups. Families and kin groups, for example, tend to lose some of their former functions, while certain former bases of grouping, such as local communities and ethnic similarities, tend to see contact between the members become attenuated.

All social groups have certain goals and values. Many of these are not in opposition to each other, as is shown by the fact that the average adult in a modern society such as ours may subscribe to the objectives of a whole range of groups without difficulty. On the other hand, modern society by its very nature also nourishes group interest in subgoals which are in some respects in apparent opposition. In democratic societies many of these subgoals are in the open; in totalitarian societies some may be "underground." Proponents of democratic tolerance hold that such diversity of group aims tends to enrich social life and that ultimate compromise permits enhancement of efforts toward the goals of the general society. The mere existence of "organized" differences, however, contains the seeds of possible malfunction in the form of internecine strife, a possibility which totalitarian systems take to be of such danger that they suppress open differences in the interests of stability or solidarity. Again we may note that "enrichment through diversity," "compromise," "stability," and "solidarity" represent values that are given different ratings in the several modern sociocultural systems.

Rivalry Between Social Categories

In addition to a wide variety of groups, modern systems also contain divisions that sociologists call social categories. These are large segments of the population whose members have a certain "consciousness of kind," but whose social contacts and positions with respect to each other are only slightly organized, if at all. Social classes and regional divisions are perhaps the most common. In the United States one of the ideal values holds that social classes should not exist. Repeated investigations have shown, however, that they do, although they are relatively "open" and although "class consciousness" is rather vague in some sectors. Entire social classes in modern society are seldom organized as groups, although groups may be formed within them, as when a club or fraternity at least tacitly restricts its membership to persons of a certain class status. Regional categories did not exist in certain earlier social systems, such as medieval principalities (Lichtenstein is a modern survival of one) whose geographical limits were confined to a fairly homogeneous type of terrain. All modern nations, however, are of such extent that they comprise geographically diverse regions. Even Belgium knows the difference between the Ardennes hill country and the flatlands to the north. In Holland, the dike-protected region of Zeeland is distinct from the lands to the north and west. Small Ecuador recognizes a distinction between coast, sierra, and eastern jungle. Differences in adaptive culture and in tradition give rise to some regional differences in values and goals. Although regions are seldom organized as wholes, they may be—as when the southeastern region of the United States constituted itself a sovereign nation in 1861 and for four years carried on a war of secession from the national system.

One must recognize another major sociocultural differentiation in modern systems, *that between urban and rural types of life.* Although settled villages and towns first appeared during Neolithic (New Stone Age) times, the modern metropolis is a phenomenon of the recent period. Cities are "organized" in the sense of having municipal governments, public services, residential rules, and so forth, yet they are not "groups" in the technical sense because they do not provide effective channels for interaction between all the members. They are better described as "organized collectivities." Communities in modern societies range along a continuum from the large metropolis, through smaller cities, suburban and "rurban" communities, towns and villages of various types, to open country neighborhoods. This variety in community pattern also gives rise to differences in values and goals. In the United States, for example, most state legislatures exhibit an organized opposition between rural and urban representatives, and in France, to cite only one more instance, the conflict between Paris and the provinces is traditional.

Two further observations must be made. One is the distinction between *voluntaristic groupings* and *required groupings.* The United States is said to be particularly encouraging to the first, and some observers judge North Americans to be a nation of "joiners." In Soviet Russia an individual does not have the choice of whether or not he will join a group such as an agricultural cooperative. He "joins" what he is told to join. It is maintained on the "democratic" side of the line that voluntary association has more strength than forced group membership, since it involves spontaneously developed values as opposed to those imposed by authoritarian control.

Many, but not all, of the groupings occurring in modern systems are organized into national *institutions.* These will be summarily analyzed after we have dealt with values and valued goals.

Improper Ordering of Goals

Values are in social systems somewhat analogous to motives in the individual. They provide the reason or impetus for social action and attitude. Goals are valued, as well as the means or instrumentalities for reaching or avoiding them. In every culture there is a "right" and a "wrong" way, or several of them, for reaching each recognized goal. Values may thus be positive or negative, and we may speak of ideal values and real or modal values. As previously mentioned, we are confining ourselves, in considering valued goals, to those which within a given system are believed to be attainable—realistically valued goals. The goals of any system, however, are usually arranged in a priority series or a rank order of value. In a crisis a subordinate goal may be sacrificed for one taking priority. In past wars, the people of the United States have placed survival of the nation above survival of individual soldiers. Goals are also placed in functional series, so that one or more is in a prerequisite relation to a principal goal. In the United States, if one wishes to become a surgeon, there are a number of educational steps—or goals—that one must take in succession before one qualifies to practice. High school graduation, college degree, medical school degree, record of completed internship, record of completed residency, passing of the "national boards," are all prerequisite goals to the major goal of recognition as a practicing surgeon. If confusion or conflict is to be avoided in a properly functioning system, the various goals must be ordered with respect to *time* and *place*. In a prerequisite series such as that of preparation to be a surgeon, neither too little nor too much time must be allowed. With respect to place (or occasion or context) the goal, say, of social relaxation or "a good time" in the American system may be properly achieved on Saturday night, but not at ten o'clock on the morning of a working day. It is all right to demonstrate one's perfection as a tango dancer on a ballroom floor, but not on a church platform. And so on.

Two goals are in opposition to each other if the attainment of one renders impossible or incomplete the attainment of the other. A system containing serious opposition produces wasteful dissipation of energy without satisfactions, or it may even fall into paralysis. Yet, in democratic systems it is believed that a certain limited goal opposition should be permitted so that the "better" may demonstrate its worth through competition. Some systems permit more deviancy than others.

Opposition Among Institutions

Large sectors of goals and instrumentalities in a modern system are organized into national institutions—economic, religious, educational, scholarly, recreational, and artistic.[1] Each has patterns for organizing the division of function of the participants, sets of goals, and customary means (including material equipment) for reaching them. The major institutions usually cut across class, ethnic, local community, and regional lines. They are relatively stable as compared with fads and whims, and when properly functioning are capable of generating large amounts of energy. If two or more major institutions in a modern system can be brought into fundamental opposition to each other, serious instabilities may be created throughout the system.

[1] Political institutions are discussed in connection with "system controls." Familial "institutions" are omitted here because they are not organized on a nationwide basis.

Because many individuals participate in more than one institution, opposition creates divided loyalties. A familiar conflict of institutional goals in the United States system, which the Russians persistently try to exploit, is that supposed to exist between "social welfare" and "economic profits."

In modern systems the "means" for reaching many goals involve machinery and other complicated material equipment plus the necessary human skills to design, build, maintain, and operate them. "Efficiency" becomes a highly rated value.

Communications Failure

Maintenance of any sociocultural system in function requires some means of *communication*. In small and relatively simple systems, such as a tribe of a few hundred members or a peasant community, the bulk of communication takes place on a personal basis by word of mouth and other forms of direct symbolization. But in a modern nation special technical elaborations are necessary, because of the size of the population and its dispersal throughout a relatively large territory. Karl W. Deutsch (1953) has offered one analysis of modern systems almost entirely in terms of communication or information theory, and Harry B. Williams (1956) has set up a similar scheme for analyzing local community disasters. It is through the media of mass communication that the members of a national society are able to keep in touch with each other and learn about and be reminded of goals and values. The press, motion pictures, and electronic communications (telegraph, telephone, radio, television) are indispensable to a modern nation. Not only must information circulate throughout the society, but communications must be maintained by some part of the system with the rest of the world if for no other reason than to perceive power threats.

From the point of view of the power potentials of a sociocultural system, it is worthy of note that communications themselves normally use relatively little energy as measured in physical units, but they are instrumental in releasing and directing large quantities of such energy. A few sentences spoken by a president or leader over radio or on television may produce the mobilization of all national energies. Breakdown in communication—perhaps a failure of warning devices—may result in catastrophe. *Input* refers to the type and quantity of messages introduced into a communications network, *output* to the type and quantity of messages actually disseminated from a given center, *feedback* to the amount and content of the messages returning to the center in response to the output. Williams (1956) has shown in his study of local natural disasters that much post-impact confusion results from failure of feedback—rescue authorities often cannot find out what has happened and what is being done in certain sectors of the disaster area. The United Nations Educational, Scientific and Cultural Organization (UNESCO) is committed to the hypothesis that many international conflicts are due to lack of adequate two-way communication across national and cultural boundaries. Through a series of projects, UNESCO is now attempting to increase mutual understanding between nations.

Two outstanding types of possible communications failure attract attention. One is technical failure of the apparatus of the mass media, which can be induced, for example, by enemy sabotage or by technical incompetence of the natives. A second type may be described as "inarticulateness"—failure of the persons involved to put their messages into words or other symbols that have the intended meaning for the receivers. Even a scientific analyst cannot be sure that he has put across his message to a sophisticated audience. One must constantly check the results and revise the presentation. How much more this is required on the sociocultural system level becomes clear when we consider Herbert Hoover's internal failures in the 1928-1932 period, for instance, or the numerous United States failures to communicate its good will abroad to Latin America in the last fifteen years. Constant checking and revision is common among the experts in the technology of communication—technologists in the electronics of radio, telephone, and TV, for example—but it appears that its necessity has been less appreciated by the formulators of the messages themselves.

Finally, in our rapid overview we come to the functions of *coordination* and *control,* whereby the energies generated by the component social units are distributed, directed, and, to some extent at least, integrated for the achievement of major goals.

Deficiencies in Coordination and Control

I mentioned earlier that human organisms as such are relatively puny producers of physical energy and that modern societies rely overwhelmingly on other sources. Normal human beings, however, are able to perform a number of other distinctive activities that in the long run have proved more important than the work they can do with their unaided muscles. They are able to develop feelings or emotions of a wide range; they are capable of imagining situations other than those immediately present to their senses; they can conceive ideas and can grasp them when they are communicated by others; they can solve problems and anticipate certain rewards and punishments; they invent and use symbols for communication and for the "storage" of their experiences in material form as well as in their "long" memories; and they organize their emotions, imagery, and ideas, and by symbols share them with their fellows. Not all individuals do these things equally well, of course, but these activities are sometimes spoken of as evidences of "psychic energy," a term which we shall use to point up the contrast with physical energy. It has been shown experimentally that there is no one-to-one relationship between physical energy and psychic energy. Although "thinking" may be unpleasant for some people, the brilliance of the ideas produced is no constant function of the number of calories absorbed, provided the organism is not in a state of advanced starvation and the individual is not unduly distracted by other bodily ailments. The results that may accrue from the delivery of an insult are not directly correlated with the number of decibels involved in offering it. And so on.

The basic function of the control agencies is to attempt to assure that the total system achieves its major goals or objectives, supports its principal real values. This requires "power." Control agencies regulate within permissible limits the organization of individuals and the various social units of the society, and from time to time they may establish new units and organization. Essentially, the organization of individuals means assigning them to their "proper" places and seeing to it that they perform the functions expected of them. Regulation of the organized interrelations of groups and categories means smoothing the pathways for their coordinated action within the system and suppressing serious tendencies to conflict. In modern systems many norms and prohibitions regarding social and individual conduct assume the form of written and codified statutes, which require specialists for their interpretation and enforcement. But a large proportion of these rules lies in nonlegalistic orders and organization charts of private organizations, and a still larger fraction, known as "common usage" or "custom," is not usually reduced to writing.

Political institutions are the control agencies in modern systems that have the exclusive right to the use of force to maintain organizational patterns and norms of conduct, and only they are permitted to maintain police and other armed forces. Even the effective use of force seems to rest on values. Death and pain are everywhere negatively valued states of affairs and members of society will conform to certain patterns in order to escape them. Deprivation of liberty by force is also negatively valued by all peoples I know. Although individuals can be forcefully removed from a situation—as when police carry rioters bodily from the street or when a criminal is executed for a capital offense—this is no way to secure cooperative action from the persons to whom the force is thus applied. It is the *fear* of death, pain, or loss of liberty, reinforced by occasional examples, that may be effective in controlling any considerable portion of a system. But force alone is comparatively inefficient, for if the populace has no positive goals toward which to strive, they do only enough to avoid the negative ones of pain, death, or imprisonment. Few people can be forced to love their country. No modern system is able to operate for long on negative sanctions alone; most people must perceive the rewards and satisfactions of "good" conduct if they are to be effective members of a sociocultural system.

We should remember that force is not the only type of negative sanction. In a modern money economy, fines are punishing and are employed by both political and nonpolitical organizations for infractions of norms. In fact any blockage of an individual or group from the attainment of an anticipated real goal may be used as a negative sanction. Influence, too, is a sort of "pressure" not formalized or legalized which may be used as a negative sanction. Office holders in organizations realize that they must "get in line" with the attitudes of their chiefs if they do not want to be discharged or skipped over for promotion. A young couple regulates its scale of living and social life according to certain norms in order to avoid being blackballed by the country club. A business organization "gets the word" that a donation to the civic auditorium fund would be a good thing, "or else." The neighbors will bring the noisy household on the block into line by refusing certain courtesies, spreading gossip, and so on.

Positive sanctions for approved conduct and attachment to goals include rewards and satisfactions of various kinds, which are provided by government agencies, other organizations, or informally. In Western Europe and the United States—at least since the beginning of the modern "welfare state" in Bismarck's Germany in the 1880's—official government has been increasingly involved in providing organized, even institutionalized, assistance in realizing the goals of previously less-favored segments of the population, as well as in regulating or curbing the excesses of certain groups believed to be contrary to the general welfare. Financial rewards and distinctions are also provided by official agencies. In England the political organization confers social distinction in the form of titles of nobility.

There are times, however, when behind-the-scenes influence controls the direction and the means of official policy and action, as shown in the Teapot Dome and Sherman Adams scandals in the United States, the Dreyfus affair in France, etc. In democratic systems, backstage influence of this type is officially disapproved.

Open and legitimate influencing of goals and policies, on the other hand, is widely recognized as important for control in modern democratic societies, and the ability to wield influence is widely sought by individuals and organizations. Advertising is an attempt by business to influence choices of the public regarding competing products, processes, or services. Mass media of all types are used by the government itself, by political parties, religious organizations, regional groups, and other segments of the population to argue or suggest in favor of their favorite values and programs. Influence is eagerly sought, and it is evident today that access to the media of mass communication is essential. Although audience's attention may be attracted by promises of future rewards held out for some goal or program, lasting influence is usually established only by accomplishment—by demonstration that the proposal delivers satisfaction. Even so, the mass media are required to "spread the news" to the public. This is one reason, of course, why a fundamental feature of totalitarian systems is control (and censorship) of the media of mass communication.

One can understand that the human control of a modern sociocultural system is in itself a very complicated process, requiring intricate organization, with its accompanying bureaucracy and administrative experts, technologized equipment, and many specialists of skill and training. As control organizations, whether public or private (such as business concerns), grow in size the sheer weight of bureaucracy itself becomes an ever-present danger of breakdown for failure of coordination.

Weakness in Leadership

Complex modern control systems also need human *leadership*. From the present point of view the most important characteristic of a leader is that he or she is able to grasp certain vital aspirations of his people, suggest what seem to be feasible ways of fulfilling them, and symbolize these goals and programs in a way that wins the people's allegiance and active cooperation. This is not the same as being a good administrator; his function is to see that a program is carried out. Some leaders do manifest administrative talents, but not all.

In today's complex civilization few, if any, individuals can be effective national or international leaders on the basis of their own intelligence or personality alone. A modern leader on a national level requires not only the equipment and skills of the mass communications systems but also idea men, researchers to fill him in on details of fact, perhaps writers to polish his language, radio and television men to improve his pronunciation and appearance, and an office staff to handle the feedback, maintain files, handle correspondence. This is true not only of political leaders but also of any individual who deals *both* with goals and with programs for reaching them and who expects to have an impact—to exert wide influence—on the system as a whole. (Leaders of armed rebellions, in order to have any chance of success, also require experts in modern armaments, supply, tactics, strategy, military administration, and discipline.) I am speaking of leaders whose influence is system-wide, not of such figures as a leader in the development of sociological theory or a leader in modern chest surgery, whose followership is a restricted, specialized segment of the total system. National or international leadership thus tends to become bureaucratized itself, a fact that renders it slow and stiff in responding to changed situations—it takes time, effort, and usually money "just to get organized," even for leadership.

This type of leadership emphasizes the function of "progress" or "reform." Another function is that required by a complex system merely to maintain itself in a "steady state" of survival, in a world of internal and external stresses. This sort of thing is not primarily concerned with new goals or new ways of achieving them. It accepts the current basic or long-term goals (although in some cases without being too clear as to what they are or imply), but is required to make choices between available alternative ways of implementing them. This is variously described as the *decision-making* process or the *policy-making* process.

In contemporary national systems this function is reserved for employees of the national government. But who makes policy in a modern government? Who decides? In presidential systems, such as that of the United States and most Latin American republics, the president himself is officially charged with responsibility for national policy decisions. In parliamentary systems the cabinet members or a committee named from it jointly assume responsibility. Few presidents or cabinet committees, however, venture to make important policy decisions without "advice." When they make such choices "on their own" they are frequently wrong. But how can the necessary information concerning the area and problem at hand be gathered and properly analyzed in a form to be useful to the policy-makers? This problem has not been successfully solved in the United States, mainly because current policy officials do not see it as a problem. There is evidence that the Soviet Union has made considerable progress in this matter, which seems to be reflected in its more accurate predictions of reactions to its policies both inside and outside its borders. (Poland and Hungary, however, testify that Russia has not learned all the lessons.) Also to be considered is the subcultural backgrounds from which policy-makers come and which may naturally be expected to influence their attitudes and decisions. It has been cogently pointed out that most of the top policy-makers in the Eisenhower administration were men well past middle age who had come from Protestant middle- or upper-middle-class backgrounds in the Middle West and Eastern seaboard regions and whose judgments tended to conform thereto.

Major Valued Goals Lose Their Holding Power

We come to the end of this brief outline of "control" in modern sociocultural systems with mention of the cathexis, or drawing or holding power, of certain valued goals. Ideally the strong, basic goals of a system would hold the allegiance of the members in such a way that specialized structures of force, influence, leadership, and policy-making would not be required. Such an ideal state, however, is in the category of utopias. Modern complex systems present such a variety of goal-choices, situations, and patterns of action that automatic compliance cannot be expected with respect to all. Yet the strong probability remains—which needs to be more fully investigated—that certain traditional values are so deep-seated in the majority of the populace that they will continue to control opinion and activity regardless of special agencies of force or influence. Perhaps the goal (state of affairs) we call "freedom for the individual" is one of these? In Latin American countries *dignidad de la persona* (personal integrity or dignity) may be analogously controlling. Political and other control agencies may rephrase such basic values and may formulate new programs for achieving them, but they will have considerable difficulty in changing them fundamentally. We must also recognize that new values of similarly strong cathecting power may appear from time to time. One such value which has apparently taken root in Western Civilization within the last thirty years is labeled "security." Much debate goes on as to whether or to what extent "security" and "liberty" are compatible with each other in the same system.

It is for this type of fundamentally cathecting value that I postulate the majority of members of any given national system would fight, regardless of the application of force, irrespective of "publicity build-ups" by means of the mass communications media, impervious to other types of "influence," whatever the constituted policy-makers might say to the contrary. It is when a people loses faith in its deepest values, in this sense, that the ultimate disaster occurs to a sociocultural system. As an example of the holding power of basic values, one may consider Poland. It has been physically overrun, battered by military forces, administratively divided, and otherwise knocked about physically and organizationally for the past three hundred years. Yet the evidence to date indicates that the "core" of Polish culture—attachment to the basic values—has yet to be stamped out. The ultimate disaster has not yet occurred.

You will understand that I am passing no ultimate judgment regarding such values of sociocultural systems. I do not say, here at least, whether "freedom for the individual" or "security" as understood in the United States, or the "core" of Polish values, or any other set of basic cathecting goals of a sociocultural system are in the ultimate sense "right" or "wrong," "good" or "bad." But I do postulate that once the cathecting power of such goals has disappeared, a situation of disaster confronts a sociocultural system until or unless other values and goals are developed to take their place functionally in the "control" of the system. Thus "control" in the final sense, I hereby suggest, lies not in specialized agencies and their formulations and manipulations but in the traditionally ingrained values of the population, or at least of its majority segment.

On the basis of the foregoing rather elementary discussion, one may perhaps begin to see a variety of points in a modern complex sociocultural system which, in theory at least, may be attacked to bring about its collapse. I have postulated that the ultimate collapse of such a system will come when its basic, universal, cathecting values lose their holding power. But I have also tried to point out that such basic values and the goals to which they are attached are supported by the achievement of subgoals throughout the system and that malfunction involving any of the subgoals or the instrumentalities for reaching them may weaken the major goals and the values attached to them. In other words, a system theoretically can be "nibbled away" as well as struck down by major blows.

The elaboration of such theory, plus the analysis of practicalities deducible therefrom, awaits further publications. It is my hope that a considerable amount of our scientific talent will devote itself to these matters, before the "opposition" provides too many further surprises for the Free World.

Part Five

RESEARCH PROGRAMING

► *fourteen*

PREVENTING DISASTROUS BEHAVIOR

George W. Baker

General Interests in Disasters

Death, suffering, and destruction are ancient concomitants of disaster. In the past, man sometimes philosophically accepted such events and their human costs[1] in the belief that disasters were imposed by a supreme being as punishment for sinful behavior. Fortunately, this belief has changed in much of modern society.

Recent interest in the prediction and control of human behavior prior to, during, and after disastrous events is associated with a civilized desire to prevent or minimize unnecessary human suffering. Complementing this humane interest is the more abstract interest of scientists in acquiring basic knowledge about how individuals and social units function under diverse forms of disaster and other environmental stresses. Properly supported and directed, these scientific efforts could ultimately insure the attainment of a fair measure of prediction and control over behavior. When this is accomplished we will have the basis for achieving a significant reduction in those deaths and injuries which are caused by non-rational or inappropriate responses to a disastrous event. That some behavior is non-rational has been adequately demonstrated in almost every completed disaster study. Failure of individuals and groups to take prompt protective action as soon as a warning is received is one of the most obvious examples; failure of organizations to utilize the best available information, techniques, and procedures in the per-

[1] Some of the costs exacted by disasters were reviewed in the special issue of *The Annals* devoted to "Disasters and Disaster Relief" (1957).

formance of their disaster duties may also result in needless human and material losses.

Relatively recent developments have already provided some degree of control for two ancient causes of disaster, economic depressions and epidemic diseases. Modern economists, eschewing the outmoded theory that depressions periodically provide natural corrective action for some of society's ills, have promoted the adoption of programs for the control of depressions. Preventive medical programs, supported by both public and private funds, have succeeded in bringing disastrous epidemics under control in many countries. In the case of natural disasters, human costs are often a function of population size, location, and concentration, so we may assume that disaster damages will tend to increase with the present population expansion and the growth of urban centers. Yet research which could lead to the prevention of non-rational individual and group behavior before, during, and after a variety of other predictable disasters has not received comparable support and interest.

Study of Behavior in Disaster

The assumption that scientific principles can be applied advantageously to the prediction and control of behavior in disaster hardly needs to be demonstrated today. It follows from the theory that much of patterned behavior or culture is socially learned, socially shared, and socially modified (Gillin, 1948). Awareness of this principle was implicit in the request which the National Academy of Sciences–National Research Council received to initiate a disaster program. The request, like so many developments of the past two decades, came from the Department of Defense. The Department's interest was based upon the realization that if atomic weapons were employed against national societies, we would require considerable new planning information for managing behavior, and upon the assumption that the behavioral scientists could provide that information. An editorial in *Science* (DuShane, 1960) suggests that the present research program has achieved at least some small progress in reducing the human costs of natural disasters. The efficiency with which some four hundred thousand coastal residents of Texas and Louisiana were evacuated prior to the arrival of Hurricane Carla in September 1961 indicates recent improvements in the response of the public and disaster agencies to warnings.[2]

When we consider that individuals, groups, and societies have been subjected to a range of disastrous events—both natural and man-made—

[2] A detailed comparative study of this event is presently being conducted by F. L. Bates and H. E. Moore.

since the beginning of time, the relatively late sustained application of scientific principles to human behavior in disasters is somewhat surprising.[3] The lag cannot be explained on the grounds that our society was slow in developing a sense of responsibility for the consequences of disasters. Soon after the establishment of the Republic, the government began providing relief for disaster victims. By the middle of the twentieth century it could be said that there were "fully half a hundred Federal agencies, bureaus, and offices which have statutory responsibility for disaster assistance either under the provisions of the Federal Disaster Act or under other statutes . . ." (Keyser, 1959). These agencies generally have been charged with responsibility for rescuing disaster victims, providing for their immediate relief, aiding their recovery, restoring damaged public facilities, and developing plans for the control and management of future disastrous events.[4] But seldom have they directly employed and supported behavioral science research for the conceptualization and execution of their responsibilities. The Weather Bureau, the agency responsible for issuing natural disaster warnings, did not employ social scientists or support behavioral science programs as late as the spring of 1962. The charter of the American National Red Cross since 1905 has carried a responsibility for preventing disasters. Its present support of behavioral science research is largely limited to the analysis of its own organizational operations. Representatives of both

[3] While even a modestly sustained systematic application of the behavioral sciences to man-made and natural disasters did not begin until the 1950's, there were a few significant pioneering works prior to that date. William James's informal observations on the 1906 San Francisco earthquake were a first modest effort by a psychologist to observe post-impact behavior (James, 1911, Chapter 9). Samuel Prince's study of the 1917 Halifax disaster was more comprehensive and systematic (Prince, 1920). The real impetus to research came with the Depression of the early thirties and the second World War, when the challenges to understand and control behavior during periods of extreme national and international stress were most urgent. Inclusion of sections on disaster in recent social science texts—e.g., Loomis (1960), Merton and Nisbet (1961), Turner and Killian (1957)—reflects the growth of research interest in this general area. The section "Disaster and Disaster Relief" in the *Encyclopedia of the Social Sciences* (Brownlee, 1937) is of some historical interest, since it illustrates the stereotypes about behavior that existed in the professional literature some years ago.

[4] The difficulty of adhering to rational considerations during the rebuilding process has been amply demonstrated: homes that have been destroyed by volcanic eruptions are often rebuilt on their original sites, and the same type of construction is often repeated in the rebuilding of homes destroyed by hurricanes. One of the most recent illustrations of this practice was provided by the disaster that struck the eastern coast of the United States in the spring of 1962 (Fair-weather Island, 1962). The extent to which sentiment has dominated site and building design selection in disaster-prone areas is a question of more than academic interest to governmental and other agencies having some responsibility for assisting individuals and other units in the rebuilding process.

agencies have expressed interest in utilizing behavioral research findings.

There is a growing desire to gain control of disaster agents. One of the current publicly supported research programs is designed to attack natural disaster agents directly. An impressive program for achieving control of weather is now underway. Current annual budgets provide millions of dollars for these projects (Moffitt, 1962). While this work may yield useful basic and applied findings, there is no reason to assume that the societal wastes annually inflicted by natural disasters will be completely eliminated. Until they are eliminated we will have a need to minimize the kinds of behavior that add to disaster costs.

Aside from a desire to prevent or reduce suffering and an interest in the accumulation of basic knowledge, the application of physical and behavioral science resources to disaster phenomena is consistent with a national trend toward a "scientific society" (Seaborg, 1962). In some fields this trend has already attained the name, "big science" (Weinberg, 1962). We need to be reminded, however, that a heavy emphasis on science does not always insure a balanced effort. To employ Glenn T. Seaborg's words, society has "ingested science but it has not yet begun to digest and assimilate it." Robert Oppenheimer (1959) has commented on the need to change the general character of our social institutions to make them become capable of managing the vast challenges and threats presented by thermonuclear energy and other developments in the physical sciences. Fortunately, there is an increasing general awareness of the need to employ behavioral science more adequately in areas where it has been neglected or sparingly applied. A most timely review of this general problem has been provided by the Panel on Behavioral Science of the President's Science Advisory Committee (Strengthening . . . , 1962).

The suggestions offered by the contributors to *Man and Society in Disaster* for the further study of disaster behavior and other stressful experiences provide several bases for making improvements at each of the critical stages in the research process, including the utilization of research findings. The suggestions affect both basic and applied research interests.

Broadened Use of Behavioral Science

If thermonuclear war occurs, Ira Cisin has stated (Chapter 2), disaster research may represent the major contribution of the social sciences to societal survival. Similar comments have been heard as the tempo of national and international crises has accelerated during the last decade. During the November 1961 American Anthropological Association meeting a resolution was passed calling for the increased use of anthropology in programs bearing on international conflict.[5] The December 1961 meeting of the American Association for the Advancement of Science (Science . . . , 1961), revealed additional support for the use of behavioral science in insuring societal survival. While these announced objectives are most laudable, considerable disillusionment and waste of professional talent will be experienced unless planning is carefully conceived and executed (Greenberg, 1962).

In addition to these timely applied interests, a number of our contributors have noted that a disaster provides an especially useful opportunity for basic research in various aspects of personality, complex organization, and culture. Since ethical considerations do not permit research personnel to expose individuals and groups to extreme stress, a disaster provides a unique laboratory for studying some research problems which cannot be simulated under normal laboratory conditions.

Given that behavioral science can significantly contribute to the understanding and control of behavior during both natural and thermonuclear disasters, we are then faced with major problems of research design having various implications for policy and management. Since a variety of other programs impose heavy competing demands on our increasingly scarce manpower resources, we can no longer trust to chance that disaster research projects will ultimately develop in the time and manner desired. Nor can we assume that research findings will always be understood and used by agencies having disaster responsibilities. Fortunately the contributors to this volume have provided several specific research hypotheses and research planning suggestions for the guidance of future projects. I will briefly review and extend some of these ideas.

Changes in Disaster Research

It is clear that the definition of disaster and the manner in which research on this subject has been conducted should be significantly broadened. Further, we need to establish and utilize a typology of disaster events, preferably one that employs the performance characteristics of the disaster agent. Both of these needs are developed by Cisin and Barton (Chapters 2 and 8, respectively). Although we have hardly exhausted the possibilities for deriving new information from the study of natural disasters, other events and agents also present fruitful research opportunities. The false alert and the hoax enable us to sample and examine behavior during a period when there should be a recogni-

[5] Resolution Calling for Anthropological Contributions to the Search for Disarmament and Peace. American Anthropological Association, n.d.

tion of the possibility that disaster could occur.[6] Since the pre-impact period provides one of the most important opportunities for significantly reducing disaster casualties, the value of increased attention to this phase does not need further argument.

As Reuben Hill and Donald Hansen (Chapter 7) point out, economic depressions and individual family disasters offer useful opportunities for research that can establish how the family unit and its members respond to periods of extreme stress. Irving Janis' (Chapter 3) work on surgery patients and Robert Wilson's (Chapter 5) discussion of the links between mental health and disaster behavior identify additional research opportunities. While Harold Guetzkow's exploration of laboratory research for the study of disaster behavior (Chapter 11) underscores simulation difficulties, the contrived experiment is not completely ruled out. Bradford Hudson's earlier work (1954a) demonstrated some of its value.

Harold Guetzkow argues for the creation of trained and strategically placed research teams which would respond to field research opportunities before the disaster agent struck or while the event was still in progress. Given the increasing reliability which can be placed on the Weather Bureau warning service, this suggestion merits serious new consideration. The difficulties imposed by post-impact recall would be considerably relieved if this suggestion were adopted.

While some of the disasters that have been studied killed as many as four to five hundred people, injured hundreds more, and damaged property costing millions of dollars, these are still relatively small compared to a potential thermonuclear disaster. None that has been studied seriously crippled a major segment of our society for even a short period or posed long-range problems of adjustment and recovery for our major social institutions. In brief, while much of the existing information may be adequate for an understanding of individual and group behavior for the time periods covered, it does not tell us enough about a total society's response to a major disaster. Allen Barton has warned us (Chapter 8) against the hazard of extrapolating from the relatively small-scale disaster to a thermonuclear war.

At least three possibilities should be explored in order to reduce these deficiencies in our planning base. First, we must analyze further some of the relatively recent large-scale disasters in other societies (e.g., the 1960 earthquake in Chile). Second, we must immediately develop plans for studying future large-scale disasters. Third, we must conduct

[6] The value of focusing on this time period through the study of nondisastrous situations has recently been fairly satisfactorily established from analyses of false air-raid alerts (Mack and Baker, 1961). Cantril's contribution (1940) demonstrated the value of studying the hoax.

a detailed examination of the extent to which accumulated disaster findings can validly be applied to large-scale disasters. Some efforts in this direction have been made in this volume. However, the task of constructing and filling in a series of societal models for understanding, predicting, and controlling thermonuclear disaster behavior is enormous.

If disaster research planning is to be as sophisticated as planning in other areas, we must soon develop several flexible research designs for specific types of disasters. Designs and models should be supplemented by the creation of skeletal interview and questionnaire schedules and validated item banks. Market and public opinion research has demonstrated the utility of these general planning considerations. Since more than a hundred disasters have already been studied (Disaster Research Group, 1961), the research instruments and the findings from these past experiences give us a satisfactory base for starting this kind of planning. The desirability of employing other research techniques besides the interview must be given increased attention. Use of projective instruments and specific safeguards against interviewer bias should be more fully explored.

If we establish more useful definitions of disaster and increase the range of events studied, we will have added reason for reconsidering the analysis of completed studies. So far, as Ira Cisin has noted (Chapter 2), there has been an exclusive concern with behavior of individuals, social units, and organizations as the dependent variable. In some future studies, the disaster itself should be treated as the dependent variable and behavior as the independent one. One hypothesis affirms that behavior is associated with the victims' own definition of the disaster, as David Schneider (1957) demonstrated in his study of Yap. But whether this holds true in our own society has not been established, and the subject requires further exploration since it has a number of ramifications.

We must extend our studies of disaster significantly through time —to behavior before and after the impact of the disaster. We need, for specific social categories in our society (e.g., the aged, children, men, women), their pre-disaster definitions of what constitutes disaster and inventories of their levels of preparedness for meeting disaster. We will fill some important gaps in our present planning base if we can collect and analyze behavioral data prior to the occurrence of a disaster, and then study the same subjects after the event.

The reason for extending research interests well beyond the immediate recovery period is equally urgent. To date, we know of only two completed major longitudinal studies of disasters (Minetown Research Team, 1961; Bates, Fogelman, and Parenton, 1962). There has been a fair amount of speculation on the long-range traumatic effects of disaster on individuals, but we cannot move very far beyond the speculative stage until our research has been appreciably broadened.

More than a decade ago, Irving Janis (1951), employing a term from medical science, suggested the value of inoculation for controlling disaster behavior. While he has continued to work with this concept at the individual level, its usefulness for guiding the "work of worrying" of social units of varying size and composition has not been developed. Plans for large-scale disasters will not be complete until research has provided useful information for controlling those periods during which dysfunctional worrying can be predicted and appropriate preventive measures taken to reduce it to a satisfactory minimum. National concern about thermonuclear disaster should offer a tremendous challenge for the initiation of research projects which would contribute to the extension of Janis' concept to larger social units.

Numerous stereotypes about human behavior in disaster (e.g., panic and looting) were partly responsible for some of the early interest in a disaster research program (Fritz, 1961). Since the inception of the program the completion of numerous empirical studies has done much to reduce the effects of these stereotypes on professional thinking. In spite of the appearance of a few popular articles to the contrary (Collier, 1962), the average reader is still exposed, through journalistic accounts of disasters, to many of the ancient beliefs that much of disaster behavior is bizarre or antisocial. It is a fact that antisocial behavior does occur to some degree. The follow-up work that has been done on Hurricane Audrey (Bates, *et al.*, 1962) confirms that some post-disaster behavior is self-centered. This does not surprise any student of personality or society. The evidence does underscore the need to take a second look at some of our early impressions of post-impact behavior. A greater reliance on quantification techniques and the longitudinal approach will enable us to establish the incidence of such antisocial behavior, as well as the incidence of the more group- and community-oriented patterns. Beyond this we need to know something about the personality traits and environmental characteristics that are associated with the occurrences of each of these two extremes.

Since many of the recent formulations of behavior under stress have not been adequately validated, they too may be creating unreasonable planning expectations. Fritz's special use of "therapeutic community" and "disaster utopia" may be in this category. Robert Wilson's comments on "disaster utopia" (Chapter 5) generally discount the efficacy of this formulation. Wilson has reminded us again of the meaning of a basic and relevant concept, culture—the patterned behavior of a particular society. Disaster behavior in a given social unit is best predicted by an understanding of the norms and values which govern the group's behavior prior to the onset of disaster. Supplementing this basic fact, as Wilson does, with the concepts of competence and environmental mastery gives us additional understanding of behavior under extreme stress.

The study of human behavior in disaster has tended to proceed in a rather non-programatic fashion. The fact that scholars traditionally prefer to work on their own special and varying research interests contributes to a kind of anarchy in scientific work.

Some of the consequences of these problems become increasingly evident when the completed work is assessed. Hiram Friedsam has noted (Chapter 6) with some surprise that few of the past studies identified ages of the respondents. While family loyalties and the conflicts which they impose on individual members were established early as being important variables in disaster behavior, the accumulated knowledge about the family has been judged by Reuben Hill and Donald Hansen (Chapter 7) to be rather meager. As we move to a consideration of larger social units we are reminded by Allen Barton (Chapter 8) as well as James Thompson and Robert Hawkes (Chapter 9) that our knowledge of organizational behavior also remains quite inadequate. Thompson and Hawkes especially noted that we know very little about the secondary organizations which are called on during the course of a disaster to perform a variety of related functions. These contributors underscored the need to increase our verified knowledge about organizational phenomena in order to rationalize and integrate competing and conflicting behavior.

The implication of this volume is that we must now program and manage the study of human behavior in disaster so that the verified knowledge essential for the prediction and control of disaster behavior can be accumulated as quickly as possible. This will involve extensive research efforts focused on discrete units, e.g., the young, the aged, families, and disaster organizations. Clearly we will not be starting from scratch in any one of these areas. The contributors to this volume alone have formulated many hypotheses for testing. We already have several models which could be examined during the course of some subsequent field and laboratory studies. The new model developed by Thompson and Hawkes on organizational behavior is especially promising. Earlier models by Harry Williams on communication behavior (1956), by Leonard Schatzman on sequence patterns (1960), as well as the two analyzed by Dwight Chapman (Chapter 10), deserve special emphasis in future empirical work.

Finally, the value of encouraging additional cross-cultural research should be underscored for its theoretical as well as practical advantages. Surprisingly few studies of disaster have been conducted outside of the United States (Disaster Research Group, 1961). Those that have been done offer considerable support for increased emphasis on conducting research beyond our own national borders.[7] The fact that the United States is playing an increasingly large international role adds to our need to learn about disaster behavior in other societies.

Implications for Policy and Management

In the earlier chapters as well as the present one some ideas have emerged with a fair amount of clarity. They have implications for both applied and basic research.

First, human behavior during periods of extreme stress can be profitably studied at the individual, group, and organizational levels.

Second, such work can be rewarding for the behavioral scholar who is interested in accumulating basic knowledge, and for the scholar or planner who is interested in applying this knowledge to individual and social aspects of disaster behavior.[8]

Third, the responsible federal agencies may not have recognized fully the extent to which some dysfunctional aspects of disaster behavior can be predicted and modified; if this is true, their effectiveness in reducing the human costs of disaster can be increased through greater emphasis on research and the application of its findings.

Fourth, disaster research has developed to the point that a fair amount of selective management by mature and perceptive scholars is essential if we are to proceed beyond the "interesting hypothesis" stage.

Fifth, it is clear that our understanding of our own national society and its culture is by no means complete. Much additional work on natural disaster behavior as well as normal behavior needs to be carefully planned and executed if we are to derive a reasonably satisfactory basis for large-scale disaster planning. The full development of the theoretically interesting and awesome idea of "induced sociocultural collapse," suggested by John Gillin (Chapter 13) is contingent upon the completion of more studies of society in and out of disaster.

Sixth, while some studies of disaster behavior have been initiated

[7] Clifford's (1956) study of the Texan and Mexican communities and David Schneider's (1957) study of Yap provide good examples of the kinds of useful information which can be derived from such studies. Tyhurst's (1957) comment on the neglect of ritual in our society offers a suggestion of the kind we might want to investigate for its possible value for managing our own disaster behavior.

[8] There is some evidence which suggests that the invidious distinction between basic and applied research may be disappearing. Robert Merton's (1961) recent discussion, "Social Problems and Sociological Theory," in *Contemporary Social Problems* helps to clarify the contributions made by both basic and applied research.

independent of the Disaster Research Group (projects at Michigan State University and the University of Texas represent notable examples), the major responsibility for the development and continuation of the research program has resided within the Group. For a number of reasons, broad participation by both public and private research agencies in this area is desirable. The position of the program within its parent organization, as well as the larger research community, would be improved if the behavioral sciences were to be included in the National Academy of Sciences–National Research Council (Strengthening . . . , 1962).

Finally, while we have no immediate hope or belief that all dysfunctional human behavior in disaster can be prevented, we are confident that much of it can be reduced if research resources are imaginatively, consistently, and adequately employed. The recent panel on behavioral science (Strengthening . . . , 1962) invited behavioral scientists to be less modest in the development of research plans. The disaster research program is one area where rapid strides can be made if this advice is followed.

In view of these several considerations, two recommendations are offered. First, since disaster research may properly be considered a part of a larger program of research on behavior under stress, studies of disastrous events should be added to some of the intramural and extramural behavioral research programs of several federal and private agencies. Second, an organizational arrangement should be established to insure (a) that personnel who direct and conduct research on human behavior in stress are cognizant of the operational needs of all agencies having disaster functions, and (b) that relevant new research findings are promptly transmitted and explained to each of the planning and operational disaster agencies. In such diverse areas as public health and atomic energy a combination of support, research talent, and organizational skill have produced dramatic societal changes during the past twenty years. If carefully programed research is similarly developed to study natural and man-made disasters, we can expect equally dramatic benefits for our society.

BIBLIOGRAPHY

ALLPORT, G. W. The historical background of modern social psychology. In G. Lindzey (ed.), *Handbook of social psychology*. Cambridge, Mass.: Addison-Wesley, 1954.

ALLPORT, G. W., & POSTMAN, L. *The psychology of rumor*. New York: Holt, 1947.

AMERICAN RED CROSS. *The Mississippi Valley flood disaster of 1927*. Washington: American Red Cross, 1928.

———. *The Ohio-Mississippi flood disaster of 1937*. Washington: American Red Cross, 1938.

ANGELL, R. C. *The family encounters the depression.* New York: Scribner's, 1936.

ASHBY, W. R. *Design for a brain.* New York: Wiley, 1952.

BACKMAN, E. L. *Religious dances.* Trans. by E. Classen. London: Allen & Unwin, 1952.

BAKER, G. W., & ROHRER, J. H. (eds.) *Human problems in the utilization of Fall-out shelters.* Disaster Study Number 12. Washington: National Academy of Sciences–National Research Council, 1960.

BAKST, H. J., BERG, R. L., FOSTER, F. D., & RAKER, J. W. *The Worcester County tornado—a medical study of the disaster*. Washington: National Academy of Sciences–National Research Council, 1955.

BALLOCH, J. Some psychological aspects of disaster studies. Paper read at Richmond Psychological Assn., Richmond, Virginia, September, 1953.

———, BRASWELL, L. R., RAYNER, JEANNETTE F., & KILLIAN, L. M. Studies of military assistance in civilian disasters: England and the United States. Unpublished report, Committee on Disaster Studies, National Academy of Sciences–National Research Council, 1953.

BASOWITZ, H., PERSKY, H., KORCHIN, S. V., & GRINKER, R. R. *Anxiety and stress.* New York: McGraw-Hill, 1955.

BATES, F. L., FOGELMAN, C. W., & PARENTON, V. J. The social and psychological consequences of a natural disaster. Unpublished manuscript, Disaster Research Group, National Academy of Sciences–National Research Council, 1962.

BEACH, H. D., & LUCAS, R. A. (eds.) *Individual and group behavior in a coal mine disaster.* Disaster Study Number 13. Washington: National Academy of Sciences–National Research Council, 1960.

BERKUN, M. M., *et al. Human psychophysiological response to stress: successful experimental simulation of real-life stresses.* Washington: Human Resources Research Office, research memo. Task FIGHTER, 1959.

BERNERT, ELEANOR H., & IKLÉ, F. C. Evacuation and the cohesion of urban groups. *Amer. J. Sociol.*, 1952, *58*, 133-138.

BERNSTEIN, S., & SMALL, S. Psychodynamic factors in surgery. *J. Mt. Sinai Hosp.*, 1951, *17*, 938-958.

BERTALANFFY, L. V. The theory of open systems in physics and biology. *Science*, 1950, *3*, 23-28.

BETTELHEIM, B. Individual and mass behavior in extreme situations. *J. abnorm. soc. Psychol.*, 1943, *38*, 417-452.

BIDERMAN, A. D. The relevance of studies of internment for the problem of shelter habitability. Appendix A of *An analysis of several surveys relative to problems of shelter habitability.* Working paper. Washington: National Academy of Sciences–National Research Council, Disaster Research Group, 1960.

BLUM, R. H., & KLASS, B. *A study of public response to disaster warnings.* Menlo Park, Calif.: Stanford Research Institute, 1956.

BORING, E. G. *A history of experimental psychology.* New York: Appleton-Century, 1929.

BOWLBY, J. *Maternal care and mental health.* Geneva: World Health Organization, 1952.

BROWNLEE, ALETA. Disaster and disaster relief. *Encyclopedia of the social sciences.* 1937, *5*, 161-166.

BROZEK, J., GUETZKOW, H., & BALDWIN, M. V. A quantitative study of perception and association in experimental semistarvation. *J. Pers.*, 1951, *19*, 245-264.

BRUNER, J. S. Personality dynamics and the process of perceiving. In R. R. Blake & G. V. Ramsey (eds.), *Perception: an approach to personality.* New York: Ronald Press, 1951.

BUCHER, RUE. Blame and hostility in disaster. *Amer. J. Sociol.*, 1957, *62*, 467-475.

BURNS, A. F. Progress towards economic stability. *Amer. econ. Rev.*, 1960, *50* (1), 1-19.

CAMPBELL, D. T. Factors relevant to the validity of experiments in social settings. *Psychol. Bull.*, 1957, *54*, 297-312.

———. Quasi-experimental designs for use in natural social settings. Unpublished manuscript, Department of Psychology, Northwestern University, 1960.

CANTRIL, H. *The invasion from Mars: a study in the psychology of panic.* Princeton, N. J.: Princeton University Press, 1940.

CARTWRIGHT, D., & ZANDER, A. Origins of group dynamics. In D. Cartwright & A. Zander (eds.), *Group dynamics: research and theory.* Evanston, Ill.: Row, Peterson, 1960.

CAUDILL, W. *Effects of social and cultural systems in reactions to stress.* New York: Social Science Research Council, 1958.

CAVAN, RUTH S. Unemployment—crisis of the common man. *Marriage fam. Living*, 1959, *21*, 139-146.

———, & RANCK, K. H. *The family and the depression.* Chicago: University of Chicago Press, 1938.

CHAPMAN, R. L., KENNEDY, J. L., NEWELL, A., & BIEL, W. C. The Systems Research Laboratory's air defense experiments. *Mgmt. Sci.*, 1959, *5*, 250-269.

Civil defense is possible. *Fortune*, December, 1958, *58*, 98-101+.

Clausen, J. A., & Yarrow, Marian R. (eds.), The impact of mental illness on the family. *J. soc. Issues,* 1955, *11* (4), whole issue.

Clifford, R. A. *The Rio Grande flood: a comparative study of border communities in disaster.* Disaster Study Number 7. Washington: National Academy of Sciences–National Research Council, 1956.

Cohn, N. *The pursuit of the millennium.* London: Secker & Warburg, 1957.

Coleman, J. S. Analysis of social structures and simulation of social processes with electronic computers. Working Paper Number 4, Department of Social Relations, Johns Hopkins University, 1960.

Collier, J. How would you act in a disaster? *Pageant,* 1962, *17* (8), 6-14.

Conference on theories of human behavior in extreme situations, February 12-13, 1955, Poughkeepsie, New York. Unpublished minutes, Committee on Disaster Studies, National Academy of Sciences–National Research Council, 1955.

Coser, L. *The functions of social conflict.* Glencoe, Ill.: Free Press, 1956.

Crane, B. G. Intergovernmental relations in disaster relief in Texas. Unpublished doctoral dissertation, University of Texas, 1960.

Crawford, F. R. Application of extra-community legal norms in a disaster situation. Paper read at American Sociological Assn., Washington, September, 1955.

———. Patterns of family readjustments to tornado disasters. Unpublished doctoral dissertation, University of Texas, 1957.

Danzig, E. R., Thayer, P. W., & Galanter, Lila R. *The effects of a threatening rumor on a disaster-stricken community.* Disaster Study Number 10. Washington: National Academy of Sciences–National Research Council, 1958.

De Fleur, M., & Larsen, O. N. *The flow of information.* New York: Harper, 1956.

Defoe, D. *A journal of the plague year.* London: Routledge, 1884.

Demerath, N. J. Some general propositions: an interpretative summary. *Hum. Organization,* 1957, *16* (2), 28-29.

Deutsch, K. W. *Nationalism and social communication.* New York: Wiley, 1953.

Diggory, J. C. Some consequences of proximity to disease threat. *Sociometry,* 1956, *19,* 47-53.

Disaster Research Group. *Field studies of disaster behavior: an inventory.* Disaster Study Number 14. Washington: National Academy of Sciences–National Research Council, 1961.

Disasters and disaster relief. *Ann. Amer. Acad. Pol. Soc. Sci.,* 1957, *309.*

Dodd, S. C. Formulas for spreading opinions. *Publ. opin. Quart.,* 1958-1959, *22,* 537-554.

Douvan, E., & Withey, S. B. *The impact of atomic energy on society: an investigation of attitudes and their determinants.* Ann Arbor: University of Michigan Survey Research Center, 1953.

Drayer, C. W. Psychological factors and problems, emergency and long-term. *Ann. Amer. Acad. Pol. Soc. Sci.,* January, 1957, *309,* 151-159.

Dulles, F. R. *The American Red Cross: a history.* New York: Harper, 1950.

DuShane, G. Donna. *Science,* 1960, *132* (3432), 923.

Eaton, J., & Weil, R. *Culture and mental disorders.* Glencoe, Ill.: Free Press, 1955.

Edwards, D., & Williams, T. D. *The great famine.* Dublin: Browne & Nolan, 1956.

Eisenberg, P., & Lazarsfeld, P. F. The psychological effects of unemployment. *Psychol. Bull.,* 1938, *35,* 358-390.

Ellemers, J. E. General conclusions. In Instituut voor Sociaal Onderzoek van het Nederlandse Volk, *Studies in Holland flood disaster 1953,* Vol. 4. Washington: National Academy of Sciences–National Research Council, Committee on Disaster Studies, 1955.

Ellemers, J. E., & in 't Veld-Langeveld, H. M. A study of the destruction of a community. In Instituut voor Sociaal Onderzoek van het Nederlandse Volk, *Studies in Holland flood disaster 1953,* Vol. 3. Washington: National Academy of Sciences-National Research Council, Committee on Disaster Studies, 1955.

Eriksen, C. W., & Wechsler, H. Some effects of experimentally induced anxiety upon discrimination behavior, *J. abnorm. soc. Psychol.,* 1955, *51,* 458-463.

Fair-weather island. *Washington Post,* April 23, 1962, p. A10.

Festinger, L. *A theory of cognitive dissonance.* Evanston, Ill.: Row, Peterson, 1957.

Fogleman, C. W. Family and community in disaster. Unpublished doctoral dissertation, Louisiana State University, 1958.

———, & Parenton, V. J. Disaster and aftermath: selected aspects of individual and group behavior in critical situations. *Soc. Forces,* 1959, *38,* 129-135.

Foley, A. S. The Lower Cameron Parish community: June to September 1957. Unpublished report, Disaster Research Group, National Academy of Sciences-National Research Council, 1957. (For official use only.)

Foreman, P. B. Panic theory. *Sociol. soc. Res.,* 1953, *37,* 295-304.

Form, W. H., & Loomis, C. P. The persistence and emergence of social and cultural systems in disasters. *Amer. sociol. Rev.,* 1956, *21,* 180-185.

———, & Nosow, S. *Community in disaster.* New York: Harper, 1958.

———, Nosow, S., Stone, G. P., & Westie, C. M. Final report on the Flint-Beecher tornado. Unpublished report, Social Research Service, Michigan State College, 1954.

Fothergill, J. E., & Lamberth, D. L. *Recruitment to the civil defense services.* Nova Scotia: Central Office of Information, Social Survey, 1950.

Fraser, R., Leslie, I., & Phelps, D. Psychiatric effects of severe personal experiences during bombing. *Proc. Royal Soc. Med.,* 1943, *36,* 119-123.

Freeman, C. D., & Cooper, D. *The road to Bordeaux.* London: Cresset Press, 1940.

Freeman, F. H., & Fenn, W. O. Changes in carbon dioxide stores of rate due to atmospheres low in oxygen or high in carbon dioxide. *Amer. J. Physiol.,* 1953, *174,* 422-430.

French, J. R. P. Organized and unorganized groups under fear and frustration. *Univ. Iowa Stud. child Welf.,* 1944, *20,* 229-308.

Freud, Anna. *Ego and mechanisms of defense.* New York: International Universities Press, 1946.

———, & Burlingham, D. *War and children.* New York: Medical War Books, 1943.

Freud, S. *The problem of anxiety.* Trans. by H. A. Bunker. New York: Norton, 1936.

Friedman, P. *Their brothers' keepers.* New York: Crown, 1957.

Friedsam, H. J. Memorandum on formal organizations in Hurricane Audrey. Unpublished report, Disaster Research Group, National Academy of Sciences-National Research Council, 1957 (a). (For official use only.)

———, Memorandum on social status as a problem in Civil Defense organization. Unpublished report, Committee on Disaster Studies, National Academy of Sciences–National Research Council, 1957 (b).

Fritz, C. E. The therapeutic features of disaster and the effects on family adjustment: some research orientations. Paper read at Groves Conference on Marriage and the Family, Washington, April, 1958.

———. Disaster. In R. K. Merton and R. A. Nisbet (eds.), *Contemporary social problems.* New York: Harcourt, 1961.

———, & Marks, E. S. The NORC studies of human behavior in disaster. *J. soc. issues,* 1954, *10* (3), 26-41.

———, & Mathewson, J. H. *Convergence behavior in disasters: a problem in social control.* Disaster Study Number 9. Washington: National Academy of Sciences–National Research Council, 1957.

———, & Williams, H. B. The human being in disasters: a research perspective. *Ann. Amer. Acad. Pol. Soc. Sci.,* January, 1957, *309,* 42-51.

Funkenstein, D. H., King, S. H., & Drolette, Margaret E. *Mastery of stress.* Cambridge, Mass.: Harvard University Press, 1957.

Galbraith, J. K. *The great crash: 1929.* Boston: Houghton Mifflin, 1955.

Galdston, I. Résumé: looking backward and ahead. In I. Galdston (ed.), *Panic and morale.* New York: International Universities Press, 1958.

Garner, H. Psychiatric casualties in combat. *War Med.,* 1945, *8,* 343-357.

Geiger, K. Deprivation and solidarity in the Soviet urban family. *Amer. sociol. Rev.,* 1955, *20,* 57-68.

Gillin, J. *The ways of men.* New York: Appleton-Century, 1948.

Glass, A. J. *Psychological considerations in atomic warfare.* Washington: Walter Reed Army Medical Center, Management of Mass Casualties, No. 560, 1955.

Glover, E. *The psychology of fear and courage.* New York: Penguin, 1940.

———. Notes on the psychological effects of war conditions on the civil population: Part III, the blitz. *Int. J. Psycho-anal.,* 1942, *23,* 17-37.

Green, J. B., & Logan, L. *The South Amboy disaster.* Chevy Chase, Md.: Operations Research Office, 1950.

Greenberg, D. S. "Science of Survival": founding meeting proceeds in confusion and ends in bitterness, chaos. *Science,* 1962, *136,* 1041-1042.

Grieve, Hilda. *The great tide: the story of the 1953 flood disaster in Essex.* Chelmsford, England: County Council of Essex, 1959.

Grinker, R. R., & Spiegel, J. P. *Men under stress.* New York: Blakiston, 1945.

Group for the Advancement of Psychiatry. *Some observations on controls in psychiatric research.* New York: Group for the Advancement of Psychiatry, 1959.

Guetzkow, H. Interaction between methods and models in social psychology. In R. Glaser *et al., Current trends in the description and analysis of behavior.* Pittsburgh: University of Pittsburgh Press, 1958.

——— (ed.). *Simulation in social science.* Englewood Cliffs, N. J.: Prentice-Hall, 1962.

Hamburg, D. A., Hamburg, Beatrix, & de Goza, S. Adaptive problems and mechanisms in severely burned patients. *Psychiatry,* 1953, *16* (1), 1-20.

Hamilton, R. V., Taylor, R. M., & Rice, G. E., Jr. *A social psychological interpretation of the Udall, Kansas, tornado.* Wichita, Kansas: University of Wichita, 1955.

Hanson, R. C. Predicting a community decision: a test of the Miller-Form theory. *Amer. sociol. Rev.,* 1959, *24,* 662-671.

Harrer, H. *Seven years in Tibet.* London: Rupert Hart-Davis, 1953.

Haveman, J. Introduction. In Instituut voor Sociaal Onderzoek van het Nederlandse Volk, *Studies in Holland flood disaster 1953,* Vol. 1. Washington: National Academy of Sciences–National Research Council, Committee on Disaster Studies, 1955.

HAWKES, R. W. The role of the psychiatric administrator. *Admin. sci. Quart.*, 1961, *6*, 89-106.

HEBB, D. O. *The organization of behavior: a neuropsychological theory.* New York: Wiley, 1949.

HENRY, W. E. Affective complexity and role perceptions: some suggestions for a conceptual framework for the study of adult personality. In J. E. Anderson (ed.), *Psychological aspects of aging.* Washington: American Psychological Association, 1956.

———, & CUMMING, ELAINE. Personality development in adulthood and old age. *J. proj. Tech.*, 1959, *23*, 383-390.

HERSEY, J. *Hiroshima.* New York: Knopf, 1946.

HILL, R., & BOULDING, ELSIE. *Families under stress.* New York: Harper, 1949.

HINKLE, L. E., JR., & WOLFF, H. G. Health and social environment: experimental investigations. In A. H. Leighton, J. A. Clausen, & R. N. Wilson (eds.), *Explorations in social psychiatry.* New York: Basic Books, 1957.

HIRSHLEIFER, J. Some thoughts on the social structure after a bombing disaster. *World Politics*, 1956, *8*, 206-227.

HO, P. *Studies on the population of China, 1368-1953.* Cambridge, Mass.: Harvard University Press, 1959.

HOFFER, E. *The true believer.* New York: Harper, 1951.

HOGAN, R. A. A theory of threat and defense. *J. consult. Psychol.*, 1952, *16*, 417-424.

HOLLINGSHEAD, A. B., & REDLICH, F. C. *Social class and mental illness.* New York: Wiley, 1958.

HOLTZMAN, W. H., & BITTERMAN, M.E. A factorial study of adjustment to stress. *J. abnorm. soc. Psychol.*, 1956, *52*, 179-185.

HORVATH, F. E. Psychological stress: a review of definitions and experimental research. *General Systems*, 1959, *4*, 203-230.

HOVLAND, C. I., & JANIS, I. L. (eds.), *Yale studies in attitude and communication:* Vol. 2, *Personality and persuasibility.* New Haven, Conn.: Yale University Press, 1959.

———, JANIS, I. L., & KELLEY, H. H. *Communication and persuasion.* New Haven, Conn.: Yale University Press, 1953.

HSU, F. L. K. *Religion, science, and human crises.* London: Routledge, 1952.

HUDSON, B. B. Anxiety in response to the unfamiliar. *J. soc. Issues*, 1954 (a), *10*, (3), 53-60.

———. *Perception of threat in relation to anxiety.* Houston, Texas: Rice Institute, 1954 (b).

———. *Observations in a community during a flood.* Houston, Texas: Rice Institute, n.d.

IDLE, E. DOREEN. *War over West Ham.* London: Faber & Faber, 1943.

IKLÉ, F. C. The effect of war destruction upon the ecology of cities. *Soc. Forces*, 1951, *29*, 383-391.

———. The social versus the physical effects from nuclear bombing. *Scient. Amer.*, 1954, *78* (3), 182-187.

———. *The social impact of bomb destruction.* Norman: University of Oklahoma Press, 1958.

Instituut voor Sociaal Onderzoek van het Nederlandse Volk. *Studies in Holland flood disaster 1953.* Washington: National Academy of Sciences–National Research Council, Committee on Disaster Studies, 1955. 4 vols.

IWAŃSKA, ALICJA. Values in crisis situation. Ann Arbor, Mich.: University Microfilms, 1957.

JAMES, W. *Memories and studies.* New York: Longmans, Green, 1911.

JANIS, I. L. *Air war and emotional stress: psychological studies of bombing and civilian defense.* New York: McGraw-Hill, 1951.

———. Problems of theory in the analysis of stress behavior. *J. soc. Issues,* 1954, *10* (3), 12-25.

———. Emotional inoculation: theory and research on effects of preparatory communications. In W. Muensterberger & S. Axelrad (eds.), *Psychoanalysis and the social sciences,* Vol. 5. New York: International Universities Press, 1958 (a).

———. *Psychological stress.* New York: Wiley, 1958 (b).

———. Psychological aspects of decisional conflicts. In M. Jones (ed.), *Nebraska symposium on motivation 1959.* Lincoln: University of Nebraska Press, 1959.

———. *Fear and adjustment mechanisms: psychological studies of war, disaster, and the threat of disease.* New York: Wiley, in press.

———, CHAPMAN, D. W., GILLIN, J. P., & SPIEGEL, J. P. *The problem of panic.* Washington: Fed. Civil Defense Admin. Bull. TB-19-2, 1955.

———, & FESHBACH, S. Effects of fear-arousing communications. *J. abnorm. soc. Psychol.,* 1953, *48,* 78-92.

———, & FESHBACH, S. Personality differences associated with responsiveness to fear-arousing communications. *J. Pers.,* 1954, *23,* 154-166.

JONES, M. *The therapeutic community.* New York: Basic Books, 1953.

KALMANOVITCH, Z. A diary of the Nazi ghetto in Vilna. *Yivo Annu. Jewish soc. Sci.,* 1953, *8,* 9-81.

KARDINER, A. Traumatic neuroses of war. In S. Arieti (ed.), *American handbook of psychiatry,* Vol. 1. New York: Basic Books, 1959.

KATZ, E., KESSIN, K., MCCOY, J., PINTO, L. J., & STRIEBY, R. Public reaction to the unscheduled sounding of air-raid sirens in a metropolis: a first glance at the data. In G. W. Baker & J. H. Rohrer (eds.), *Human problems in the utilization of fallout shelters.* Disaster Study Number 12. Washington: National Academy of Sciences–National Research Council, 1960.

KENDRICK, T. D. *The Lisbon earthquake.* Philadelphia: Lippincott, 1957.

KENNEDY, J. L. A "transition-model" laboratory for research on cultural change. *Hum. Organization,* 1955, *14* (3), 16-18.

KEYS, A., BROZEK, J., HENSCHEL, A., MICHELSEN, O., & TAYLOR, H. L. *The biology of human starvation.* Minneapolis: University of Minnesota Press, 1950.

KEYSER, C. F. *Federal disaster relief manual.* Prepared for the Committee on Government Operations, U. S. Senate. Washington: United States Government Printing Office, 1959.

KILLIAN, L. M. The significance of multiple-group membership in disaster. *Amer. J. Sociol.,* 1952, *57,* 309-314.

———. *Evacuation of Panama City before Hurricane Florence.* Washington: National Academy of Sciences–National Research Council, Committee on Disaster Studies, 1954 (a).

———. Some accomplishments and some needs in disaster study. *J. soc. Issues,* 1954 (b), *10* (3), 66-72.

———. *A study of response to the Houston, Texas, fireworks explosion.* Disaster Study Number 2. Washington: National Academy of Sciences–National Research Council, 1956 (a).

———. *An introduction to methodological problems of field studies in disasters.* Disaster Study Number 8. Washington: National Academy of Sciences–National Research Council, 1956 (b).

KILLIAN, L. M., & RAYNER, JEANNETTE F. *An assessment of disaster operations following the Warner Robins tornado.* Washington: National Academy of Sciences–National Research Council, Committee on Disaster Studies, 1953.

KLAUSNER, S. Z., & KINCAID, H. V. *Social problems of sheltering flood evacuees.* New York: Columbia University Bureau of Applied Social Research, 1956.

KOMAROVSKY, M. *The unemployed man and his family.* New York: Dryden Press, 1940.

KOOS, E. *Families in trouble.* New York: King's Crown Press, 1946.

KORNHAUSER, W. *The politics of mass society.* Glencoe, Ill.: Free Press, 1959.

KRIS, E. Morale in Germany. *Amer. J. Sociol.*, 1941, *47*, 452-461.

KUHLEN, R. G. Changing personal adjustment during the adult years. In J. E. Anderson (ed.), *Psychological aspects of aging.* Washington: American Psychological Association, 1956.

LAMMERS, C. J. Survey of evacuation problems and disaster experiences. In Instituut voor Sociaal Onderzoek van het Nederlandse Volk, *Studies in Holland flood disaster 1953*, Vol. 2. Washington: National Academy of Sciences–National Research Council, Committee on Disaster Studies, 1955.

LAZARUS, R., DEESE, J., & OSLER, S. F. The effects of psychological stress upon performance. *Psycho. Bull.*, 1952, *49*, 293-315.

LEACH, E. R. *Political systems in Wighand Burma.* Cambridge, Mass.: Harvard University Press, 1954.

LECKY, P. *Self-consistency.* New York: Island Press, 1951.

LEIGHTON, A. H. *My name is legion: foundations for a theory of man in relation to culture.* New York: Basic Books, 1959.

———, CLAUSEN, J. A., & WILSON, R. N. (eds.). *Explorations in social psychiatry.* New York: Basic Books, 1959.

LEMONS, H. Physical characteristics of disasters: historical and statistical review. *Ann. Amer. Acad. Pol. Soc. Sci.*, January, 1957, *309*, 1-14.

LEVENTHAL, H., CARRIGER, BARBARA K., HOCHBAUM, G. M., & ROSENSTOCK, I. M. Epidemic impact on the general population in two cities. In I. M. Rosenstock, G. M. Hochbaum, & H. Leventhal, *et al.*, *The impact of Asian influenza on community life.* Washington: Department of Health, Education, and Welfare, Public Health Service, 1960.

LEWIN, K. Frontiers in group dynamics. *Hum. Relat.*, 1947, *1*, 143-153.

———. *Field theory in social science.* New York: Harper, 1951.

LIKERT, R. A motivational approach to a modified theory of organization and management. In M. Haire (ed.), *Modern organization theory.* New York: Wiley, 1959.

LINDEMANN, E. Observations on psychiatric sequelae to surgical operations in women. *Amer. J. Psychiat.*, 1941, *98*, 132-139.

———. Symptomatology and management of acute grief. *Amer. J. Psychiat.*, 1944, *101*, 141-148.

LINTON, R. Age and sex categories. *Amer. sociol. Rev.*, 1942, 7, 589-603.

———. The natural history of the family. In Ruth Nanda Anshen (ed.), *The family: its functions and destiny.* New York: Harper, 1949.

LITWAK, E. Geographic mobility and extended family cohesion. *Amer. sociol. Rev.*, 1960 (a), *25*, 385-394.

———. Occupational mobility and extended family cohesion. *Amer. sociol. Rev.*, 1960 (b), *25*, 9-12.

LIVINGSTON, L., KLASS, B., & ROHRER, J. *Operations Walkout, Rideout, and Scat.*

Washington: National Academy of Sciences–National Research Council, Committee on Disaster Studies, 1954.

Logan, L., Killian, L. M., & Marrs, W. *A study of the effect of catastrophe on social disorganization.* Chevy Chase, Md.: Operations Research Office, 1952.

The London Times Literary Supplement, November 6, 1959.

Loomis, C. P. Social systems under stress: disasters and disruption. Paper read at Groves Conference on Marriage and the Family, Washington, April, 1958.

———. *Social systems: essays on their persistence and change.* New York: Van Nostrand, 1960.

Luria, A. R. *The nature of human conflicts.* New York: Liveright, 1932.

MacCurdy, J. T. *The structure of morale.* New York: Macmillan, 1943.

McGregor, D. The major determinants of the prediction of social events. *J. abnorm. soc. Psychol.,* 1938, *33,* 179-204.

Machlup, F. Statics and dynamics: kaleidoscopic words. *Southern J. Econ.,* 1959, *36,* 91-110.

Mack, R. W., & Baker, G. W. *The occasion instant: the structure of social responses to unanticipated air raid warnings.* Disaster Study Number 15. Washington: National Academy of Sciences–National Research Council, 1961.

Malcolm, D. G. (ed.). *Report of system simulation symposium.* New York: American Institute of Industrial Engineers, 1958.

March, J. G., & Simon, H. A. *Organizations.* New York: Wiley, 1958.

Marks, E. S., & Fritz, C. E. Human reactions in disaster situations (3 vols.). Unpublished report, National Opinion Research Center, 1954.

Marks, R. W. The effect of probability, desirability, and "privilege" on the stated expectations of children. *J. Pers.,* 1951, *19,* 332-351.

Massoti, L. H. Disaster variable index. Unpublished manuscript, Department of Psychology, Northwestern University, 1960.

Meerloo, J. A. M. People's reaction to danger. In I. Galdston (ed.), *Panic and morale.* New York: International Universities Press, 1958.

Menninger, K. A. Psychological aspects of the organism under stress. *J. Amer. Psychoanal. Assn.,* 1954 (a), *2,* 67-104, 280-309.

———. Regulatory devices of the ego under major stress. *Int. J. Psycho-Anal.,* 1954 (b), *35,* 412-420.

Menninger, W. C. Psychological reactions in an emergency (flood). *Amer. J. Psychiat.,* 1952, *109,* 128-130.

Merton, R. K. *Social theory and social structure* (rev. and enlarged ed.). Glencoe, Ill.: Free Press, 1957.

———. Social problems and sociological theory. In R. K. Merton and R. A. Nisbet (eds.), *Contemporary social problems.* New York: Harcourt, 1961.

———, & Kitt, Alice S. Contributions to the theory of reference group behavior. In R. K. Merton & P. F. Lazarsfeld (eds.), *Continuities in social research: studies in the scope and method of "The American soldier."* Glencoe, Ill.: Free Press, 1950.

———, and Nisbet, R. A. (eds.). *Contemporary social problems.* New York: Harcourt, 1961.

Meyner doubtful on shelter plans. *New York Times,* March 20, 1960, p. 50.

Miller, D. C. The prediction of issue outcome in community decision-making. *Proc. Pacific Sociol. Soc.,* 1957, *25,* 137-147.

Miller, J. G. Toward a general theory for the behavioral sciences. *Amer. Psychologist,* 1955, *10,* 513-531.

MILLER, N. E. Comments on theoretical models illustrated by the development of a theory of conflict. *J. Pers.*, 1951, *20,* 82-100.

MINETOWN RESEARCH TEAM. Individual and group reactions to disaster and unemployment. Unpublished manuscript, Dalhousie University, 1961.

MOFFITT, D. A. Weather makers. *Wall Street Journal,* April 10, 1962, pp. 1, 12.

MOLS, R. *Introduction à la démographie historique des villes d'Europe du XIV*e *au XVIII*e *siècle.* Louvain: Univer. de Louvain, 1955.

MOORE, H. E. Some emotional concomitants of disaster. *Ment. Hyg.*, 1958 (a), *42,* 45-50.

———. *Tornadoes over Texas.* Austin: University of Texas Press, 1958 (b).

———, & CRAWFORD, F. R. Waco-San Angelo disaster study: report on second year's work. Unpublished report, Department of Sociology, University of Texas, 1955.

———, & FRIEDSAM, H. J. Reported emotional stress following a disaster. *Soc. Forces,* 1959, *38,* 135-139.

MURRAY, H. A. *Explorations in personality.* New York: Oxford University Press, 1938.

NAGAI, T. *We of Nagasaki: the study of survivors in an atomic wasteland.* New York: Duell, Sloan & Pearce, 1951.

NATIONAL ANALYSTS, INC. *Study of public reactions to the explosion at Sylvania Laboratories in Queens, New York.* Washington: National Academy of Sciences–National Research Council, Committee on Disaster Studies, 1956.

NATIONAL OPINION RESEARCH CENTER. An airplane crash in Flagler, Colorado. In *Conference on field studies of reactions to disasters.* Chicago: National Opinion Research Center, 1953.

NAUTA, L. W., & VAN STRIEN, P. J. A study of community re-integration. In Instituut voor Sociaal Onderzoek van het Nederlandse Volk, *Studies in Holland flood disaster 1953,* Vol. 3. Washington: National Academy of Sciences–National Research Council, Committee on Disaster Studies, 1955.

NEARMAN, M. J. *A biblography of the products of the Disaster Research Group.* Washington: National Academy of Sciences–National Research Council, Disaster Research Group, 1959.

NICHOLSON, G. E., JR., & BLACKWELL, G. W. *Game theory and defense against community disaster.* Washington: National Academy of Sciences–National Research Council, Committee on Disaster Studies, 1954.

NOHL, J. *The Black Death.* New York: Ballantine Books, 1960.

ORNE, M. T. The nature of hypnosis: artifact and essence. *J. abnorm. soc. Psychol.,* 1959, *58,* 277-299.

OPPENHEIMER, J. R. The importance of new knowledge. In D. Wolfle (ed.), *Symposium on basic research.* Washington: American Association for the Advancement of Science, 1959.

PACE, N., *et al. Physiological studies of infantrymen in combat.* Los Angeles: University of California Publications in Physiology, vol. 10, no. 1, 1956.

PARSONS, T. Age and sex in the social structure of the United States. *Amer. sociol. Rev.*, 1942, 7, 604-616.

———. *Structure and process in modern societies.* Glencoe, Ill.: Free Press, 1960.

PEPITONE, A., DIGGORY, J. C., & WALLACE, W. H. Some reactions to a hypothetical disaster. *J. abnorm. soc. Psychol.*, 1955, *5,* 706-708.

PERRY, HELEN S., & PERRY, S. E. *The schoolhouse disasters: family and community as determinants of the child's response to disaster.* Disaster Study Number 11. Washington: National Academy of Sciences–National Research Council, 1959.

PERRY, S. E., SILBER, E., & BLOCH, D. A. *The child and his family in disaster: a study of the 1953 Vicksburg tornado.* Disaster Study Number 5. Washington: National Academy of Sciences–National Research Council, 1956.

PETERSON, V. Panic: the ultimate weapon? *Collier's,* August 21, 1953, *132,* 99-109.

POLIAKOV, L. *Harvest of hate.* Syracuse, N. Y.: Syracuse University Press, 1954.

POWELL, J. W. Interview protocols of victims of the toxicological disaster in Atlanta, 1951. Unpublished. Disaster Research Group, National Academy of Sciences–National Research Council, 1951.

———. A poison liquor episode in Atlanta, Georgia. In *Conference on field studies of reactions to disasters.* Chicago: National Opinion Research Center, 1953.

———. Gaps and goals in disaster research. *J. soc. Issues,* 1954 (a), *10* (3), 61-65.

———. An introduction to the natural history of disaster. Baltimore: University of Maryland Psychiatric Institute, 1954 (b).

———, & RAYNER, JEANNETTE. *Progress notes: disaster investigation July 1, 1951–June 30, 1952.* Edgewood, Md.: Army Chemical Center, Chemical Corps Medical Laboratories, 1952.

———, RAYNER, JEANNETTE, & FINESINGER, J. E. Responses to disaster in American cultural groups. In *Symposium on stress (16–18 March 1953).* Washington: Walter Reed Army Medical Center, Army Medical Service Graduate School, 1953.

PRINCE, S. H. *Catastrophe and social change.* New York: Columbia University Press, 1920.

PRINS, S. A. The individual in flight. In H. B. M. Murphy (ed.), *Flight and resettlement.* Paris: UNESCO; New York: Columbia University Press, 1955.

PROJECT EAST RIVER. *Report of the Project East River.* New York: Associated Universities, 1952.

QUARANTELLI, E. L. The nature and conditions of panic. *Amer. J. Sociol.* 1954, *60,* 267-275.

———. A note on the protective function of the family in disaster. *Marriage fam. Living,* 1960, *22,* 263-265.

RAKER, J. W., WALLACE, A. F. C., RAYNER, JEANNETTE F., & ECKERT, A. W. *Emergency medical care in disasters: a summary of recorded experience.* Disaster Study Number 6. Washington: National Academy of Sciences–National Research Council, 1956.

RAYNER, JEANNETTE F. *Hurricane Barbara: a study of the evacuation of Ocean City, Maryland, August 1953.* Washington: National Academy of Sciences–National Research Council, Committee on Disaster Studies, 1953.

———. Studies of disasters and other extreme situations—an annotated selected bibliography. *Hum. Organization,* 1957, *16* (2), 30-40.

RIECKEN, H. W. A program for research on experiments in social psychology. Paper delivered at the Behavioral Sciences Conference, University of New Mexico, 1958.

———, *et al.* Narrowing the gap between field studies and laboratory experiments in social psychology. *SSRC Items,* 1954, *8,* 37-42.

RIGGS, MARGARET M., & KAESS, W. Personality differences between volunteers and nonvolunteers. *J. Psychol.,* 1955, *40,* 229-245.

RINGELBLUM, E. *Notes from the Warsaw ghetto.* Ed. and trans. by J. Sloan. New York: McGraw-Hill, 1958.

ROBBINS, R. H. *The encyclopedia of witchcraft and demonology.* New York: Crown, 1959.

ROHRER, J. H. A generalized experimental design for studying aspects of mental health. In W. Line & Margery R. King (eds.), *Mental health in public affairs.* Toronto: University of Toronto Press, 1956.

ROSE, E., & FELTON, W. Experimental histories of culture. *Amer. sociol. Rev.*, 1955, *20*, 383-392.

ROSEN, JACQUELINE L., & NEUGARTEN, BERNICE L. Ego functions in the middle and later years: a thematic apperception study of normal adults. *J. Gerontol.*, 1960, *15*, 62-70.

ROSENBERG, M. J. Cognitive reorganization in response to the hypnotic reversal of attitudinal affect. *J. Pers.*, 1960, *28*, 39-63.

ROSOW, I. L. Conflict of authority in natural disaster. Unpublished doctoral dissertation, Harvard University, 1955.

REUSCH, J., & PRESTWOOD, A. Anxiety—its initiation, communication and interpersonal management. *Arch. Neurol. Psychiat.*, 1949, *62*, 527-550.

SCHACTER, S. *The psychology of affiliation.* Stanford: Stanford University Press, 1959.

SCHATZMAN, L. A sequence pattern of disaster and its consequences for community. Unpublished doctoral dissertation, Indiana University, 1960.

———, & STRAUSS, A. Social class and modes of communication. *Amer. J. Sociol.*, 1955, *60*, 329-338.

SCHELSKY, H. *Wandlungen in der deutschen Familien in der Gegenwart.* Stuttgart: Enke-Verlag, 1954.

SCHMIDEBERG, M. Some observations on individual reactions to air raids. *Int. J. Psycho-Anal.*, 1942, *23*, 68.

SCHNEIDER, D. M. Typhoons on Yap. *Hum. Organization*, 1957, *16* (2), 10-15.

SCHWARTZ, S., & WINOGRAD, B. Preparation of soldiers for atomic maneuvers. *J. soc. Issues*, 1954, *10* (3), 42-52.

Science and human survival. *Science*, 1961, *134* (3496), 2080-2083.

SCOTT, W. A. *Public reaction to a surprise civil defense alert in Oakland, California.* Ann Arbor: University of Michigan Survey Research Center, 1955 (a).

———. Unpublished interview, study on public reaction to surprise civil defense alert. Ann Arbor: University of Michigan Survey Research Center, 1955 (b).

SEABORG, G. T. A scientific society—the beginnings. *Science*, 1962, *135* (3503), 505-509.

SELLTIZ, CLAIRE, *et al. Research methods in social relations* (rev. ed.). New York: Holt, Dryden, 1959.

SELYE, H. *The physiology and pathology of exposure to stress.* Montreal: Acta, 1950.

———. *The stress of life.* New York: McGraw-Hill, 1956.

SHANNON, D. A. (ed.). *The great depression.* Englewood Cliffs, N.J.: Prentice-Hall, 1960.

SHERIF, M. Integrating field work and laboratory in small group research. *Amer. sociol. Rev.*, 1954, *19*, 759-771.

———, & SHERIF, CAROLYN W. *Groups in harmony and tension.* New York: Harper, 1953.

SHILS, E. A., & JANOWITZ, M. Cohesion and disintegration in the Wehrmacht in World War II. *Publ. opin. Quart.*, 1948, *12*, 280-315.

SINHA, D. Behavior in a catastrophic situation: a psychological study of reports and rumours. *Brit. J. Psychiat.*, 1952, *43*, 200-209.

———. Psychological study of catastrophes. *Patna Univer. J.*, 1954, *8*, 51-60.

SJOBERG, G. Contradictory functional requirements and social systems. *J. conflict Resolution*, 1960 (a), *4*, 198-208.

———. *The preindustrial city: past and present.* Glencoe, Ill.: Free Press, 1960 (b).

———, & CAIN, L. D., JR. Negative values and social action. *Alpha Kappa Deltan*, 1959, *29*, 63-70.

SKINNER, B. F. *Science and human behavior.* New York: Macmillan, 1953.

SNYDER, R. C. Personal communication. November, 1960.

SOLOMON, P., *et al.* Sensory deprivation. *Science*, 1959, *129*, 221-223.

SOROKIN, P. A. *Man and society in calamity.* New York: Dutton, 1942.

SPIEGEL, J. P. Psychological transactions in situations of acute stress. In *Symposium on stress (16-18 March 1953).* Washington: Walter Reed Army Medical Center, Army Medical Service Graduate School, 1953.

———. The English flood of 1953. *Hum. Organization*, 1957, *16* (2), 3-5.

STERN, K., WILLIAMS, GWENDOLYN, & PRADOS, M. Grief reactions in later life. *Amer. J. Psychiatry*, 1951, *108*, 289-294.

Strengthening the behavioral sciences. *Science*, 1962, *136* (3512), 233-241.

STRODTBECK, F. L. Husband-wife interaction over revealed differences. *Amer. sociol. Rev.*, 1951, *16*, 468-473.

SULLIVAN, H. Psychiatric aspects of morale. *Amer J. Sociol.*, 1941, *47*, 277-301.

Symposium on stress (16-18 March 1953). Washington: Walter Reed Army Medical Center, Army Medical Service Graduate School, 1953.

TAEUBER, IRENE. *The population of Japan.* Princeton, N.J.: Princeton University Press, 1958.

THOMPSON, J. D. & MCEWEN, W. J. Organizational goals and environment: goal-setting as an interaction process. In D. Cartwright & A. Zander (eds.), *Group dynamics: research and theory* (2nd ed.). Evanston, Ill.: Row, Peterson, 1960.

THOMPSON, J. D., & TUDEN, A. Strategies, structures and processes of organizational decision. In J. D. Thompson *et al.* (eds.), *Comparative studies in administration.* Pittsburgh: University of Pittsburgh Press, 1959.

THRALL, R., COOMBS, C., & DAVIS, R. L. *Decision processes.* New York: Wiley, 1954.

TIRYAKIAN, E. A. Aftermath of a thermonuclear attack on the United States: some sociological considerations. *Soc. Probl.*, 1959, *6*, 291-303.

TITMUSS, R. M. *Problems of social policy.* London: H. M. Stationery Office and Longmans, Green, 1950.

Tornado warning. *Disaster*, February, 1948, 2, 5+.

TORRANCE, E. P. What happens to the sociometric structure of small groups in emergencies and extreme conditions. *Group Psychother.*, 1957, *10*, 212-220.

———. A theory of leadership and interpersonal behavior under stress. In B. Bass and L. Petrullo (eds.), *Leadership and interpersonal behavior.* New York: Holt, Rinehart & Winston, 1961.

TOWNSEND, P. *Family life of old people.* London: Routledge, 1957.

TURNER, R. H., AND KILLIAN, L. M. *Collective behavior.* Englewood Cliffs, N.J.: Prentice-Hall, 1957.

TYHURST, J. S. Individual reactions to community disaster. *Amer. J. Psychiat.*, 1950-1951, *107*, 764-769.

———. Research on reaction to catastrophe. In *Transactions of the conference on morale and prevention and control of panic.* New York: New York Academy of Medicine and the Josiah Macy, Jr., Foundation, 1951.

TYHURST, J. S. The role of transition states—including disasters—in mental illness. In *Symposium on preventive and social psychiatry.* Washington: Walter Reed Army Institute of Research, 1957.

———. Research on reaction to catastrophe. In I. Galdston (ed.), *Panic and morale.* New York: International Universities Press, 1958.

U.S. CONGRESS, JOINT COMMITTEE ON ATOMIC ENERGY, SPECIAL SUBCOMMITTEE ON RADIATION. *Biological and environmental effects of nuclear war.* Washington: U.S. Government Printing Office, 1959.

U.S. STRATEGIC BOMBING SURVEY. *Summary report (European War).* Washington: U.S. Government Printing Office, 1945.

———. *Summary report (Pacific War).* Washington: U.S. Government Printing Office, 1946.

———. *Civilian Defense Division final report.* Washington: U.S. Government Printing Office, 1947 (a).

———. *The effect of bombing on health and medical care in Germany.* Washington: U.S. Government Printing Office, 1947 (b).

———. *The effects of strategic bombing on German morale* (2 vols). Washington: U.S. Government Printing Office, 1947 (c).

———. *The effects of strategic bombing on Japanese morale.* Washington: U.S. Government Printing Office, 1947 (d).

UNIVERSITY OF MICHIGAN SURVEY CENTER. Civil Defense in the United States 1952: a national study of public information and attitudes about civil defense. Unpublished report, 1952.

UNIVERSITY OF OKLAHOMA RESEARCH INSTITUTE. *The Kansas City flood and fire of 1951.* Chevy Chase, Md.: Operations Research Office, 1952.

VAN DIJK, K., & PILGER, J. Communications in the stricken area in February, 1953. In Instituut voor Sociaal Onderzoek van het Nederlandse Volk, *Studies in Holland flood disaster 1953,* Vol. 1. Washington: National Academy of Sciences–National Research Council, Committee on Disaster Studies, 1955.

VAN DOORN-JANSSEN, M. JEANNE. A study of social disorganization in a community. In Instituut voor Sociaal Onderzoek van het Nederlandse Volk, *Studies in Holland flood disaster 1953,* vol. 3. Washington: National Academy of Sciences–National Research Council, Committee on Disaster Studies, 1955.

VAUGHAN, ELIZABETH. *Communities under stress.* Princeton, N.J.: Princeton University Press, 1949.

VERNON, J. A. *Project Hideaway.* Battle Creek, Mich.: Office of Civil and Defense Mobilization, 1959.

VERNON, P. E. Psychological effects of air raids. *J. abnorm. soc. Psychol.,* 1941, *36,* 457-476.

VOLKART, E. H. Bereavement and mental health. In A. H. Leighton, J. A. Clausen, & R. N. Wilson (eds.), *Explorations in social psychiatry.* New York: Basic Books, 1957.

WALLACE, A. F. C. *Tornado in Worcester: an exploratory study of individual and community behavior in an extreme situation.* Disaster Study Number 3. Washington: National Academy of Sciences–National Research Council, 1956.

WALLER, W., & HILL, R. *The family: a dynamic interpretation.* New York: Dryden Press, 1951.

WEBER, M. *The theory of social and economic organization.* New York: Oxford University Press, 1947.

WEINBERG, A. M. The federal laboratories and science education. *Science,* 1962, *136* (3510), 27-30.

WESTIE, C. M. Problems encountered in disaster research. Paper read at Michigan Sociological Assn., Wayne State University, Detroit, November 1954.

WHITE, R. W. Motivation reconsidered: the concept of competence. *Psychol. Rev.,* 1959, *66,* 297-333.

WILLIAMS, H. B., JR. Communication in community disasters. Unpublished doctoral dissertation, University of North Carolina, 1956.

WILLIAMS, J. D. The nonsense about safe driving. *Fortune,* September, 1958, 118, 119+.

WITHEY, S. B. *Survey of public knowledge and attitudes concerning civil defense.* Ann Arbor: University of Michigan Survey Research Center, 1954.

———. *Some factors influencing public reaction to civil defense in the U.S.* Ann Arbor: University of Michigan Survey Research Center, 1956.

WITTKOWER, E. *A psychiatrist looks at tuberculosis.* London: National Association for the Prevention of Tuberculosis, 1949.

———. Psychological aspects of physical illness. *Canad. Med. Assoc. J.,* 1952, *66,* 220-224.

WOLFENSTEIN, MARTHA. *Disaster: a psychological essay.* Glencoe, Ill.: Free Press, 1957.

Working definition of mental health. Unpublished memorandum, National Conference on Mental Health Teaching in Schools of Public Health, Arden House, 1959.

YOUNG, M. The role of the extended family in a disaster. *Hum. Relat.,* 1954, 7, 383-391.

ZAWADZKI, B., & LAZARSFELD, P. The psychological consequences of unemployment. *J. soc. Psychol.,* 1935, *6,* 224-251.

ZBOROWSKI, M. Cultural components in responses to pain. *J. soc. Issues,* 1952, *8* (4), 16-30.

ZINSSER, H. *Rats, lice and history.* Boston: Little, Brown, 1935.

INDEX